SELF-FULFILLING PROPHECIES
Social, Psychological, and
Physiological Effects of Expectancies

SELF-FULFILLING PROPHECIES
Social, Psychological, and Physiological Effects of Expectancies

RUSSELL A. JONES
University of Kentucky

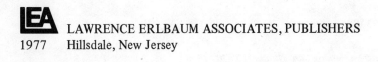

LAWRENCE ERLBAUM ASSOCIATES, PUBLISHERS
1977   Hillsdale, New Jersey

DISTRIBUTED BY THE HALSTED PRESS DIVISION OF
JOHN WILEY & SONS
New York   Toronto   London   Sydney

Lawrence Erlbaum Associates, Inc., Publishers
62 Maria Drive
Hillsdale, New Jersey 07642

Distributed solely by Halsted Press Division
John Wiley & Sons, Inc., New York

ISBN 0-470-99301-4

Library of Congress Catalog Card Number: 77-11134

Printed in the United States of America

Contents

Preface

Most prefaces appear to have been written after the books they begin have been completed. At least, that is what a biased, unsystematic sampling of the books on my bookshelves leads me to believe. I suppose that's fine from the reader's point of view. It should make for clarity and an extremely high correlation between what the preface says the book is about and what the book actually contains.

This preface, however, is being written before the book. As a consequence, there is a distinct possibility that no one will ever read it. The book, in short, may never get completed, and, if it does, there may be no imaginative, intelligent, and creative publishers to be found. However, I assume these two obstacles can be overcome.

The purpose in writing this preface first is to record what I hope the book will accomplish. I hope that the book will explicate the ramifications of statements such as, "I assume these two obstacles can be overcome." In simpler language, I have become convinced that expectations often lead to their own fulfillment. I hope to bring together evidence from a variety of sources and disciplines to shed light on some of the intrapersonal and interpersonal processes involved.

R.A.J.

Acknowledgments

It is a genuine pleasure to express my appreciation for the help of Debby Mills, Dorothy Manon, Ruth Stanton, and Martha Lancaster. Each has contributed mightily in converting my handwriting to a neat and accurately rendered manuscript. I would also like to thank Joanne Basehart, Debby Mills, and Ruth Stanton for their aid in checking quotations and verifying references.

The following people were kind enough to read and critique various sections of the first draft of the manuscript, and the final version has benefitted greatly from their comments: Norman H. Anderson, Judith Phillips Archambo, Joanne Basehart, David Bricker, Audrey Burnham, John V. Haley, Reid Hastie, Lawrence E. Hinkle, Jr., Kathleen Miller, Robert Noble, Stephan G. West, Jean Wiese, and James Zolman. I am especially indebted to Jack W. Brehm for his thoughtful and detailed comments on the entire first draft.

1
Self-Fulfilling Prophecies

The ultimate function of prophecy is not to tell the future, but to make it.
Wagar, 1963, p. 66

I first became interested in the processes involved in self-fulfilling prophecies several years ago when I was a faculty member in the psychology department of a newly opened college. There were only six members of the department at that time, and one of our major tasks for the year was to hire two or three more faculty members. The usual procedure was to have a candidate visit the campus for a day and talk with each of us individually for an hour or so. After the candidate left we would get together—supposedly to arrive at a consensus as to whether or not we would offer him or her a job.

It was incredible. It was as if each of us had talked to a different candidate, and this happened with nearly every person we interviewed. Only on the real duds or geniuses was there even the semblance of agreement as to their merits or lack of them. For the vast range in between, there were usually six conflicting opinions.

I found this intriguing, but then convinced myself that it was not so surprising after all. We simply had different ideas about what constituted a "good" colleague. We also had various motives, some of which were rather devious, for liking or not liking a particular candidate. For example, the older members of the department wanted to hire young superstars and the younger members wanted older superstars. Nobody wanted a superstar for a peer. And, for a while at least, such explanations seemed to suffice.

As the year progressed, however, it became obvious that something else, something more subtle, was operating. On the basis of information about where the candidate had gone to school, whom he or she had worked with, letters of recommendation, and other data we collected before a candidate's visit, we were each forming definite expectations about what the candidate was going to be like. Further, our expectations were usually quite different. For example, one of my colleagues thought that we should do anything necessary to hire a particular candidate who was getting her Ph.D. in social psychology at a well known university. In contrast, I thought that the social psychologists there were fakers who were engaged in trivial research and, consequently, one could not reasonably expect anyone graduating from that institution to know much about research or scholarship. Thus, before we ever saw the real, live candidates themselves, we had each developed clear-cut expectations about what they were going to be like.

It did not stop there, however. When the candidates did arrive, we seemed to treat them differently, and it appeared that how we treated any particular candidate was more a function of the expectations we had about the candidate than of anything the candidate said or did. The candidates from prestigious schools and those with impressive vitae did not appear to be questioned as closely about the details of their research. We seemed to assume that they had tended to all those little points of design and procedure that can make or break an experiment. We seemed to encourage such candidates to talk about the more interesting theoretical issues and, consequently, they themselves gave the impression of being more interesting and promising. Other candidates, for whom one or more of us had less favorable expectations, would get flooded with questions about abstruse statistical issues—to see if they knew what they were talking about—and their presentations would become bogged down in uninteresting detail. Hence, even if they did know their material perfectly, they appeared overly concerned with minutiae and much less interesting and/or promising.

I began to see how important expectations were and how we often behave in ways that insure our expectations will be fulfilled. Thus alerted, I began to see examples of the power of expectations everywhere I turned and in everything I read. Since my own interest in the topic began with expectations about the characteristics of others, I began digging through the research literature pertinent to such expectations. As I shall try to make clear in the chapters that follow, a sequence of relationships began to take shape in my mind, a sequence beginning with these expectations about others. I have organized the material in subsequent chapters in what I judged to be a logical sequence, given such a starting point. The sequence is, in fact, the order in which I explored these topics. As I got into the literature on a given issue, certain questions occurred that led naturally, or so it seemed to me, to the next issue. As an overview of the chapters that follow, let us take a brief look at the chain of reasoning that ties them together. As we shall see, there are several weak links, but pointing out those weaknesses and suggesting how they can be strenghtened is, of course, part of the purpose of the book. The chain begins, as I did, with expectations about the characteristics of others.

EXPECTATIONS ABOUT OTHERS

It appears to be the case that, during the course of our experience with others, we learn to expect certain characteristics to co-occur. As Rosenberg and Jones (1972) point out, these expectations about others generally consist of: (a) the *categories* we employ to describe the range of abilities, attitudes, interests, physical features, traits and behaviors that we perceive in others; and (b) the *beliefs* we hold concerning which of these perceived characteristics tend to go together and which do not. One way to sensitize people to the existence of such beliefs is to pose a question such as, "What do you think of a wise, cruel man?"—a jarring inconsistency for most people. For most people, wise men are generally kind, old, and perhaps jaded, but never cruel.

While on a general level the existence of such interpersonal expectations seems quite plausible, there are many questions one might raise about them and, in Chapter 2, we begin by looking at how these expectations are organized and how they have been studied in the past. A number of studies of impression formation have demonstrated that people quite readily attribute additional characteristics when given only one or two items of information about another person. Further, the characteristics that will be inferred—on the basis of no objective evidence—are quite predictable and can be related to a number of characteristics of the inferrer. People, in general, seem to have implicit theories of personality, theories about what characteristics or behaviors are likely to be related, and they use these implicit theories to fill in gaps in their knowledge of others. In Chapter 2 and the first part of Chapter 3, we shall explore these built-in expectancies. In doing so, we shall be forced to consider several methodological issues, such as the merits of free-response formats. As we shall see, one of the major hindrances of research on implicit theories and stereotypes has been the use of procedures that restrict respondents to a fixed format and/or a preselected vocabulary. Such procedures often fail to provide respondents with categories that are relevant or meaningful with respect to their particular expectations.

Once we have established the pervasiveness and nature of these interpersonal expectancies, the questions of interest become whether or not such expectancies are translated into action and, if so, how? An anecdote that hints at several of the processes involved in such translation comes from Liebow (1967):

... owners of small retail establishments and other employers frequently anticipate employee stealing and adjust the wage rate accordingly. Tonk's employer explained why he was paying Tonk $35 for a 55–60 hour workweek. These men will all steal, he said. Although he keeps close watch on Tonk, he estimates that Tonk steals $35–$40 a week. What he steals, when added to his regular earnings, brings his take home pay to $70 or $75 per week. The employer said that he did not mind this because Tonk is worth that much to the business. But if he were to pay Tonk outright the full value of his labor, Tonk would still be stealing $35–$40 per week and this, he said, the business simply would not support (pp. 37–38).

By expecting Tonk to steal, his employer defines the employment situation in such a way—paying a substandard wage—that Tonk has to steal to support himself, confirming the employer's expectation. The employer's assumption that Tonk would steal regardless of what he was paid remains untested; it could be true or false.

Many years ago Merton (1957) defined a self-fulfilling prophecy as ". . . in the beginning, a *false* definition of the situation evoking a new behavior which makes the originally false conception come *true*" (p. 423). There appears to be no reason, as Krishna (1971) has recently pointed out, to accept such a restrictive definition. Harking back to Thomas's theorem (see Thomas and Thomas, 1928) that "If men define situations as real, they are real in their consequences" (p. 1104), Krishna points out that, in determining social reality, beliefs have consequences whether they are true or false. Whether or not Tonk would have stolen had he been paid a wage of $75 is irrelevant. His employer believed that he would and so paid a wage of only $35.

In the second half of Chapter 3, some research on psychological and psychiatric diagnosis is examined in search of an answer to the questions of whether beliefs and expectations about others can and do have an effect on their subsequent behaviors. Studies of the influence of the examiner on the results of psychodiagnostic testing indicate that the expectations of the examiner play a significant role in determining the outcome of testing. Further, the circumstances of testing and knowledge of "extraneous" characteristics of the client also appear to play a role in the outcome of the diagnostic process. Different examiners both see different cues in the same patient and use the same cue to infer different things. Different diagnoses, of course, have dramatically different effects on the client's subsequent behavior.

In an attempt to understand how this stage of affairs is perpetuated, the final section of Chapter 3 is devoted to an examination of some of the pitfalls that interfere with information processing in personality assessment. Clinicians—and others—appear prone to a number of biasing influences that range from ignoring base rate data when attempting to decide if two variables are related to mistaking their own premature inferences for fact to relying on judgmental heuristics that lead to erroneous inferences. An attempt is then made to put all this into focus by relating it to the theoretical systems of George Kelly and Egon Brunswik. These two offer perspectives on clinical judgment within which the evidence seems to make sense and within which there is explicit appreciation of the importance of the perceiver's own beliefs and expectations.

Interpersonal expectations appear, under many circumstances, to influence both the behavior of the person holding the expectation and the behavior of the person about whom the expectation is held. In Chapter 4, we shall focus on both of these by examining some research pertaining to the labeling perspective on deviant behavior. The key to the labeling perspective is the reaction of others to those who violate society's rules and norms. Most such violations appear to be transitory and are ignored, but when public labeling of the rule-breaker as a deviant occurs, intrapersonal (activation of previously existing stereotypes about such deviants) and interpersonal (communication of these expectations and negative affect) processes may push the "deviant" individual into secondary or career deviance.

As an example of how these processes operate, we shall look at the available evidence on involuntary institutionalization of those who have been labeled "mentally ill." The evidence appears to indicate the operation of a presumption of "illness" that is reinforced in numerous ways: perfunctory sanity hearings, failure to meet legal criteria for commitment, and institutional arrangements that strip away the social amenities and props by which the committed might maintain the appearance of normality. In general, it appears that the so-called "mentally ill" suffer, to a large extent, from the expectations of others.

We shall then look at some of the ways in which an individual who holds a given expectation about another can communicate that expectation to the other in such a manner as to increase the probability that the expectation will be validated. It appears that the cues employed to communicate expectancies are manifold and range from the most subtle, minute aspects of behavior to gross and dramatic interpersonal confrontations. From mutual glances to avoidance of eye contact, from name calling to name dropping, from cooperation to competition: almost all aspects of behavior can be employed to let someone know what we think of them and, in particular, how we see them in relation to ourselves.

In thinking about all of the verbal and nonverbal cues and maneuvers we employ that communicate to others, often unintentionally, what we expect of them, it occurred to me that there are few totally purposeless interactions between people. People interact with each other for reasons and much of what is involved in the various interpersonal tactics and strategies, the assumption of roles and the attempts to maneuver others into complementary roles, the variations in self-presentation can be seen as attempts to achieve their own goals and purposes. Thus, if individual goal attainment were an operative factor behind interpersonal self-fulfilling prophecies it seemed important to look at some of the variables influencing individual goal-setting and goal-directed behavior.

EXPECTATIONS ABOUT ONE'S OWN BEHAVIOR

People can be viewed as continually attempting to impose some sort of order and coherence on the events in which they find themselves immersed. In order to survive we must extract some meaning from our experience so that we can understand, anticipate, and, thus, exercise some control over life's experiences. We do this by making choices—choices about how to interpret events, choices among alternative courses of action, choices among evaluations of our actions. In Chapter 5, an attempt is made to develop the idea that the outcome that follows the choice of a particular course of action is, in part at least, a function of the expectation or perceived probability that the outcome of interest will result. The question is, if one perceives that one is very likely to succeed at a particular task, does that perception ipso facto increase the probability that one will in fact succeed?

A prior question, however, concerns the determinants of the perceived probability of an outcome itself, and, in the first half of Chapter 5, these determinants will be explored in some detail. As one might expect, the most important determinant of the subjective probability of success on familiar tasks is one's own past experience on the task. On such tasks, the simple knowledge that one has succeeded or failed, even if one cannot accurately evaluate and adjust one's performance, is sufficient to determine one's subjective probability of success. Further, the evidence seems to indicate that we must distinguish between one's level of aspiration and one's overall subjective probability of goal attainment. The latter appears to be a better index of one's degree of encouragement or discouragement.

But what about unfamiliar tasks, tasks on which we have no experience? As we shall see, it appears that on such tasks we evaluate our chances of success by comparing ourselves with others. These comparisons result in an interesting asymmetry in the form of an assumed similarity "upwards," that is, the average person apparently believes he or she is a little better than average. The general result of this asymmetry is an elevation of the subjective probability of success when the objective probability is below .5. The evidence also indicates that other variables also influence the subjective probability of success: the value of the goal, the amount of effort already expended, and the amount of time remaining for goal attainment.

In the last half of Chapter 5, a theoretical model is developed to relate one's subjective probability of success to the objective probability of success and the likelihood that one will expend whatever effort or exercise whatever skill necessary to insure success. Beginning with two antagonistic cognitive processes, wishful thinking and anticipatory face-saving, which are assumed to vary in relative dominance from person to person, it is postulated that these two processes combine to distort the objective probability of success. The general result is an overestimation of low objective probabilities and an underestimation of high objective probabilities. Further, individual differences in the relative dominance of these two processes are shown to affect the proportion of the objective probability continuum that is over or underestimated. The greater the relative dominance of wishful thinking, the greater the proportion of the objective probability continuum that is overestimated. The greater the relative dominance of anticipatory face-saving, the greater the proportion of the objective probability continuum that is underestimated. The interesting questions, of course, are whether or not these expectations for one's performance get translated into behavior and, if so, how the antecedent perceived probability of success makes a difference in subsequent behavior. Drawing on Cofer and Appley's (1964) anticipation-invigoration mechanism, Chapter 5 ends with a discussion of how the subjective probability of success relates to effort expended in pursuit of the goal. The hypothesis is developed that, as the subjective probability of success increases, the likelihood that one will do whatever is necessary to insure success also increases.

The model developed in Chapter 5 is, then, an attempt to specify the psychological processes underlying intrapersonal and, by extension, interpersonal self-fulfilling prophecies. I have repeatedly been struck by the fact that goals people both desire and have the ability to achieve are often relinquished, abandoned without a real effort to attain them. On the other hand, people who appear to have no more, or even less, ability, often achieve those very goals. How could this be accounted for? The answer, or so it seemed to me, was that those who relinquished their goals somehow became convinced that they could not achieve them and, hence, did not try as hard as they might have had they had greater faith in the efficaciousness of their efforts. The model developed in Chapter 5 is an attempt to articulate the components involved in such an apparently simple answer and to formulate the answer in such a way that it can be tested. The basic idea contained in the answer is not, of course, new. As Eisenberg (1972) puts it:

> ... pessimism about man serves to maintain the status quo. It is a luxury for the affluent, a sop to the guilt of the politically inactive, a comfort to those who continue to enjoy the amenities of privilege. Pessimism is too costly for the disenfranchised; they give way to it at the price of their salvation (p. 124).

Given the theoretical model developed in Chapter 5, the question of interest becomes one of evidence and, in Chapter 6, the pertinent evidence relating one's subjective probability of success to performance is reviewed. As we shall see, it appears that prior success not only tends to raise one's subjective probability of success for future performance, but such increases in the subjective probability of success are followed by improved performance. On the other hand, prior failure appears to lower one's subjective probability of success and such decreases are followed by poorer performance. Further, the evidence seems to indicate that one's subjective probability of success has two components: a dispositional and a situational component. The former appears to be most influential in determining initial performance on an unfamiliar task. As one gains experience on a task, the influence of the dispositional component fades and the situational component, as determined by one's experience on the task at hand, becomes a better predictor of performance.

In going through the literature on feedback, it will become apparent that the perceived reasons for one's success or failure are more important in determining future performance than success or failure per se. Failure may, in fact, lead to an increase in one's subjective probability of success and improved performance if the failure is attributed to luck or lack of effort. Further, feedback of success or failure may not always mean what it is intended to mean. It is necessary to know the particular goal or level of performance a person is striving to attain in order to understand how feedback will be interpreted and what effect it will have on performance. We shall also examine some research on the discrepancy between expectancy and performance, and we shall offer an interpretation of the data in terms of the effects of uncertainty on variability in responding. Similarly, we shall look at some data on the relationship between anxiety and performance that point to maximum distraction, arousal, and response variability when the perceived probability of success is at an intermediate level. The argument will be developed that such behaviors decrease the likelihood of a successful performance if compared with the behaviors of someone with a high subjective probability of success and, simultaneously, increase the likelihood of a successful performance if compared with the behaviors of someone with a low subjective probability of success. From the work on anxiety, which focuses on the intermediate levels of perceived probability, we shall turn to a topic concerned with the effects of very low levels of the subjective probability of success. The work on learned helplessness indicates that a very low perceived probability of success is a motivational disaster. The important, and still-open question about the helplessness research is the extent to which such effects generalize and influence the dispositional component of one's subjective probability of success.

Chapter 7 is an effort to extend the work on expectancies even more intrapersonally. Beginning with some data on placebos and ending with some observations on death and dying, we shall see that expectancies produce effects ranging from pain relief to an increase or decrease in one's general susceptibility to illness and may even influence death itself. We shall explore some physiological and endocrine responses that could link various psychosocial stimuli, such as expectations, to disease. We shall also review a number of studies that indicate that expectations of failure or of being unable to cope produce in humans the sorts of physiological responses that, if prolonged, could lead to malfunctions and disease.

Finally, in Chapter 8, we shall outline some of the implications for future research of the material covered in the preceding chapters.

2
Implicit Theories of Personality

Everyone has a set of beliefs about what people are like. Examples of such beliefs abound in literature, in movies, and in everyday conversation. Further, casual observations suggest that these beliefs differ in some respects from person to person, even though there may be large areas of overlap between the belief systems of any two people. The purpose of this chapter is to explore in some detail the research that bears on these beliefs about people. We shall begin by reviewing several early studies of impression formation, studies that demonstrate the influence of previously existing beliefs on the perception of others. We shall then examine some more recent research on how people organize their beliefs about others and how they use cues in conjunction with their "assumptive worlds" to attribute characteristics for which they have no evidence to others. Along the way, we shall consider a couple of methodological issues, such as how one could determine the veridicality of these beliefs about people and how these beliefs can best be studied in an unbiased manner. We shall also examine individual differences in these believed-in associations among characteristics of others and how such individual differences relate to the perceiver's own personality and situation in life.

We are assuming, then, as a working hypothesis, that everyone has some beliefs about the nature of personality. As noted in the preceding chapter there are really two components involved: (1) the categories that one uses in his or her perceptions of the characteristics of others; and (2) the beliefs about which of these perceived characteristics tend to go together and which do not. These two components constitute the rudiments of a theory of personality. It is apparent, however, that most people are under little pressure to make *explicit* either the categories into which they code the characteristics of others or their beliefs about which of these categories are related; hence, the term *implicit* theories of personality. Bruner and Tagiuri (1954) and Cronbach (1955) appear to be among the first to have used the term itself, but it is clear that the idea has been around a long time and has appeared under a lot of different aliases. For example, Newcomb (1931) and Guilford (1936, 1954) have described a tendency of people to package information and took this as an indication that people do have conceptions about what characteristics "go together" in others. They viewed these conceptions as sources of error in making judgments about people and the bias was termed the logical error in judgments. Presumably, if one knows that another is intelligent, it would be logical to also assume that he or she reads a lot. Such an assumption could lead to error, however, because there are many intelligent people who do not read a lot.

Even earlier than Newcomb's and Guilford's descriptions of the logical error was Thorndike's (1920) description of the halo effect. The halo effect is simply a high correlation among several judgments about a person that is due to a tendency of people to judge each of another's characteristics in the light of an overall impression of goodness or badness. The halo effect and the logical error were considered things to be corrected for, not as processes of interest in their own right. Koltuv (1962) notes that only gradually was there a shift toward studying such artifacts as possible indices of cognitive organization. The evolution of interest in these "errors" seems to have followed the three stages of ignorance, coping, and exploitation described by McGuire (1969).

> At first, the researchers seem unaware of the variable producing the artifact and tend even to deny it when its possibility is pointed out to them. The second stage begins as its existence and possible importance become undeniable. In this coping phase, researchers tend to recognize and even overstress the artifact's importance. They give a great deal of attention to devising procedures which will reduce its contaminating influence and its limiting of the generalizability of experimental results. The third stage, exploitation, grows out of the considerable cogitation during the coping stage to understand the artifactual variable so as to eliminate it from the experimental situation. In their attempt to cope, some researchers almost inevitably become interested in the artifactual variable in its own right. . . . Hence the variable which began by misleading the experimenter and then, as its existence became recognized, proceeded to terrorize and divert him from his main interest, ends up by provoking him to new empirical research and theoretical elaboration (pp. 15–16). (Copyright 1969 by Academic Press, New York. Reprinted by permission.)

During the 1920s and 1930s, when interest in the errors discovered by Thorndike, Newcomb and others was groping through the second of the stages described by McGuire, Gestalt psychology was beginning to establish itself as a dominant orientation within the field. According to Boring (1950), "The most concise way to characterize Gestalt psychology is to say that it deals with wholes. . . . The Gestalt psychologists . . . were convinced that it is really always wholes that are given in experience to conscious man" (p. 588). According to the Gestaltists, one sees a tree, not an array of different colored patches of light; one learns a melody, not a string of individual notes. Solomon Asch, a social psychologist then at Swarthmore, was much influenced by the Gestalt orientation and, in 1946, he published a paper on impression formation that has since become a classic in the study of implicit theories of personality.

IMPRESSION FORMATION

Asch took the point of view that when we form an impression of another we do not see that person as simply a summation of a number of different character-istics. Rather, we interpret each of another's characteristics in the light of all that we know about that person; we see the whole and not each part.

To demonstrate his point Asch carried out and reported a series of studies. In his first experiment, two groups of subjects heard a list of characteristics which were supposedly descriptive of a person. The characteristics heard by the two groups of subjects were identical except for one term. One group was read: *intelligent, skillful, industrious, warm, determined, practical, cautious*. The second group heard: *intelligent, skillful, industrious, cold, determined, practical, cautious*. Both groups of subjects were then asked to write brief sketches of the person described and to check (on a provided form) those additional qualities or characteristics that the described person would be likely to have. The resulting differences in impression were dramatic. Subjects for whom *warm* had been included in the list were much more likely to describe the stimulus person as generous, wise, happy, good-natured, humorous, sociable, popular, humane, altruistic, and imaginative.

Asch's basic result has held up through a series of replications which have utilized different subjects and/or less artificial stimulus materials (Kelley, 1950; Mensch and Wishner, 1947). Kelley, for example, told students in classrooms that he was "interested . . . in the general problem of how various classes react to different instructors" (p. 433) and gave the students a biographical note contain-ing some information about a visiting instructor. The information given to all students was the same, with one exception. For half, the visiting instructor was described as *warm* and for the other half *cold*. The instructor then actually appeared and led the classes in a 20-minute discussion following which the students wrote free descriptions of him and rated him on 15 scales. Those subjects given the warm preinformation consistently rated the instructor more favorably.

One of the lines of research triggered by Asch's study has had to do with the question of meaning change. That is, does the intelligence of a warm and intelligent person differ in meaning from the intelligence of a cold and intelligent person? There is, in fact, a continuing controversy on this issue. In an impressive series of experiments, Anderson (cf. 1971, 1974) and his associates have demon-strated that if one defines meaning as the placement (scale value) of the word in question along a dimension of judgment, there is little evidence that the word's meaning changes as a function of context. What may happen, however, is that the weight or importance of a particular word in determining the overall judgment may vary as a function of the words with which it is associated.

Although the change-of-meaning issue is interesting in its own right, it is actually somewhat different from what we shall be concerned with. We shall explore some questions related to the issue of whether people have different expectations for, say, an *intelligent—warm* person than they do for an *intelligent—cold* person. As Higgins and Rholes (1976) put it:

> Anderson . . . has stated that 'word mixture does not imply meaning change any more than a mixture of sweet and sour solutions implies chemical change". . . . However, even if word mixture does not imply change in literal meaning, any more than hydrogen has a different nuclear structure when combined with oxygen than when combined with sulphur, one still cannot predict the nature of the combination solely from a knowledge of its components, any more than one can predict the smell of hydrogen sulphide from a knowledge of the smell of sulphur and hydrogen alone (pp. 432–433).

The expectations about an intelligent cold person are, according to Higgins and Rholes, a function of three things: one's knowledge of the literal meanings of *intelligent* and *cold*, one's knowledge of grammatical relationships, and one's past experience with people who could be described as intelligent and cold. Let us go back to Asch's study and pursue these issues in more detail.

In one of his additional studies, Asch demonstrated that manipulation of *polite—blunt* in the stimulus materials, instead of *warm—cold*, made little difference in the resulting impressions formed by subjects. He interpreted this, in conjunction with the large differences obtained by *warm—cold*, as evidence that *polite—blunt* was a peripheral characteristic, whereas the warmth or coldness of a person was a central characteristic. Presumably, a central characteristic is one, the absence of which "makes a difference." Hair color would probably not be central for most people (except, perhaps, gentlemen), whereas intelligence would be. Another way of phrasing this is that Asch seemed to be saying that people have no clear conceptions or assumptions about characteristics that "go with" peripheral traits, whereas they do have definite assumptions about characteristics that accompany central traits.

Wishner (1960) was concerned with the question of how one could know on an a priori basis which traits would be central and which peripheral for a given group of people. In looking over Asch's results, it seemed to Wishner that the reason *warm—cold* made such a difference in the resulting impressions and *polite—blunt* did not was because *warm—cold* was correlated with the scales on which Asch asked subjects to rate their impressions, whereas *polite—blunt* was not. What this means, of course, is that if Asch had used a different set of scales for subjects to rate their impressions, he would have gotten a different result. To check on this possibility, Wishner first constructed some rating booklets using 53 bipolar scales that had been employed by Asch. He then had 214 students who were taking introductory psychology to simply rate their lab instructors (eight different instructors) on these scales. As he had hypothesized, there was a significant relation between the size of correlations between *warm–cold* and the check list items and the magnitude of the differences on those items in impressions by the warm and cold groups in Asch's original study.

To further demonstrate his point, Wishner constructed a new checklist composed of items having high and low correlations with *polite–blunt*. He then repeated Asch's *polite–blunt* study and found large differences in the resulting impressions as a function of varying *polite–blunt* in the list of traits read to subjects. Thus, it appears that "A trait is central for those traits correlated with it and peripheral for those traits uncorrelated with it" (p. 108). As Hastorf, Schneider, and Polefka (1970) have pointed out,

> Wishner's article is often interpreted as being critical of Asch, but actually it has merely put Asch's argument on firmer grounds. . . . The most important feature of Wishner's analysis is that he has provided us with a working model of the implicit personality theory. It is simply a correlation matrix among traits, a matrix we all carry around with us. Each of us has an idea of what traits are closely or not so closely related to other traits (p. 41).

To review for a moment, it does seem that, as Asch and Wishner demonstrated, people have definite beliefs about certain traits going together. Further, we may take Wishner's correlation matrix as a tentative working model of what an implicit theory of personality is like. Next, it seems appropriate to try to refine our working model.

The Multidimensional Nature of Implicit Theories

Various researchers have arrived at an appreciation of the pervasiveness of implicit theories by diverse routes. For example, Norman (1963) had groups of subjects rate each other on twenty scales. For each of the twenty scales, instructions required participants (in groups of 6 to 16) to pick out one-third of the other group members who best exemplified the characteristic denoted by one end of a given scale (say, *adventurous*) and another third who best exemplified the other end of the scale (*cautious*). Five factors emerged from these peer ratings and were labeled as follows:

1. Extroversion
2. Agreeableness
3. Conscientiousness
4. Emotional Stability
5. Culture

These same five factors were obtained when the procedures were carried out with a number of different subject samples and had even been obtained earlier by different investigators (Tupes & Christal, 1958, cited in Passini and Norman, 1966). These repeatedly obtained and highly similar results seemed to be saying that the five factors account for variations in how people behave.

It apparently occurred to Norman, however, that if this same five-factor "... structure could be obtained from groups of subjects (raters and ratees) with virtually no opportunity for prior interaction or observation, then the inference that the previously obtained results veridically reflected attributes of the ratees would certainly be questionable" (Passini and Norman, 1966, p. 45). To check on this possibility, Passini and Norman used essentially the same rating procedure that Norman had used earlier, except that subjects were asked to rate others on the basis of less than 15 minutes acquaintance and without previously having had a chance to even talk to those they were rating. Comparison of the results indicated that, when subjects are rating complete strangers, the factor structure that emerges is highly similar to that obtained from raters who knew a great deal about each other. Passini and Norman (1966) conclude that

> ... if we accept the position that each rater brings to the situation an implicit personality theory which in certain aspects is similar to that of the other persons in the group and if observable features of the dress and manner of the participants are sufficient to provide an entree to one or more components of each of these common attribute clusters, then the interrater agreement and factorial structures obtained in the present study begin to seem a little less incredible (p. 48).

Taking the demonstration a step further, Hakel (1969) did away with the ratees. That is, he simply gave subjects a questionnaire with a number of items such as: Suppose a person is ____. How likely is it that he is also ____? The blanks were filled in with the adjectives which had defined Norman's 20 scales, and subjects were asked to rate the likelihood of all possible co-occurrences. The results, again, were essentially the same as in Norman's studies. Hakel, of course, attributes the results entirely to the eyes of the beholders, that is, the operation of the raters implicit theories of personality.

D'Andrade (1965) has shown that simply asking subjects to rate the similarity in meaning between all possible pairs of the terms used in Norman's (1963) study results in essentially the same five-factor structure. Similarity and differences in meaning are, no doubt, incorporated into implicit theories. *Frank* and *open* might both be inferred about another who is *honest* simply because they are all similar in meaning. As we shall see, however, similarity of meaning cannot account for many of the patterns of relationships obtained in studies of implicit theories. As a case in point, Bruner, Shapiro, and Tagiuri (1958) found that inferences from *intelligent* are made to many traits that "... are by no means *denoted* by intelligent, certainly not in the dictionary or even in the thesaurus sense" (p. 280).

The studies by Norman, Passini, and Hakel help refine our model of implicit theories in the following two senses. First, an implicit theory is not simply a random correlation matrix of relationships among traits. Rather, it is a matrix that has an underlying structure or organization. Secondly, this underlying structure can be extracted and made explicit. The technique used in the above studies was factor analysis and, as we shall see, there are a number of related techniques that enable us to determine how implicit theories are organized. It is also worth noting that the studies by Norman and Passini demonstrate that one's implicit theory influences how he or she interprets and rates the actual behavior of others.

Armed with a somewhat refined model of an implicit theory as a correlation matrix with an underlying dimensional (factorial) structure let us go back and see if this will help us clarify the notion of a central trait.

Asch's (1946) manipulation of *warm–cold*, while making large differences in attribution for most of the characteristics on his checklist, did not influence responses to some of the checklist items. For example, subjects were about equally likely to describe the stimulus person as reliable, important, persistent, serious, strong, and honest regardless of whether he had been described to them as warm or cold. Asch does not really interpret this lack of difference on some items, but simply says that "... if we assume that the process of mutual influence took place in terms of the actual *character of the qualities* in question, it is not surprising that some will, by virtue of their content, remain unchanged" (p. 264, emphasis added). The content of the unchanged items is presumably somehow different from the content of the items influenced by *warm–cold*. One possible way of conceptualizing such content differences is in terms of the structure of an implicit theory.

If we conceptualize a dimensional structure underlying one's implicit theory, then to the extent that the various dimensions are orthogonal, they contribute different areas of content to the theory. Visualizing such a model, Jackson (1962) suggested that it might then be possible to assign formal meaning to "centrality ... for example, a trait would be considered central if it was highly loaded on a 'large' dimension, that is, a dimension accounting for a large proportion of the variance" (p. 185). Jackson seems to have ignored an apparently important determinant of centrality, however, that of context. Is a given characteristic "central" for all time and place for a given perceiver? A study by Rosenberg, Nelson, and Vivekananthan (1968) indicates that context is crucial—a notion in keeping with Asch's original Gestalt formulation.

Rosenberg et al (1968) utilized multidimensional scaling to obtain geometrical representations of the relationships among a set of 64 traits, a set that included 39 traits taken from Asch (1946) and Wishner (1960). What multidimensional scaling does is to take measures of relatedness among the items of interest (e.g., judgments of how likely an honest person will also be clever) and represent those measures in a geometrical configuration so that one can visualize the relationships. The method of interpreting such geometrical configurations involves empirical "fitting" of axes (dimensions), which account for variations among the items of interest. The measures of relatedness among all possible pairs of the 64 traits were obtained by asking subjects to sort the traits into categories and to let each category be descriptive of a person that they knew. A count was then made of the number of times any two traits were put together in the same category.

The assumption is that the more often any two traits occurred together, the more closely related they were perceived to be.

Once the scaling had been carried out with these relatedness (distance) measures, the traits were rated on several properties, and multiple regression was employed to locate the best fit of each of these properties (dimensions) in the obtained configuration of traits. Rosenberg et al (1968) found that a two-dimensional configuration interpreted with the properties *good social–bad social* and *good intellectual–bad intellectual* seemed to adequately account for the variations among the 60 traits. This two-dimensional framework is presented in Figure 2.1.

Comparing their results to Asch's *warm–cold* study, Rosenberg et al (1968) point out that the context traits presented to subjects—intelligent, practical, determined, skillful, industrious, cautious—that is, those "common to both lists are all from the positive end of the intellectual desirability dimension, whereas 'warm' and 'cold' have very similar values (near the neutral point) on this dimension. The trait inferences *not* affected by the substitution of 'cold' or 'warm' are more or less also on the positive side of the intellectual desirability dimension" (pp. 292–293).

Thus, the question of centrality as Asch conceived it has been changed to a suggestion that a characteristic is important as an organizer of one's impression of another to the extent that that characteristic stands out as begin unique among the characteristics of the other. If this is true, then taking a pair of antonyms from the poles of the intellectual *good–bad* dimension (e.g., *industrious–lazy*) identified by Rosenberg et al (1968) and presenting them in a context of social good traits (e.g., warm, sociable, good-natured, humorous) should make *industrious–lazy* the central characteristic. This was done by Zanna and Hamilton (1972), who also repeated the original Asch experiment in the same study. As anticipated *industrious–lazy* was central when presented in a context of social good traits just as *warm–cold* was central when presented in a context of intellectual good traits. As Zanna and Hamilton (1972) note, "Centrality is not a property of certain traits, but—rather—is a function of the inferential relationships among a set of traits" (p. 354).

This way of looking at centrality might be restated by using the notion of cues. Some characteristics, qualities, or behaviors of others serve as cues to additional characteristics that these others might possess. There has been a fair amount of research on what cues people use to form impressions of others and even some theorizing as to how they go about utilizing cues.

Cues and Attributions

There are a number of ways one could approach the subject of what cues people use in making inferences about the personalities of others. Theoretically, at least, anything that a perceiver believes to be related to some aspect of personality

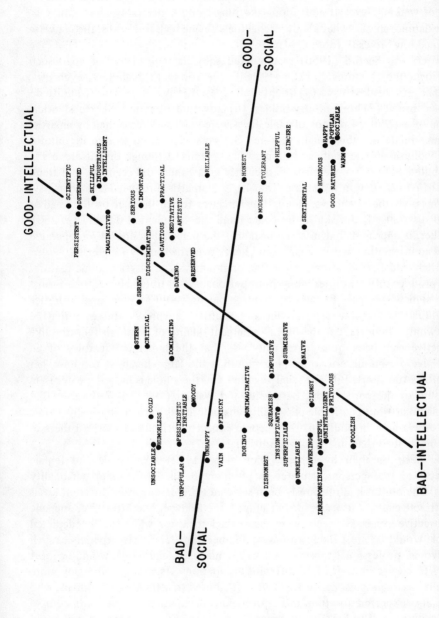

FIG. 2.1 Two-dimensional configuration of 60 traits showing best fitting properties of social desirability and intellectual desirability. (From Rosenberg et al., 1968, p. 290. Copyright 1968 by the American Psychological Association, Reprinted by Permission.)

could serve as a cue. Dress, type of car another drives, types of music listened to, way of walking, level of education—anything could conceivably serve. There is, for example, an old belief about intellectuals having high foreheads; the converse assigned low brows to football players.

Stritch and Secord (1956) manipulated subjects perceptions of eight such physiognomic features: (1) heavy–light eyebrows; (2) high–low eyebrows; (3) hair groomed–messy; (4) bright–dull eyes; (5) eye wrinkles; (6) knitted–relaxed brow; (7) horizontal wrinkles; (8) curvature of mouth. Three identical prints of each of 24 photos of male faces were made and retouched by an artist to manipulate the above eight features. Subjects were asked to rate the photos on 18 physiognomic traits and 25 personality traits. Although the differences in attributed personality were not particularly great, there did seem to be a trend toward *consistency* in judgment. That is, ". . . an artist produced change in, say, heaviness of the eyebrows, causes the perceiver to see the hair on the head as more disarranged, the skin more coarse, and the complexion darker" (p. 280). Further, it appeared that in some instances the personality impression operated by as an integrating factor: coarse skin, heavy eyebrows imply roughness.

Stritch and Secord attempted a fine grain analysis of physiognomic features that produce different inferences about personality. As noted above, their results were somewhat weak. Perhaps the average person is not so precise as to notice individual features like, say, heaviness of another's eyebrows. Rather, it may be that what is important is the overall emergent quality of another's features, like attractiveness. It is quite often the case that the individual features of an attractive person are not so hot; her mouth is too large, her nose too long, her eyebrows too short. But put it all together and the whole is indeed greater than the sum of the parts. Dion, Berscheid, and Walster (1972) hypothesized that people do attribute desirable personality characteristics to such physically attractive others and, in addition, that people expect physically attractive others to lead better lives than unattractive individuals.

To check on their hypothesis, Dion et al (1972) asked male and female subjects to rate persons depicted in photographs on 27 different personality traits. The photos had previously been selected to represent three different levels of attractiveness, and each subject judged one average, one attractive, and one unattractive other. Subjects were also asked to assess which of the depicted people would be most likely to have a number of different life experiences such as divorce, professional success, or a happy marriage, and which would be most likely to engage in each of 30 different occupations. As anticipated, many more socially desirable personality traits were attributed to attractive individuals, who were also expected to attain more prestigious occupations, to be more competent spouses, and to have happier marriages. These differences were not affected by the sex of the person making the judgments or by the sex of the person about whom the judgments were being made. Dion et al (1972) point out that the results are "perfectly compatible with the 'What is beautiful is good' thesis" (p. 289).

There have been a number of studies in this tradition. Luft (1957), for example, asked college students to fill out a personality test (the California Test of Personality) as though they were a married, 30-year-old man, with two children. Some of the students were told that the man made $42.50 a week, and others were told that he made $250.00 per week. Regardless of their own family income level, the students attributed more unfavorable personality characteristics to the low income man than an actual group of low income men attributed to themselves. Pheterson, Kiesler, and Goldberg (1971) found that women students at Connecticut College used the sex of an artist as a cue to the artist's "technical competence" and "artistic future." That is, when judging paintings entered in a contest, these women downgraded the artist more when told that the artist was female than when the artist was described as male (the paintings were the same in both cases, of course).

Such research is of interest and can be used for a number of purposes, not the least of which are political and humane for the last two studies cited. However, one begins to get a feeling of discomfort in reading through the literature on cue utilization in personality judgments. How valuable is it to keep piling up instances of different cues and what people infer from them? There is material for hundreds of such experiments in the daily life of most people. What about judgments of smokers as opposed to nonsmokers, drinkers versus nondrinkers, lipstick wearers versus nonwearers (this one has been done), style of dress (so has this), type of car driven? Here is a field for rampant empiricism and advertising image builders. After all, what type of man does read Playboy?

What would result if all these studies were carried out? A not very useful catalogue of cues and a lot of disillusioned researchers. What we really want is an understanding of cue utilization, not simply more examples. We need to know the how and why of cue utilization. In short, we need some coherent theoretical statements about what is involved.

Theories Pertinent to Cue Utilization

One of the things that scares people off when someone starts discussing theory, is that they envision some elaborate, hard-to-understand superstructure made up of varying amounts of hot air and gas, which—perhaps because of such a composition—rarely touches ground. Such a preconception is unfortunate, because theories are important and it is necessary to use them to achieve any sort of integration of knowledge. Such a preconception is also, usually, just plain wrong. As we shall see most of the theories we will discuss below are elegant in their simplicity and not in the least hard to understand.

Theories vary in scope. Some seek to explain only a small portion of the cue utilization process, while others are much broader and sweeping in terms of what they seek to explain. Cohen (1961), for example, was concerned with a single aspect of impression formation, the purpose for which the impression is being formed. Making use of Zajonc's (1960) concepts of "transmission tuning" and "reception tuning," Cohen reasoned that these two sets or types of orientation to deal with information should make a difference in how one handles information about another person. In transmission tuning, the individual expects to have to communicate the impression to others; hence, he or she needs to be able to articulate that impression clearly and concisely. Such an orientation would tend to lead one to ignore or minimize inconsistencies and form a definite impression. In reception tuning, on the other hand, the individual expects to continue to receive information; hence, he or she is more likely to suspend judgment, thus forming a less clear-cut impression.

Cohen gave subjects a list of traits supposedly descriptive of another person. Half of the subjects were told that, after reading the traits, their job would be to communicate to others all they could about the person described by the traits. The remaining subjects were told that, after reading the traits, they would find out how others perceived the person described by the traits. Since Cohen also anticipated that highly contradictory material (traits) would exaggerate the different influences of the two sets, half of the subjects in each of the above two conditions read a list of traits that were highly contradictory and half read a list that contained only moderate contradictions. As expected, subjects in the transmission set condition were more likely to exclude one or the other aspect of information when it was highly contradictory. Also, subjects set to receive information had greater desires for more information and for information on both sides. Thus, it appears that the purpose for which an impression is being formed does make a difference.

Others have concerned themselves with similarly specific theoretical questions pertinent to the cue utilization process. Blanchard (1966), for example, addressed the question of relevance of the information (cue) to the type of attribution being made. It stands to reason that we need pertinent cues in order to make accurate predictions about another. If I am trying to decide whether or not I think a particular person will make a good colleague, I really do not care how many children he or she has or what section of the country he or she was born in; those facts are simply not relevant. On the other hand, I would be interested in knowing the person's research interests, intelligence, and, probably, general energy level. It comes as no surprise that Blanchard found accuracy of predictions to be higher when the cues given judges were relevant to the predictions being requested.

The theorists who have been most influential, however, have formulated somewhat broader conceptions about the processes involved in making inferences about others. Notable among these are Bruner (1948), Heider (1958),

...lation between the observed act and ...
...the act appears to have been forced by th... ...ibuted characteristic
... Davis use the term "correspondence" to re... ...g in which it occurs.
...ed act and the underlying attributed charac... ...he extent to which
...y the inference. An inference is "correspondent" ...are similarly de-
...the number of noncommon effects following the ...nverse function
...d social desirability of these effects. ...; and (b) the
...mmarizing their position, Jones and Davis (1965) presen...
...(Table 2.1). It is important to understand that the perceiv... following
...d as attempting to understand *why* a person acted in a particul... ...ferer) is
...e specifically, is attempting to determine if the evidence warrants a... ...y and,
...particular disposition to that person. As the table shows, ...ution

> . . . actions which lead to effects deemed highly desirable to most persons cannot h...
> ...ut be trivial from an informational point of view. Also, when the number of noncom...
> mon effects is high, the perceiver cannot escape from the ambiguity of the data in
> making inferences either to common or idiosyncratic personal characteristics. In line
> with the stated theoretical relationship, the high correspondence cell is that in which
> assumed desirability and the number of noncommon effects are both low.

Jones and Davis incorporate two further concepts into their theory, "personalism" and "hedonic relevance," which we will not go into, but which deal with the implications of a particular action for the perceiver.

The most direct descendent of the Heider and Jones and Davis formulations of how we go about making inferences is the work of Kelley (1967). In analyzing the problem of how a person goes about deciding that he or she has a valid impression of another, Kelley lists four criteria: (1) distinctiveness; (2) consistency over time; (3) consistency over modality; and (4) consensus. Thus, we may feel confident that George is an antisemite if he responds with hostility to any mention of Jews, but not to blacks, if he has responded in this manner ever since we have known him, if he responds with both verbal and nonverbal indices of hatred, and if everyone who knows him agrees that he hates Jews. It is important to point out that Kelley, Jones and Davis, and Heider are all dealing with the

TABLE 2.1

Effect Desirability and Effect Commonality
as Determinants of Correspondence[a]

		Assumed desirability	
		High	Low
Number of noncommon effects	High	Trivial ambiguity	Intriguing ambiguity
	Low	Trivial clarity	High correspondence

[a]From Jones and Davis, 1965, p. 229.

...1964), Sherif ...

Secord and Bac 7).

(1965) and Kell as his basic premise
Heider (195 edict and control it, b
reality, and ts to relatively unchanging un
behavior an perties of his world" (p. 79). Th
disposition me to understand if I assume that
a cat, it However, if I *know* that the person is
plain m understand the action unless I could
could of the person, something in the environment
"out ten by the cat. Maybe the cat had rabies. Accordi
just me or action is dependent upon a combination of
ou ntal forces and the personal force can further be conceiv
wer factor and a motivational factor. Heider (1958, p. 8
relations as follows:

that the re
declines as
Jones and
an obser
scribed
of: (a)
assume
In s
table
view
mor
of

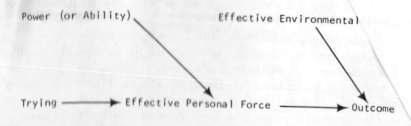

If we know that someone has published ten articles in the last two years and we want to infer something about the quality of the person's efforts, we might first look at the journals in which he or she has published. If the publications are in prestigious journals that have notoriously high rejection rates, its going to be difficult to attribute the productivity to a weak restraining environmental force. Hence, we are likely to infer high quality (or that the person has ability). On the other hand, if the publications are in vanity press journals that take anything from anybody, we are likely to infer that the quality is not so good. The restraining environmental force here is weak and anybody could do the same if they simply tried. Of course, to be safe, we should actually read the work; there is a lot of low quality material in the best journals and an occasional gem in the worst.

Building on Heider's basic premise, Jones and Davis (1965) developed a theory to explain some of the processes mediating the gap between observing a particular act of another and attribution of a particular disposition to the other. Basic to their conception is the idea that a given act represents a choice and that any effects of the act which are common to all choice alternatives could not be the determinants of why the given act was chosen. As does Heider, they also assume subjective validity of one's impressions and are not concerned with objective veridicality. That is, they are not concerned with whether or not George is really an antisemite, but with how one convinces oneself about George.

It should be clear that, in discussing the above attribution theories, we are not really talking about the internal relations within an implicit theory of personality. Rather, we are attempting to throw some light on how a given cue or observed act is tested by the perceiver to determine if it allows tapping into his or her implicit theory and making additional inferences about the perceived.

The first state, the one that Heider, Jones and Davis, and Kelley attempt to analyze, is essentially a process of categorization. Without formulating unique models, a number of others have commented on the categorization process and how it might be triggered. Secord and Backman (1964) argue that intensive observation and analysis of a number of situations involving person-perception suggest several inference processes. One, referred to as temporal extension, takes place when a perceiver regards a momentary characteristic of the perceived as if it were an enduring attribute. To translate this into Kelley's terms, the perceiver assumes consistency over time on the basis of insufficient evidence. Another process may be triggered when the perceived resembles a familiar person. Again, on the basis of such an insufficient bit of evidence, the perceiver may attribute characteristics of the familiar acquaintance. Secord and Backman also identify two additional types of inference based on analogy:

1. Metaphorical generalization occurs when qualities inherent in the stimulus information presented by the perceived are generalized to personality judgments (e.g., coarse skin implies a coarse person).
2. Functional generalization occurs when the perceiver makes an inference from the function of some observed attribute of the person (e.g., thin, compressed lips imply the person is not very talkative).

The feature common to the various attribution theories and inference processes is that, during this initial stage, we essentially take the epistemological position proposed by Allport (1966) of *heuristic realism*. That is, "the person who confronts us possesses inside his skin generalized action tendencies (or traits) and that it is our job scientifically to discover what they are" (p. 3). Once we do decide that we have enough evidence to attribute a given disposition or characteristic to another, as Warr and Knapper (1968) point out, we immediately assume sets of both episodic and dispositional expectancies about that person.

As for how the latter relationships come into being, the most straightforward interpretation is a simple associationist hypothesis. One could use such learning theories as those of Skinner, Hull, Guthrie, or Watson to build a case for how concepts like *wise* and *kind* come to be associated or to be believed to be related. However, the learning theory that is most congenial and most directly relevant seems to be Tolman's (1932).

Tolman called his theory of learning *purposive behaviorism*, and, as the term implies, there is a definite cognitive emphasis to his theory. Using the results of a series of animal and human experiments, Tolman developed a conception of expectancy (Hilgard, 1956), which included the following aspects:

1. The organism brings to a problematic situation various systematic modes of attack, based largely on prior experiences.
2. The cognitive field is provisionally organized according to the hypotheses of the learner, the hypotheses which survive being those which best correspond with reality, that is, with the overall texture of the environment. These hypotheses or expectancies are confirmed by success in goal achievement.
3. A clearly established cognitive structure is available for use under altered conditions (p. 210).

The keys to the concept of expectancy, as we wish to use it, involve an assumption that trying to determine what another is like is a problematic situation with which everyone has had experience and an assumption that we behave as scientists when confronted with this situation. That is, we take some systematic hypothesis-generating and -testing approach. It should be noted that Tolman (1932) replaces the classic concept of reinforcement with the notion of confirmation. "If an expectancy is confirmed, its probability value is increased; if an expectancy is not confirmed, its probability value is decreased (i.e., it undergoes extinction)" (p. 202).

It might be useful, in order to clarify the above, to describe a hypothetical situation. Let us assume that, when nothing is known about the relationship between two personality characteristics (*A* and *B*), we take .5 as the probability that a person who "has" *A* will also "have" *B*. Let *A* be *kindness* and *B*, *determination*. Suppose we see a man who has his arm around a crying child. Our first task is to try to decide what is going on. Is he comforting or molesting the child? Checking around for cues, we see a broken toy on the sidewalk and a guilty looking toddler peeking out from behind the bushes.

The man is "obviously" trying to console the child. The following day, we see the same man retrieving a stranded cat from a tree limb. We might consider these two instances sufficient to attribute to the man a quality of kindness. In inquiring around the neighborhood about our good samaritan, we learn that he is a self-made man who came from a poverty-stricken family and worked nights to put himself through college. We begin to entertain the hypothesis that there may be some relation between kindness and determination. The next kind and determined person we meet confirms our hypothesis and increments our perceived probability of there "really" being a relation between the two to something a little above .5. If half of the kind people we meet are determined (confirmation) and half not determined (disconfirmation), we will sooner or later relinquish our hypothesis of a relationship.

By such processes, we build up our correlation matrix of perceived relationships among traits. Since we continue to exist and (most of us) continue to learn, the processes continue throughout life and our implicit theories are constantly being revised. Since so many of our experiences are shared with others or are very similar to experiences many people have, it comes as no surprise that there are large areas of overlap among the implicit theories of different people. One feature that many implicit theories seem to share and that may be of significance in determining if implicit theories influence behavior toward others is the evaluative dimension.

The Evaluative Dimension

Does our liking or disliking another person influence the characteristics we attribute to him or her? Are our friends flexible and intelligent, but our enemies wishy-washy and cunning? It will be recalled that Thorndike's (1920) halo effect was precisely this tendency to judge each of another's characteristics in the light of an overall impression of goodness or badness. While the behavior of one's friend may be exactly the same as the behavior of one's enemy, the interpretations or the "meaning" of the behavior may differ.

Perhaps the most well known investigations into the nature of meaning are those of Osgood and his associates (Osgood, Suci, and Tannenbaum, 1957). The primary instrument that Osgood has employed in his studies of connotative meaning is the semantic differential. For the uninitiated, the semantic differential is simply a generic name given to any series of bipolar rating scales on which subjects are asked to rate a concept (like *motherhood*). Employing a wide variety of rating scales, concepts, and subject populations over a number of years, factor analyses of the ratings have repeatedly revealed three dimensions of connotative meaning: evaluation, potency, and activity. The evaluative dimension is usually defined by contrasts such as: good–bad, clean–dirty, beautiful– ugly, kind–cruel. The potency dimension is usually defined by contrasts such as: hard–soft, masculine–feminine, severe–lenient, strong–weak, heavy–light. The activity factor is usually identified by: fast–slow, active–passive, excitable–calm, rash–cautious. The evaluative factor appears to be consistently the largest, to account for the greatest amount of variation in meaning.

The success with the semantic differential in uncovering stable dimensions of connotative meaning prompted an attempt by Osgood and Ware (Osgood, 1962) to develop a personality differential. Forty-five college students were asked to rate, on 30 scales, 6 personality concepts, such as *me* or *my best friend*. Separate factor analyses of the ratings for each of the six concepts again turned up variants of evaluation, potency, and activity, which were labeled, respectively, morality, toughness, and volatility. Thus, evaluation (in the guise of morality) appeared to be an important aspect of judgments about people as well as an aspect of the more general connotative meaning.

To further refine their inspection of evaluation in personality judgments, Osgood and Ware asked two samples of subjects to make judgments about the likelihood of co-occurrence of 34 general personality traits taken from Allport and Odbert (1936). That is, subjects were asked to make judgments in a format similar to that cited earlier in the study by Hakel (1969): A person who is: mature is likely to be: impulsive ____; ____; ____ ; ____; ____; ____; logical. The results of "The factor analyses of these two samples of scale-on-scale judgments yielded such large evaluative factors (58% and 69% of total variance, respectively) that little else could be determined" (Osgood, 1962, p. 25).

In a third study, an attempt was made to deflate the dominant evaluative factor by deliberately choosing diverse scales on which subjects were to make ratings of forty concepts. Again, however, evaluation (morality) emerged in the factor analyses of the ratings, although it accounted for a smaller proportion of the variation in those ratings. Thus, evaluation appears to be an important organizing force in implicit theories of personality; even when attempts are made to downplay its role, it continues to emerge.

Suppose, however, that subjects were not asked to rate others on specific scales. Suppose subjects were encouraged to think more abstractly and pull together the common characteristics of people whom they have liked and the characteristics of people whom they have disliked. Would the characteristics attributed under these conditions still have strong evaluative connotations? If so, this would seem to be better evidence for the importance of an evaluative dimension in implicit theories because it is less artificial than having person concepts rated on scales. After all, one of the lessons of Wishner's (1960) study was that, if we choose the rating scales properly, we can get just about any result we want.

Pastore (1960) asked subjects to judge the characteristics of people whom they have liked or disliked. Relative to liked others, disliked others were judged: to have fewer friends, to elicit less agreement for their opinions, to be less interested in travel, to eat more, to possess a personality more determined by hereditary factors, to be more influenced by prestige, and so on. In short, a long list of specific characteristics were seen as significantly differentiating liked from disliked others. In a second study, Pastore obtained similar differences from another sample of subjects—indicating that the effects were not peculiar to the particular people who participated in the first study.

In a third experiment, Pastore attempted to manipulate liking or disliking for another by using a procedure similar to Asch's (1946). That is, he selected sets of traits that would elicit a positive or negative attitude toward a person who was described by the traits. One group of subjects was asked to respond to a stimulus person described as sincere, tactful, sympathetic, cooperative, self-confident, and another group of subjects responded to a stimulus person described as cunning, cynical, selfish, untrustworthy, blunt. Here, even more extreme differences in resulting impressions were obtained than in his first study. It is interesting to note that Pastore placed more faith in the results of his first study because, "it could be claimed that the rated impressions were contained in or could be directly inferred from the traits themselves" (p. 159). Yes, indeed.

Thus, the evaluation we place on another person, whether we like or dislike them, is related to the characteristics we attribute to them. If we like a person we attribute desirable qualities to them, or do we like a person because of the desirable qualities? Both directions operate, no doubt, but here we are not concerned with the research that has used *liking* as a dependent variable. Rather, we are concerned with research that has asked for attributions of additional characteristics to liked and disliked others, research that has manipulated the desirability of the characteristics of a stimulus person and asked for additional attributions, and research that has attempted to determine the underlying dimensions or factors of implicit theories (such as that of Norman and Osgood).

Lott, Lott, Reed and Crow (1970), for example, asked subjects to think of three persons: one liked, one disliked, and one toward whom they felt neutral. Using the 200 most meaningful traits from Anderson's (1968) evaluatively scaled list, subjects were asked to decide which of the three people they were thinking of was most appropriately described by each of the traits. Liked others were described with more favorable traits than neutral persons and disliked others were described using less favorable traits than those used to describe neutral persons. Also, the greatest number of words were used to describe liked persons, fewer for neutral persons, and least for disliked persons.

There is an interesting asymmetry to the evaluative dimension in implicit theories, which is suggested by the Lott et al (1970) results. If the 200 words from Anderson's list contained approximately equal numbers of positively and negatively evaluated traits (which Lott et al aver), then subjects appear to see more traits (both positive and negative) being implied by positive traits than by negative traits. Could it be that, when we like someone, we like them even though we recognize their negative characteristics but, when we dislike someone, we are less willing to give them credit for having any positive characteristics? Such a result could be accounted for by Newcomb's (1947) notion of autistic hostility. That is, when we dislike (or, are hostile to) someone, we avoid them; it is not very rewarding to be around them. Hence, we have less opportunity to learn that they may have many shining features and be fine upstanding pillars of the community. On the other hand, when we like someone, it is rewarding to be around them. Hence, we spend more time with them and sooner or later we discover that they have certain negative characteristics. Such duel processes would also explain the finding that, just in terms of total numbers of words, Lott et al found more attributions to liked others, a finding they interpret in terms of the greater salience of liked persons.

The evidence begins to appear overwhelming that evaluation is an important organizing principle in implicit theories of personality. Before turning to other substantive aspects of implicit theories, however, we need to address some methodological issues that we have skirted in the last few sections. The first of these is a point that was raised specifically in connection with research on the evaluative dimension.

METHODOLOGICAL ISSUES

Peabody (1967) has argued that the primary reason evaluation has appeared as such a strong factor in implicit theories of personality and trait inferences is that "... there has been a failure to distinguish clearly between evaluative and descriptive aspects of judgment which are normally confounded with each other" (p. 2). In an attempt to demonstrate that evaluation is really of secondary importance, Peabody constructed sets of traits which consisted of:

1. A given descriptive attribute which was positively evaluated (say, *alert*);
2. Its opposite which was also positively evaluated (*relaxed*);
3. A trait descriptive of the same attribute as the first, but which was negatively evaluated (*tense*);
4. A negatively evaluated opposite of the latter (*lethargic*). A number of such sets were constructed which, in tabular form can be represented as:

		Descriptive attribute	
		X	Un-X
Evaluation	+	Modest	Confident
	−	Self-disparaging	Conceited

Subjects were then asked to make inferences in which they were "given a single trait (the 'antecedent term') and a choice between two alternative traits. In relation to the antecedent term (e.g., *cautious*), the two alternatives would be: (a) similar in evaluation and dissimilar on the descriptive attribute (e.g. *bold*); and (b) dissimilar in evaluation and similar on the descriptive attribute (e.g. *timid*) ..." (Peabody, 1967, p. 5). In every case, on such items, subjects inferred traits that were descriptively similar to the antecedent term and evaluatively dissimilar to the antecedent term, a result that led Peabody to conclude that evaluation "tends always to be secondary to" descriptive aspects of judgment.

Even if his data were unimpeachable, that is a slight overgeneralization. Such overgeneralizations often serve as goads, challenges for someone to find the fatal flaw in the data or analysis. But before looking at the follow-up studies, there are two more results of Peabody's that are of interest.

In addition to the inferences within the specially constructed sets, subjects also made inferences across sets. That is, from an antecedent term in one set (e.g., *modest*), they would infer to a scale defined by two terms from another set (e.g., *alert–tense*). Here evaluative similarity was the usual result, occurring on approximately two-thirds of 3450 such items. Peabody, of course, discounts this result because it is impossible to tell if evaluative similarity is operating directly or if it is simply a by-product of descriptive similarity. One other result of interest is that, from a given antecedent term, subjects demonstrated a great deal of agreement as to the direction of inference. "Far from restricting inferences only to closely related terms, subjects demonstrated a very extensive *common* network of inferences" (p. 6, emphasis added). Thus for unselected inferences, evaluation dominates as an organizing principle once again and there is a great deal of overlap among the implicit theories of the subjects.

Peabody (1967) did carry out a factor analysis of the inference data in which an evaluative factor failed to appear. Rosenberg and Olshan (1970) have pointed out that by using correlation coefficients as his measure of intertrait relatedness, Peabody inadvertently threw out information about the evaluative dimension.

> That is, since each bipolar scale contains an evaluative component (a favorable trait at one end and an unfavorable trait at the other end) and since all the scales were oriented the same way for scoring (seven-step scales with the unfavorable end being scored as 1), most if not all of the information about evaluative similarity between any two traits is contained in the difference between their means over the scales. The product–moment correlation of the average ratings across the scales, which Peabody used in his factor analysis, discards the differences between the means and reflects only the similarity in the shape of the profiles" (Rosenberg and Olshan, 1970, p. 620).

A reanalysis of Peabody's data using a more appropriate index of intertrait relatedness yielded a strong evaluative dimension.

In another follow-up to Peabody's study, Felipe (1970) found that when subjects were making inferences from a trait (e.g., *rude*) to scales defined by bipolar terms with the same descriptive quality but different evaluative signs (e.g., *stingy–thrifty*) that evaluative consistency predominates. In 305 out of 321 such inferences, or 95 percent, the results confirm evaluative consistency predictions. On the other hand, when subjects were infering from a concept to scales composed of descriptively bipolar terms that had the same evaluative sign (e.g., *stingy–extravagant*), 82 percent of the resulting inferences were in the direction of descriptive consistency. Finally, when evaluative and descriptive consistency were put in opposition, the evaluative consistency hypothesis again appeared to do better. However, as Felipe points out, his study was designed "to sample cognitive structures that would be difficult to balance descriptively, by using a large number of inference items involving concepts that have minimal descriptive overlaps with scales. . . . The findings strongly indicate that apparently strong support for either descriptive or evaluative consistency theories . . . may be gathered in a study depending on the proportion of descriptively related trait terms used" (p. 633–634). Thus, we seem to have another case of the old truism: the results depend on the method of measurement.

It seems to me that the entire issue of evaluative versus descriptive similarity is something like a snark hunt. Felipe's paraphrase of Peabody's (1967) starting point is that "subjects would prefer affectively unbalanced cognitions so long as they are descriptively consistent, to the reverse" (p. 627). Think about that for a moment. That's like saying subjects would prefer having their left hand amputated to having their right hand amputated—what subjects would really prefer is to keep *both* hands! If I know that a person is opportunistic, I am going to infer additional characteristics that are *both* affectively and descriptively consistent with that characteristic.

If I did make such inferences a legitimate concern would be how these inferences compared with what the person is "really" like. Earlier we made a case for the building up of implicit theories—our correlational matrices with their underlying structure and organizing principles, such as evaluation—through experience. To what extent, then, do our theories reflect that experience?

Veridicality

At first glance, the question of veridicality of implicit theories might appear to be a direct descendant (or the ghost itself) of the old studies on "accuracy" or the "ability to judge people" which abounded during the 1940s and 1950s. However, as Hastorf et al (1970) point out, the accuracy studies were

... directed not so much toward our ability to assess accurately the personality traits of others as toward the identification of the kinds of perceivers who are particularly sensitive to the enduring characteristics of others. ... The motivation of those who conducted the early accuracy studies was very pragmatic: accurate judges may well occupy special positions in various social groups by virtue of their ability—or at least, it might be beneficial if they did (pp. 25–26).

Studies of veridicality have not been concerned with identifying "sensitive perceivers" per se but with the (admittedly related) more general question of whether the ways in which perceivers organize their beliefs about the relationships among characteristics correspond to the ways in which these characteristics really co-occur in others.

We have already mentioned several pertinent studies. For example, Luft (1957) had college students fill out a personality test as they believed a man who earned $42.50 a week would, while others filled it out as they believed a man who earned $250.00 a week would. Actual low income men who filled out the test had significantly different personality patterns from those projected by the students. Thus, the students beliefs about the relationships between earning $42.50 per week and the various personality aspects tapped by the test were in error. There are a number of possible explanations for this finding: one that is particularly appealing is that knowledge of how much a person makes is simply not a relevant cue to judgments of, say, how sensitive that person is.

Blanchard (1966) attempted to manipulate the relevance of the information given an observer being asked to make predictions about another. He administered a pool of 300 interest items distributed over five scales (e.g., *aesthetic, science*) to a criterion group. He then asked a group of judges to predict how certain members of the criterion group had responded to 20 specific items. Before judges made their predictions, however, they were given some information about how these people had responded to 10 other items. In some cases, the 10 items were highly related to those 20 on which predictions were requested, and, in other cases, the 10 items were not closely related to the 20. As anticipated, the judges were quite accurate when the cues were relevant and quite inaccurate when the cues were irrelevant.

Comparisons of data from Norman (1963) and Passini and Norman (1966) also bear on the question of veridicality. It will be recalled that the same five-factor structure emerged in the Passini and Norman study when subjects were rating others on the basis of less than 15 minutes acquaintance as had emerged in the Norman study. In the latter, raters had had a great deal of prior contact with each other. This similarity of results might be taken as evidence that the implicit theories of the raters in the Passini and Norman study were veridical; the raters obviously had not had time to really get to know those whom they were rating.

A study by Stricker, Jacobs, and Kogan (1970) also yields some evidence for the veridicality of implicit theories. In the study, high school girls sorted items from a personality test into categories on the basis of "belonging together because they refer to the same characteristic" (p. 157). These categories were then compared with results from studies in which the same items had been administered to subjects who were to indicate which were descriptive of themselves. Using this "self-report" as the criterion, the categories obtained from sorting on the basis of "belonging together" were very similar to the criterion.

There are other data bearing on the question of veridicality, but we may have encountered a red herring. Let us go back for a moment and see if the issue of veridicality should be pursued. Is the issue important to our purpose? We want to demonstrate that expectations about other people exist, are organized in certain ways, and are dependent upon or related to certain other characteristics of the perceiver. These are only preliminary to demonstrating that such expectations influence our behavior toward the others about whom we hold these expectations.

Thus, the issue of veridicality of implicit theories is not directly pertinent to our purpose. To paraphrase Krishna (1971), our purpose is to develop the position that expectations have consequences because they exist and regardless of whether they are accurate or inaccurate. Why, then, have we bothered to discuss veridicality at all?

There are two reasons. First, it was argued earlier that implicit theories are built up through experiences with actual others. Hence, it is important to note that there does appear to be evidence that indicates *some* correspondence between the way people "are" and the way they are believed to be. Second, the issue of veridicality makes salient a theme that has been recurring throughout our discussions. That is, the results of research on implicit theories have been closely tied to (biased by?) the techniques of measurement employed. Asch's (1946) claim that *warm–cold* was a "central" characteristic, for example, was due to the particular traits on his checklist. Had he used a different checklist to begin with, he might never have published that paper. Before one could legitimately study veridicality of implicit theories, then, it would be necessary to obtain representations of those theories which are uncontaminated by the method of measurement.

The Free Response Approach

As we have seen, much of the work on implicit theories has required subjects to rate others on a list of predetermined scales, to infer from a given trait which of two additional traits (also given) would another be likely to have, or to sort a previously selected group of traits into categories. The major problem with such procedures, which restrict respondents to a fixed format and/or a preselected vocabulary, is that they may fail to provide the respondents with categories that are relevant or meaningful with respect to their particular perceptions. This problem has been recognized for many years and, as we shall see, a number of researchers have attempted to solve the problem. What the problem calls for is the approach taken by phenomenologists.

According to MacLeod (1947), "the phenomenological method in social psychology as in the psychology of perception . . . is the attempt to view phenomena in their entirety and without prejudice, to distinguish the essential from the nonessential, to let the phenomena themselves dictate the conceptual framework and the further course of the inquiry" (pp. 207–208). This statement is deceptively simple. The phenomenological method is extremely difficult to put into practice. How, for example, is one to distinguish the essential from the nonessential? How are we, mere mortals that we are, to view anything without prejudice? Perhaps a newborn baby can view things without prejudice, but no adult can, regardless of race, creed, or place of national origin. But given at the outset that a pure phenomenological approach is impossible, an unattainable ideal, we can, at least, try to approximate it.

In the study of implicit theories, many researchers have been attracted to the phenomenological approach and have usually taken the first step of asking subjects for "free," "open-ended," or "unconstrained" descriptions of others as a substitute or accompaniment to rating the others on a series of standard scales. Asch (1946), for example, asked subjects in his *warm–cold* experiment to write out a brief descrption or sketch of the person who had been described to them with one of the lists of seven traits. Asch used these sketches to illustrate some of the characteristics of how subjects organized their impressions and reinterpreted certain specific traits of the stimulus person, like *intelligent* in light of whether the stimulus person was also *warm* or *cold*. While Asch used the sketches effectively to buttress his arguments about the gestalt or holistic quality of the impressions formed, the sketches were not themselves used for any purpose other than plausible illustration.

Kelley (1950), in his follow up of the Asch study, also asked subjects to write out free descriptions of the instructor who had previously been described to them as warm or cold. Again, however, the free descriptions were not themselves subjected to detailed analysis but were simply read to glean some impressions of how the subjects organized their perceptions of the instructor. The treatment of the free response data in the Asch and Kelley studies, while interesting, does not really give us much information or new insights into the nature of implicit theories. If this were the best that the phenomenological approach had to offer, we could quickly go on to the next topic. Things began to pick up during the 1950s, however, as researchers began to push the free response approach.

Between 1954 and 1957, such eminent social psychologists as Allport, Bruner, Hastorf, and Tagiuri all published persuasive arguments that the study of person perception and impression formation would be greatly enriched by the study of how people spontaneously categorize others. The essence of their arguments is the notion that, in order to "understand" another, we need to know how that person perceives and interprets the world. In order to obtain this understanding, it is necessary to avoid putting words into the subjects' mouths, asking them to make inferences from traits they seldom, if every, employ in thinking about others, or asking them to sort a group of traits which they do not use into categories. All of these and related procedures may distort the resulting picture of the subjects' implicit theories.

Suppose, for example, that someone thinks of others in terms of how practical, friendly, honest, and hard-working they are. If you then ask such a person to infer whether practical others are likely to be polite or blunt, the person will have to fall back on something other than his or her implicit theory to make the judgment. In the person's implicit theory, *practical* has never been associated with either *polite* or *blunt*. The person would rely on the meanings of the terms (cf., D'Andrade, 1965) and reason that "politeness is sort of a superficial friendliness and practical people are friendly, so I guess a practical person would be polite." In short, the response would reflect the descriptive similarity (Peabody, 1967) between the presented scale and one facet of the person's implicit theory, but it would be false to take the response as indicating that, in the person's naive implicit theory (before being asked to make the inference), there was a relationship between *practical* and *polite*. The person had never used the term *polite* in thinking about others.

A study of particular pertinence here is one by Allport (1958). One of the things that concerned Allport was the artificiality of giving subjects long series of bipolar scales defined by traits that they may or may not have ever used to think about the personalities of others and asking them to make ratings on those scales. He reports a study in which 93 students were asked "to think of some one individual of your own sex whom you know well . . . describe him or her by writing in each space provided a word, a phrase, or a sentence that expresses fairly well . . . some essential characteristic of this person" (p. 254). Ninety percent of the subjects found ten spaces to be completely sufficient, and, on the average, the subjects felt that seven "essential" characteristics could capture their beliefs and impressions of the person described. One might begin to wonder what the results of studies really mean when subjects are asked to rate their acquaintances on hundreds of scales. "Perhaps what we need is fewer units than we now use, but units more relevant to individual structural patterns" (Allport, 1958, p. 253).

Partly as a result of the urgings by Bruner and Tagiuri (1954), Hastorf, Richardson, and Dornbusch (1958), Tagiuri (1958), and Allport (1958), people began to study "the perceptual categories that are actually employed by, and thus relevant to, the perceiver under consideration" Hastorf et al (1958, p. 55). Sarbin (1954), for example, had selected students in a classroom stand for ten seconds while their classmates wrote down the first three words that "came to mind" about the person standing. Females were significantly more likely to think of words which represented inferred qualities or traits such as aggressive, warm, hostile, and logical, while males were more likely to think of purely descriptive terms like tall, girl, and gray clothes.

One question that might occur when we give subjects so much freedom to select the terms they will use in describing others is the extent to which the terms employed are reflections of their implicit theories or are simply reflections of what the stimulus person is "really" like. That is, students in a classroom would presumably have some knowledge of their fellows. Hence, when John stands up, one may think of athlete *and* intelligent even though one believes that most athletes are unintelligent. Dornbusch, Hastorf, Richardson, Muzzy, and Vreeland (1965) addressed themselves to this question of the relative influence of the perceiver and the perceived. They solicited information from boys and girls in summer camps. Each child was interviewed twice and, in each interview, was asked to describe two other children who shared his or her tent. A set of 69 content analysis categories was developed and the descriptions reliably coded into these categories. Without exception, there was greater category overlap when one child was describing two others than when two children were describing the same other child. This finding held up even when the two descriptions from a given child were elicited a week apart. Thus, there are at least some conditions under which our implicit theories play more of a role in our perceptions of others than the actual characteristics of the others.

Although many researchers have attempted to utilize free response data to come to grips with the nature of implicit theories, the main reason that this approach has not received more emphasis is the difficulty in handling the data. What do you do with an open-ended description of another once you have it? How do you go about representing the relationships among the categories of descriptive information which are present? As we have seen, Sarbin (1954) simply divided the words used by subjects into two categories: inferred and descriptive. This is not really an adequate solution for at least two reasons: (1) the two categories are completely arbitrary—someone else might impose another classification, and (2) we are unable to say anything about the correlational network, which we are still using as our working model of an implicit theory.

The beginnings of a solution to these two problems were contained in a paper by Baldwin which was published in 1942. Baldwin employed a technique which he called personal structure analysis to analyze such free-response data as that contained in diaries and letters. The technique was based on two assumptions involving frequency and contiguity of units. The more often a given item appeared in the material to be analyzed, the more important it was assumed to be, and the repeated appearance of two items in close proximity was taken as evidence that they were perceived to be related. Baldwin employed his technique to analyze a series of letters from an elderly lady named Jenny in which she wrote about many things that concerned her, but mainly about her son (Ross), his friends, and their relationships to her. Baldwin prepared a long list of categories; the categories must be prepared anew for each individual to be analyzed and are based on prior knowledge of what the material contains. Defining an incident as a small temporal segment of the letters in which Jenny was writing about one general topic, two items or categories were said to be contiguous if they both appeared in the incident. The more often two categories appeared contiguously, the more closely related they were taken to be in Jenny's view of things. Baldwin was then able to represent these co-occurrences graphically.

The figure below is taken from Baldwin (1942, p. 175). In the figure, a line connecting two categories means they were significantly related in the letters. The location of the categories in the diagram is arbitrary.

Baldwin's technique was a valuable start, but, as a tool for investigating implicit theories of personality, it has serious problems. Perhaps most serious is the lack of procedures for looking at the underlying organization of the categories. We can get a picture of which categories are related, but, with a large number of categories, it would be very difficult to keep track of recurring themes—like what kinds of things are related to *unfavorable*. It appears that Jenny did employ an evaluative dimension, but did she also employ status as an organizing principle in her implicit theory and, if she did, was status independent

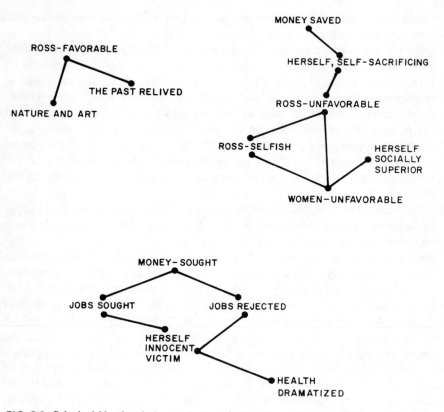

FIG. 2.2 Principal ideational clusters in Jenny's life. (From Baldwin, 1942, p. 175. Copyright 1942 by the American Psychological Association. Reprinted by Permission.)

of evaluation? Personal structure analysis does not allow us to answer such questions.

Recently, Rosenberg and Sedlak (1972), Jones and Rosenberg (1974), and others have employed advances in multidimensional scaling (Kruskal, 1964a, 1964b; Shepard, 1962a, 1962b); to determine if the organizing principles of subjects' implicit theories can be extracted from their free-response descriptions of others. For example, Jones and Rosenberg (1974) asked fifty students to "think of five people whom you *know* rather *well*.... Then describe each of these people as accurately as possible using a simple list (words or short phrases) of characteristics" (p. 218). Each item in a subject's lists was taken verbatim and two items were grouped into a category only if they contained the same basic morpheme. For example, *snob* was grouped with *snobbish* but not with *stuffed shirt*. For the 99 most frequently occurring categories in the descriptions, an index of co-occurrence was calculated to reflect how frequently two categories were used to describe the same persons. The more often two categories were used jointly, the closer together they were assumed to be in the implicit theories of the subjects.

The scaling of trait categories indicated that four dimensions were needed to interpret the relationships among the 99 most frequently occurring descriptive categories. These properties were: (1) evaluation; (2) hard—soft; (3) impulsive—inhibited; and (4) introverted—extraverted. Thus, there appear to be four common dimensions among the implicit theories of the subjects sampled by Jones and Rosenberg, and one of these shared organizing principles is our old friend evaluation.

The appearance of shared or common dimensions in the implicit theories of subjects does not, however, preclude the possibility of idiosyncratic organizing principles. In fact, one of the most interesting aspects of implicit theories is the extent of individual variations, a topic we take up in the next section. Before doing that, let us summarize this section with the following statements:

1. In the study of implicit theories, distortions have often been introduced by the methods investigators have used, such as adjective check lists and rating scales.
2. Many people have advocated the use of free response descriptions in the study of implicit theories, but few have actually employed such data.
3. There is some evidence that, even when free response data are utilized, there are some conditions under which the perceiver's implicit theory plays a more important role in perception of others than the actual characteristics of the perceived.
4. Some techniques have been developed that allow researchers to extract the underlying factors or organizing principles from free-response data just as earlier researchers were able to do with rating-scale data. What the free response approach really brings out, however, is the existence of individual differences in implicit theories.

INDIVIDUAL DIFFERENCES

One of the prime contentions put forward by Warr and Knapper (1968) is that person perception and object perception involve basically the same processes. Although they appear to overemphasize the similarity and do not really do more than acknowledge counter-arguments, it does seem that when we begin to look at the influence of values, needs, attitudes—in short, individual differences—that object and person perception are surprisingly similar. This similarity was brought into sharp focus about 30 years ago.

The New Look in Perception

In the period immediately following World War II, there was a great deal of interest in what came to be known as the "new look" in perception. According to Jones and Gerard (1967),

> The basic argument of the new-look perception psychologist was that perceptions are often erroneous, and that the errors bear some systematic relation to such intrapersonal variables as expectancies, current motive states, stable value patterns, mood, preferred defensive mechanisms, . . . The strategy was to inject those variables into the traditional settings of perceptual research and to measure the resulting distortion. (p. 230).

It often happens that a particular approach or theory fits in so well with what common sense and everyday experience dictate that it is difficult to believe that anyone could ever have believed otherwise. How could anyone have believed that values, moods, and other personality factors did not influence perception? Yet the very expression "*new* look" clearly implies that someone, somewhere, did not believe that personality was relevant to perception.[1] The truth is that for decades most experimental psychologists tried to study humans as if they were passive receivers and processors of information.

In the late 1940s and early 1950s, Bruner, Postman, McClelland, and their colleagues carried out a number of studies which demonstrated that the human perceiver is anything but passive. Subjects in the experiments appeared to approach the perception of ambiguous stimuli (such as blurred images briefly exposed on a screen) with sets of hypotheses about what it was they were seeing. According to Bruner (1951),

> The concept *hypothesis* is best likened to such terms as *determining tendency, set, Aufgabe*, and *cognitive predisposition*. It may be regarded as a highly generalized state of readiness to respond selectively to classes of events in the environment. We may characterize it as generalized, for it is a form of tuning of the organism that may govern all cognitive activity carried out during its period of operation (p. 125).

Such hypotheses, then, can lead one both to quicker and more accurate perception, but can also lead one to delayed and erroneous perception. Suppose that, in our implicit theory of personality, we believe there is a high likelihood that a woman who is physically attractive is also sensual. If we *see* a physically attractive woman, our hypothesis then (or our set or expectation) is that she is sensual. If in fact she really is, then our hypothesis will lead to quicker and more accurate perception by predisposing us to interpret her smile as an invitation, her movements as suggestive. If, however, she really is not sensual, our hypothesis can lead to delayed recognition of that fact by inducing us to read things into a

---

[1] Some have claimed that "new look" came from women's fashion changes in the late 1940s, changes that sent hemlines plunging. Hence, like incurable girl watchers, new look perception psychologists became interested in things that were hidden from view.

simple friendly smile that are not there, by making us wonder what she really meant by saying "How are you?"

Bruner (1951) states that a basic property of such perceptual hypotheses is what he refers to as *strength*, and he lists three theorems relevant to this concept:

1. The stronger a hypothesis, the greater its likelihood of arousal in a given situation
2. The greater the strength of a hypothesis, the less the amount of appropriate information necessary to confirm it
3. The greater the strength of a hypothesis, the more the amount of inappropriate or contradictory information necessary to infirm it (p. 126).

To pursue our example and translate *strength* into the language of our earlier discussion of implicit theories, let *strength* refer to likelihood of co-occurrence. If a person believes there is a high likelihood that physically attractive women are sensual, then his is a strong hypothesis or one with high strength. If, on the other hand, he believes there is only a slightly better than 50–50 chance that physically attractive women are sensual, then his is a weak hypothesis or one with low strength.

When the letch with his strong hypothesis sees a physically attractive woman, the expectation of sensuality is almost sure to be aroused. Once aroused, only a smile (perhaps) would be necessary to confirm it, and things may have to progress through denials (playing hard to get) to a slap in the face before his hypothesis is infirmed. When the hypothesis is not so strong, it is less likely to be aroused by any particular physically attractive woman, and, if aroused, it will take much more than a smile to confirm it, while the slightest possible expression of coldness would infirm it. The ambiguity inherent in most social situations sometimes makes confirmation or disconfirmation of such hypotheses about others extremely tricky. How these hypotheses actually influence social interaction is a topic we will pursue later.

The question of interest is whether there are individual differences in the hypotheses that people entertain about what characteristics co-occur in others and if such individual differences are related to other aspects of personality. The "new look" approach is nothing more than a paradigm for investigating such individual differences. As Bruner himself (1951) has pointed out:

If we wish to work on personality factors in perceiving, then we must concentrate upon the investigation of those environmental cues which are appropriate to the confirmation of *hypotheses which reflect basic personality patterns*. By and large, these environmental cues are *not* size cues or color cues or brightness cues. They are cues which aid more directly in our interpersonal adjustment: the apparent warmth or coldness of people, the apparent threateningness of situations, the apparent intelligence or apparent sincerity of others. . . . In studying size, for example, we may speak of "distortion" in terms of deviation of judgments from "actual" or physically measurable size. There is no such "base measurement" of apparent personal warmth. What we must do, then, is to utilize instead judgments by different groups or different individuals under different

The approach advocated by Bruner, comparison of the social judgments made by different groups of subjects, was, in fact, the first approach utilized by students of individual differences in implicit theories.

Global Personality Variables

When people interested in personality and perception begin casting about for a variable that will "make a difference," they often fall back on sex. Males and females differ in so many ways that it is a safe bet that they will differ with respect to variable X. True to form, one of the first variables psychologists investigated in relation to individual differences in implicit theories was sex. In a study that was mentioned earlier, Sarbin (1954) asked various students to stand for a few seconds while their classmates wrote down the first three words they thought of in relation to the person standing. Grouping the words into those that were purely descriptive (e.g., girl, color of clothes) versus those that represented inferred qualities (e.g., logical, hostile), Sarbin found that females were more likely to use the latter while males were more likely to use the former. It is not really clear what this finding means. If it was true that females had more friends and/or were better acquainted with the other students in the class, the finding might simply reflect this fact. That is, if you know someone well, you are more likely to know whether they are logical or not than if you don't know them well. If you don't know them well (males), you rely on their external appearance. Hence, the finding may say nothing about individual differences in implicit theories.

A study by Shapiro and Tagiuri (1959) avoided the problem of possible differential prior acquaintance of males and females with the stimulus persons by asking 240 male and 240 female undergraduates to each make inferences from one of four stimulus traits to a list of 59 reponse traits. For example, a given subject was asked to infer how likely a person who was intelligent would also be _____ (for each of the 59 response traits). Surprisingly, there seemed to be little difference in the distribution of inferences as a function of the sex of the inferer. There was some evidence that "for women subjects the preponderant emphasis of definite inferences [i.e., leaving out the *may* or *may not be* inferences] is on such qualities as *efficiency, responsibility*, and *practicality*. For men, intellectual qualities emerge more clearly in their impressions: *humor, wit, imagination. Enthusiasm* also stands out for men" (p. 135). Unfortunately, there is no way of knowing if even these slight differences are due to differences in implicit theories of males and females. It may be that when the stimulus person is left unspecified, as it was here, men and women tend to think of men and women, respectively, when given a trait from which to make inferences. A possible reason for the high degree of similarity among males and females is that Shapiro and Tagiuri employed only four traits from which subjects were to make inferences and these traits were all extremely common ones (intelligence, inconsideration, consideration, and independence) about which widespread, stereotypical beliefs may exist.

Beach and Wertheimer (1961) carried out an investigation that promised to overcome both the ambiguities of an unspecified stimulus person and the lack of a range of traits. Subjects were asked to describe 12 others, one for each of the intersections defined by the variables well known–not well known, higher–equal–lower status, and same–opposite sex. For example, at the top of each of 12 otherwise blank pages were instructions such as, "Think of a person who is the same sex as you, whom you know well, and whom you consider of higher status than yourself. . . . Describe this person" (p. 369). The information in the descriptions was then coded into 13 categories: (1) appearance; (2) background; (3) job and income; (4) behavior toward the describer; (5) behavior toward others; (6) the describer's reaction to the described; (7) others' reaction to the described; (8) temperament; (9) self-concept and emotional adjustment; (10) morals and values; (11) abilities; (12) motivation; (13) activities and interests.

The results suggested strong differences in the descriptions as a function of both the sex of the describer and the relationship between the describer and the described. For example, male subjects made greater use of *abilities* when describing males as opposed to females and greater use of *behavior toward the describer* when describing females rather than males. Female subjects tended to use categories emphasizing social skills and adjustment; also, when describing physical appearances, females were more likely than males to employ evaluative terms. There are a number of other results from this study which could be cited. However, questions might be raised about the value of such a list. Beach and Wertheimer themselves appear to view their results as being of interest primarily from a methodological point of view, that is, "These results suggest that when selecting scales or dimensions upon which [the subject] is to be required to make judgments about [others], one must keep in mind that these dimensions are not going to be applicable to all [others] and [subjects]" (p. 373).

The latter is a valid point to make and it is one that was, hopefully, made in an earlier section of this chapter. But do studies such as those by Sarbin (1954), Shapiro and Tagiuri (1959), and Beach and Wertheimer (1961) really give us any firm knowledge about individual differences in implicit theories? They seem more to hint at knowledge, to whet one's appetite for understanding. Basically there are two problems with such studies. First, they focus on an aspect of personality that is too global. Sex differences encompass a range of variables, only some of which may be relevant to implicit theories. It's like the old joke about a sociological variable being the sum of 15 psychological variables.

Secondly, they seem to be starting at the wrong point. Rather than simply selecting any personality variable at hand and seeing if people who differ on that variable also differ in their implicit theories, it would be much more parsimonious to derive from personality concepts specific hypotheses as to why and how that variable would make a difference in implicit theories. Presumably, if we conceive of the human organism as an integrated system, there should exist definite relationships among the various subsystems. If perception functions as an aid to personal adjustment, as the new look perceptionists would have us believe, there should be some systematic relationships among an individual's preferred modes of adjustment and his or her implicit theory of what others are like.

Theory-Based Selection of Subjects

During the 1950s, a personality syndrome that was the focus of a great deal of discussion and research was authoritarianism (Adorno, Frenkel-Brunswik, Levinson, and Sanford, 1950). A person exhibiting an authoritarian personality was supposedly characterized by submissiveness to authority figures, rigidity, belief in things mystical and supernatural, opposition to subjectivity, exaggerated condemnation of sexual deviance, and a host of other "bad" things.

Scodel and Mussen (1953) reasoned that a person high in authoritarianism would not be likely to be particularly sensitive to the characteristics of others. In fact, descriptions of the authoritarian syndrome seemed to emphasize that the authoritarian divided people into "those like me" and "others." Others, of course, included blacks, Jews, foreigners, sexual deviates, anybody, in short, who might have a different set of values. If authoritarians are given no basis for tapping into the "others" category, they will assume that someone they are interacting with is pretty much like themselves. To check on their analysis, Scodel and Mussen paired high and low authoritarian subjects of the same sex and instructed each pair to discuss radio, television, and movies for 20 minutes. Following the discussion, each subject was instructed to fill out some personality measures of authoritarianism as he or she felt the other subject would respond to it. As anticipated, the high authoritarian subjects estimated their partner to be about as authoritarian as they themselves were. On the other hand, low authoritarian subjects estimated their partners to be considerably more authoritarian than themselves. While this result is intriguing and makes sense in terms of the personality dynamics associated with authoritarianism, it is ambiguous for a couple of reasons. For one, it may not mean that nonauthoritarians are more sensitive to the characteristics of others; they may simply be more cautious. The estimates of the nonauthoritarians very closely corresponded to the overall mean of the group from which the highs and lows had been selected.

A second problem, and one of particular pertinence here, is that, by using the overall estimated scores, Scodel and Mussen have obscured the very thing we are interested in, the differential patterns of characteristics attributed to others by authoritarians and nonauthoritarians. Kirscht and Dillehay (1967) review a number of similar studies on the social perceptions of authoritarians vs. non-authoritarians and find a similar problem. Of the "patterns about social perception derived from authoritarianism, there is little evidence supporting specific relationships" (p. 84).

We might look at it from the other side and ask if authoritarians are more sensitive to certain cues in the behavior of others. Jones (1954) hypothesized, among other things, that authoritarians would be more sensitive to certain attributes of power in a prospective leader than would subjects low in authoritarianism. Navy recruits who had been selected on authoritarianism (highs and lows) heard a mock interview with a "platoon leader," following which they recorded their impressions of him. Some recruits heard an interview with a passive leader, while others heard an interview with a forceful leader. In contrast to expectations, recruits low in authoritarianism saw the forceful leader as *more* powerful than did recruits high in authoritarianism. Although Jones appeared to be surprised by this result, it seems exactly what should have been anticipated. A subject low in authoritarianism should have a lower threshold for cues relevant to the perception of force and power. These are things that, by definition, are not a part of his life. Hence, when he hears a mildly forceful person, he attributes greater power by a process akin to a contrast effect (Sherif and Hovland, 1961).

A number of later studies have taken variables correlated with authoritarianism and essentially replicated the format of the Scodel and Mussen (1953) study. Burke (1966), for example, found that subjects high in dogmatism estimate others to be about as dogmatic as they themselves, whereas subjects low in dogmatism estimate others to be considerably more dogmatic than themselves. Again, such studies tell us nothing about the differential patterns of characteristics attributed by dogmatic versus nondogmatic subjects.

There is an old saying about walking before running, a moral that suggests looking for studies that have investigated differential attribution of one characteristic before proceeding to those dealing with differential attribution of patterns. Bossom and Maslow (1957) hypothesized that subjects who were themselves emotionally secure would be more likely to perceive warmth in others than would insecure subjects. *Secure* and *insecure* were defined by responses to the Maslow S-I Test for security. The participants in their study were asked to judge 200 photographs in terms of whether the persons depicted in the photos were "very warm", "warm," "cold," or "very cold." As anticipated, secure judges made a greater percentage of attributions of "warm" and "very warm" than did insecure judges. As Bossom and Maslow (p. 148) point out, however, the result is ambiguous. Since they did not know whether the faces were "really" warm or cold, the differences in attribution of the secure and insecure subjects may be due to: (1) differential accuracy; (2) habitual expectations in interpersonal relationships; or (3) Freudian projection. The second possibility, of course, is the one of interest for our purposes.

A study by Benedetti and Hill (1960) gets around at least one of the problems of interpretation of the Bossom and Maslow results. Benedetti and Hill administered the Gordon Personal Profile to a large group of students at the University of New Mexico and divided the students into high, middle, and low subgroups on the basis of their sociability scores. Each subject was then read a list of traits that were supposedly descriptive of another person, following which they selected from a list of 20 pairs the 20 traits that best fitted their impressions of the stimulus person. One-half of the subjects in each of the sociability groups was read the list: *intelligent, skillful, industrious, sociable, determined, practical, cautious*. The list read to the remaining subjects had *unsociable* substituted for *sociable*. The mean numbers of subjects in each condition who attributed the preferred trait of each trait pair to the stimulus person are summarized in Table 2.2.

Thus, when another is described as "unsociable," subjects attribute different characteristics to the other as a function of their own level of sociability. The failure to find a similar result (though in the opposite direction) when another is described as "sociable" is puzzling. It could be due to a number of factors. For example, subjects who are themselves examples of a particular characteristic (high in sociability) may be more discriminating among others with respect to sociability than are subjects who are not examples of the particular characteristic (those middle and low in sociability). This is another way of saying that personality variables may not be symmetrical. Those high in authoritarianism, sociability, security, or what have you may not simply be mirror images of those low in authoritarianism, sociability, or security.

An example of the sorts of problems of interpretation that can arise from such an asymmetry is contained in a study by Gardner and Barnard (1969).

TABLE 2.2[a]

	Subject's sociability		
	High	Middle	Low
Sociable	32.35	30.75	30.25
Stimulus Person			
Unsociable	12.30	17.00	21.60

Mean Number Attributing Preferred Traits
[a](From Benedetti and Hill, 1960, page 279. Copyright 1960 by the American Psychological Association, Washington, D.C., Reprinted by Permission).

These authors started with the reasonable assumption that "a very important difference among individuals is level of intelligence, and person perception as a domain with important cognitive elements should be related to levels of intelligence" (p. 213). To check on this, they selected three groups of subjects on the basis of IQs: a group of retardates (mean IQ = 76.7), an average group (mean IQ = 99.8), and a gifted group (mean IQ = 132.6). Each subject was asked to rate 34 faces on 15 bipolar scales. For each subject, the ratings were then intercorrelated and the resulting correlation matrix factor analyzed. While several of the results are in line with what was anticipated, several surprising things appeared. For example, the retardates were more similar to the gifted than were the average subjects in how consistently the scales were used over the series of 34 photos. One might hypothesize that consistency means different things for a retarded and for a gifted child, but there is no way of knowing within the context of this study. Another problem is that the Gardner and Barnard study again tells us nothing about differential patterns of characteristics, which may or may not constitute the implicit theories of intelligent, average, and retarded subjects.

Perhaps we are not looking at the "right" personality variables. There is no reason to expect that every personality variable should make a difference in the implicit theories of people. The new look perceptionists placed a great deal of emphasis on two relatively specific chronic modes of adjustment, which they believed characterized people to varying degrees, perceptual vigilance and perceptual defense. Using these two concepts as the basis for defining a relevant personality variable, psychologists have labeled as repressors those people who use avoidance and denial of potential threat and conflict as a primary mode of adaptation. Sensitizers, on the other hand, are people who are alert to potential threat and conflict. Altrocchi (1961) hypothesized that sensitizers would assume more dissimilarity when describing others than would repressors. Subjects were student nurses who described themselves and three randomly chosen students in one of their training groups on an interpersonal check list. The only differences in assumed similarity between self and others were due to differences in the self descriptions of repressors and sensitizers and *not* to differences in the perception of others. Shrauger and Altrocchi (1964) pointed out early in their review of the literature on the personality of the perceiver in person perception that," Despite the generally held assumption that one's perceptions of others are partially shaped by his own personal characteristics, it will be seen that there has been little research devoted directly to this topic and that contributions to the area have been scattered and unsystematized" (p. 289). With one or two exceptions, the studies cited in this section would tend to support that pessimistic conclusion. But, perhaps, the problem is more with the method of approach than any inherent intractability or even nonexistence of the phenomenon.

We have already pointed out a number of problems with the research in this section. Many authors, notably those interested in the social perceptions of authoritarians, simply did not ask the "right" (for our purposes) question. There are problems of asymmetry of many of the personality variables on which subjects have been selected, a subproblem of the more general lack of specificity and precision of definition of many personality variables. There are many personality variables which are, no doubt, irrelevant to differences in implicit theories of personality.

Suppose, then, that we turn our approach around. Instead of selecting subjects on the basis of some personality variable that should make a difference in their implicit theories and seeing if we can identify those differences, let us first see if we can identify stable individual differences in implicit theories and then figure out the additional personality characteristics associated with the different implicit theories. One of the nice features of this approach is that it will not constrain us to personality variables for which there are preexisting standardized measurement devices.

Cues and Types of Judges

Several years ago Jackson and Messick (1963) pointed out that complex domains such as person perception require measurement procedures that can reasonably be assumed to be capable of adequately capturing or representing the complexity inherent in the domain. Traditional unidimensional scaling methods are likely not to be appropriate to the study of implicit theories. Earlier our working model of a person's implicit theory was described as a "believed" correlation matrix with an underlying dimensional structure, the number of dimensions corresponding to the number of different ways the traits or components of the matrix are perceived to differ. Most of the research cited in this section has taken that model seriously and has utilized factor analysis or some variant of multidimensional scaling in order to discover the dimensions of subjects' implicit theories and/or how the subjects themselves differed.

There have been some who claimed that even utilizing these more sensitive measurement techniques, individual differences in implicit theories appear small and insignificant. Kuusinen (1969), for example, had 39 students make peer ratings of each other on a number of bipolar personality scales. The ratings were intercorrelated and factor analyzed yielding a seven-factor structure for the students as a whole. The structure underlying each individual's ratings was then compared to the group structure, and Kuusinen concluded that the group structure and individual structures were "sufficiently similar" so that individual variations could be disregarded. Hamilton (1970), in examining Kuusinen's results, felt that this conclusion was unwarranted.[2] To check on his impression,

---

[2] One of the problems with this type of research is that clear-cut decision aids are few. How similar must two structures be to be taken as being essentially the same? Nobody knows.

Hamilton gave seven male college students a list of 15 role figures (e.g., firemen) and asked them to differentiate the figures on a large set of bipolar attributes. Intercorrelations among the scales were determined, factor analyzed for each subject, and five factors retained for each subject. "No two subjects had a total congruence of all five factors and in only 5 out of 21 cases did two subjects have four factors in common" (p. 264). It should be noted that such strong individual differences in implicit theories appeared *in spite of* Hamilton's use of role figures as the stimuli to be rated, stimuli that would presumably increase homogeneity among subjects.

Thus, the basic approach appears to be more promising than preselection of subjects who differed on some personality variable. The question now becomes: can we identify, through some variant of this approach, subgroups of subjects who differ in the types of information that they find to be most salient in making interpersonal judgments? Hamilton and Gifford (1970) constructed 52 personality profiles such that each profile gave nine items of information about a young man. Four items of information were biographical or demographic, while the other five items were personality, that is, the man's standing on each of five bipolar personality scales. Subjects were asked to study each profile and then make a judgment as to how liberal or conservative the person was. Based on a factor analysis of the correlations of each subjects' liberal—conservative ratings with those of each other subject, six subgroups of subjects were identified in terms of the cues they placed most reliance or emphasis on. These six subgroups were:

1. relied on the stimulus person's race-using "black" as a cue to liberalism;
2. relied on degree of cultural refinement and home region of the country;
3. relied on biographical cues and ignored personality;
4. relied on conscientiousness and responsibility of the stimulus person;
5. relied on race in conjunction with emotional stability;
6. relied on extraversion of the stimulus person in inferring liberalism.

One of the problems with the Hamilton and Gifford results is the overlap among the six identified groups, but the study does seem to be a step in the right direction.

A very similar study is one by Wiggins, Hoffman, and Taber (1969). Wiggins et al. carry the research a giant step further, however, by not only identifying subgroups of judges but by additionally differentiating the subgroups on the basis of other personological characteristics. The judgment or attribution of interest in this case was intelligence, and the stimuli were profiles of college students, each of which involved nine cues coded on scales from 0 to 100: high school grade rating, ambitiousness, degree of self-support, correctness of written expression, responsibility, mother's education, study habits, emotional anxiety, and credit hours per semester. Subjects were asked to judge similarity with respect to intelligence of the stimulus persons represented by selected pairs of profiles and to judge the intelligence of each stimulus person on a nine-point scale. Eight subgroups of subjects were identified in terms of the cues they placed most emphasis on in making judgments of intelligence. The first two groups relied most heavily on either high school grade rating or English effectiveness. Subjects who relied on these cues tended to themselves be intelligent, to be conventional with respect to religion, to be low in ethnocentrism, and to have good mechanical comprehension. A third group of subjects placed emphasis on responsibility and study habits in making their judgments of intelligence. These subjects were themselves not particularly intelligent, but were rather authoritarian and religiously conventional. According to Wiggins et al. (1969), the "remaining subject groups were small [but] the fact that their cue weights differ appreciably from one another and from the other larger groups would seem to indicate important, if idiosyncratic, differences in perceptual viewpoints of intelligence" (p. 56).

There have been a number of similar studies within this realm. Sherman and Ross (1972), for example, asked subjects to rate the similarity of 20 American politicians who had been selected so as to cover a large portion of the range of the political spectrum (from Wallace to McGovern). Seven types of variations were perceived among the politicians and these variations were systematically related to the liberalism of the subjects making the judgments. For example, the more conservative a subject was, the less likely he was to use a hawk–dove dimension in differentiating the politicians. Liberal subjects were likely to place great emphasis on the power of the politician within his own party as a basis for differentiation.

Thus, data seem to be accumulating that indicate clear and definite relationships between the personality of the perceiver and how he or she organizes beliefs about others. We have only scratched the surface, citing studies that show individual differences in implicit theories to exist (Hamilton, 1970), which identify subgroups of perceivers in terms of the cues utilized to make judgments of liberalism (Hamilton and Gifford, 1970), which relate cues perceivers use to make judgments of intelligence to other aspects of the perceivers' personalities (Wiggins et al., 1969), and which show that an aspect of the perceivers' personality is related to the variations they perceive among a set of standard stimulus figures (Sherman and Ross, 1974). Although some additional research could be cited in this section, our purpose here is simply to make a plausibility argument. We are not interested in citing every piece of research that documents a relationship between a specific cue utilized to make attributions about others and some aspect of the perceiver's personality. Both domains (cues and aspects of personality) are probably infinite. Hopefully, we have not been so selective that we have failed to make our point that definite relationships do exist between the personality of the perceiver and how beliefs about others are organized. The point, of course, is that everyone's implicit theory is organized along dimensions that make sense in terms of his or her past experience with others.

It should follow that, as one's situation in life changes, as one gains new experience, salient interpersonal expectations also change, and these expectations are likely to be organized in terms of current preoccupations and social interactions. For example, Friendly and Glucksberg (1970) reasoned that novices in a particular culture often lack an understanding of the way full-fledged members of the culture view things. Full-fledged members of the culture may seem to make discriminations and differentiations that are lost on newcomers. An example is the old standby about Eskimos being able to discriminate (and having words for) a large number of different kinds of snow. But more than this, Friendly and Glucksberg were also interested in whether experience in a particular culture or subculture led to perceptions of differential associations among related objects. Do Eskimos, to continue with the example, perceive certain atmospheric conditions as being associated with one type of snow, but not with others?

With the aid of undergraduate informants, Friendly and Glucksberg selected 20 trait names that were peculiar to their particular college culture (e.g., "Ivy Type," "Meatball," "Lunch") and asked one group of freshmen (novices in the culture) and one group of seniors (old hands) to sort these traits, along with 40 additional personality characteristics. The structures underlying the perceived relationships were then obtained separately for the two groups. For the freshmen, two dimensions were adequate to account for the variations that they perceived among the 60 terms. Seniors, on the other hand, perceived these same two variations, but also a third. The latter variation had to do with socially approved behavior for students at that particular institution, a discrimination that freshmen did not yet make.

Thus, it again appears that the ways in which people organize their interpersonal expectations are related to their situations in life. Seniors had swallowed the party line in a sense, they organized things as "going together" in ways that newcomers to that particular subculture did not. As Kelly (1955) has argued and as Friendly and Glucksberg (1970) have empirically demonstrated, we are continually reconstruing, reorganizing, and placing alternative constructions on our perceptions of others. Our interpersonal expectations and the things we perceive as "going together" in others continue to change.

SUMMARY

In this chapter, we have explored some research bearing on the existence and nature of our beliefs about other people, beliefs about what characteristics and/or behaviors of others are likely to be related. Some early studies seemed to find evidence that there are perceived relationships among various characteristics of others. However, for many years these relationships were viewed as simply sources of error, as biases that interfered with accurate perceptions of others. Only gradually was there a shift toward studying such "artifacts" as possible indices of cognitive organization.

Beginning in the 1940s, a series of studies on impression formation provided clear evidence for the existence of expectations about associations among characteristics of others. Further, these expectations are not simply random collections of beliefs about relationships among traits and behaviors. Rather, they can be conceptualized as a "believed-in" correlation matrix of associations, a matrix with an underlying dimensional structure or organization. We also saw that one widely shared property that people use to organize these beliefs about others is evaluation and, as we shall see in the following chapters, the evaluative dimension is of major significance in determining if implicit theories influence behavior toward others.

Armed with this somewhat refined working model of an implicit theory of personality, we then went back and examined the issue of "centrality." It appears that a particular characteristic is important as an organizer of one's impression of another to the extent that that characteristic stands out as being unique among the characteristics of the other. This lead us to a discussion of cues and attribution processes because another way of stating the above is that some characteristics, qualities, or behaviors of others are more likely to serve as cues to additional characteristics that these others might possess. Our primary interest, however, was what the literature on cues and attributions might tell us about the preexisting perceived relationships among characteristics and how these perceived relationships develop and change. It appears that trying to determine what another is like is a problematic situation with which everyone has experience and when confronted with this situation we take a systematic hypothesis generating and testing approach. Unfortunately, as we shall see in the next chapter, we do not always behave as "good scientists" should. That is, our implicit theories are not as responsive to disconfirming data as, perhaps, they should be.

Of course, the important questions are:

1. *Why* are some characteristics more likely than others to serve as cues about additional characteristics?
2. Is there any way we can know a priori which cues will be important for a particular perceiver?

Both of these questions have to do with how one's implicit theory is organized, what categories are employed in perceiving others and what relationships are believed to exist among the categories. In the last half of the chapter, we have explored these two questions by looking first at some methodological problems that hindered early research on the categories people actually employ and how these categories are organized. We then turned our attention explicitly to the issue of individual differences in implicit theories, and data seem to be accumulating that indicate clear and definite relationships between the personality of the perceiver and both the cues employed and how beliefs about others are organized.

3
Stereotypes and Psychological Diagnosis

In the last chapter, we explored "built-in" expectancies, the beliefs that people hold about which characteristics of others go together. In the present chapter, we begin to shift our focus outward: first, by examining research on expectancies about particular categories of people (stereotypes) and, then, by scrutiny of one process by which people are categorized (psychological–psychiatric diagnosis).

STEREOTYPES

The term *stereotype* was originally employed in the printing and newspaper industries to refer to a one-piece metal sheet that had been cast from a mold taken of a printing surface, such as a page or set type. The term was adopted over 50 years ago by Walter Lippmann (1922) to refer to the "pictures in our heads" of various racial, national, religious, and other ethnic groups. The connotation that Lippman evidently intended was that of an unvarying form or pattern, of fixed and conventional expression, and of having no individuality, as though cast from a mold. As a point of departure, then, let us say that to stereotype a particular group means thinking about and referring to members of that group as though they were all the same. The initial studies of stereotypes employed a methodology that attempted to assess these aspects of the process.

The Rise and Fall of the Adjective Checklist

Cauthen, Robinson, and Krauss (1971b) point out that since 1930 there have been over 200 published articles dealing with stereotypes. That number continues to rise, and the methodology employed in one of the first studies of stereotypes (Katz and Braly, 1933), the adjective checklist, continues to be the most popular and widely employed. In the Katz and Braly study, 100 Princeton undergraduates were asked to select from a list of 84 adjectives those which they believed characterized each of ten racial and national groups (Germans, Italians, Irish, English, Negroes, Jews, Americans, Chinese, Japanese, Turks). When the student had finished selecting words for all ten groups, he was asked to go back over the lists and mark those five on each list he thought "most typical" of the group in question. The latter traits were employed in the analyses.

Although there were other aspects of the study, the treatment of the data seized upon and perpetuated in hundreds of subsequent studies was a simple tabulation of traits most frequently assigned to each group. At intervals of 18 years, the Katz and Braly study was even repeated at Princeton, employing the same 84 trait adjectives and asking for attributions to the same ten groups (Gilbert, 1951; Karlins, Coffman, and Walters, 1969). The data generally show a decline in the willingness of students to stereotype groups by picking "characteristic" adjectives. It is less than clear, however, what such data mean. Are students of the late 1960s less inclined to stereotypic thinking? Or, are they simply more aware that it is "bad" to hold stereotypes about certain groups? Given the inherent ambiguity of such studies, why bother to mention them at all?

There are several reasons. First, by the way in which the data have been handled in such studies, a new component has ipso facto been incorporated into the popular definition of stereotype. It has come to mean a consensually agreed-upon set of characteristics thought to be descriptive of the members of some group. Although some authors have done so (cf., Secord and Backman, 1964, p. 73), there appears to be no compelling reason for accepting the criterion of consensus as an aspect of our definition of stereotypes. I can have a stereotype of college administrators which need not be shared by anyone. As with implicit theories of personality, there may be large areas of overlap among the stereotypes of different people, but, again, there may not be.

A second reason for mentioning the adjective checklist studies is that the issues that have developed within this line of research all seem to point to the message hinted at in the last sentence above, that is, that stereotypes are simply aspects of an individual's implicit theory of personality. In the following sections, we will review a number of issues that have developed out of the adjective checklist studies. Our goal is to demonstrate the basic conceptual and empirical similarities of the work on stereotypes to the work on implicit theories of personality.

As a starting point, think about what has resulted from adjective checklist studies: a not-very-informative catalogue of traits attributed to certain categories of people at certain points in time by certain subjects. While this might be useful for historical purposes (Gergen, 1973), it does not tell us much about the processes involved or about the functional significance of stereotypes. Analogously, we pointed out in the last chapter that it seemed pointless to pile up instances of different cues utilized in personality judgment. This led into a discussion of attribution theories, in the attempt to throw some light on how a given cue or observed act is tested by the perceiver to determine if it allows him to attribute a particular disposition, thus tapping into his implicit theory and making additional inferences about the perceived. With stereotypes, the basic process seems very similar, that is, there are certain cues (such as skin color) and behaviors (such as speaking with an accent) that serve the observer by allowing a particular categorization of the perceived. Once this categorization has been made (disposition attributed?), the component parts of the stereotype are invoked.

Stereotypes as Categorical Responses

Going back to our definition of an implicit theory as a perceived correlation matrix of relationships among characteristics, a stereotype might be considered a *region* of one's implicit theory, to which access is gained by a small number of cues, within which the correlations among components approach unity and which has relatively few connections with other regions. A similar view is shared by Cauthen et al. (1971b, p. 118). The differences between stereotypes and other regions within one's implicit theory are matters of degree, then, and not kind.

Secord, Bevan, and Katz (1956) were concerned with one aspect of our definition of stereotype: whether there are certain necessary and sufficient cues that result in attribution of the full-blown stereotype regardless of the strength of the cue itself. As they phrase it, "Are light Negroes and dark Negroes stereotyped to the same degree? Or, is there, instead, a quantitative relationship between the degree to which a Negro possesses 'Negroid' physical characteristics and the extent to which stereotyped traits are attributed to him?" (p. 78).

To check on this question, ten Negro and five white photos were selected to form a continuum of increasing "Negroidness" as determined by ratings on eight physiognomic characteristics such as hair texture, lightness of complexion, and fullness of lips. High school students were then asked to rate each photo on a number of personality traits, which had been selected from those attributed to Negroes in Gilbert's (1951) replication of the Katz and Braly study. As anticipated, the photos of Negroes were rated significantly less alert, honest, responsible, refined, intelligent, thrifty, and significantly more superstitious, lazy, emotional, untidy, and immoral. Ratings on these traits were combined to obtain a total score on personality stereotyping. Of interest here is the finding that the stereotype score for a given photo remained essentially unchanged with increasing Caucasian appearance *as long as the photo was identified as Negro*. "In fact, data ... indicate that the two whitest Negroes are as heavily stereotyped as the darkest Negroes, in spite of the probability that, if the photograph of the lightest Negro has been shown in a context of white photographs only, he most likely would not have been recognized as a Negro" (p. 80). Thus, the

Secord et al. study provides some tentative evidence for the notion of a stereotype as a region within one's implicit personality theory, in which the components are inferred in toto, once the region has been tapped into.

There are several sources of ambiguity in the Secord et al. (1956) results, however. First, the presence of five photos of whites may have led subjects to contrast the supposed attributes of whites and Negroes hence producing, artifactually, what appears to be the full-blown stereotype for all the Negro pictures. Another difficulty is that only one set of stimulus materials (photos) was used, and there may have been something peculiar about the two "whitest" Negroes in the series.

To clarify these and some other issues, Secord (1959) selected a second set of photos which, again, were ranked in terms of increasing Negroidness. These photos were rated by four groups of subjects on both favorable and unfavorable traits that were either relevant or irrelevant to the "typical" Negro stereotype. The four groups differed in terms of whether they rated only Negro photos or Negro and white photos and whether the photos they rated were identified or unidentified by the experimenter as containing only Negro or Negro and white photos. The results indicated that as long as the person depicted in the photo is racially identified (by the perceiver or by the experimenter) as Negro, he is stereotyped. Further, it apparently did not matter whether subjects were judging only Negro photos or were judging Negro and white photos. That is, "the reasonable hypothesis that a mixed series of Negro and white photographs should produce a tendency to contrast the two groups in making stereotype ratings is not confirmed" (Secord, 1959, p. 313). It is also worth noting that on traits irrelevant to the "typical" stereotype, many of the Negro photos were reacted to more favorably than the white photos, but they were categorized nevertheless on the traits defining the Negro stereotype. In line with our position that stereotypes are simply regions of one's implicit personality theory, Secord (1959) argues that:

> . . . there is a reasonable probability that categorization of other persons is important not only in the case of Negroes, but instead is a widespread process in person perception. Certainly it is not feasible to observe and grasp each individual in all his uniqueness and still carry on the smooth, fast-moving interaction with other persons which is characteristic of most everyday relationships. A reasonable assumption is that each perceiver has a set of person categories (of which stereotypes are the most obvious) into which he classifies those with whom he interacts (p. 313).

Another pertinent, but unfortunately ambiguous, bit of evidence comes from a study by Secord and Berscheid (1963). In that study, subjects were asked to make inferences of the form cited in Chapter 2. From Secord and Berscheid (1963) an example is:

A person is *lazy*. How likely is it that he is also:
Sportsmanlike
0 1 2 3 4 5 6 7 8 9 10
impossible   certain (p. 68).

Subjects made these ratings with the person unspecified and again, at a later session, with the person specified as being Negro. Half of the traits, in both sessions, were traits associated with the Negro stereotype in the Katz and Braly study. There were a number of findings, but most relevant here are "The main results . . . [which] strongly support the notion of implicit personality theory that the perceiver's associations among traits are stable. While some shift in mean ratings occurs because of categorization of a person as Negro, associations between cue-trait and judged trait remain markedly consistent whether the stimulus person is Negro or white" (p. 75). This result is ambiguous for the following reason. When the race of the person was unspecified, Secord and Berscheid made the assumption that "the normal frame of reference of S in response to the word *person* would be that the stimulus person would be white" (p. 69). However, for traits closely associated with the Negro stereotype, that assumption may be invalid. That is, when a subject saw the statement "A person is happy-go-lucky. How likely . . . ," he or she may have assumed that "person" referred to a Negro. Thus, it would be worthwhile to gather similar trait inference data, in which the race of the stimulus person is clearly specified in all instances.

At issue, of course, is the referent that one calls to mind when asked to make such inferences. Higgins and Rholes (1976) hypothesize "that a person receiving a verbal description of some stimulus will, through the use of his or her stored information about the world, call to mind information concerning the type of stimulus to which the verbal description *as a whole* refers" (p. 423). For example, Bayton, McAlister, and Hamer (1966) asked subjects to select from a list of 85 adjectives those that they believed to be descriptive of each of four groups: upper-class whites, upper-class negroes, lower-class whites, lower-class negroes. In contrast to the negative stereotype of Negroes that had appeared in scores of studies (cf., Brigham, 1971), upper-class negroes were characterized as intelligent, ambitious, industrious, neat, and progressive. On the other hand, both lower-class negroes and lower-class whites were described as ignorant, lazy, loud, and physically dirty. It was not the case, however, that race had no influence on the attributions. Upper-class whites, but not upper-class negroes, were described as being pleasure-loving and sophisticated. Upper-class negroes, but not upper-class whites, were described as ostentatious. When information in addition to ethnic group membership is provided, however, it apparently has the effect of changing the referent that is brought to mind and the different referents may be associated with different expectations.

It does appear, then, that stereotypes can be considered as categorical responses that are invoked in response to particular referents. In this sense, it seems reasonable to consider stereotypes as regions within one's implicit theory to which access is gained by specific cues, regions within which the correlations among components approach unity and that have relatively few external connections with other regions. However, an important question about such regions remains. That is, to what extent do people really "think" in terms of stereotypes. Perhaps checking adjectives on a list as typical of a given group merely means that subjects can recognize what Karlins et al. (1969) called the social stereotypes of that group. What we want to know about, of course, is their own personal stereotype.

The Free-Response Approach

What is needed is a way of asking subjects to describe various ethnic groups without putting words into their mouths or at the tips of their pencils. As Ehrlich and Rinehart (1965) point out:

Most of the studies of intergroup imagery, insofar as they use stereotype check lists or their variants, commit two types of instrument errors. First, the answer programs frequently fail to permit the researcher to distinguish between a respondent's *knowledge* of group stereotypes and the respondent's personal *endorsement* of such stereotypes. Second, the answer options frequently fail to tap the salient and personal aspects of the respondent's intergroup imagery (pp. 565–566).

In an attempt to meet the second of these two criticisms, Ehrlich and Rinehart asked 85 students at Ohio State to check those adjectives on a list they believed to be descriptive of Turks, Russians, Negroes, Japanese, Alorese (a Ringer), Jews, and Americans. A second group of 85 students was simply asked to write out the characteristics they believed each of these groups possessed. That is, they were not given prepared checklists, but blank pages. Excluding data from the presumably unknown group (the Alorese), students given the open-ended format produced a total of 2,378 traits, or an average of less than 5 per student per group. On the other hand, students filling out the adjective checklists for the same groups produced 6,863 traits, or almost 14 per student per group. It is also important to note that overlapping—the same traits being attributed to a given group by students using the two different methods—accounts for only 13 percent of the total number of traits. As Ehrlich and Rinehart point out, it seems apparent that data from the two groups of respondents indicate meaningful aspects of intergroup imagery may be distorted and obscured by the use of adjective checklists: ". . . the specific traits employed on the stereotype check list are not salient terms in the vocabularies of the respondents administered the open-ended format" (p. 567). This point has been confirmed in several other studies (cf. Eysenck and Crown, 1948).

Adjective checklists, then, appear to *force* subjects into employing stereotypes and making apparent attributions that they do not spontaneously associate with a given ethnic group. This is an important point to keep in mind, because one of the more interesting issues in stereotype research has centered around the question of veridicality. Is it the case that stereotypes are to some extent *accurate* generalizations about groups? In pursuing this question, the lesson of the present section is that we must be wary of using adjective checklists as sources of generalizations that we wish to assess for veridicality.

Stereotypes and the Kernel of Truth Hypothesis

In the last chapter, the question of the veridicality of implicit theories was raised, and it was indicated that, while pertinent and while there was some evidence for veridicality, the question was really somewhat peripheral. The reason given for this was that our purpose is to develop the position that expectations have consequences because they exist, regardless of whether they are accurate or inaccurate. Making the same point with respect to stereotypes, Cauthen et al. (1971b) note that "Implicit in our use of stereotype is the old conception of W. I. Thomas that if a situation is defined as real, then it is real in its consequences" (p. 104).

With stereotypes of ethnic groups, however, the question of veridicality takes on a little more importance. Components of stereotypes of particular ethnic groups can be and have been incorporated into the institutional structure of society, thereby creating an appearance of veridicality. As Ashmore (1970) points out:

> At a societal level, the self-fulfilling prophecy works by creating a political, economic, and social structure which dooms outgroup members to an inferior position. This structure in America has aptly been called *institutional racism*. . . . For example, in the days of slavery black people were regarded as intellectually inferior and consequently were seldom taught to read and write. Without education, the slaves were indeed less intellectually sophisticated than the masters. In short, the stereotype of the black person led to discriminatory practices which produced black people congruent with that stereotype (p. 287).

The idea that stereotypes of ethnic groups may *to some extent* be accurate is known as the "kernel of truth" hypothesis. Campbell (1967) argues that there are sound theoretical reasons for expecting that stereotypes may have such kernels of truth in them. In an analysis that employs a combination of Hullian learning theory and phenomenological social psychology, he points out that stereotypes can reflect both the character of the group being described and, projectively, the character of the person holding the stereotype. This point, which is quite congenial with the position being developed here, is illustrated with the notion of *stimulus intensity*, an important determinant of response strength in Hull's theory. As Campbell points out, Helson's (1964) adaptation level theory leads us to expect that perceptual contrasts provide strong stimuli and the greater the contrast, the more intense the perceptual stimulus. Thus, "the greater the *real* difference between groups on any particular custom, detail of physical appearance, or item of material culture, the *more* likely it is that that feature will appear in the stereotyped imagery each group has of the other" (p.

821, emphasis added). Campbell goes on to note that "the more opportunities for observation and the longer the exposure to the outgroup, the larger the role of real differences in the stereotypes. . . . To state it in opposite terms: The more remote and less well known the outgroup, the more purely projective the content of the stereotype" (p. 821). The term *projective* here is used to refer to the perceiver's *own* drives, habits, and incentives (D, H, and K in Hullian terms).

Pursuing the learning theory approach, Campbell notes several additional ways in which real group differences may be incorporated into stereotypes and in which these same differences are likely to be distorted and exaggerated by the intrapsychic components of Hullian theory (D, K, and H). For example, those characteristics actually invoked in intergroup interaction are likely to provide the strongest stimuli relevant to each group's perception of the other and, hence, to be incorporated into the stereotype that each has of the other. One of the major points to be developed in the following chapter is that, in *any* interaction—whether it be with some "outgroup" member or not—each participant brings a set of goals, desires, and expectations about how the interaction should proceed. To the extent that one's goals and desires are thwarted or facilitated by those with whom one is interacting, it should be the case that certain of their characteristics will be seized upon and, if necessary, distorted to "explain" what occurred in the interaction. If we fail to understand what the Chinese gentleman meant by a particular statement, he is simply inscrutable; we, of course, are not dumb.

There are several additional points to Campbell's analysis. A particularly important one is that the Hullian H (habit strength or familiarity), which is a key determinant of response strength, provides a way of accounting for the persistence of stereotypes once the initial "kernel of truth" has vanished. With each invocation of the stereotype, its strength is incremented, and the associative bonds between group membership and particular characteristics are strengthened. As Campbell (1967) puts it, "For a given individual, . . . the more familiar he is with making prejudiced statements, the easier such a statement will appear on any given occasion—or the more readily the stereotyped difference will be perceived. . . . Once a stereotype or perception of differences is established, less real difference is required to maintain . . . it" (p. 822).

Given, then, that there are sound reasons for expecting stereotypes to have, at least, *begun* with kernels of truth, what empirical evidence exists? Brigham (1971) cites several studies that lead him to conclude that "ethnic stereotypes can have 'kernels' of truth, at least in a convergent validity sense, that is, agreement between several groups as to the traits that characterize a particular object group" (pp. 25–26). As Brigham himself notes, such evidence may not provide an adequate test of the hypothesis. Just because both Californians and Georgians think New Yorkers are rude and inconsiderate doesn't mean they really are. Such consensual validity would be particularly suspect in those cases where long standing, widely disseminated stereotypes exist.

Another potential type of data that might bear on the kernel of truth hyothesis concerns the reciprocal stereotype held by two groups. Harding, Proshansky, Kutner, and Chein (1969) point out that:

> When members of two different ethnic groups are asked to rate both themselves and each other in the Katz and Braly manner two things usually happen. The first is that the array of characteristics selected by group X as most typical of itself is similar to the array selected by group Y as most typical of group X. The second is that socially desirable characteristics are more likely to be emphasized in a group's description of itself, while undesirable characteristics are more likely to be stressed in descriptions of the group by members of another group (p. 8).

Thus, the evaluative versus descriptive similarity controversy about implicit theories of personality appears to be an issue in the study of stereotypes also. Bruner (1956), for example, cites some evidence that a group of Dakota ranchers were perceived by nearby Hidatsa Indians to be "stingy and selfish," whereas the ranchers perceived themselves to be "thrifty and provident."

Such data are interesting and, inductively, offer more support for our point that stereotypes are simply regions of ones implicit personality theory. That is, they point up another issue that is common to both fields. However, it is not clear that they can be used as evidence for the kernel of truth hypothesis. The problem is that it becomes very nearly circular (ellipsoidal?) to accept a person's image of the ethnic group to which he belongs as the "reality" against which to compare an outsiders image of that same group, especially when the two images were developed, in part, in mutual interaction.

Inkeles and Levinson (1969) discuss a type of data that could be used, were it available, to test the kernel of truth hypothesis. The question they address is that of "national character." "To what extent do the patterned conditions of life in a particular society give rise to certain distinctive patterns in the personalities of its members?" (p. 418). Although bits and pieces of evidence exist that are pertinent to this question, the varying methodologies employed and nonoverlapping foci of the investigators make comparisons impossible. Much of the research consists of anthropological descriptions of single societies or comparisons of different peoples on a single characteristic (e.g. McClelland, 1961, on need for achievement). In short, the basic research that would make studies of national character usable to test the kernel of truth hypothesis has not been done. As Inkeles and Levinson (1969) point out, "If national character refers to modes of a distribution of individual personality variants, then its study would seem to require the psychological investigation of adequately large and representative samples of persons *studied individually* . . . most assessments of national character have not proceeded along these lines" (p. 425).

Good, hard data pertinent to the kernel of truth hypothesis, then, are relatively scarce. Why should this be so? Brigham (1971), Mackie (1973), and Campbell (1967) argue that, in spite of theoretical reasons for believing that real group differences are often incorporated into stereotypes and, hence, for believing that stereotypes may contain kernels of truth, social scientists have defined stereotypes as inaccurate. The source of this somewhat hasty definition appears to spring from humanitarian concerns, but, as Campbell (p. 823) notes, saying that all stereotypes of group differences are false puts us in the silly and noncommon-sensical position of saying that all groups are on the average identical. If all are equal, must all be alike? The kernel of truth hypothesis remains largely untested, then, but the apparent reluctance to face this question raises the last issue we would like to discuss in connection with stereotypes: whether prejudice is a necessary concomitant of stereotypes.

Prejudice and Stereotypes

According to Ashmore (1970), "Prejudice is a negative attitude toward a socially defined group and toward any person perceived to be a member of that group" (p. 253). "Negative attitude" apparently refers to an *overall* negative attitude. If I have a negative evaluation of one facet of members of a particular group—say, that they take themselves too seriously—but have a positive evaluation of the other characteristics I attribute to them (working for a good cause, intelligent, concerned about their sisters), then I would not be considered prejudiced against the group. Concerning the origins of prejudice, Ashmore's review of the evidence leads him to believe that realistic-group-conflict theory (the notion that prejudice arises from intergroup conflict and competitiveness) "is the best explanation of when and how prejudice originates, though it is certainly not the whole story" (p. 263). This coincides rather nicely with one of the points made in the last section, that is, that reciprocal stereotypes appear to originate in actual intergroup contact. Perhaps there is some relation between prejudice and stereotype.

If there is a relation, it has kept itself well hidden. Lambert, Hodgson, Gardner, and Fillenbaum (1960) asked French and English speaking Canadian students to attribute characteristics to speakers reading a passage in either French or English. There was no relationship between attitudes toward the outgroup (French for English students and English for French students) and the traits attributed to the speakers. A similar result is reported by Anisfeld, Bogo, and Lambert (1962). In the latter study, subjects listened to eight speakers who either spoke in "flawless" or "accented" English. Again there was no relation "between the differential ratings of the guises and any personal or attitude variables" (p. 229). Brigham (1971) points up another bit of negative evidence. He notes that: "Under the Katz and Braly paradigm, subjects have been willing (at least in the earlier studies) to stereotype virtually all ethnic groups. Unless some type of pervasive outgroup prejudice is postulated, it would appear that this indicates the presence of stereotyping without prejudice" (p. 28). Cauthen et al. (1971a) found that the words constituting the Negro stereotype were not evaluated any more or less positively when attributed to whites. Although the evidence in their study is itself mixed and open to serious methodological questions, Saenger and Flowerman (1954) state that "The characteristics commonly ascribed to Jews . . . [fail to explain] the hostility directed toward them" (p. 222).

We could continue, but, in spite of occasional bits of evidence to the contrary (cf., Secord et al. 1956), the weight of the evidence appears to indicate that there is no simple relation between prejudice toward a group and stereotypes of the group. As Secord and Backman (1964) point out, ". . . a stereotype does not simply consist of the assignment of a set of attributes to a category of persons on the basis of consistency with a positive or negative feeling toward that person category" (p. 73).

Summary

The major purpose of the foregiong discussion of stereotypes has been to illustrate that stereotypes are no different, in principle, from the types of interpersonal expectancies discussed in Chapter 2. Stereotypes are simply regions within one's implicit theory of personality, for which the pertinent cues are markers of ethnic group membership. The definition of stereotypes as regions within one's implicit theory has been reinforced and supported by demonstrating that the same issues have arisen in stereotype research as in research on implicit theories: free versus constrained responses, cues and attributions, and veridicality. The attempt, in short, has been to break down the distinction between stereotypes and implicit theories. The two bodies of research have proceeded almost completely independent of each other. Synthesis of the two lines should at least avoid duplication of effort and at best be productive of new approaches to old problems. For example, there has been almost no research on individual differences in cues utilized to make stereotype attributions comparable to the Wiggins et al. (1969) study of implicit theories. There has been only a beginning of research on the multidimensional nature of stereotypes. The question of veridicality of stereotypes has received much less attention in stereotype research than it deserves (cf., Brigham, 1971, p. 31). More generally, applying the notion of implicit theories to expectations about ethnic group members carries the implication that these expectations—like other regions of one's implicit theory—are subject to revision, are artificial constructions, and are subject to the same criteria for evaluation (internal consistency, testability, parsimony, validity).

An ethnic group can be defined as any group that is distinguished from others by such things as its customs, characteristics, language, or general style of life. Stereotypes of ethnic group members have been shown to be in part a function of the perceiver, the method of measurement, and their interaction. There is one particular ethnic group, however, that has been the subject of so much discussion, speculation, concern, and research that we have reserved a special section for it. The question of interest is the extent to which perceptions of, and expectations about, this particular group are a function of the perceiver.

PSYCHOLOGICAL DIAGNOSIS

The group consists of those who, for one reason or another, are subjected to the interviewing, testing, and observation that constitutes the process of psychological diagnosis. We could circumvent such a circumlocution by saying the group consists of the so-called mentally ill, but that both prejudges the result of diagnosis and employs a metaphor which is not acceptable to many people. In any event, it may strike some as inappropriate to discuss this topic in the same chapter that we discuss stereotypes and prejudice. After all, what could a psychological assessment carried out by a trained professional who (usually) is genuinely concerned about the well being of the "patient" have in common with stereotyping? In this section, we will try to demonstrate that psychological diagnosis and stereotyping have a great deal in common.

The similarities have been commented on before. Kostlan (1955) pointed out in a discussion of psychodiagnosis that: "The present-day nosological categories, for all their disadvantages, are highly useful, empirically derived stereotypes" (p. 486). We shall see about the usefulness, but with the assertion that they are stereotypes we have no argument. Our purpose here is to look at the evidence. Does the research support the proposition that the process of psychological categorization as carried out by trained professionals is influenced by the same variables which influence our day-to-day perceptions and expectations about others? As we have seen in the last section and in the previous chapter, there are strong individual differences in our perceptions of others. Translating this into the psychological assessment setting, the question becomes: does the personality of the examiner influence the outcome of psychological diagnosis?

Examiner Influence on Test Results

For many years, a major component of psychological diagnosis has been the administering and interpretation of various tests. These tests are many and varied and range from the Rorschach, in which the person being tested responds to a series of inkblots by describing what he or she "sees," through more objective personality inventories such as the Minnesota Multiphasic Personality Inventory (MMPI) in which the person answers a series of questions about preferences and thoughts, to standard intelligence tests. Some of the more popular tests among psychodiagnosticians have been the Rorschach, the MMPI, the Thematic Apperception Test, various forms of an Incomplete Sentence Test, various IQ tests, and certain tests that require the examinee to draw things. The model implicit in the administration of such tests is that the only variable is the "personality" of the examinee. Thus, any differences in the Rorschach protocols, for example, produced by two different people are presumed to reflect differences in their personalities, differences in their preoccupations and concerns.

Much of the early research on examiner influence was addressed to the viability of such a model. Is it legitimate to assume that the only variable is the examinee's personality? Are examiner's interchangeable? Much of the early research was also nonexperimental. That is, what often happened is that someone who was interested in the question would go through the files of a hospital or clinic and extract the test protocols and results. The results for different examiners would then be compared.

An example of such research is a study by Baughman (1951), in which 633 Rorschach protocols were secured from the files of an outpatient clinic. All of the examinees were male veterans, and the Rorschach had been administered to various numbers of these veterans by 15 different examiners. Thus, the average examiner had administered the Rorschach to about 42 of the 633. Baughman compared the results by examiners in 22 different scoring categories and found significant examiner differences in 16 out of the 22 categories. According to Baughman (1951), "The differences found in this study can be related to two major factors: (1) differences in the characteristic subject—examiner relationships created by the examiner; and (2) differences in scoring conceptions" (p. 247).

During the 1940s and 1950s, there were numerous studies such as Baughman's. One difficulty with these studies, as Levy (1956) has pointed out, is that we have no way of knowing how examinees were assigned to examiners. The assignment was generally non-random and, hence, we are unable to evaluate the extent to which selection factors play a role in the results. A number of studies, however, have essentially replicated Baughman's result under conditions of random assignment and have gone on to take a somewhat closer look at the processes involved.

Gibby (1952), for example, was interested in the "stimulus value of the examiner" with special reference to the Rorschach inquiry. Gibby used the term "inquiry" to refer to the questions asked by the examiner to clarify the subject's or examinee's responses to a given Rorschach card or section of a card. As a comparison standard, Gibby analyzed the Rorschach records of 240 Veterans Administration patients who had been assigned to one of 12 different examiners. This part of the study was essentially the same as Baughman's study, and the results were, as anticipated, that strong and significant differences appeared in the protocols as a function of the person administering the Rorschach. In the second part of Gibby's study, preexisting records were not employed. Instead, 135 subjects were randomly assigned to nine examiners who administered the Rorschach. In addition, the inquiries were standardized by having each examiner ask a set number of questions. The results were the same as in the other group, strong and significant differences in the protocols as a function of the examiner. Similar results have been reported in a number of other studies (cf., Miller, Sanders, and Cleveland, 1950).

What are some of these differences? Filer (1952) tabulated the references to four categories in 156 reports of 13 male clinicians at the Detroit Mental Hygiene Clinic. The four categories were: (1) hostility; (2) hostility turned inward; (3) passive dependency; and (4) feelings of inferiority. In addition, each examiner's behavior was rated in terms of ascendency, depression, intropunitiveness, extropunitiveness, and inpunitiveness. A number of results emerged. For example, examiners who stress hostility turned inward in their reports of patients tend themselves to be rated as depressed and intropunitive. Examiners who stress inferiority or passive dependency in their reports of patients were themselves rated as being more ascendant than examiners who "saw" fewer feelings of inferiority among their patients. Filer (1952) concludes that "the three most frequently mentioned defense mechanisms in reports are more characteristic of the clinicians than their patients" (p. 336). Filer's results are suggestive, but, unfortunately, not conclusive. The problem of nonrandom assignment of patients to examiners clouds the interpretation, and it is not clear from Filer's report of his study who rated the examiners' behavior and under what conditions those ratings were made.

Results similar to Filer's are reported in a study by Sanders and Cleveland (1953), which is somewhat less ambiguous. Sanders and Cleveland administered the Rorschach to 9 second-year graduate students in psychology and then trained these same graduate students to administer the Rorschach. Each of these 9 examiners was then assigned 30 "normal" subjects to be tested. Following the administration of the Rorschach, each of the 270 subjects (i.e., 9 × 30) was given a questionnaire and asked to respond to a number of items concerning his feelings about the examiner. These questionnaires were completed after the examiner had left the room and were sealed in an envelope. The 270 Rorschach records were scored blindly, without knowing which examiner had administered the Rorschach. Of 38 scoring categories on the Rorschach, 20 yielded significant examiner differences. Further, examiners who appeared anxious to their subjects elicited significantly more general responsiveness from their subjects. Examiners who appeared hostile to their subjects were more likely to elicit responses of passivity and stereotypy from their subjects. These and a number of similar differences lead Sanders and Cleveland (1953) to conclude that ". . . the personality of the examiner is significantly related to the type of Rorschach protocol which he obtains when his technique has been standardized and his subjects have been selected at random" (p. 47).

One might argue that the Rorschach, being the most unstructured of the various tests used in psychological diagnosis, is particularly susceptible to the kinds of effects cited above, Hence, to substantiate the argument that psychological categorization is subject to the same sorts of biases and preconceptions that appear to exist in our day-to-day perceptions of others, we need to broaden our base of support and consider other "diagnostic" instruments. At the same time, we need to consider whether there are characteristics—other than the examiner's personality—of the testing situation that can bias the results.

The Circumstances of Testing

Holt (1961) conceptualizes clinical judgment as "the informal application of the creative, inquiring intelligence to human problems as principally conveyed through words" (p. 381). Another way of saying this is that the "essence of clinical work lies in dealing with verbal meanings" (p. 370) and the clinicians task is one of interpretation. Holt casts clinical judgment into the framework of systematic scholarship and discusses the various modes of analysis available to the clinician to check out his or her hypotheses and interpretations. A clear implication of Holt's discussion—and one consistent with our discussion of stereotypes and implicit theories—is that the interpretation of a given act or response by a subject in the testing situation is likely to depend on other acts or responses by the subject.

Suppose that a person who was being administered the Rorschach behaved in a warm, congenial, and accepting manner. Further, suppose that this person gave precisely the *same* responses to the Rorschach as another person who behaved in a cool, aloof, and rejecting manner. Would the diagnosis for these two people differ? A study by Masling (1957) indicated that indeed they would. Masling trained two female undergraduates by having them memorize two sets of responses to the Rorschach and to be either warm or cold while giving these responses. The examiners were eight psychology graduate students in a seminar on projective techniques. Each examiner administered the Rorschach to each accomplice (1 warm and 1 cold), and each accomplice played warm versus cold an equal number of times. Once the examinations were completed, two judges were asked to determine for each "thought unit" in the examiners' reports whether the examiner was making a positive, negative, or other statement about the subject. As anticipated, the interpretations for both accomplices were far more positive when the accomplices had given their responses in a warm manner than when they had given the same responses in a cool, aloof manner.

As Masling (1959) notes, and as was pointed out above, the ambiguity inherent in a projective test such as the Rorschach may make it particularly susceptible to such "interpretation" effects. Consequently, Masling set out to see if such effects occur with intelligence testing. Again two female accomplices were trained to act in a warm or a cool manner. Again a set of answers was prepared for each accomplice to memorize; the script this time consisted of answers to three subtests (Information, Comprehension, and Similarities) of the Wechsler—

Bellevue IQ test. Each accomplice had a different script, but each gave the same answers regardless of whether she was responding warmly or coldly. The examiners were ten psychology graduate students who had completed a course in the administration and scoring of intelligence tests. Each examiner administered the three subtests to each accomplice, and the accomplices alternated in playing the warm or the cold role. For each accomplice, four of the five examiners who tested them when they were answering "warmly" gave them scores higher than the mean, while four of the five with whom they interacted while they were answering "coolly" gave them scores lower than the mean. Remember that each accomplice always gave the *same* answers, regardless of her style (warm or cold). Analysis of the recorded transcripts of the testing sessions revealed that the examiners made significantly more reinforcing statements to the accomplices when they were behaving warmly, and they asked significantly more questions when the accomplices were behaving warmly. This latter finding is interesting and directly relevant to the material we will discuss in the next chapter but, unfortunately, it muddies the claim made by Masling that the accomplices always gave the *same* answers regardless of whether they were answering warmly or coldly. How did the accomplices handle the greater number of questions when they were behaving warmly?

A study by Hersh (1971), however, indicates that the major result obtained by Masling may be a real one. Hersh points out that psychological testing is seldom a dyadic situation. Usually there is a third party hovering somewhere in the background, the person who requested that the testing be done. Often this third party is someone of some status and authority: a guidance counselor, a judge, a psychiatrist, a teacher. The point, as amplified by Towbin (1960), is that the referring agent usually has some purpose in mind and often communicates a preliminary assessment to the person administering the test. Hersh's question was whether or not such preliminary assessments can affect the outcome of testing. To examine this question, 14 male and 14 female graduate students were employed as testers. Fifty-six boys and girls from a summer Headstart program were randomly assigned to one of two "teacher-referral-report" groups. For the children assigned to the positive referral condition, the examiner received a handwritten note supposedly from the child's teacher, which stressed the child's high academic ability and general social skillfulness. For the children assigned to the negative referral condition, the note stressed the child's relatively poor standing academically and apparent lack of social skills. The examiners administered the Stanford–Binet Intelligence Test to the children after having read the referral note; each examiner tested one child from each condition. During the testing, the examiner's behavior was observed and recorded. The examiners scored a higher mean IQ for the children assigned to the positive referral condition ($\bar{X}$ = 93.5) than for those assigned to the negative referral condition ($\bar{X}$ = 88.0). Further, when the examiners began testing a child for whom they had just read a positive referral note, they began the child at a significantly higher year level[1] than when they began testing a child for whom they had just read a negative referral note.

There are two points that need to be raised here. First, in spite of the widespread use of tests such as the Rorschach, the MMPI, and various IQ tests, most clinical judgments are based on interviews with clients or patients or subjects, not on specific tests. Secondly, the usual concern of psychological diagnosis is with a relatively global categorization of the patient or client or subject, and not with his or her score on a specific test. Thus, it is of some interest to see if the sorts of suggestion or cueing effects demonstrated by Hersh occur with more global judgments—such as whether another is "neurotic" or "psychotic"—based on interview data.

To check on this, Temerlin and Trousdale (1969) wrote a script of an interview with a relaxed, confident, productive man who had made an appointment with a psychotherapist to discuss therapy because he was intellectually curious. They then hired a professional actor to play the role and tape recorded his "interview" with a therapist. The taped interview was then played for several large groups of subjects including undergraduates, law students, clinical psychology graduate students, practicing psychiatrists, and practicing clinical psychologists. For the experimental groups, at some point before listening to the interview, it was suggested that the person to be interviewed "looked neurotic, but was actually quite psychotic." This suggestion was part of the instructions for some experimental groups and was a casually dropped remark by a confederate for other experimental groups. Several control groups were employed. In one, subjects were asked to make a diagnosis based on the same interview, but after hearing that the patient "looked like a normal, healthy man." In a second control group, the diagnosis was made with no prior suggestion. In a third control group, there was no prior suggestion and the interview was described as having been a "personnel interview," that is, outside of a clinical setting. Diagnoses were made anonymously by subjects' checking a counterbalanced list of psychoses and neuroses (with descriptive definitions). In addition, all subjects were asked to write a noninferential description of the interviewee. The results were astounding and somewhat scary. Diagnostic differences between the experimental and control groups were highly significant, whether combined or considered individually. Diagnosis of some form of "mental illness" ranged from 84 percent to 100 percent in the experimental groups. Such diagnoses were made by 0 percent to 43 percent of the subjects in the control groups. Further, not a single experimental subject (out of a total of almost 300) wrote a descriptive rather than inferential report of the interviewee. Not a single experimental subject described the behavioral basis for his diagnosis. Temerlin and Trousdale (1969)

---

[1] Stanford—Binet items increase in difficulty, corresponding (roughly) to age levels.

conclude that "inference, unchecked by systematic and repeated observations of behavior, may produce gross errors of interpersonal perception" (p. 28).

One of the problems with the Temerlin and Trousdale study and with a similar study reported by Temerlin (1968), is that only one stimulus person was employed. The suggestion appeared to produce dramatic differences between the experimental and control groups, but rather than being purely a function of the suggestion, the differences may be due to an interaction between the suggestion and the particular stimulus person employed. Hence, it would be nice to have some additional data. In a recent discussion of the literature on behavior classification, Phillips and Draguns (1971, p. 467) point out that research on the clinician's diagnostic activity seems to converge in suggesting that social distance is a mediating variable. They note that the middle-class diagnostician is likely to employ different categories for lower class "patients" and is likely to note fewer symptoms in the process of assigning lower-class patients to those categories. The point here is that the kind of "suggestion" employed in the Temerlin and Trousdale study is relatively artificial and would be pretty unlikely to occur in most testing situations. The kind of "suggestion" alluded to by Phillips and Draguns, that is, preexisting beliefs of the middle-class diagnostician about how the "lower classes" behave, for example, is much more likely to occur.

The difficulty with studies of preexisting beliefs of diagnosticians, generally, is that there are many uncontrolled variables. An example of a study that attempted to shed some light on the influence of these preexisting beliefs (implicit suggestions?) is one by McDermott, Harrison, Schrager, and Wilson (1965). McDermott and his colleagues examined the records of 450 children who had been referred to the University of Michigan's Children's Psychiatric Hospital. On the basis of their father's occupation, the children were divided into a middle-class group, a skilled blue-collar group, and an unskilled group. It was found that poor school "adjustment" was significantly more likely to be the reason for referral among the unskilled group than among the other groups. However, there was also a significantly longer delay in referral of the unskilled group to the clinic after the point in time when their problems first became apparent. Another pertinent finding, reported by McDermott, Harrison, Schrager, Wilson, Killins, Lindy, and Waggoner (1967) and based on data from the same hospital, is that "both mental retardation and chronic brain syndrome were diagnosed *less frequently* than expected in the children of unskilled or chronically unemployed parents as compared to all other classes" (p. 311). McDermott et al. (1967) speculate that it may be that "teachers . . . interpret the presence of certain symptoms differently when they occur in children from different socioeconomic classes. Behavior which may be considered cause for referral in the upper end of the socioeconomic scale may be attributed to 'cultural deprivation' at the lower end" (p. 315).

Thus, it begins to look as if psychological testing and interviewing conducted by professionally trained psychiatrists and psychologists are subject to many of the same types of biasing effects as are the impressions we form of other people in our day-to-day experience. The expectations of the tester, as cued by various "irrelevant" characteristics of both the testing situation and the testee, appear to influence the outcome of testing. To further elucidate the manner in which this occurs, we need to look at what research has been done on the diagnostic process itself.

Studies of the Diagnostic Process

In an attempt to look at the types of information (cues) sought out by psychiatrists in arriving at a diagnostic decision, Gauron and Dickinson (1966) selected three actual cases from the records of a psychiatric hospital for presentation to each of 12 psychiatrists. With each case, a list of 40 categories of information that was available on that case was also presented. The categories included such items as: age, sex, reason for referral, results of projective tests, past school performance. Each psychiatrist sequentially requested items of information and, after receiving each new item, he was to make a decision as to the most probable diagnosis at that point and to rate his certainty about the diagnosis. The reason for referral was clearly perceived to be the most important category. Further, a general pattern in terms of information ordering emerged: orienting information such as age, sex, and reason for referral was first re- quested, followed by requests for information about past history, followed by mental status categories (results of projective testing). Of particular interest here, however, is an index derived by Gauron and Dickinson to look at category importance. They defined a category of information as being *actually important* if it either suggested the diagnosis that ended up as the final diagnosis or increased the probability of the diagnosis that ended up as the final diagnosis. They then correlated this index of *actual importance* with the psychiatrists' own direct ratings of category importance and found that the two were not related. Gauron and Dickinson (1966) use this to argue that "... In actual fact the psychiatrist derived the clues underlying his diagnosis from sources other than he thought he did" (p. 230).

To a practicing psychiatrist, the diagnostic situation in the Gauron and Dickinson study must have seemed extremely contrived and artificial, since it requested items of information about a client one at a time and made several ratings and a decision following each new item. The main objection of the psychiatrists to the entire study was, in fact, that they could not see and interview the patients themselves. "They felt uncomfortable because they could not obtain their own personal impression of the patient upon which they could base their diagnosis. This in itself is an interesting commentary on the current state of affairs within psychiatry in that one evaluator cannot 'trust' the impressions of another one" (Gauron and Dickinson, 1966, p. 231). That, of course, is exactly what we are talking about.

As part of an earlier, related study, Newton (1954) asked a group of clinical psychologists to make judgments about the "adjustments" of each of a group of patients, based either on the basic data sheets or the Rorschach protocols for each patient. These two judgments were made with a considerable degree of reliability (.94 for the basic data sheets and .73 for the Rorschach protocols). However, there was no relation between the psychologists' judgments of adjustment from the Rorschach and their judgments of adjustment from the basic data sheets. Thus, one's "diagnosis" may be as much a function of the particular instrument the clinician employs as it is of one's "actual" adjustment. But, let's not jump to conclusions on the basis of one or two studies.

Another way of looking at the problem is to ask whether the professionally trained clinical psychologist or psychiatrist has an expertise about the behavior of others that is not shared by, say, an equally intelligent layman. Luft (1950) reports two experiments that bear on this question. Although he does not elaborate, Luft's conceptual framework appears to have been very similar to the one employed here. He utilized the method of *controlled cross-prediction*, in which material is extracted from an actual case history and a judge or diagnostician is asked to predict from known behavior (part of the material) to behavior not known (another part of the same case material). Luft assumed that ". . . the bridge between the two samples of behavior is made up of the impressions or implicit hypotheses conceived by the judge" (p. 756). In his first study, Luft asked five clinicians and five physical scientists to listen to a case conference summary about a patient presented by the patient's therapist. Following this, each of the listeners was asked to respond to a standard personality questionnaire as the patient would. A number of the listeners did significantly better than chance[2] in terms of the number of items correctly predicted, that is, they answered more items as the patient himself had actually answered them than could be expected on the basis of chance. However, the clinicians were no more accurate than the nonclinicians.

In a second study, Luft asked four groups of judges (20 psychiatrists, 18 social workers, 28 clinical psychologists, and 28 physical scientists) to read the transcripts of a one-hour diagnostic interview for each of two different patients. The judges then attempted to predict patients' responses to both a sentence completion test—for example, "I am happiest when _____.")—and an objective test. Again, no single group of judges was reliably superior. Luft concludes that "Prediction from such material may therefore call for general intelligence rather

[2] It is not clear if Luft used an appropriate comparison here. Stereotype accuracy (Cronbach, 1955) may have produced the result he refers to. It would be nice to know the extent to which the patient's own responses differed from those of an "average person" on the questionnaire. That is, chance may be an inappropriate base line.

than special clinical understanding" (p. 757). I would phrase it somewhat differently and say that the hypotheses formulated on the basis of cues contained in such material tap into shared aspects of the implicit personality theories of the judges.

If we conceptualize clinical judgment as a process of categorization, a process in which certain cues or combinations of cues are used to refine the placement of "... the patient from a supraordinate stereotype (i.e., class of events) to more subordinate ones as increments of information are accumulated" (Kostlan, 1955, p. 486), then it becomes important to know whether or not the clinical judge employs a given combination of cues consistently. Another way of phrasing this is to ask if, for a given judge, a consistent judgmental strategy can be identified and separated from the judge's unreliability.

Studies of the reliability of the diagnostic process done with actual patients face-to-face with actual clinicians are few. The reasons for this are obvious. If we define *reliability* as being the repeatability of a diagnostic categorization made by a clinician of a client whom he or she has interviewed in depth, tested, and gathered auxiliary information about, there is no way we can ask the clinician to erase all that and repeat the entire process to see if the same diagnosis results. What we can do is see if different clinicians, when confronted with the same case material, make the same diagnosis. Note that this is different from the sorts of examiner influences described in the section on the examiner's influence on test results. There, the examiner's own personality characteristics may have partially determined the actual responses given by clients, that is, different examiners may have elicited different responses. Here we are interested in whether the diagnoses that result differ as a function of the diagnostician when the material on which the diagnoses are based is the same.

As part of a larger study, Goldfarb (1959) selected 100 cases from the files of a Veteran Administration hospital and removed all identifying information from the reports. The reports contained extensive material on each patient: life history data, referral information, and the results of testing. Four psychiatrists were asked to read through the cases and make a diagnostic judgment for each. A number of diagnostic categories were available and there was significant variability among the four judges in their assignments to the various categories. Based on this and some related data, Goldfarb (1959) summarizes by saying, "The fundamental question raised in this study was whether or not the diagnoses given to groups of patients depended to a significant degree upon which clinician made the evaluation. The results suggest that the answer to this question is substantially 'yes' " (p. 396). Grosz and Grossman (1968) report a similar result based on a study of the diagnostic decisions of five psychiatric residents who evaluated comparable samples of 23 to 36 female patients. The residents appeared to differ systematically in their tendencies to note consistently high or consistently low levels of "abnormalities" in their patients.

The above studies might be criticized on several grounds. For example, psychiatric residents are *not* experienced clinicians. They are generally considered to be students who are just beginning to specialize in psychiatry. Hence it should come as no surprise that they make systematic errors in diagnosis. Further, one might argue that the above studies, while suggestive in pointing to the existence of differences, do not really identify those differences beyond the global stage of noting that they exist. Is it the case that different diagnosticians believe different characteristics to be associated with the same cues or do different clinicians actually "see" different cues in the same client? Let's take this question in stages. First, are there certain commonly employed sources of information about clients that lead to more valid[3] inferences about the clients?

Kostlan (1954) addressed this somewhat more restricted question by utilizing four commonly employed diagnostic instruments in a *fractional omission* design (Brunswik, 1949). In a fractional omission design, each of several cues thought to be utilized in making a judgment is systematically eliminated one at a time, and the judgment made with each individual cue missing can be compared to the judgment made with all cues present. The idea is to find the optimal cue or combination of cues. The four cues of interest to Kostlan were the Rorschach, the MMPI, the Stein Sentence Completion Test (SCT), and a social case history. Kostlan obtained these items of information about five male outpatients, each of whom was currently undergoing individual psychotherapy. To establish his criterion, Kostlan presented all of the available material on each of the five outpatients to eight experienced clinical psychologists and asked them to make a series of 283 true–false judgments about each patient. Any of the 283 items on which six or more of the eight judges agreed for a particular patient were defined as "internally valid" for that patient, and these were the items the judges were asked to predict. Twenty clinical psychologists, each with at least two years of psychodiagnostic experience were then employed as judges. Five conditions were set up as illustrated below:

Condition	Information available	Missing
1	MMPI, SCT, case history	Rorschach
2	Rorschach, SCT, case history	MMPI
3	Rorschach, MMPI, case history	SCT
4	Rorschach, MMPI, SCT	Case history
5	Age, marital status, occupation, education, source of referral	Everything else

Each judge saw the material from one of the patients under one of the five conditions, but neither a patient nor a condition was repeated for any judge.

[3] Again we are plagued by a criterion problem. In most studies in the literature, *validity* is defined by the extent to which judgments agree with a panel of experienced clinicians who have "total" information about the client. Such a criterion has obvious drawbacks, many of which we are in the process of discussing here.

There were a number of results, two of which are of particular interest here:

1. Under each of the five experimental conditions, the judges were able to make inferences that were more accurate than chance, that is, more than 50 percent[4] correct predictions on the "valid" items.
2. When deprived of the case history, clinicians can make no more accurate inferences than they can on the basis of minimal information, that is, condition (5).

As Meehl (1959) summarizes this result, ". . . clinicians knowing only the age, marital status, occupation, education and source of referral of a patient (that is, relying essentially upon the *Barnum effect* for their ability to make correct statements) yield an average of about 63 percent correct statements about the patient. If they have the Rorschach, Multiphasic, and Sentence Completion Tests *but are deprived of the social case history*, this combined psychometric battery results in almost exactly the same percentage of correct judgments" (pp. 115–116).

The answer to our question, thus, appears to be that some of the commonly employed cues used by clinicians in the "assessment" of personality, that is, the Rorschach, the MMPI, and the Sentence Completion Test, are not likely to increase the validity of clinical judgments beyond that gross level of categorization that can be attained with face sheet data (age, sex, education, occupation, and source of referral). One study, of course, is insufficient evidence. But there are others that can be used to buttress the argument.

Sines (1959) obtained four major kinds of data on a number of applicants to a VA Mental Hygiene Clinic: a lengthy Biographical Data Sheet (BDS), an MMPI profile, an interview report, and Rorschach responses. The clinicians who were to serve as diagnosticians received this information sequentially and, after each new source of information, the diagnostician sorted 97 personality–behavioral statements according to how descriptive each statement was of the patient. Thus, the diagnosticians performed four such sorts for each patient. For all patients, the BDS Was seen first by their diagnostician, and the order of the other three types of information was systematically varied. The criterion to be predicted by the diagnosticians for each patient was a sort of the same 97 statements carried out by the patient's own therapist after the patient had been in therapy for ten interviews or sessions. As a base line against which to compare the results, several judges sorted the 97 items in terms of how descriptive they were of an "average patient." For two-thirds of the cases, the correlation between the fourth sort by the diagnostician, that is, the sort he made after he had seen all four kinds of data, and the sort performed by that patient's therapist after ten sessions was greater than that between the "average patient"

---

[4] Patterson (1955) points out that the measure of chance success should not have been 50 percent correct, but the proportion correctly answered on the basis of the knowledge that the person was *a clinic patient*.

sort and the therapist's sort. Further, the sorts made by the diagnosticians when the only types of information they had were the BDS and the interview were significantly more valid (agreed with the therapist's sorts) than sorts made on the basis of the BDS plus Rorschach or BDS plus MMPI. It appears that, across the board, omitting the Rorschach was associated with greater validity than including it. Sines points out that, in general, there appears to be a consistent positive relationship between the amount of information a diagnostician has and the accuracy of his judgments. However, ". . . the absolute improvement from initial (BDS) to final clinical sort was quite small" (p. 488).

Another point that should be noted about Sines' data is that, for only two-thirds of the cases, the correlation between the fourth sort by the diagnostician and the therapist's sort after ten sessions was greater than the correlation between the "average patient" sort and the therapist's sort. A more forceful way to make this point is to rephrase it to indicate that for one-third of the patients ". . . the application of a stereotype personality description based upon actuarial experience in this particular clinic provided a more accurate description of the patient than the clinician's judgment based upon any, or all, of the available tests, history, and interview data!" (Meehl, 1959, p. 116). In an extensive review of the literature on attempts to predict suicide, Lester (1970) reaches a similarly pessimistic conclusion about the usefulness of standardized personality inventories and projective tests.

It is possible that the criterion Sines used was inadequate. Maybe a psychotherapist who has had ten sessions with a patient does not really "know" the patient yet. Horowitz (1962), in a study very similar to Sines's, used as her criterion a description of each patient by a therapist who had seen the patient for a minimum of 20 hours of psychotherapy. The criterion for each patient was obtained by asking the therapist to sort 32 socially desirable and 32 socially undesirable statements into categories according to how descriptive they were of the patient. Groups of clinician—judges were then asked to sort the 64 statements about the target cases on the basis of either biographical data only or on the basis of biographical data plus the results of the Rorschach, TAT, and Sentence Completion Test. In line with earlier results, Horowitz (1962) found ". . . projective data were useful only insofar as they enabled the clinicians to place the patients into a grossly defined subgroup of the general psychiatric population" (p. 255).

We could continue to cite evidence, but presumably the point has been made. In spite of what is claimed for the usefulness of projective data, clinicians do not improve their accuracy of prediction or categorization by employing such data. Apparently the important cues or, at least, the cues utilized, are contained in other aspects of the clinical situation. To go back to the question raised earlier, then, we still need to know whether clinicians actually "see" different cues in the same patient or whether they "see" the same cues, but believe them to be associated with different things, that is, different diagnostic categories.

In a series of studies Katz, Cole, and Lowery (1969) addressed themselves to precisely this question, that is, whether diagnostic ". . . disagreements among clinicians are a function of differences in their actual perceptions of the patient or are simply a matter of their assigning different designations to patients on whose symptoms and behavior they are in agreement. (p. 937). In one study, 25 psychiatrists and psychologists viewed standard interview situations, that is, all the raters viewed the same patients at the same time and rated those patients on a set of psychiatric symptom scales. Katz et al. then separated out those three patients for whom the clinicians were agreed on the diagnosis and found that the ". . . patterns of symptoms and behavior manifested by these three patients were distinct" (p. 938). Thus, there is a little evidence that clinicians can use different cues to arrive at a common diagnosis. This is not surprising; each patient may have exhibited a different subset of the overall set of cues taken to indicate their common problem.

But what about the case where clinicians disagree in their diagnosis? In another study, Katz et al. (1969) asked 44 experienced psychiatrists to view an interview with a psychiatric patient and rate the symptoms exhibited. Based on their diagnosis of the patient as being either "schizophrenic" or "psychoneurotic," the psychiatrists were separated into two groups. Katz, et al. then compared the symptoms that these two groups reported "seeing" in the patient and found that the sets of symptoms reported by the two groups were very similar. Thus, there is some evidence that different clinicians use the same symptoms as the basis of different inferences. In further studies, Katz et al. note that on some occasions clinicians report seeing different patterns of symptoms as being present in standardized videotaped interviews. The implication here is that clinicians are attending to, and thus utilizing, different cues. Thus, it appears that clinicians both see different cues in the same patient and use the same cue to infer different things.

Mistakes and differences in psychiatric and psychological diagnosis are common. As we have seen, the diagnostic process suffers from many of the same biases, distortions, preconceptions, and expectations as our day-to-day perceptions of others. So far, however, we have been mainly descriptive. Let us take a step back from demonstrations of the existence of diagnostic biases and see if we can achieve an understanding of a few plausible processes that might account for such biases.

Pitfalls of Information Processing in Personality Assessment

One of the keys to understanding psychological (or physical) diagnosis is an appreciation of the probabilistic relationship between cues and the characteristics or entities one infers from these cues. Another way of stating this is that there is seldom an absolute one-to-one relation between a given cue and an inferred characteristic. Given such a state of affairs, it becomes incumbent upon the would-be diagnostician to determine exactly which cues can be relied upon. This is more easily said than done.

The problem appears to be one of simply learning which event or events are associated with which cue. For years, learning theorists have pointed out and demonstrated empirically that, when a given event follows the presentation of a given cue, the association between the two is strengthened. Conversely, when the cue is not followed by the event, the association between the two is weakened. But what happens to the association when the event appears or does not appear in the *absence* of the signal? Apparently, these important bits of evidence pertinent to the association are ignored. Some evidence exists that people do, indeed, ignore aspects of evidence that should be taken into account in order to decide if two events are related. Ward and Jenkins (1965), for example, constructed a series of problems having to do with the relationship between rain and cloud seeding. If we cast the data for the type of problem they were concerned with into a contingency table it might look something like this:

	Rain	No Rain
Seeded	75	25
Not seeded	50	50

The entries in each of the four cells are the number of days on which rain followed seeding (75), rain occurred in the absence of seeding (50), and so forth. Of interest here is that when subjects received the information contained in such a table on a trial-by-trial basis—a series of statements such as: "On the first day the clouds were seeded and it rained"—they were generally very inaccurate in deciding whether or not seeding was related to the probability of rain. In fact, only 17 percent of such subjects followed a logically defensible rule for making the judgment. As Ward and Jenkins (1965) note, "In general, our results lend support to the conclusion that statistically naive subjects lack an abstract concept of contingency that is isomorphic with the statistical concept. Those who receive information on a trial-by-trial basis, as it usually occurs in the real world, generally fail to assess adequately the degree of relationship present" (p. 240). One strategy that many subjects appeared to follow was to place undue reliance on only those instances which confirm that a relationship exists, that is, those days on which seeding was followed by rain and not seeding was followed by sunshine. What they should have done, of course, is compare the probability of rain when clouds were seeded with the probability of rain when clouds were not seeded.

One could argue that Ward and Jenkins[5] were unrealistic in expecting subjects to take in, store, retrieve, and appropriately compare such a large amount of information. It is true that subjects who were provided a summary of the information in the form of a contingency table such as the one above did

[5] The Ward and Jenkins study was simply chosen as an example. There are a number of other studies which have yielded comparable results about the lack of understanding of what is needed to conclude that a relationship exists between two variables (cf., Smedslund, 1963, 1966).

significantly better in judging whether or not a relationship existed than did subjects exposed to the information on a trial-by-trial basis. Further, one might argue that naive subjects are not, after all, trained diagnosticians, who are generally much better educated and, perhaps, more knowledgeable, and who may even have had formal training in statistics and probability.

On the other hand, one could argue that the task facing the clinician who has a hunch about a particular cue being related to a particular problem is much more complex and difficult than the Ward and Jenkins task. First of all, he or she will probably not be exposed to all the necessary information. People who do not have the problem are not likely to see the clinician. Hence, the clinician will never know whether or not they have the symptom. Secondly, even the information the clinician does obtain relevant to the relationship of interest is likely to be gathered over the course of months or years rather than in a single experimental session. The problems introduced by these extended time periods are obvious.

One thing does seem clear, however, and that is that a practicing clinician who would like to check out a hunch about a relationship between a behavioral cue, say, and a personality disposition by observing how these covary in the next x number of patients who display the cue is going to end up making an inaccurate assessment. For as we noted above and as Wason (1960) points out, ". . . scientific inferences are based on the principle of eliminating hypotheses, while provisionally accepting only those which remain. Methodologically, such eliminative induction implies adequate controls so that both positive and negative experimental results give information about the possible determinants of a phenomenon" (p. 129). At the very least, our clinician would have to determine for *all* patients whether or not they have the particular disposition, regardless of whether or not they display the cue.

Unfortunately, there are other sources of error that plague the attempt to determine relationships between symptoms or cues and personality characteristics in addition to the failure to secure the necessary control or base rate data. A line of research begun some years ago by Chapman (1967) has identified a type of error that appears to be particularly widespread in psychological assessment situations. Chapman's study was a relatively simple verbal learning type of experiment in which subjects were shown pairs of words projected on a screen for a couple of seconds and were later asked to recall how many times particular pairs had been shown. For example, one series consisted of 12 word-pairs, each shown 10 times for a total of 120 presentations. The 12 word-pairs were constructed by pairing each of the four words on the left below with each of the three words on the right:

Boat	Tiger
Lion	Eggs
Bacon	Notebook
Blossoms	

As can be seen, two of the resulting word pairs are strong associates: *lion–tiger* and *bacon–eggs*. When asked to recall how frequently each of the 12 word-pairs had been presented in the series, subjects significantly overestimated the number of times that such strong associates had been shown.

In a follow-up study, Chapman and Chapman (1967) attempted to extrapolate this finding to the clinical test situation. Specifically, they felt it had some applicability to "One of the most puzzling and distressing problems that confronts clinical psychology today . . . the persistent report by many psychodiagnosticians of clinical observations which, by objective evidence, clearly appear to be erroneous" (p. 193). To be more precise, the Chapmans were concerned about the continued reports that certain responses to projective tests were correlated with certain "problems," such as homosexuality, when the research evidence appeared to indicate no relationship. The finding concerning overestimation of strong associates in the Chapman and Chapman study suggested that, perhaps, ". . . these systematic errors are produced by variables inherent in the stimuli observed, and are of such a nature that entirely naive observers who view psychodiagnostic materials would report the same erroneous correlates of patients' symptoms" (pp. 193–194).

To check on this, Chapman and Chapman first collected 45 responses to the Draw-a-Person test from both psychotic patients in a state hospital and psychology graduate students. They then constructed six-symptom statements, for example, "He is suspicious of other people," and asked a number of practicing clinicians, most of whom used the DAP test regularly, to indicate the essential characteristics of pictures drawn by men with each symptom. Next, they presented the 45 drawings to college students, with each drawing *arbitrarily* paired with two of the six-symptom statements. Following the presentation of all 45 pictures, subjects were asked six questions, one for each symptom statement. Each question asked them to list the characteristics of the drawings made by persons who had that symptom. It is important to remember that for these college students the symptom statements had been arbitrarily paired with the drawings.

The result of interest here is the comparison between the drawing characteristics that the practicing clinicians said were typical of patient's with each symptom and the drawing characteristics that the naive college students said were typical of people with each symptom. In all, there were 15 drawing characteristics identified by at least 15 percent of either the clinicians or the students as being typical of patients with at least one of the symptoms.

For each of the 15 drawing characteristics, the symptom for which the clinicians most often reported it as a correlate was the same symptom for which the naive observers most often reported it. . . . For example, both the clinicians and the naive observers reported broad-shouldered, muscular figures more often as a correlate of the symptom "He is worried about how manly he is" than for any other of the six symptoms, and both groups reported drawings with atypical eyes more often for the symptom "He is suspicious of other people" than for any other symptom (p. 198).

The interpretation the Chapmans prefer for this similarity is that, in the absence of any true association between particular symptoms and particular drawing characteristics, both clinicians and naive students were relying on preexisting associative links between manliness and broad shoulders, for example. In subsequent research reported in the same article, they asked undergraduates to rate the strength of association between the problem areas identified in the six-symptom statements and various parts of the body. As anticipated, the correspondence between these ratings and the drawing characteristics most often associated with the six symptoms was very high. For example: "... 'eyes' are a stronger associate to 'suspiciousness' than to any other symptom, and ... [in the earlier study] drawing characteristics mentioning 'eyes' were listed as an illusory correlate of that same symptom more often than any other symptom" (p. 200).

In a series of subsequent studies the Chapmans (1969) and others (Golding and Rorer, 1972; Starr and Katkin, 1969) have demonstrated similar illusory correlation effects with the Rorschach and the Incomplete Sentence Blank. Further, these effects appear to be relatively resistant to extinction, that is, they persist under conditions that place a premium on accuracy and even in the face of negative evidence. In all of these studies, the erroneous beliefs about relationships between test responses and particular psychosocial problems, that is, the illusory correlations, were interpreted in terms of preexisting associative links between aspects of the test responses and connotations of the psychosocial problems.

In his original article, however, Chapman (1967) postulated a second basis for illusory correlations. In addition to finding overestimation of the frequency of word-pairs for which there was a preexisting associative link (*lion–tiger*), Chapman also found that the frequencies of word-pairs made up of atypically long words (e.g., *blossoms–notebook*) were also overestimated. Chapman interpreted the later finding as being due to the "distinctiveness" of pairing two long words in a series in which most of the word-pairs were two short words or one short and one long word. Unfortunately, this appears to be more a description of what happened than an explanation.

Recently, Tversky and Kahneman (1973) have called attention to a judgmental heuristic that may explain both sources of illusory correlations. Judgments of the frequencies with which various classes of events have occurred are common, and the basis for many such judgments appears to be a simple law of repetition: the more frequently an event has occurred, the stronger the associative links to that event. Strength of association to the event is later used as an aid or clue in making judgments of the event's frequency. The ease with which instances of a particular class of events can be brought to mind has been termed *availability* by Tversky and Kahneman (1973), who point out that "Availability is an ecologically valid clue for the judgment of frequency because, in general, frequent events are easier to recall or imagine than infrequent ones" (p. 209).

There are things other than repetition, however, that affect the availability of a particular class of events. Anything that makes a particular class more salient or distinctive than related classes will make that class more available. Since, in general, frequent events are more available in memory than infrequent ones, bias occurs when the frequencies of related classes do not correspond to the ease with which those classes can be retrieved from memory. Thus, to return to the Chapman and Chapman (1967) study, in judgments of the frequency with which pairs of words had been presented subjects erred by overestimating the frequency of pairs such as *lion–tiger*, for which there was a preexistent association and by overestimating the frequency of pairs composed of atypically long words. Rather than implicating two different bases for the formation of illusory correlations, Tversky and Kahneman (1973) point out that these data may be viewed as indicating that

> . . . illusory correlation is due to the differential strength of associative bonds. The strength of these bonds may reflect prior association between the items or other factors, such as pair distinctiveness, which facilitate the formation of association during learning. Thus the various sources of illusory correlation can all be explained by the operation of a single mechanism—the assessment of availability or associative strength (p. 224).

In addition to the errors that assessment of availability can introduce into interpretations of projective test results, they may result in a chain of further mistakes. That is, a number of studies have indicated that premature conclusions about what another person is "really" like can interfere with appropriate utilization of new information about the person. For example, Dailey (1952), in a series of experiments, asked subjects to read autobiographical sketches written by stimulus persons and to predict how the stimulus person would respond to specific items on a personality inventory. The criterion in each case was how the stimulus person had actually responded. Some subjects made predictions after reading half the autobiography and again after reading all of it. Other subjects made predictions only after reading all the information. The latter group did significantly better or, as Dailey puts it ". . . premature conclusions on the basis of a small amount of data can apparently prevent the observer from profiting as fully from additional data as he would without the premature decision" (p. 142). In later experiments, Dailey attempted to manipulate the importance of the information on which the premature conclusions were based and, as expected, premature decisions were most detrimental when based on unimportant information. Further, simply allowing subjects to pause after reading some information (and think about it!) had a biasing effect similar to asking for personality predictions on the basis of only a small amount of information. Dailey concludes that, in situations ". . . involving repeated evaluations by observers of the same persons, validity may be lost by the cumulative tendency of understanding to affect itself adversely, *to diminish as it is expressed*" (p. 151).

The clinical–psychotherapeutic situation is, of course, one in which an observer–clinician does make repeated observations and evaluations of the same persons over time. According to D'Andrade (1974), such situations are "... subject to a special effect analogous to that of an illusion; an effect in which there is a reliable and systematic distortion of judgments" (p. 161). D'Andrade's argument is that, when an observer relies on his or her long term memory in making assessments of a number of different people each of whom performed a number of different behaviors, the characteristics and behaviors that the observer considers to be similar are likely to be recalled as applying to the same person. If such a systematic distortion were operative, it would have serious implications for the clinician engaged in psychodiagnosis and psychotherapy. Consider the psychotherapist. During a week, he or she may see 20 to 40 patients for an hour each and, while the therapist may take some notes or even record some sessions, by and large the hours are spent in conversation with the patients. If there is a tendency for observers to remember similar behaviors as having been performed by the same others under such circumstances, then over a few months the therapist will have built up partially erroneous pictures of various clients. The hostile and aggressive Mr. Brown will be remembered as the one who got into that scrape on the street and beat his wife and earlier got suspended from high school for fighting when, in fact, it was Mr. Smith who beat his wife.

To check on the possibility that such distortions do occur, D'Andrade made a search for published studies of group interaction in which there was both immediate recording of ongoing behaviors of the group members and judgments based on memory of who had done what during the group interactions. He found two such studies. Analysis of the patterns of correlations among the various attributed behaviors in both studies revealed that observers' and participants' memories for what occurred in the group interactions are systematically biased by a tendency to recall similar behaviors as having been performed by the same person when, in fact, they were not. As D'Andrade (1974) points out, the implication here is that, "With this type of memory error, any attempt to discover how human behavior is organized into multibehavior units . . . which is based on data consisting of long-term memory judgments will result in conclusions which primarily reflect the cognitive structure of the raters" (pp. 175–177). Unfortunately, one way of conceptualizing the task of psychodiagnosticians and psychotherapists is to discover how an individual's behavior is organized into multibehavior units.

In this section, a few of the pitfalls that interfere with accurate information-processing in personality assessment have been examined. There are others that could be cited. For example, Regan, Straus, and Fazio (1974) found that behaviors consistent with one's expectations of another tend to be perceived as dispositional properties of the other, whereas inconsistent behaviors are perceived to be due to the situation. Hopefully, enough has been said to make the point that clinical judgment is *not* the passive receipt and processing of information about one person by another person. In order to change this into an affirmative statement, that is, what clinical judgment *is*, it might be helpful to look at some of the ways in which clinical judgment has been conceptualized.

Perspectives on Clinical Judgment

There have been numerous theoretical and metatheoretical statements about what is involved in clinical judgment. Two positions that are particularly congenial with both the point of view taken here and the evidence of the preceding sections are the schemas of George Kelly and Egon Brunswik. Although the viewpoints of these two differ in many fundamental respects, they both place heavy emphasis on the importance of the cognitive structure which the perceiver—the clinician—brings to the task of understanding another.

George Kelly was a practicing psychotherapist who developed a theoretical perspective, which he called *The Psychology of Personal Constructs* (1955). The basic philosophical position underlying Kelly's perspective was termed *constructive alternativism*, the position that "... whatever nature may be, or however the quest for truth will turn out in the end, the events we face today are subject to as great a variety of constructions as our wits will enable us to contrive. ... Events do not tell us what to do, nor do they carry their meanings engraved on their backs for us to discover. For better or worse, we ourselves create the only meanings they will ever convey during our lifetime" (Kelly, 1966, cited in Bannister and Mair, 1968, pp. 6–7).

Kelly assumed that in the attempt to bring order to the events surrounding them, each person developed their own idiosyncratic, hierarchically organized system of personal constructs. A construct is simply a dichotomous abstraction that the person has made of the similarities and differences among events in the onrushing stream of stimuli surrounding them. The key, of course, is that different people make different abstractions from the "same" events. To say that a person's system of constructs is hierarchically organized means that some constructs are more important than others and it is the interrelationships *among* constructs that are of central concern. "A single construct by itself would allow no predictions, since it is along the line of interrelationships *between* constructs that predictions are made. Only when constructs are interrelated and organized into some kind of system can they form the bases for consistent or useful anticipations" (Bannister and Mair, 1968, p. 15). If we know that someone construes others in terms of a like me—not like me construct, we need to know how the perception that another is not like me relates to other aspects of the person's construct system. What is that perception likely to imply?

It is important to note the similarities between Kelly's notion of a hierarchically organized set of personal constructs and the notion of an implicit theory of personality. The relationships among constructs define a network of interrelated expectations or anticipations that is essentially the same as the correlation matrix with its underlying dimensional structure that was described in Chapter 2. Given such a conception of cognition, it follows that Kelly viewed clinical judgment as a process of attempting to understand the constructions that a client has placed on reality. Understanding how another construes his or her interpersonal world is preliminary to helping the other chart a more satisfying course of behavior through that world. The idea that one's perceptions are tentative and subject to reconstruction is basic to Kelly's argument, as it is to the notion of implicit theories of personality.

A related perspective on clinical judgment has its origins in the work of Egon Brunswik. Brunswik was an experimental psychologist who, early in life, developed an appreciation for the fact that different people may see the "same" situation in different ways. Tolman (1956) reports that Brunswik's father was Hungarian and his mother Austrian. As a consequence, Brunswik could read both Hungarian and German and, in reading the history of the Austro–Hungarian Empire in these two languages, he was impressed by the discrepancies between the two versions. Whether or not this early understanding of varying perspectives is really implicated in his later theoretical stance is open to debate. The example, however, fits rather nicely into the system he did develop.

Brunswik's basic point about perception was that the perceiver's knowledge of the environment is of a probabilistic nature. His system or theoretical stance is, in fact, referred to as *probabilistic functionalism*. As Hammond (1966) points out, Brunswik's system ". . . is a form of functionalism because its main focus is on the adaptive interrelation of the organism with the environment" (p. 16). In attempting to understand, adapt to, or come to terms with the environment, the person must employ signs or cues given off by various aspects of the environment. The task is complicated by the fact that the various cues given off by an aspect of the environment are not all equally trustworthy. There is a hierarchy among these cues in terms of the extent to which they validly represent some aspect of the person's ecology. Further, the person may place undue reliance on a poor cue and may ignore or place only little reliance on cues which are ecologically valid.

Brunswik's theoretical position may be illustrated with his lens model. Consider the example depicted in Figure 3.1, in which the lens model is applied to the task of judging another's intelligence from four cues: height of forehead, score on Scale D of the MMPI, shoe size, and score on an IQ test. As can be seen in the figure, our hypothetical judge is placing equal reliance on cues 1 and 4—IQ score and forehead height—when the ecological validities of these two cues differ considerably. In the example, forehead height is uncorrelated with intelligence $(r_{e_4} = .0)$, whereas the IQ scores are highly correlated with intelligence $(r_{e_1} = .8)$. Further, the judge depicted in the figure is using the third cue as though it were positively correlated with intelligence $(r_{s_3} = .4)$ when, in fact, it is negatively correlated with intelligence $(r_{e_3} = -.5)$.

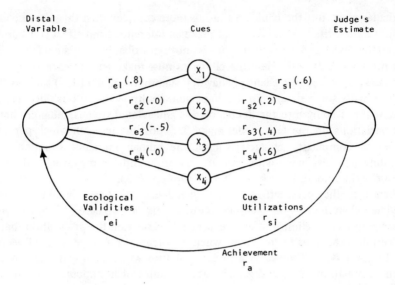

Distal
Variable

Cues

Judge's
Estimate

$r_{e1}(.8)$ X_1 $r_{s1}(.6)$

$r_{e2}(.0)$ X_2 $r_{s2}(.2)$

$r_{e3}(-.5)$ $r_{s3}(.4)$

$r_{e4}(.0)$ X_3 $r_{s4}(.6)$

X_4

Ecological
Validities
r_{ei}

Cue
Utilizations
r_{si}

Achievement
r_a

CUES: X_1=Score on IQ test

X_2=Shoe Size

X_3=Score on scale D of MMPI

X_4=Height of Forehead

ECOLOGICAL VALIDITIES: Correlation between the given cue and the
variable to be estimated (Distal Variable).

CUE UTILIZATION: Correlation between the given cue and the Judge's
estimate.

ACHIEVEMENT: Correlation between the judge's estimate and the variable
estimated.

FIG. 3.1 An example of Brunswik's lens model with four cues employed in making
judgments of intelligence.

An extension of the lens model by Hammond, Wilkins, and Todd (1966) to
the interpersonal learning situation, such as that involved when a clinician is
attempting to learn how a particular client is responding to the cues in his or her
environment, is, conceptually, very close to Kelly's perspective, in which the
clinician's first task is to learn how the client construes his or her environment.
Applying the Hammond et al. (1966) analysis to the clinical setting, the task
facing the clinician is one of discovering how the client responds to or utilizes

particular cues. But the clinician's task is more complex than this, because he or she must first discover the cues and make an inference from effect (the cues) to cause (the distal variable); *then* there is another probabilistic system (the client) that must be dealt with. Here the clinician must make an inference from cause (the cues) to effect (the client's behavior). Hammond et al. (1966) support their analysis with some data from a two-person, multiple-cue, probability learning task. Without going into the details of this and related studies, the point here is that variations on the lens model make ". . . possible research which permits a degree of complexity characteristic of the human inference situation while providing a precise analysis of both the situation and the organism's inferential process" (Hammond, Hursch, and Todd, 1964, p. 455).

There are other perspectives on clinical judgment that are related to the point of view taken here. For example, Sarbin, Taft, and Bailey (1960) present a six-stage model of clinical inference which ". . . rests on the proposition that we use certain categories or 'modules' when we organize our experience of people" (p. 22). A module "serves as a molar structure which is already in existence when stimulation of the organism occurs and which imposes some holistic imprint onto the perception" (p. 27). As we have seen in the preceeding sections, the clinician, no less than the client, organizes his or her experience of people and, hence, develops certain implicit expectations and beliefs. To phrase this in Brunswikian terms, the clinician develops a set of cue-utilization coefficients, which may or may not match the ecological validities of the cues and may or may not correspond to the cue-utilization coefficients of the client with whom he or she is interacting. In Kelly's terms, both the clinician and the client have systems of personal constructs, which may or may not be organized in the same way. Hence, clinical judgment is the process of discovering how the client construes reality. It is the process of pinning down the environmental and interpersonal cues to which the client is responding and developing an appreciation for what the client takes those cues to mean.

Summary

In the Summary section on page 62, the discussion of stereotypes was summarized by pointing out that the evidence seemed to indicate that stereotypes are no different, in principle, from the sorts of interpersonal expectancies discussed in Chapter 2. The evidence on psychological and psychiatric diagnosis forces a similar conclusion. We have examined studies on the influence of the examiner on the results of psychodiagnostic testing indicating that the examiner plays a significant role in determining the outcome of testing. Further, the circumstances of testing are not irrelevant to the outcome, and studies of the diagnostic process indicate that different examiners both "see" different cues in the same patient and use the same cue to infer different things. Clinicians, in short, disagree on diagnosis, even when given the same information about a client. Further, these disagreements are at least in part a function of the preexisting conceptual schemes (implicit theories) that clinicians bring to the diagnostic situation.

We then turned to a brief examination of some of the ways in which this state of affairs perpetuates itself by looking at a few of the pitfalls that interfere with information-processing in personality assessment. Clinicians, and others, appear prone to a number of biasing influences from ignoring base rate data, when attempting to decide if two variables are related to mistaking their own premature inferences for fact, to relying on judgmental heuristics, which lead to erroneous inferences. These biases are compounded by the fact that our impressions of others appear much less responsive to additional information, especially contradictory information, once we have developed clear expectations about what another is like. Finally, we attempted to put all this in focus by briefly describing the systems of Kelly and Brunswik. These two offer perspectives on clinical judgment within which the evidence we have examined makes sense and within which there is explicit appreciation of the importance of the clinician's own beliefs and expectations.

Unfortunately, the view of psychological and psychiatric diagnosis taken here is not shared by everyone. In a slight hyperbole, Szasz (1970) points out that ". . . today, particularly in the affluent West, all of the difficulties and problems of living are considered psychiatric diseases, and everyone (but the diagnosticians) is considered mentally ill" (p. 4). The interesting question for our purposes is: What are the consequences of this? What, if anything, happens when someone is labelled mentally ill or psychotic or neurotic or, more generally, deviant? This is the topic we take up next.

4

Labeling and the Communication of Expectations

In the preceding chapters we have concentrated on the cognitive consequences of attributing a particular characteristic to someone. Further, we have concerned ourselves almost exclusively with the cognitive consequences for the inferrer. Specifically, we have looked at additional characteristics which the inferrer assumes to be true about the target of his or her attribution. In the present chapter we shall shift both of these focal points. First, we are going to look at behavioral consequences of attributing a particular characteristic to someone and, second, we are going to look at the behavioral consequences for the target of the initial attribution. There are several provocative lines of research that are pertinent to these new foci. One of the more interesting ones has been concerned with the study of deviant behavior.

DEVIANCE AND THE LABELING PERSPECTIVE

The labeling perspective on deviance is not particularly concerned with the origins of deviant behavior. That is, it does not concentrate on such questions as why one person and not another robs a bank or becomes a prostitute or starts taking drugs. It is assumed that there can be many sources of deviant acts. Scheff (1966), for example, discusses four such sources. The labeling perspective, however, takes the deviant act—whatever it may be and whatever its source—as a given and focuses on what occurs after the act has been committed. One of the leading spokesman for the labeling perspective defines behavior as deviant "... *to the extent that* it comes to be viewed as involving a *personally discreditable* departure from a group's normative expectations, *and* it *elicits* interpersonal or collective reactions that serve to 'isolate,' 'treat,' 'correct,' or 'punish' individuals engaged in such behavior" (Schur, 1971, p. 24). The key to this perspective on deviance, then, is the reaction of society to the individual who commits some act that violates normative expectations and not simply the action of the individual per se. There are a number of ways to illustrate that the action of the deviating individual is not all there is to deviance.

Hollander (1958), for example, introduced the concept of idiosyncrasy credit to account for the fact that in many groups a double standard seems to operate. That is, newcomers or initiates into the group often are expected to toe the line and conform rigidly to the group's expectations, while oldtimers appear much more lackadaisical in their adherence to group norms. Hollander's argument is that old-timers have built up credit by their proven support of the group in the past and are allowed minor deviations. It is important to note that the notion of idiosyncrasy credit implies that groups have a sliding definition of deviance which is, in part, a function of other characteristics of the deviating individual.

The Theoretical Position

Let us be a little more explicit about the various factors involved in labeling theory. The basic ideas have been around a long time, although they have been expanded and elaborated upon by many people including Lemert (1951), Erikson (1966), Goffman (1961), and others. We will not attempt to cover all contributions to the labeling perspective here, but will concentrate on the works of several of the more important spokesmen.

Becker's (1963, 1973) statements about the labeling approach to deviance emphasize that there is more to deviance than a simple act or acts of alleged wrongdoing. The observation at the heart of Becker's approach is the elementary but profound one that different groups (cultures, societies) judge different things to be deviant. Thus, groups create deviance by making rules which, when broken by an individual, constitute deviance. An entire cast of characters is involved, including the rule breaker, those whose business it is to enforce the rule(s), and those who made the rule(s). Consequently, Becker (1973) now believes that interactionist theory is a more appropriate name than labeling theory. The rule-making group, of course, generally has some reason for making a particular rule and, once made, such rules often take on a moral character—the group's view of the world is threatened by those who break the rule. As Becker points out, ". . . the study of deviance [is] essentially the study of the construction and reaffirmation of moral meanings in everyday social life" (p. 184).

Of particular interest here is Becker's use of the concept of *career* as a descriptive handle for the sequence of events he claims often ensues once an individual is labeled as a deviant. The concept *career* ". . . refers to the sequence of movements from one position to another in an occupational system made by any individual who works in that system" (1973, p. 24). Depending on the circumstances, deviant careers that begin with the experience of being caught breaking some rule and publicly labeled as a deviant may proceed all the way to what Becker believes to be the final step in such a career, the joining of an organized deviant group. Such a career may abort, of course, at any of several points, and it is here that the reaction of the group or society is crucial. If one is caught breaking a rule but is not publicly labeled as deviant, one can slip back into respectable society. On the other hand, if one is held up to public scorn as, say, a thief or a forger or an adulterer, then more than the legal penalty may be extracted by one's (former) friends, business associates, and relatives. One may be pushed by society into an entirely new, and usually degraded, style of life as a result of being publicly labeled.

Becker's use of the concept of career is very similar to Lemert's (1951) concept of secondary, as opposed to primary, deviation. Primary deviation is simply some aspect of a person's behavior that is contrary to generally accepted norms but is not believed to be bad or immoral by the person. Secondary deviation, however, consists of responses the person is pushed or forced into by the reactions of others to his or her primary deviation. A young boy with excessively long hair (primary deviation) may be kidded and ridiculed by his peers until he flails out at them or isolates himself in his room, both of which would be examples of secondary deviation. The result of either or both of these examples of secondary deviation is a compounding of the youngster's problem. Now he begins to accrue a reputation as a troublemaker ("always fighting") or a weirdo ("he just sits in his room"), and pretty soon neighbors are counseling their children to stay away from him.

Thus, the keys to the labeling approach are:

1. The idea that particular types or categories of people are *expected by others* to display certain additional characteristics and/or to be consistently deviant.
2. Once we have discovered that another is a certain type, we react to them in ways that push them into secondary and/or career deviance, thereby confirming our initial expectations.

The labeling approach to deviance has proven itself useful in understanding a number of different areas, from juvenile delinquency to the culture developed by dance musicians (Becker, 1963). The area in which the labeling approach appears to be in greatest vogue, however, is in the phenomena surrounding the so-called mentally ill.

The theorist who has been most explicit in spelling out how the labeling approach applies to the mentally ill is Scheff (1966, 1974). At the core of Scheff's analysis is a distinction between *rule-breaking*, which he uses to refer to violations of social norms or expected modes of behavior, and *deviance*, which he uses to refer to particular acts that have been labeled publicly as violations of social norms. Thus, any given rule-breaking behavior may or may not be considered as deviant, depending on the reaction of others. If they ignore it, it is not deviance. If they point their finger and proclaim it to be so, then it is deviance. Scheff's argument is that all societies have many rules or social norms and an accompanying vocabulary for labeling violations of these norms. One is expected (norms) to eat and drink in moderation. If one violates these norms, he or she becomes a glutton or a drunkard.

However, there are other rules that are so embedded in our every activity they "go without saying." That is, there are some rules that seem so much a part of our conceptions of reality that violations of these rules seem strange or uncanny. Partly because such rules are central to our conceptions of what reality ought to be, our vocabularies for labeling violations of these rules are relatively undeveloped. Scheff refers to the breaking of these rules for which we have no clear-cut labels as *residual rule-breaking* and argues that we tend to lump various sorts of residual rule-breakers into the category mentally ill.

What is an example of the type of residual rule-breaking that might get labeled mentally ill? One that Scheff (1966) and Goffman (1961) focus on is the expectation that an adult in the presence of others should be involved or engaged in doing something—assuming, of course, that he or she is awake. When adults stare vacantly at a wall, appear not to hear those around them, look at others with blank, expressionless faces, or in other ways appear withdrawn and not in contact with what is going on around them, they are likely to be labeled crazy. Scheff points out that such residual rule violations do not in themselves bring forth censure. They are likely to create problems, however, when performed in inappropriate contexts or by people who are socially unqualified. The college professor who wears bedroom slippers to class and lets his sentences trail off unfinished as though he were in deep thought may get a reputation as absent-minded. The junior executive at IBM who forgets to tuck in his shirt tail and stares out the window for most of the morning may not be dealt with so magnanimously.

In a series of nine propositions, Scheff (1966) presents the outline of a model that attempts to make explicit some of the processes by which residual rule-breaking may be stabilized and incorporated into the rule-breakers' self-definition as "mental illness." It is important to note that residual rule-breaking may arise from several different sources, including external stress, organic sources, and even free choice of the rule-breaker. However it arises, most residual rule-breaking is transitory, and, even if others notice it, they write it off as due to the rule-breaker's having a bad day or being tired or being under a lot of pressure lately. Scheff does spell out a number of variables that influence the probability that residual rule-breaking will be denied or ignored, including the degree and visibility of rule-breaking, the power of the rule-breaker, and the community tolerance level. If the residual rule-breaking is not denied, however, a public labeling of the residual rule-breaking as mental illness may occur, and, unlike alleged criminals, the "mentally ill" appear to be presumed guilty until proven innocent. (We shall try to document this point below.)

Once the public labeling of the residual rule-breaker as mentally ill has occurred, Scheff argues that a number of forces come into play. First, both the residual rule-breaker and those around him have preexisting stereotypes about the mentally ill that are continually reaffirmed by the news media, popular fiction, and the people around them (cf., Nunnally, 1961). These stereotypes feed into the expectations that others now have for the rule-breaker's behavior and influence both the response cues that they give to the rule-breaker and the vocabulary with which they refer to the rule-breaker. Secondly, the residual rule-breaker, who is at the hub of interpersonal confusion surrounding such crises, is likely to be extremely stressed and suggestible. As a result, he or she may incorporate into their self-conception the role expectations that are being thrust upon them from all sides. Their self-control may be impaired and episodes of compulsive behavior ensue. Others, of course, may fall into a pattern of rewarding the residual rule-breaker for acting like he or she is really mentally ill.

A flow chart depicting the sequence of stages that Scheff believes results in the stabilization of such residual rule-breaking into a career of mental illness is depicted in Figure 4.1. It is important to note the feedback loops in the figure, or, as Scheff refers to them, the "deviation amplifying" loops. For example, as the self-control of the residual rule-breaker is weakened in the stressful and upsetting situation surrounding his or her being labeled as mentally ill, episodes of compulsive behavior may ensue. The latter, of course, may create new crises and further convince others that the rule-breaker is, indeed, mentally ill.

Sarbin offers an interesting observation, which fits in rather nicely with Scheff's notions about the reactions of others helping to stabilize mental illness. After discussing the medical metaphor from which the concept of "mental illness" developed, Sarbin (1967) notes that ". . . because of the inherent vagueness in the concept of mind, its assumed independence from the body, and its purported timelessness (derived from the immortal soul), there is a readiness to regard this special kind of sickness as permanent" (p. 451). It does appear to be the case that people react to those labeled mentally ill as if they are permanently disabled. Along this line, Szasz (1970) argues that in criminal cases, when a successful insanity plea results in commitment to a mental institution, the defendant is better off not to make that plea. This is because what constitutes mental illness is so vague and the belief that whatever it is it's permanent is so widely held, the person involuntarily committed to a mental institution is likely to spend a much longer time behind bars than if he or she had gone to prison. Chu and Trotter (1974) offer some data on this point that indicate that Sarbin and Szasz may be on to something. In 1965, 94 percent of all prisoners in federal prisons of the United States had been incarcerated for five years or less. However, over half (53 percent of the 2,349 patients at the federally created State Mental Hospital in Washington, D.C. had been in-patients for 10 years or more, and 37 percent had been in-patients for 20 years or more.

It should be obvious that these data are far from conclusive. There are several sources of ambiguity, including such questions as whether this particular hospital is representative of all state hospitals and whether the population served by this hospital is representative of the population served by all federal prisons. Further,

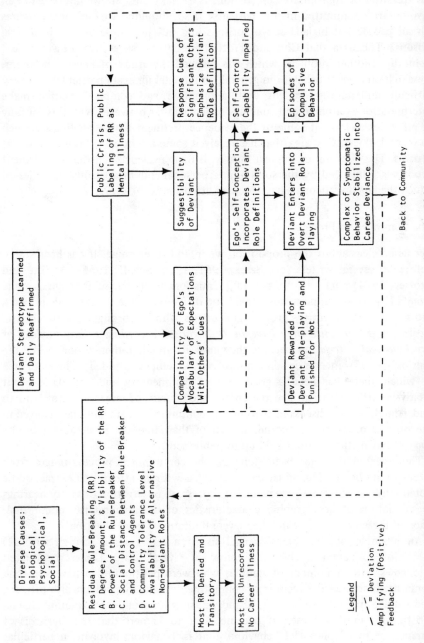

FIG. 4.1 Stabilization of deviance in a social system. From Scheff, 1966, p. 100. Copyright, 1966, by Thomas Scheff. Reprinted by Permission.

93

the question of appropriate comparisons is a sticky one—are we interested in all involuntarily committed mental patients? If so, shouldn't we look at the figures for all people put in jails and/or prisons and not just those housed in federal prisons? The data that Chu and Trotter present are suggestive, however, and point up another problem which has plagued the study of deviant behavior. Research on deviant behavior in general, and mental illness in particular, is a very difficult undertaking, fraught with ambiguities and complexities that make interpretations tentative and conclusions few and far between. With this warning in mind, let us look at some of the evidence pertinent to the labeling approach to mental illness. One area that has received some attention is the commitment process. The question of interest here is: Is there evidence that the commitment process is influenced by the sorts of interpersonal and intrapersonal variables on which the labeling theorists have focused attention?

The Commitment Process

Let us be clear about the proposition we intend to examine. It has been stated before by several writers (cf., Szasz, 1961, 1970; Scheff, 1966). As Chu and Trotter (1974) phrase it, "In general, admissions to state mental hospitals come from a large 'residual population' made up of the poor, the aged, the abandoned, the members of minority groups, and others who are brought for psychiatric treatment *not because they have been diagnosed according to any medical or psychological criteria* but because they have disturbed, bothered, or shocked the sensibilities of someone or some group" (p. 43, emphasis added). This is an area in which there has been a great deal of commentary and speculation, but relatively little research. The reason for the paucity of research is not hard to understand. We are discussing involuntary commitments, and anyone involved in the process of depriving another person of their freedom might justifiably be wary of having their actions held up to public scrutiny.

The research that has been done on the commitment process ranges from intensive studies of individual cases, coupled with an attempt to extract some potentially generalizable aspects of the process, to observation of sanity hearings to tabulation of demographic characteristics of the involuntarily committed. Each of these types of research has severe limitations, as we shall see.

An example of the intensive analysis of a few cases is Lemert's (1962) discussion of paranoia. Over the course of several years, Lemert conducted interviews with a number of families who were petitioning to have someone committed, studied the records of commitments made by public health officers, and studied in depth eight cases of individuals with prominent paranoid characteristics. From these cases, it became clear to Lemert that the diagnosis of paranoia is based on social behaviors, that is, behaviors involving a particular type of relationship to another person or persons, such as, hostility, aggressiveness, suspicion, envy, stubbornness, or jealousy. At first, others regard the aggressiveness and hostility as simply a variation of normal behavior, but, if it persists, the person displaying such behavior soon comes to be regarded as someone with whom others do not wish to be involved, and a process of exclusion begins. This exclusion and isolation, of course, gives the individual something to be suspicious and aggressive about, and the process spirals down-ward into ever greater detachment of the individual from the surrounding social network. Lemert (1962) notes that many paranoid persons realize that they are being pushed out but, "... as channels of communication are closed to the paranoid person, he has no means of getting feedback on consequences of his behavior, which is essential for correcting his interpretations of the social relationships and organization which he must rely on to define his status and give him identity" (p. 14). The strained social relationships and lack of com-munication with others resulted, in Lemert's cases, in exclusion, definition as a crank, and, in some instances, involuntary commitment as insane.

The importance of a social network of friends and family as a potential buffer against involuntary commitment is further implicated in some work by Rushing (1971). Rushing was interested in what he refers to as the *resource–deprivation hypothesis* suggested by Scheff (1966), that is, the idea that "... individuals with limited social and economic resources have limited power and are more apt to be involuntarily confined than individuals whose resources and power are less limited" (p. 513). To check on this he examined the ratio of involuntary to voluntary commitments as a function of socioeconomic, occupational, and marital status of patients entering three state mental hospitals in Washington between 1956 and 1965. Involuntary commitment was more likely the lower the socioeconomic status of the patient, for manual than for nonmanual workers, and for single than for married individuals. Further, analysis of the conjunctive effects of these variables indicate that, "... regardless of low resources in one status variable, high resources in another may effectively prevent institutionaliza-tion proceedings" (p. 523). Rushing's result is suggestive, but somewhat ambiguous. The problem, of course, is lack of knowledge about base rates and severity of social/emotional disturbances in the various categories of the popula-tion. The use of the ratio of involuntary to voluntary commitments was an attempt to hold these constant, but there is no reason to believe that voluntary commitments accurately reflect base rates of social/emotional disturbances across social classes.

Some research by Linsky (1970) bears on this latter point. Linsky was interested in the influence of the homogeneity of 27 community areas in Washington state on the rates of voluntary and involuntary hospitalization of mental patients. Utilizing political, economic, and racial indices of community homogeneity, he found that community homogeneity was essentially unrelated to level of disturbance, as measured by such markers as suicides, deaths from duodenal ulcers, and alcoholism. However, the more homogeneous the com-munity, the greater the number of voluntary admissions. Linsky argues that, in homogeneous communities, there is greater consensus about what constitutes mental illness, and this results in greater pressure on individuals to voluntarily[1] accept hospitalization when they behave in particular ways.

Since the individual in question is part of the community and privy to the consensus about what, for them, constitutes mental illness, he or she may label themselves even before others do. Krauss (1968) has argued that "schizophrenia" is frequently the end result of a self-fulfilling prophecy in which two primary components are central: 1) the experience of intense subjective discomfort and; 2) the necessity of understanding the nature and meaning of the discomfort. The danger is that, if individuals accept a self-definition of "madness" as a way of understanding or, at least, labeling what is going on in their emotional crises, they become ". . . entrapped by a network of self and societal expectations and interactions into maladaptive behavior patterns which futher isolate them from productive roles in the society and which consign them to even lower levels of self-adjustment" (p. 243).

Implicit in Scheff's model (Figure 4.1) and in the above argument by Krauss is a theory of self-labelling that has received a fair amount of attention. In a series of important studies, Schachter and his colleagues (cf., 1971) have explored the implications of the general proposition that arousal (cf., intense subjective discomfort) in the absence of an understanding of the source of that arousal is likely to be labeled in terms of the situation in which the person finds himself/herself. As Schachter (1971) puts it, ". . . given a state of physiological arousal for which an individual has no immediate explanation, he will 'label' this state and describe his feelings in terms of the cognitions available to him. To the extent that cognitive factors are potent determiners of emotional states, one might anticipate that precisely the same state of physiological arousal could be labeled 'joy,' or 'fury,' or any of a great number of emotional labels, depending on the cognitive aspects of the situation" (p. 4). The evidence generally appears to support this proposition.

The cognitive aspects of the situation most salient for many residual rule-breakers are the reactions of others and, as we mentioned earlier, the others generally have poorly developed vocabularies for categorizing residual rule-breaking. The result is that the others tend to think of and talk about the residual rule-breaker as if he or she were "crazy." Thus, the commitment process which, theoretically, is supposed to be a series of steps by which others can determine if the individual meets the legal criteria of insanity, is likely to be doubly detrimental for the residual rule-breaker. The others will confirm their presumption of craziness, and the individual's self definition is likely to mirror the others' reactions.

There have been several studies of the commitment process that used court records and examined the outcome of the proceedings as a function of such

[1] Note that "voluntary" commitments are considered to result from group pressure.

variables as age, race, and sex of the individual and composition of the examining panel. Haney and Michielutte (1968), for example, in a study of competency hearings in Florida in 1965, found that the older an individual for whom such a hearing was held, the greater the chances that the individual would be judged incompetent. Further, the individual was significantly more likely to be judged incompetent when the examining committee included a psychiatrist than when it did not. Unfortunately, we have no way of knowing whether older individuals were really any more or less competent or whether psychiatrists were called in on only the more difficult cases. Again, the data are suggestive, but ambiguous.

Some research by Wenger and Fletcher (1969) overcomes at least one of the problems in the above study. Wenger and Fletcher observed and took notes on admissions hearings for 81 persons against whom petitions had been filed for incarceration in a state mental hospital. The purpose of each of these hearings was to determine if the individual was "sane." The median time for the hearings was 5.03 minutes! Of those individuals who did not retain a legal counsel to represent them at the hearing, over 92 percent were admitted, whereas, of those who did retain a lawyer, only 27 percent were admitted. It is, of course, possible that the "saner" individuals were more likely to hire a lawyer, as Gove (1970) has noted, and that this accounts for the result. Wenger and Fletcher attempted to check on this by having observers[2] categorize each prepatient as to whether or not the legal criteria of insanity were met in his/her case. "The patients classified as borderline or as criteria-not-met, and who had legal counsel, were more likely to be released than similar patients not represented by a lawyer" (p. 71).

Given the extraordinarily brief hearings and the dramatic effect of having a lawyer, it is beginning to appear as if there is a presumption of insanity when an individual gets caught up in the commitment process. The individual's sanity or insanity is, of course, what the commitment proceedings are supposed to ascertain. Some further evidence comes from a study of a psychiatric screening agency by Wilde (1968). The particular agency that Wilde studied received petitions for commitment from several sources, but apparently acted as the active decision-maker only when a petition was received from a member of the general public. Around 6,000 such petitions were received annually, and about 2,000 of these were approved, that is, the individual against whom the petition was filed was committed. Three points are of interest here. First, the agency never saw or interviewed the person against whom the petition was filed—the alleged deviant. Secondly, some agency interviewers had a significantly higher rate of petition approval than others. Thus, if we assume there were no selection factors operating in the assignment of interviewers, then the chances of having the petition approved are a function of the interviewer assigned and this, of

---

[2] It is still possible that the observers were biased since they could obviously see that the prepatient did or did not have a lawyer.

course, has nothing to do with the alleged deviant's degree of sanity or insanity. Finally, when the petitioner just showed up at the center, the petition was less likely to be approved than if the petitioner called and made an appointment ahead of time. The meaning of this is unclear, however, since it may simply indicate that those who call and made appointments have considered the situation more carefully and have more deliberately marshalled the evidence to support their petition. Those who just show up may do so on the spur of the moment or in a fit of anger at the person they would have committed. One further problem is that Wilde's study was of only one agency—perhaps his findings bear little relation to what generally happens.

Unfortunately, the evidence continues to grow indicating that similar phenomena are widespread. Scheff (1966) points out that there appear to be two principal legal grounds for involuntary commitment of individuals as "insane": 1) that the individual is dangerous to others; and 2) that the individual is severely "mentally impaired." Scheff attempted to assess psychiatrists' evaluations of patients on these two criteria by asking 25 psychiatrists who made admissions examinations in three mental hospitals to fill out a questionnaire about the first 10 patients they examined in June 1962. Of these patients, there were 164 who were involuntarily committed. Of the 164, 102, or 62 percent, were rated as neither dangerous nor severely impaired. Gove (1970) argues that Scheff's conclusion here is based solely on an arbitrary decision about where to place the cutting point on the rating scales and that he might have shown that most of the patients were insane had he placed the cutting point elsewhere. Scheff (1974) has replied to this criticism by pointing out that Gove disregarded the problem posed by the study, that is, ". . . whether or not patients were being committed illegally" (p. 447).

In another study, Scheff (1966) reports data from questionnaires filled out by the staff of the "public mental hospitals in a Midwestern state" (p. 130) about a systematic sample of patients ($N = 555$). The hospital official legally responsible for the patient interviewed the patient and filled out a questionnaire about the patient. Examination of the ratings of these officials (often, but not always, psychiatrists), in terms of the degree of mental impairment of the patient and the patient's dangerousness to others, led Scheff to conclude that 43 percent of the patient population's presence in the hospital cannot readily be explained in terms of their psychiatric condition.

Scheff (1966) points out that an ". . . important norm for handling uncertainty in medical diagnosis [is] that judging a sick person well is more to be avoided than judging a well person sick" (p. 105). In physical medicine, this norm is usually a safe one since tentative diagnoses of physiological problems cause little if any difficulty for the individual beyond the time and expense of having additional tests made. When carried over into psychiatry, however, this norm creates a presumption of illness which is very difficult for the individual who is the object of psychiatric scrutiny to combat. Part of the problem, of course, is inherent in the vagueness of what really constitutes mental illness. As we have seen, the research that has looked into the commitment process appears to indicate that this presumption of illness is real and has real consequences. Sanity hearings are often perfunctory, and the outcomes appear to have little to do with the individual's mental state.

Given the ambiguities of several of the studies cited above and the need for more precise and better controlled research, it still appears that, taken together, the researches indicate that a sizeable number of mental patients are shuttled through the commitment process and incarcerated largely because of the expectations of others—the presumption of illness focussed on anyone appearing before sanity hearings. The question then becomes, what happens once these people have been incarcerated. Do the expectations of others continue to play such a pernicious role in their lives or do they find themselves in situations where others—the doctors, nurses, and attendants who staff mental hospitals— take the time to understand and relate to them and, perhaps, discover that they are not so crazy after all?

Life on the Wards

The manner in which a patient arrives on the ward can, of course, convey information about the patient. Someone who voluntarily signs into a mental hospital might reasonably be taken by the staff to be someone with the right attitude, that is, someone who has already acknowledged that they have a problem and who apparently believes that the type of treatment they will receive in such an institution will be of benefit to them. Hence, we might anticipate that the staff would have relatively favorable expectations about such patients, expectations that they would be easier to work with, that they would be more accepting of the psychiatric line, and that they would be more conforming to staff wishes and directives. On the other hand, involuntary entry may be taken by the staff to mean something quite different. A patient who has been forcibly incarcerated in a mental hospital may not even believe that he or she has a problem much less that psychiatric treatment is called for. Hence, we might anticipate that the staff would have relatively unfavorable expectations about such patients, expectations that they will be difficult to work with, that they will not be accepting of the psychiatric line, and that they will be little concerned about pleasing the staff and behaving in accordance with staff directives.

Some research by Denzin and Spitzer (1966) indicates that these two modes of entry into the mental hospital do indeed trigger different expectations on the part of the staff and that these expectations are in operation before the staff ever see the individual patient. As a preliminary step in their study, Denzin and Spitzer asked 50 psychiatric nurses and aides to list the characteristics of a "good" or "ideal" psychiatric patient. From these open-ended descriptions, they selected 18 adjectives and used the adjectives to construct a semantic differential measure of self-presentation on which patients could be rated. They then prepared four brief descriptions of a 35-year-old male first-admission mental patient and randomly assigned these descriptions to 66 psychiatric nursing staff members. The nursing staff were to read the description they had been assigned and rate the patient on the self-presentation scales. The four descriptions differed only in the patient's mode of entry into the hospital: (1) voluntary entry—self/family referral; (2) involuntary entry—family referral; (3) voluntary entry—community agency/court referral; and (4) involuntary entry—community agency, court referral. As anticipated, voluntary entry led to significantly more favorable ratings on expected self-presentation of the patient.

In a subsequent study, Denzin (1968) made an attempt to look at some of the consequences of such favorable initial expectations on the part of the staff. Specifically, he hypothesized that patients who initially appear to be accepting of the psychiatric line would be given more positive prognoses, receive more personal therapy each week, and be released from the hospital more quickly than patients who initially appear to hold unfavorable attitudes toward the psychiatric line. Denzin asked 10 psychiatrists in a state hospital to fill out a brief questionnaire about each new patient admitted during a specified time interval. A total of 73 patients were rated, once at the time of hospitalization and again several weeks later. The psychiatrists were asked for a prognosis (good—fair—poor) on the initial ratings and for information on the number of hours of therapy with the patient on the second ratings. In addition, the questionnaires contained a number of items about the psychiatrist's perceptions of the patient's attitudes (for example, their attitudes toward psychiatric hospitals and mental illness). As anticipated, the more favorable the patient appeared to be toward psychiatry and toward his role as a mental patient, the more favorable the initial prognosis, the more personal therapy the patient received, and the more quickly the patient was released from the hospital. Denzin (1968) believes that a somewhat circular process is involved here:

> The therapist selectively perceives information about the patient which he uses to determine how the patient is accepting the "psychiatric line." He then acts toward the patient on the basis of this information and in his actions communicates his impressions of the patient. . . . Possessing something less than complete knowledge about treatment and his role as patient, the inmate will frequently respond to the therapist in terms of these interpretations. This reciprocal response of the patient tends to confirm the therapist's initial inference (pp. 355–356).

Unfortunately, the circular contingencies of life on the wards of a mental hospital involve a great deal more than the initial expectations of the staff about how particular patients are going to fare. A detailed analysis of the ways in which almost every aspect of the structure and functioning of a mental hospital operate so as to deny even the possibility that any of the inmates are "sane" or "normal" is provided by Goffman (1961). Goffman spent a year doing field work as a member of the staff (assistant athletic director) of a large mental hospital. He specifically chose not to become an inmate for his participant observation so that his freedom to move about the entire hospital campus (300 acres) would not be impeded.

Goffman focuses most of his attention on the mental patient's self and the manner in which both the institution and staff strip away all supports for the patient's self. He points out that mental hospitals ". . . disrupt or defile precisely those activities that in civil society have the role of attesting to the actor and those in his presence that he has some command over his world—that he is a person with 'adult' self-determination, autonomy, and freedom of action" (p. 43). This disruption and defiling are well begun even before the patient is fully admitted. The admissions process is often what Goffman refers to as a *betrayal funnel*, where the soon-to-be patient finds himself odd man out in a triad consisting of a psychiatrist, the patient's next of kin, and the patient. The next of kin, who may have suggested hospitalization, is not likely to be able to provide a realistic picture of what life in the hospital will be like and the extent to which the patient's personal freedom will be curtailed. Hence, one side effect of the admissions process is that the patient is likely to become embittered about and distrustful of his closest relation. At each stage of the admissions process, there is indeed a further loss of adult free status: the patient's personal possessions are taken away; institutional clothes are issued; and a barrier is placed between the individual and the free world.

Once on the ward, a forced deference to all staff is usually extracted from the patient, a deference that may be incompatible with the individual's self-conception. Further, the staff (and other inmates) automatically assume the right to use an intimate form of address, and all information about the patient is readily available in a file to which even the lowliest staff have access. Goffman points out that in many mental hospitals there is a practice of all-level staff conferences, in which patients are discussed and the line to be taken with particular patients is decided. "Since the differential image of himself that a person usually meets from those of various levels around him comes here to be unified behind the scenes into a common approach, the patient may find himself faced with a kind of collusion against him" (p. 160). Other aspects of life on the wards deny the individuality of the patient; all activities are regimented and usually done in the company of a number of others, thus, the patient is not allowed control over his or her own time and energy. Those who had been work-oriented on the outside become demoralized because there is nothing to do but sit or only petty activities that can be engaged in, such as watching TV, and these only at specified times.

The result of all this, according to Goffman, is that the patient attempts to find ways of expressing distance between his or her self and the surroundings, ways of symbolically saying, "I'm not like this," and "I don't belong here."

From the patient's point of view, to decline to exchange a word with the staff or with his fellow patients may be ample evidence of rejecting the institution's view of what and who he is; yet higher management may construe this alienative expression as just the sort of symptomatology the institution was established to deal with and as the best kind of evidence that the patient properly belongs where he now finds himself. In short, mental hospitalization outmaneuvers the patient, tending to rob him of the common expressions through which people hold off the embrace of organizations—insolence, silence, *sotto voce* remarks, un-cooperativeness, malicious destruction of interior decorations, and so forth; these signs of disaffiliation are now read as signs of their maker's proper affiliation. . . . Furthermore, there is a vicious circle process at work. Persons who are lodged on "bad" wards find that very little equipment of any kind is given them—clothes may be taken from them each night, recreational materials may be withheld, and only heavy wooden chairs and benches provided for furniture. Acts of hostility against the institution have to rely on limited, ill-designed devices. . . . And the more inadequate this equipment is to convey rejection of the hospital, the more the act appears as a psychotic symptom, and the more likely it is that management feels justified in assigning the patient to a bad ward (pp. 306–307).

Goffman's description of life in a mental hospital is a damning one. There are, however, problems involved in accepting his view. First, Goffman was himself the only observer and, although he frequently buttresses his points with quotations from other works, these quotations are frequently from fiction or the retrospective accounts of ex-mental patients. The potential biases and interpretive problems introduced by these facts are rather obvious. Secondly, Goffman freely admits (1961) that he ". . . came to the hospital with no great respect for the discipline of psychiatry nor for agencies content with its current practice" (p. x). Even so, his description is very compelling. The process of self-mortification that he argues is woven into the very fabric of the mental hospital would indeed seem to make the sane appear insane. It should be the case, then, if the circular contingencies we have been discussing are, in fact, operating, that normal or sane people who take up residence in a psychiatric ward and act "normally" would go undetected. On the other hand, "If the sanity of such pseudopatients were always detected, there would be *prima facie* evidence that a sane individual can be distinguished from the insane context in which he is found. Normality (and presumably abnormality) is distinct enough that it can be recognized wherever it occurs, for it is carried within the person" (Rosenhan, 1973, p. 251).

To check on which of these alternatives occurred, Rosenhan and seven co-workers became participant observers by gaining admission to the psychiatric wards of 12 different hospitals. Each pseudopatient gained admission by claiming to hear voices saying such things as "empty," "hollow"—a symptom chosen because of its similarity to the self-questioning that occurs when people wonder about the meaningfulness of their lives. The only other alteration for the participant observers was that they employed pseudonyms and, in several cases, gave false occupations to protect their true identity.

As soon as they had been admitted, all pseudopatients began to behave normally; they stopped simulating any symptoms. "That their behavior was in no way disruptive is confirmed by nursing reports. . . . These reports uniformly indicate that the patients were 'friendly,' 'cooperative,' and 'exhibited no abnormal indications' " (p. 252). Each pseudopatient had been told upon entry that he would be discharged when he convinced the staff that he was sane. They stayed an average of 19 days—at least one stayed as long as 52 days—but not one of the pseudopatients was ever detected. Not one was ever deemed sane by the staff.

During the course of their stays, the pseudopatients took notes and systematically recorded what went on in the wards: the number and types of drugs given (these were people with no bodily or "mental" problems, yet they were administered over 2,000 pills!); the amounts of time that staff spent on the ward; and the behaviors of their fellow patients. One of the things that became clear from the notes is that:

> Once a person is designated abnormal, all of his other behaviors and characteristics are colored by that label. . . . One psychiatrist pointed to a group of patients who were sitting outside the cafeteria entrance half an hour before lunchtime. To a group of young residents he indicated that such behavior was characteristic of the oral-acquisitive nature of the syndrome" (p. 253).

It apparently never occurred to the psychiatrist that life in a mental ward is incredibly dull and that there is not much to look forward to other than mealtime.

Aside from the reinterpretation of normal behaviors so that they would fit into what the staff "knew" about the pseudopatients, the pseudopatients quickly began to experience depersonalization and self-mortification. Several of the intake physical exams were given in semi-public rooms; staff would often discuss a patient within his hearing range; staff would avoid eye contact with patients and fail to acknowledge their questions; morning attendants often woke patients with, "Come on, you m___-f___s, out of bed!" (p. 256). All of these behaviors by the staff have the effect of defining the situation in a particular way, a way that includes the pseudopatients only as mental cases—not as persons. Had the pseudopatients expressed their indignation at such treatment and demanded the normal respect due any other person, this in itself would be interpreted as further evidence of their "craziness." As Rosenhan (1973) notes, "The Hospital itself imposes a special environment in which the meanings of behavior can be easily misunderstood" (p. 257).

Given that the daily round of life in a mental hospital has such an insidious self-demeaning character and that the grounds on which many of the patients are admitted are somewhat shaky to begin with, one begins to wonder exactly what it is that these people suffer from. The point here, of course, is that these people are in part suffering from the expectations of others. In order for these expectations to influence behavior, they must be communicated, and we have already mentioned a number of the subtle and not-so-subtle ways in which such communication takes place. But more is involved than a simple transmission of knowledge about what expectations exist for the other's behavior. There is a communication of expectations via a process of projecting specific situational definitions coupled with interpersonal influences. The goal, of course, is to make the other behave as expected. Let us examine the processes involved in a little more detail.

COMMUNICATION OF EXPECTATIONS

There are several lines of evidence that bear on the questions of how expectations are communicated and how situations are defined so as to make those expectancies come true. Since the previous sections have, of necessity, dealt with some rather tentative and soft data, it might be best to begin with a line of research that has attempted a fine-grained analysis and documentation of the process of expectancy communication.

Expectations and Experimenter–Subject Interaction

For several years there has been a rising tide of experimental and quasi-experimental studies (Campbell and Stanley, 1966) on the importance of expectations in interpersonal behavior. Much of this research has been carried out or stimulated by Robert Rosenthal (1966). Although people had long been aware of the influence of expectations in perception, one of the more important findings from Rosenthal's research was that even in apparently well-controlled laboratory settings, experimenters who expected their subjects to respond in certain ways were more likely to obtain those responses than were experimenters who had no such prior expectations.

For example, in a number of studies, Rosenthal and his colleagues (1966) asked experimenters to administer a person–perception photo-rating task to subjects. Experimenters were to show a series of photos to each subject and ask the subject to rate each photo as to "whether the person pictured has been experiencing success or failure" (p. 144). The ratings were to be made on a scale running from −10 (extreme failure) to +10 (extreme success). The photos had previously been selected so as to actually be neutral on this scale. Some experimenters were led to believe that the subject's ratings would average about +5, and other experimenters were led to believe they would average about −5. It was found, repeatedly, that experimenters with the former expectation obtained significantly more positive photo ratings from their subjects than experimenters with the latter expectation. As Rosenthal (1966) points out, "Since the experimenters had all read from the identical instructions, some more subtle aspects of their behavior toward their subjects must have served to communicate their expectations to their subjects" (p. 149).

The search for what these more subtle aspects might be began almost immediately and still continues. One hypothesis that suggested itself to Rosenthal was that the experimenters were shaping the subjects' response by a process of operant conditioning (Skinner, 1938). That is, experimenters with the expectation that subjects' responses would average about +5 were reinforcing only positive ratings with signs of approval, whereas experimenters who expected ratings to average −5 were reinforcing only negative ratings from their subjects. However, analysis of studies that had demonstrated the experimenter expectancy effects (Rosenthal, 1966, pp. 290–291) revealed that the effects occur on the first photo rated by subjects making it unlikely that experimenters were shaping the subjects' responses. Other studies reported by Rosenthal (pp. 287–289) indicate that expectancy effects occur on the photo-rating task even when the subjects cannot see the experimenter, that is, when the experimenters simply read the instructions while seated behind a screen out of the subjects' line of sight.

If expectancy effects occur on the first photo rated and even when the experimenter cannot be seen, there must be something crucial about the manner in which the experimenter instructs the subject. In a detailed analysis of filmed interactions, in which experimenters were administering Rosenthal's person–perception task to individual subjects, Friedman (1967) found that each of the following correlated positively with the subjects' tendency to perceive success in the neutral photos: 1) the number of glances exchanged between the experimenter and the subject in the interaction period; 2) the number of times the experimenter glanced at the subject in the instruction period; 3) the longer the duration of the instruction period; 4) the longer the duration of the prerating period; 5) the longer the duration of the rating period; and 6) the longer the duration of the total experiment. Thus, it appears that the tendency for the subject to perceive success in the photos is related to exchanging glances with the experimenter and to time.

Friedman offers a rather convincing argument about what he thinks the nature of these relations to be. Citing Goffman and Simmel on the importance of mutual glances in social interaction, he suggests that, in exchanging mutual glances with the experimenter, the subject comes to feel more accepted as a person. The experimenter is treating him with respect and interest. Similarly with time: the longer the experimenter takes to deliver the instructions, the more likely the subject is to feel that the experimenter is interested in him and in making sure that he understands what is required. The more likely, in other words, the subject is to feel that his interaction with the experimenter has been a successful interpersonal encounter. Thus, Friedman's interpretation led to a projection hypothesis: "The subject sees in the photos what his interaction with the experimenter leads him to feel himself" (p. 56).

Jones and Cooper (1971) offer some evidence pertinent to Friedman's interpretation of the processes involved in communication of expectancies on Rosenthal's photo-rating task. In the first of two experiments, Jones and Cooper gave subjects false feedback immediately prior to the photo-rating task, indicating that they had either done exceptionally well, about average, or rather poorly on a high-level intelligence test they had just completed. The prediction, of course, was that those subjects who were told they had done very well on the intelligence test would be most likely to perceive success in the photos, while those who thought they had done very poorly would be least likely to perceive success in the photos. As anticipated, subjects who had experienced success prior to viewing the photos reliably rated the faces pictured as more successful than subjects who had experienced failure prior to viewing the photos. In the second experiment, an attempt was made to directly manipulate the subjects' mood by having some experimenters look at some subjects many times (at least 30) while reading the instructions, and other experimenters look at their subjects as little as possible. Subjects in the former condition again perceived the faces as significantly more successful.

It appears that projection[3] does play a role in the communication of expectancies on the person–perception task. This does not imply that projection is the only mediating process or that visual cues are exclusively involved—we have already mentioned that this is not so. Further, Duncan and Rosenthal (1968) have presented evidence that unintentional voice inflections of the experimenter can play an important role in producing biased ratings of the photographs. Even so, the above studies add to a large body of data documenting the affective significance of the mutual glance. For example, Exline and Winters (1965) found that receipt of a negative evaluation from another was followed by a sharp decrease in mutual glances exchanged with the other. Receipt of a positive evaluation led to a slight increase in mutual glances. It has also been shown that the relation between eye-contact and positive affect for another may be direct or inverse, depending on the nature of the verbal exchange involved (Ellsworth & Carlsmith, 1968). Such experimental data give added weight to the observations by Goffman and Rosenhan about avoidance of eye contact between staff and mental patients. Such avoidance in itself conveys an affective message.

One might argue, however, that Rosenthal's photo-rating task is relatively circumscribed and that results obtained with such a task are not really generalizable to the "real world." It may be true, on the other hand, that there are many interpersonal expectations that begin their realization by simply making the object of the expectations feel disliked and unworthy or liked and respected. But is there evidence that aspects of interaction other than eye contact play a role in the communication of expectancies? A line of research stemming from the experimenter expectancy studies bears directly on this question.

Expectations and Teacher–Pupil Interaction

In a study that has aroused considerable controversy and criticism, Rosenthal and Jacobson (1968) attempted to test the proposition that children in a classroom would show greater intellectual growth if their teacher expected such

---

[3]Actually, Holmes (1968) defines the type of projection discussed by Friedman as *attributive projection*. Attributive projection is said to occur when the person sees others as having the same trait he is aware of in himself.

growth than if the teacher had no such expectation. In the spring of 1964, all of the children at Oak School who would return in the fall (kindergarten to fifth grade) were given a disguised intelligence test. The procedure was described as ". . . further validating a test which predicts the likelihood that a child will show an inflection point or 'spurt' within the near future" (p. 66) in intellectual ability. At the end of the summer, the school teachers were informed that certain pupils had indeed been identified as "spurters" and that they could expect these pupils to do quite well. The pupils who were so identified to the teachers had in fact been randomly selected from among their classmates. Several months later, the students were again given the IQ test and intellectual growth was defined as the difference between IQ's at the time of the pretest (the preceding spring) and the post test. The main result was that among first and second graders, those who had been identified to their teachers as "spurters" did indeed show significantly larger gains in IQ than their classmates who had not been so designated.

The Rosenthal and Jacobson study met with severe criticism from a number of authors (cf., Snow, 1969; Thorndike, 1968). Much of the criticism was deserved. For example, the IQ test employed was one which had not been adequately standardized for use with young children and these were the only children who showed significant gains in IQ. The study has, however, been replicated in various settings many times in recent years. Rosenthal (1973) points out that, "As the evidence continues to accumulate showing that one person's expectation of another person's behavior can come to serve as a self-fulfilling prophecy, it becomes less and less useful to conduct studies that do nothing but increase still further the very high probability that such effects do occur" (p. 24). Even some of Rosenthal's erstwhile critics now agree that ". . . the question for future research is not whether there are expectancy effects, but how they operate . . ." (Baker and Crist, 1971, p. 64).

Unfortunately, this latter question is one to which Rosenthal and Jacobson paid little attention. They do speculate about it, however. Toward the end of their book they propose an "interaction-quality hypothesis" to account for the processes involved, that is, the idea that when a particular child is expected to show IQ gain, the teacher may treat the child in a more pleasant, friendly, encouraging, and supportive manner. Such treatment may make school more pleasant for the child as a result of which he or she shows more enthusiasm for the work, takes a greater interest, attends more closely to what the teacher says, and, sure enough, learns more.

Rubovits and Maehr (1971) designed a study specifically intended to gain some evidence on the interaction-quality hypothesis. Twenty-six female undergraduates were each assigned to teach a lesson plan on "television" to randomly selected groups of four sixth and seventh graders. Before the actual teaching session with her group of four, each teacher was given a seating chart with the names of the students, their IQ's, and a note indicating whether they were from the school's gifted or regular track. In each group of four, two were identified as gifted and two as nongifted. An observer sat behind the students during the teaching sessions and coded the teachers' behavior in terms of the amounts of attention, elaboration, encouragement, ignoring, praise, and criticism directed toward the individual students. Although there was no difference in the amount of attention paid to the gifted versus nongifted students, significantly more statements were requested of gifted students and the statements of the gifted students were praised significantly more often than were those of the nongifted. Rubovits and Maehr believe that the greater participation demanded of the gifted students gives them the opportunity to clarify their thoughts more through dialogue with the teacher, and, by their having to articulate their ideas more precisely, they come to understand those ideas better. It would have been nice if Rubovits and Maehr had included some sort of test to see how much the students did learn as a check on their interpretation.

A study by Chaikin, Sigler, and Derlega (1974) produced results very similar to those of Rubovits and Maehr. Chaikin et al. assigned undergraduates the task of teaching a brief lesson on home and family safety to a 12-year-old. Some of the teachers were led to believe that the pupil was very bright; others were given no information about the pupil; and still others were led to believe that the pupil was somewhat slow. During the actual teaching session the teachers' face and body movements were recorded simultaneously on a split-screen video tape. The video tapes were then rated on a number of nonverbal indices. Teachers who had been led to believe that their pupil was very bright were found to lean forward more during the interaction, to look their pupils in the eye more, to nod their heads up and down more, and to smile more than did those who either had no prior expectancy about their pupils or who expected them to be somewhat slow. Again, however, it is unfortunate that the Chaikin, et al. design did not allow for the assessment of what effect these behaviors had on the pupils—the roles of pupils were played by confederates. It does seem plausible that such nonverbal indicators may actually make the learning task more enjoyable and interesting for pupils with the consequence that they do, indeed, learn more.

That this is the case is indicated in an experiment by Beez (1968) in which 60 graduate students in education served as teachers. The pupils in this case were 60 five- and six-year-old boys and girls from a Headstart program. Prior to seeing a child, the teacher was given a phony evaluation, which either emphasized that the child appeared to be doing very well or very poorly in his or her educational activities. Positive and negative evaluations were randomly assigned to pupils, of course. The teacher—pupil interaction was then observed and rated for ten minutes, while the teacher attempted to teach the pupil as many as possible of a series of 20 symbols. Of interest here are the findings that teachers with favorable expectations about their pupil translated these expectations into dramatic and overt changes in their teaching style, that is, they tried to teach significantly more symbols to their pupils than did teachers who had unfavorable expectations. As a result, children about whom favorable expectations had been generated actually learned significantly more symbols than children for whom the expectations were less favorable. An interesting and unanticipated finding was that teachers who had unfavorable expectations about their pupil explained the meanings of particular symbols more often and gave more examples than teachers who had favorable expectations about their pupil.

It may be that teachers become overly exacting when they believe they are dealing with a low ability pupil, that is, they may not be willing to take minimal knowledge as sufficient for such pupils, but feel they must make sure he or she has got it, which slows down the learning process. Another possibility is that teachers are less punitive to low ability pupils, that is, they may withhold negative feedback from such pupils because they expect less of them to begin with. There is, in fact, some evidence that, in a simple learning task in which a teacher was to teach a particular discrimination to pupils who were either competent or incompetent, lower levels of shock were administered for mistakes when the pupil was believed to be less competent (Lanzetta and Hannah, 1969). Milder negative feedback, of course, is less likely to impress on a learner that a mistake has been made—particularly if it is known that stronger negative feedback is available. Under such circumstances, mere mild negative feedback may actually be taken as a sign of improvement.

Implicit in the above and, generally, in studies of the process by which teachers' expectations are communicated to their students is an assumption that the students are themselves alert to any cues the teacher may give off about what behavior is desirable. Further, it is generally assumed that the pupils are motivated to win the approval of their teachers or, at least, avoid disapproval and, thus, respond to the cues emitted by the teachers. In other words, the teacher–pupil interaction appears to be susceptible to arousing that anxiety-toned concern that M. J. Rosenberg (1965) has termed *evaluation apprehension*. With particular reference to experimenter–subject interactions, Rosenberg has noted that many experimental situations are likely to arouse such a concern on the part of the subject, that is, a concern that he or she win a positive evaluation from the experimenter.

Using Rosenthal's photo-rating task, Minor (1970) has demonstrated that experimenters fail to obtain results in line with their expectations when the subjects are not experiencing evaluation apprehension. Minor employed 15 male graduate students as experimenters, some of whom were led to expect that their subjects would make ratings which would average about +5 and some expected ratings of about −5. Subjects were 39 male and female student volunteers who were either led to believe that they would be psychologically maladjusted on the task if they did not do well (high-evaluation apprehension) or who were told that they were part of a control group whose data would simply be lumped together with everyone else's (low-evaluation apprehension). The results appear in Table 4.1. As Minor (1970) notes, "The data suggest that subjects who were not concerned about their performance failed to respond to the expectancy-

TABLE 4.1
Mean Ratings of the Neutral Photographs[a,b]

		Experimenters' Expectations	
		+5	−5
Subjects'			
evaluation	High	+.16	−1.06
apprehension	Low	−.78	− .59

[a]Interaction: $F = 9.67, df = 1/38, p < .001$
[b]From Minor, 1970, p. 331. Copyright 1970 by the American Psychological Association, Washington, D.C. Reprinted by permission.

indicating cues; whereas those who were concerned did avail themselves of these cues" (p. 331).

Thus, the ability and/or interest of the subjects in responding to interpersonal cues may be an important ingredient necessary for the successful communication of expectations. If the attention span of subjects—pupils is too short, if they lack motivation to win the approval of experimenter—teachers, or if they are incapable of detecting the cues emitted by others, there is little reason to believe that the expectancies of others will have any effect on their behavior. Along this line, it is of interest to note that a study by Anderson and Rosenthal (1968) carried out in a state school for the mentally retarded yielded only minimal support for the influence of interpersonal self-fulfilling prophecies. In fact, this study yielded some negative support for the operation of such prophecies since "The boys who were both expected by their counselors to bloom intellectually and exposed to the tutoring relationship . . . showed a *decrease* in reasoning IQ" (p. 480). On the other hand, boys in the favorable expectancy condition did gain significantly more than those in the control condition on ratings of self-help.

For a number of reasons, it is difficult to know how to interpret the Anderson and Rosenthal study. For example, apparently the volunteer students who were to tutor the boys were not the ones who were exposed to the expectancy manipulation. Rather, the names of the boys expected to blossom were given to their day-camp counselors. The study is mentioned here—in spite of such ambiguities—for two reasons. If we assume that the mentally retarded are below average in their ability to detect and interpret interpersonal cues, then the study is at least consistent with the notion that objects of interpersonal expectations must be capable of picking up emitted cues in order for those expectations to be successfully communicated and, hence, fulfilled. Secondly, the study is a caution against believing that expectations are everything. To tell counselors in a school for the mentally retarded that certain of their charges can be expected to blossom intellectually may produce only incredulity. Even so, there does appear to be a wide latitude within which expectancy effects may operate and within which retrospective interpretations may occur. Consider the following study by Meichenbaum, Bowers, and Ross (1969).

Meichenbaum et al. conducted an intensive analysis of the classroom behaviors of 14 adolescent females who were inmates at a training school for juvenile offenders. Six of the 14 were selected to be identified to the four teachers involved as late bloomers and, for five weeks, observers, who were unaware of the purpose of the study or the expectancy manipulation, recorded teacher–pupil interactions and the appropriateness of the girls' behaviors. The group of six girls who were identified as those expected to show intellectual gains consisted of three girls for whom the teachers had themselves previously indicated high expectations of academic potential and three for whom they had previously indicated low expectations. Of interest here is that:

> Initially, the teachers expressed some surprise about the inclusion of the three girls for whom they had prior low expectancy. Then, very quickly, one of the group reported some relatively insignificant observations she had made of a low-expectancy girl which indicated that she had potential. The other teachers who had been talking about the girl as having limited potential followed the lead and started to describe other situations which justified the fact that these girls were intellectual bloomers" (pp. 308–309).

Observers' ratings of the appropriateness of classroom behavior indicated that the behaviors of the expectancy group improved significantly more than those of the other group.[4] Further, on later objective examinations, the expectancy group performed significantly better.

Although the results of the above studies are generally more similar to the types of expectancy effects that occur in everyday life than those obtained with Rosenthal's photo-rating task, there is still a great deal of artificiality involved that may limit the generalizability of the results. A less artificial type of expectation that has been well documented and may have detrimental effects is the belief of many white middle-class teachers that lower-class black students will perform poorly in academic subjects. In one of the few studies that has attempted to look at the effects of such an expectation on teacher–pupil interaction, Rubovits and Maehr (1973) asked each of 66 white female undergraduates enrolled in a teacher training course to teach a brief lesson on television to groups of four seventh and eighth graders. In each group of four students there were two white and two black students. As in the previous Rubovits and Maehr study (1971), an observer categorized each teacher's behavior on an observational schedule. Unfortunately, it was not possible to keep the

---

[4] During a pretreatment period prior to the study, the two groups had been matched on teachers' expectancies of academic potential, level of appropriate classroom behavior, and amount of teacher attention received.

observer blind as to the race of the student which may, of course, have introduced a bias in the results. With this note of caution, it is of interest to note that white students received significantly more attention than black students. Further, fewer statements were requested of black students, more statements of the black students were ignored, and black students were praised less and criticized more. These results do not appear to be due to differential spontaneity of black and white students, because there was no difference between blacks and whites in student-initiated interaction.

Most of the research on teacher–pupil interaction as a function of teacher expectations has focussed primarily on the influence of positive expectations— expectations that certain pupils were to blossom. The studies by Rubovits and Maehr are, to some extent, exceptions, but they point to the need to look more closely at what is involved in the communication of negative expectancies. Is the process simply one of (relative) ignoring those about whom the negative expectancy is held, while positive expectancies are actively communicated by a variety of verbal and nonverbal indicators? Our earlier discussion of the labeling approach to mental illness indicated that the processes involved in letting those so stigmatized know their place are anything but passive. Let us look at some of the evidence on the communication of negative expectancies.

Expectations and the Stigmatized

According to Goffman (1963) there are three general types of stigma: abominations of the body, blemishes of individual character, and tribal stigma such as race and religion. Goffman believes that these widely varying types of imperfections have essentially the same sociological consequences and that regardless of the source or nature of an individual's stigma, the problem that he or she must continually confront is one of acceptance. Part of the problem, from the point of view of the stigmatized person, is that he or she has usually learned and incorporated the viewpoint of unstigmatized or normal persons about what it takes to be normal. Hence, the stigmatized individual is likely to be aware that others construct what Goffman (1963, p. 5) refers to as *stigma-theories*, that is, systems of expectations about what blind people or the mentally ill or paraplegics are like.

A major source of difficulty is that others usually incorporate into their expectations about the stigmatized a variety of imperfections in addition to the original one. As a result, there is likely to be a double uneasiness during contacts between those with visible or known-about stigma and normals who can either observe or know about the others' stigma. The normal in such a situation may be uneasy because he or she does not know quite how to treat the stigmatized individual and may believe that people with such stigma—whatever it may be—are not quite whole people. The stigmatized individual may be uneasy because he or she knows what the other is thinking and knows that he or she must be very careful to appear normal. To see if such uneasiness was really characteristic of interactions with the stigmatized, Kleck, Ono, and Hastorf (1966) recruited 40 male high school students for a study supposedly concerned with physiological reactions during face-to-face interaction. The subjects were run individually and, while having their galvanic skin response monitored, were assigned the task of interviewing another subject (actually a confederate) who had either walked in or arrived in a wheelchair. The wheelchair employed had a false bottom so that the confederate's left leg could be inserted in such a way as to appear as if it had been amputed. There are several results of interest. First, as indicated by the GSR index, subjects showed a significantly greater decrease in skin resistance—presumed to be an indication of emotional arousal—when the confederate entered in a wheelchair than when he simply walked in. Further, subjects interviewing the confederate in the wheelchair tended to terminate the interaction sooner and, in a similar pilot study, subjects committed considerably more errors in procedure when the confederate was in the wheelchair. It does appear as if the subjects were somewhat less at ease when interviewing the apparent amputee. There are two slight ambiguities here, however: (1) apparently, only one confederate was employed; and (2) he, obviously, knew what condition was being run at any given time. Hence, one might argue that the results may be peculiar to this particular person—perhaps only he makes others uneasy when he is in a wheelchair or perhaps he unintentionally behaved differently when he was in the wheechair.

A later study by Kleck (1969), using female subjects and two confederates who alternated playing a handicapped (in a wheelchair) and nonhandicapped fellow subject, found some evidence that normal subjects place themselves at a greater physical distance from the other when interacting with a handicapped as opposed to a normal other. It is interesting to note the discrepancy between this rather unobtrusive, nonverbal index of interpersonal distance and the finding that in this same study subjects rated the handicapped other more positively than the nonhandicapped. Kleck notes that the source of this positiveness on the ratings may inhere in a general norm in our society to be kind to disadvantaged persons. The nonverbal behavior of the subjects suggests, however, that they may not quite feel what they say they feel. As Goffman (1963) notes, the stigmatized person is expected ". . . to reciprocate naturally with an acceptance of himself and us, an acceptance of him that we have not quite extended him in the first place. A *phantom acceptance* is thus allowed to provide the base for a *phantom normalcy*" (p. 122).

This phantom acceptance extended to the stigmatized may be relatively transparent and obvious even to the stigmatized, although those extending it are likely to deny that it is not genuine. Laing and Esterson (1964) cite the following example from their investigation of the families of eleven supposed schizophrenic patients:

> Subsequently, Ruby's feeling that 'people' were talking about her disparagingly began to develop in earnest. As we have noted, she was told this was nonsense [by her family]. They told us that everyone was 'very kind' to her 'considering.' Her cousin was the most honest. 'Yes, most people are kind to her, just as if she were coloured' (pp. 134–135).

Some experimental evidence by Farina, Chapnick, Chapnick, and Misiti (1972) also indicates that people are not able to effectively monitor the less overt aspects of their reactions to those who are "different."

Thus people appear to be ill at ease around the mentally and physically handicapped and there is some indication that they attempt to cover their dis-ease with a patronizing kindness that is not really felt. The question remains, however, as to the source of the tension and strain that characterizes interaction with the stigmatized. Is it a function of what others believe about and expect from the stigmatized, or is it really brought about by the peculiarity of the behaviors emitted by the stigmatized?

In an attempt to glean some evidence on this question, Farina and Ring (1965) recruited 30 previously unacquainted pairs of male undergraduates to participate in an experiment in which the pairs were to operate a tilt-roll game for 50 consecutive trials. The tilt-roll game is one in which a marble or small ball is placed on a surface that can be tilted in two directions (forward-backward and side-to-side) by moving pairs of knobs. The object is to maneuver the marble along a curving path while avoiding a series of holes placed beside the path. Prior to interacting over this task, each of a pair of subjects was given some false background information about their partner which described him as either normal or emotionally disturbed. Based on this information, three conditions were set up: (1) both interactants believed their partner was normal; (2) one believed his partner was normal, while his partner believed he was emotionally disturbed; and (3) both believed their partner was emotionally disturbed. Of interest here is the finding that subjects who received information that their partner was emotionally disturbed were significantly more likely than those who thought their partner normal to report that the partner had hindered the joint performance. This occurred in spite of the fact that, on the task itself, the former group did objectively better than the latter. Farina and Ring (1965) point out that ". . . believing an individual to be mentally ill strongly influences the perception of that individual; this is true in spite of the fact that his behavior in no way justifies these perceptions" (p. 50).

There have been a number of additional experimental studies of interactions betwee normals and stigmatized subjects. The results are not entirely clear cut, but there is a fair amount of evidence that people are made ill at ease by the mere presence of the stigmatized and that being stigmatized has something of the character of a central trait (cf., Chapter 2), in that the perceptions and expectations of others appear to be organized around the stigma whether it is physical, mental, or—in Goffman's term—tribal. There is also some evidence that the interpersonal effects of stigma may be mitigated or enhanced as a function of the extent to which the stigmatized is seen as responsible for his or her "blemish" (e.g., Farina, Holland, and Ring, 1966).

There is another side to the story, however. Earlier the point was made that the stigmatized are themselves aware of the viewpoint of others, that is, that others feel uncomfortable around them, attribute all sorts of additional imperfections to them, and, generally, believe that they are not quite real people. This raises the rather interesting possibility that the reactions of others to the stigmatized may in part be a function of the expectations of the stigmatized. That is, the stigmatized individual, believing that he or she is disliked or thought inferior, consequently may behave in ways that bring about such feelings on the part of the others.

To focus on the effects of the belief that one is perceived to be either mentally ill or homosexual, Farina, Allen, and Saul (1968) set up a very simple three-condition experiment. Subjects were recruited in pairs, and one member of each pair was told that the purpose of the experiment was to investigate the impact *on the other student* of believing he was working with a stigmatized person. The subject was then asked to copy over in his own handwriting a brief life history, which indicated that he was either relatively normal (the control condition), an overt practicing homosexual, or an ex-mental patient who still had severe emotional problems. The experimenter then left to take this life history to a nearby room where the other student was waiting so that he could read it, following which the two subjects would be brought together to interact over a cooperative task. In *all* conditions, what the experimenter actually took to the other subject was a life history which indicated that the subject with whom he was about to interact was relatively normal. Thus, in two conditions, one subject believes that the other thinks he is stigmatized when, in fact, the other does not. The interactions between the pairs of subjects were recorded and, although a number of findings emerged, the main point of interest here is that, in the control group, the subjects who *received* the written life history talked for a longer time and tended to initiate more conversations with the other subject than did the subjects who received the life history in the other two conditions. In other words, when a person believes he is stigmatized, he apparently gives off interpersonal cues that lead others to talk less to him and to initiate fewer conversations with him. As Farina, et al. put it, "If an individual believes he is perceived in an unfavorable way by another person, his behavior in a subsequent interaction is affected independently of the other person's actions in the situation" (p. 178).

Thus, not only may one's expectations about another influence one's own behavior, they may actually lead the other to behave differently simply because the other is aware that such expectations exist. One might well point out here, however, that we have been discussing very special, and even unusual, situations:

interactions with the stigmatized; teacher–pupil interactions, in which teachers have been given artificial expectations about particular pupils; and results obtained on a photo-rating task, which is so ambiguous that subjects may be extraordinarily sensitive to any cues given off by the experimenters. What about other, less artificial situations? What about interactions between equals? In all of the studies cited above there has been a strong asymmetry: teacher–pupil, experimenter–subject, deviant–labeler, and stigmatized–normal. Do similar sorts of effects occur in general, everyday social interaction?

Expectations in Social Interaction

The question of interest here is the same as in the three preceding sections: how do expectations get communicated? How do we let others know what we believe their place to be? Berne (1961) argues that it is difficult not to let others know what we expect of them. He points out that "A great deal of linguistic, social, and cultural structure revolves around the question of mere recognition: special pronouns, inflections, gestures, postures, gifts, and offerings are designed to exhibit recognition of status and person" (p. 85).

As an example, consider one facet of this process by which we recognize another, the manner in which we address them. Ervin-Tripp (1969) notes that in our culture there are certain widely understood rules for how we should address people in different circumstances. When one of the parties to an interaction wants to define the other and the situation in a certain way, it can be done, in part, by the form of address. Consider a young, attractive, well-dressed, professional woman carrying an attaché case along a street in a business district. The accepted manner for a stranger to address her might be something like, "Excuse me, Ms., I . . ." Other forms of address, particularly those beginning with exclamations or a reference to her physical attractiveness, would be viewed as attempts to redefine her from a professional woman into a sexual object. By her style of dress and her attaché case, she is projecting a certain image of herself and a certain definition of the situation.

As Watzlawick, Beavin, and Jackson (1967) point out, a person may offer others a definition of self in ". . . many possible ways, but whatever and however he may communicate on the content level, the prototype of his metacommunication will be 'This is how I see myself' " (p. 84). Others, of course, may or may not accept the projected image:

What's your name, boy?
Dr. Poussaint. I'm a physician.
What's your first name, boy?
                        (Poussaint, 1967, p. 53, cited in Ervin-Tripp, 1969, pp. 97–98).

As Ervin-Tripp points out, there was no problem of communication in this interchange. Both parties were acutely aware of what was going on. "Both were familiar with an address system which contained a selector for race available to both black and white for insult, condescension, or deference, as needed. Only because they shared these norms could the policeman's act have its unequivocal impact" (p. 98).

For the most part, however, the self-images and situational definitions that people project are accepted, even if only temporarily and even if they are not believed in by others. The hesitancy that people apparently experience about calling what may appear to them to be a bluff, that is, a projected image of self or situation on the part of another which is unwarranted, stems from at least two sources. First, it seems safe to assume that most people prefer to avoid unnecessary interpersonal conflict and want interaction with others to run its course smoothly. Hence, we usually say nothing when someone presents a slightly exaggerated view of their own virtues and pretends to unattained accomplishments or drops a few well-chosen names. Secondly, and perhaps more important in everyday interaction, it is often quite difficult for one to tell whether or not the self and situational definitions projected by another are appropriate. We frequently have no clear contradictory evidence and, under such circumstances, the most reasonable course of action is to accept the other at face-value—we assume that he or she is what they appear to be and treat them accordingly.

The important point for our purposes is that persons who communicate a given situational and/or self definition for themselves have, in effect, delineated both what can be expected from them in the situation and what they expect from those with whom they are interacting. Thus, impressions and situations are "managed" for a purpose, and the techniques people employ in their attempts at impression management are simply techniques for communicating expectancies, expectations about how they are to be treated and how they intend to treat others. In a series of works reporting his own participant observations interspersed with illustrative citations from biographies, autobiographies, fiction, and even occasional experimental results, Goffman (e.g., 1959, 1961, 1963, 1974) has depicted in detail many of the nuances and subtleties of the arts of situational definition and impression management. The metaphor with which Goffman is most closely identified is contained in the phrase, "All the world's a stage." Individuals and/or teams of individuals are conceived of as staging performances in virtually all of their day-to-day activities. These performances are geared to specific audiences and are intended to project particular definitions of both the situation and the performer's self. Each performer attempts to control or manage the available information about themselves and the situation to insure that the audience perceives the intended message. Goffman pursues this dramaturgical metaphor relentlessly in *The Presentation of Self in Everyday Life* and interprets much of our daily experience with theatrical concepts such as: settings, appearance, performances, front region, back region, communication out of character, audience.

The focus of much of Goffman's work can be summarized by understanding his distinction between an impression that one *gives*, that is, the conscious attempts by the person to convey or project a particular body of information about oneself or the situation, and an impression that one *gives off*, that is, the not-so-conscious cues and nuances which may destroy the definition of the situation that one wishes to maintain. For example, the projected definition of being dispassionate and objective and taking part in an intellectual discussion may fall apart when one's voice breaks or a particularly cutting remark escapes. The consequences of such inadvertently given off impressions are severe. As Goffman (1959) puts it:

> Given the fact that the individual effectively projects a definition of the situation when he enters the presence of others, we can assume that events may occur within the interaction which contradict, discredit, or otherwise throw doubt upon this projection. When these disruptive events occur, the interaction itself may come to a confused and embarrassed halt. Some of the assumptions upon which the responses of the participants had been predicated become untenable, and the participants find themselves lodged in an interaction for which the situation has been wrongly defined and is now no longer defined. . . . Society is organized on the principle that any individual who possesses certain social characteristics has a moral right to expect that others will value and treat him in an appropriate way. Connected with this principle is a second, namely that an individual who implicitly or explicitly signifies that he has certain social characteristics ought in fact to be what he claims he is (p. 12).

The most important thread running through Goffman's work, then, is the concept of *information management*. The individual is seen as attempting to control the information about him or herself to which the audience has access.

The extent to which attempts at impression management are conscious can vary from those features of personal style and habit that appear so routine that they have slipped from awareness to overt, active attempts to present oneself in a particular light. Gibbins (1969), for example, presents evidence that the messages conveyed by particular types of women's clothing are clearly perceived and, within a given social group, consensus exists about the characteristics of women who wear particular items of apparel. Presumably, the clothes that a person wears become a part of his or her daily routine, and the messages conveyed by one's manner of dress may indeed have slipped from awareness. On the other hand, there is the possibility that failure to attempt to convey anything by one's manner of dress in itself conveys something. As Watzlawick et al. (1967) argue, all behavior has communicational significance and since behavior has no opposite, it is impossible not to communicate. It is, of course, possible to attempt to miscommunicate and such miscommunication may take several forms, including the sort of overt, conscious manipulation attempted by Plath (1971) during an encounter with one of her psychiatrists: "I began to feel pleased at my cleverness. I thought I only need tell him what I wanted to, and that I could control the picture he had of me by hiding this and revealing that" (pp. 106–107).Whether conscious or unconscious, impression management can be tricky and, as Goffman notes, one is constantly in danger of giving off cues that will destroy the projected image.

The most important part of impression management, of course, is how one attempts to define the relationship(s) between oneself and the other person(s) in the situation. For example, if the other person perceives that he or she is liked and respected, this may lead to quite different consequences from those that occur when the other person perceives that he or she is disliked. The interesting point is that the initial perception of being liked may be quite groundless, but may lead to behaviors such as cooperativeness and politeness, which induce the liking thought to be present at the outset. Hence, if one successfully conveys that the others in the situation are liked, the consequences are likely to be quite different from those that follow when one successfully conveys that the others in the situation are disliked.

Jones and Panitch (1971) offer some evidence pertinent to the above in the context of the Prisoner's Dilemma game. The Prisoner's Dilemma game is a mixed-motive game usually played by two people for a series of trials. On each trial, each player is confronted with a choice between a cooperative and a competitive response and is also faced with the puzzle of what the other player will choose on that trial, since the outcome of a given trial is determined by what both players choose. An example of the basic structure is depicted in Figure 4.2. As can be seen in the figure, if mutual cooperation occurs on a given trial, both players win a moderate amount (+5); if mutual competition occurs, both players lose (−5). There is also the opportunity for exploitation of a cooperative opponent, that is, by making a competitive choice when one's opponent makes a cooperative choice. Jones and Panitch (1971) found that among male dyads, those who were given false information at the beginning of the game to the effect that their partner liked them made significantly more cooperative choices during the game and were really rated as significantly more likeable after the game by their partners than were those who were initially led to believe that their partners disliked them. It does appear that, for male subjects at least, ". . . one person's conception of being liked or disliked . . . initiate[s] a chain of events resulting in another person's actually liking or disliking him" (p. 364).

		Player A: Cooperative	Player A: Competitive
Player B	Cooperative	+5* / +5	+10 / 0
	Competitive	0 / +10	-5 / -5

*Above the diagonals in each cell is A's payoff, below is B's payoff.

FIG. 4.2 An example of the Prisoner's Dilemma Game.

An important qualification of the Jones and Panitch result is that the same effects failed to occur with pairs of female subjects. There are several possible explanations for this, but one that is particularly pertinent to the argument being developed here involves general expectations about appropriate behavior for males and females. For a female subject to learn that, on the basis of a very brief preexperiment interaction, her opponent likes her may be relatively uninformative about what her opponent really thinks, since females are generally expected to be more pleasant and accepting in social interaction than are males.[5] Hence, a positive evaluation from a female may not be as likely to be taken at face value as a positive evaluation from a male. There is, in fact, some evidence that, when interacting with their children, mothers are more likely to smile regardless of the content of what they are saying than are fathers (Bugental, Love, and Gianetto, 1971).

The direct, verbal communication of affect—even by a third party as in the Jones and Panitch study—is relatively rare in social intercourse. Thus, the question of interest is how the perception that one is liked or disliked arises and how is the affect which another may experience communicated? These, of course, are the prior questions to what effect the perception of being liked has. One must perceive that one is liked or disliked before that perception can have any effect. Wiener and Mehrabian (1968) point out that with respect to the communication of affect, little attention has been paid to the particular words a person uses to refer to objects and other persons even though one's choice of words can tell us a great deal about his or her feelings toward the person or event being referred to. Wiener and Mehrabian introduce the concept of *immediacy* and argue that immediacy is an aspect or channel of verbal communication that carries important information about the speaker's affective state.

Nonimmediacy is defined as "any variations in word usage which indicate differences in the degrees of separation or non-identity among the communicator, the addressee, the object of communication or the communication itself" (p. 31). Consider the following examples which are arranged (roughly) on a continuum of immediacy to nonimmediacy:

We . . .
He and I . . .
John and I . . .
Mr. Smith and I . . .
Mr. John Smith and I . . .
That person with whom I . . .

---

[5] For this explanation to account for the male—female differences in the Jones and Panitch (1971) study, it is necessary to assume that a negative evaluation from a female opponent is no more devastating for females than a negative evaluation from a male opponent is for males.

In addition to choice of nouns and pronouns, nonimmediacy or separation of the speaker from the person or object referred to, can be indicated by other linguistic components such as verb tense, the order in which objects are introduced in a communication, the frequency with which reference is made to certain persons or objects, and various other linguistic devices, all of which are intended to put some distance between the speaker and the person or object referred to.

Wiener and Mehrabian (1968) review several studies in which subjects were asked to write out descriptions of others whom they either liked or disliked. Using a content analysis scheme based on their conception of immediacy— nonimmediacy, the descriptions reveal that, when subjects dislike the person being described, they use more nonimmediate verbalizations. It is important to note that this is different from referring to the person being described in negative terms, or attributing more negative characteristics, or even saying things such as "I dislike him." One can, in fact, convey negative affect toward another person while saying positive things about them. Further, Weiner and Mehrabian review several studies which indicate that ". . . speakers apparently use different vocal patterns to communicate different feelings, and, furthermore, addressees can reliably, although far from perfectly, interpret these vocal behaviors" (p. 69).

There are ways, then, in which interpersonal affect can be communicated, ways which are subtle enough to avoid a direct confrontation and breakdown of interaction when the affect happens to be negative, but which nonetheless get the message across. Communication of interpersonal affect, however, may be a sufficient condition, but does not appear to be a necessary condition for the sort of interpersonal self-fulfilling prophecies we are discussing. One's own behavior may induce responses in others that make the original behavior appropriate. Kelley and Stahelski (1970) point out that some people exert an influence on their social worlds in such a way that what they are reacting to in others has been determined by their own behavior.

In a series of studies employing variations of the Prisoner's Dilemma game, Kelley and Stahelski (1970) identified groups of subjects who indicated, prior to the game, that they intended to be either cooperative or competitive in the game itself. Subjects were then paired off in one of three ways: two competitive players, two cooperative players, or one competitive and one cooperative player. After playing for a number of trials, the players were asked, individually, about what they believed their opponents initial orientation had been. "The most common kind of error . . . consisted of a judgment by the competitor . . . that his cooperative partner was also a competitor" (p. 68). Further, analysis of trial-by-trial choices indicated that, when paired with a competitor, the initially cooperative players had indeed become competitive. Kelley and Stahelski term this a behavioral assimilation effect, and they review some evidence which suggests that an overassimilation may occur, that is, when paired with a competitively oriented partner, the initially cooperative person behaves even more competitively than the competitor. On the other hand, when two cooperative players were paired, they maintain cooperation throughout the game.

One implication of these findings is that cooperators and competitors will develop different views of what other people are like, that is, cooperators will be aware that there is variability in orientation with some being cooperative and some competitive. Competitors will not be aware of this variability since they force all those with whom they interact to be competitive. This, as Kelley and Stahelski point out, is based on the assumption that the goals and orientations people adopt for themselves in laboratory tasks, such as the Prisoner's Dilemma, reflect the goals and orientations they generally adopt in interpersonal encounters. Kelley and Stahelski review some old data from studies using the F-scale (Adorno et al., 1950) which lend some plausibility to the above assumption. As noted in Chapter 2, people scoring low on the F-scale (nonauthoritarian) tend to see others as being heterogeneous in their degree of authoritarianism, whereas those scoring high on the F-scale tend to see everyone as being authoritarian like themselves. Further, the evidence appears to indicate that in the Prisoner's Dilemma game, people scoring low on the F-scale tend to be cooperative in play and, when playing opposite a high F-scorer, to be behaviorally assimilated to the high scorer who tends to be competitive in play. The evidence is certainly not conclusive, but it is intriguing.

> One wonders whether, in general, the belief that other people are very much alike may not be a clue that the person holding that belief plays a very influential causal role in his interpersonal relationships. . . . The interactional process described here would . . . constitute a mechanism by which the authoritarian interpersonal orientation is a self-fulfilling prophecy, maintaining and justifying itself by causing the person to experience a world in which the orientation is shared and, therefore, necessary and justified (Kelley and Stahelski, 1970, pp. 88–89).

From the point of view of the competitor or the high F-scorer, the difficulty appears to stem from what Watzlawick et al. (1967) refer to as the punctuation of the interaction sequence. *Punctuation* refers to the manner in which one organizes his or her perception of the sequence of events in an interaction, and disagreement about how to punctuate a given sequence of events appears to be the source of many interpersonal conflicts. Watzlawick et al. (1967) give the following example:

> Suppose a couple have a marital problem to which he contributes passive withdrawal, while her 50 percent is nagging criticism. In explaining their frustrations, the husband will state that withdrawal is his only *defense against* her nagging, while she will label this explanation a gross and willful distortion of what "really" happens in their marriage: namely, that she is critical of him *because of* his passivity. . . . Represented graphically,

with an arbitrary beginning point, their interaction looks somewhat like this:

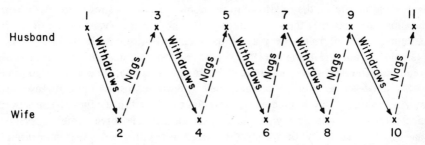

It can be seen that the husband only perceives triads 2–3–4, 4–5–6, 6–7–8 . . . where his behavior (solid arrows) is "merely" a response to her behavior (the broken arrows). With her it is exactly the other way around; she punctuates the sequence of events into the triads 1–2–3, 3–4–5, 5–6–7 . . . and sees herself as only reacting to, but not determining, her husband's behavior (pp. 56–57). (Copyright 1967 by W.W. Norton & Co., New York. Reprinted by Permission.)

Such punctuation of a sequence of behaviors serves to help the individual make sense out of what is going on and helps organize the ongoing interaction. As illustrated above, however, it is important to realize that the different participants in an interaction may punctuate the sequence differently and, hence, may end up with totally different views of what has occurred in the interaction—even though they both observe precisely the same behaviors.

It appears that the behavior of an individual engaged in social interaction cannot be interpreted except as part of a system, a system which is in part composed of the behavior of the other person or persons with whom the individual is interacting. Once this is clearly understood—that a behavior can only be studied and interpreted within the interaction or context in which it occurs—then, as Watzlawick et al. (1967, p. 46) points out, terms such as *sanity* and *insanity* or *mental illness* and *deviancy* become meaningless as attributes of individuals. What is usually referred to by these terms is a particular form of ongoing relationship. Laing and Esterson (1964) make essentially the same point in their presentation of the cases of supposed schizophrenics—in each of their cases the actual behaviors of the individual diagnosed as schizophrenic make eminent sense when viewed in relation to the covert and overt behaviors of the individual's entire family. With reference to the interview material collected from the family of one of their patients, Laing and Esterson (1964) comment that, once the attribution of illness is made, it comes ". . . to be taken as a fact, and . . . she is treated accordingly. Such is the spell cast by the make-believe of everyone treating her as if she were ill, that one has constantly to pinch oneself to remind oneself that there is no evidence to substantiate this assumption, except the actions of the others" (p. 203).

As we have seen, the actions of others may communicate a number of things to the object of these actions. Generally speaking, however, what they communicate is the nature of the relationship the communicator desires to maintain with the other, the role that the communicator wishes to assume vis-à-vis the other. In assuming different roles, we may actually exhibit different characteristics. For example, Sarbin and Kamiya (1952) asked each of a number of male and female volunteers to enact three different roles. In the first role, they were to interact with a same-sex peer; in the second, they interacted with an opposite-sex peer; and, in the third, they interacted with an older male authority figure. The task in each interaction was simply to get acquainted and the three stimulus persons, that is, the persons with whom they were interacting were the same for all subjects. The interactions were observed and rated by groups of judges who recorded their impressions of the personality characteristics of the subjects. The results indicate that the judges perceived the subjects to have different characteristics as a function of whom they were interacting with. For example, tabulations of the attributions demonstrate that:

> When the male social objects were interacting with a like-sex peer, the qualities *informal, honest,* and *sincere* were inferred by the judges. . . . When enacting the role vis-à-vis the opposite-sex peer, the three qualities just listed *do not* appear regularly. Instead the qualities *well-mannered* and *intelligent* survive the counting process. In the third role, where the social object appears with an older male, only one adjective meets the criterion of communality without appearing as a quality of the other roles, *ambitious* (Sarbin, 1954, pp. 254–255).

The implication of findings such as those by Sarbin and Kamiya is that we do present different selves to different others. Several personality theories are, in fact, predicated on this (cf., Carson, 1969; Sullivan, 1953). Leary (1957), for example, makes explicit his belief that all human behavior is interpersonal and, consequently, the interpersonal is "the most crucial and functionally important dimension of personality" (p. 12). Although some would disagree with Leary's assumption that all interpersonal behaviors are efforts to avoid anxiety and maintain self-esteem, it seems clear that there are few totally purposeless interactions between people. It appears that people do bring goals to interaction and much of what is involved in the various interpersonal tactics and strategies employed, the altercasting and role assumptions, and the variations in self-presentation can be seen as attempts to achieve their own goals and purposes. Thus, if individual goal attainment underlies the factors involved in interpersonal behavior, we need to look at some of the variables which influence goal-setting and goal-directed behavior. That is the topic we shall take up next.

SUMMARY

In this chapter we have examined some of the ways in which the sorts of interpersonal expectations discussed in Chapter 2 and the first part of Chapter 3 influence behavior. Interpersonal expectations appear, under many circumstances, to influence both the behavior of the person holding the expectation and the behavior of the person about whom the expectation is held. As we have seen, the key to the labelling perspective on deviancy—as illustrated by our discussion of mental illness—is the reaction of others to those who violate society's rules and norms. Most such violations appear to be transitory and are ignored, but when public labeling of the rule-breaker as a deviant occurs, various intrapersonal (previously existing stereotypes about such deviants) and interpersonal (communication of expectations and negative affect) processes may push the deviant individual into secondary or career deviance.

As an example of how these processes operate, we then looked at the available evidence on involuntary institutionalization of those who have been labeled mentally ill. The evidence appears to indicate the operation of a presumption of illness, which is reinforced in numerous ways: perfunctory sanity hearings, failure to meet legal criteria for commitment, and institutional arrangements that strip away the social amenities and props by which the committed might maintain the appearance of normality. In general, it appears that the so-called mentally ill suffer, to a large extent, from the expectations of others.

We then turned to an examination of the ways in which an individual who holds a given expectation about another can communicate that expectation to the other in such a manner as to increase the probability that the expectation will be validated. It appears that the cues employed to communicate expectancies are manifold and range from the most subtle, minute aspects of behavior to gross and dramatic interpersonal confrontations. From mutual glances to avoidance of eye contact, from name-dropping to name-calling, from cooperation to competition—almost all aspects of behavior can be employed to let someone know what we think of them and, in particular, how we see them in relation to ourselves. The results of these attempts at placing the other include both a definition of one's own role in the interaction and the development of what Goffman (1959) refers to as a *working consensus*, that is, a definition of the interaction situation that the participants implicitly agree to sustain (temporarily, at least). Goffman also argues that the emergence of a working consensus is usually engineered by one of the interactants for the purpose of inducing the others present to act "voluntarily" in accordance with the former's plan or purpose. Thus, the factors underlying *intra*personal goal-setting and striving may be an important key to *inter*personal self-fulfilling prophecies.

5
Expectancies and Goals

Other things equal, does the belief that one can do something influence the likelihood of actually getting it done? Further, what are the determinants of such beliefs, beliefs that one can shape the course of events? What are the processes through which such beliefs are realized? These are some of the questions to be pursued in the present chapter. Before looking at the pertinent data and theories, however, it might be well to make explicit a basic orientation underlying much of what follows.

The stream of events in which we find ourselves caught up each day can be viewed as an endless sequence of choices. We choose the clothes we put on each morning, what we eat or don't eat for breakfast, whether we walk or ride to work, the route we take—all the way to what time we turn out the light at night. Even though many of our choices are constrained and even if we maintain that the freedom of choice is an illusion, the fact remains that the feeling of having choices is real and we do believe ourselves to be continuously choosing. Implicit in the concept of choice is the notion of anticipation. A choice between alternative actions, or between action and inaction, or between alternative thoughts is, in effect, a choice between alternative futures—different events follow.

Granting this assumption that we have the feeling of being able to exercise freedom of choice, we may then ask if there is any overriding principle by which to understand the totality of each of our choices. The point of view taken here is a familiar one (cf., Brehm, 1966; White, 1959) that has recently been reemphasized by Burgers (1975). As Burgers puts it, ". . . the feeling of having a certain freedom of choice carries with it a motivation of fundamental importance. . . . We try to make our choices in such a way that in the next instant we shall still have some freedom. . . . The basic principle of motivation is thus: conservation of some measure of freedom; to which we may add: extension of potentialities for action, that is, extension of freedom" (p. 195). Kelly (1955) makes a similar statement in his *Choice Corollary*—that people make their choices in ways which appear to them to extend the system they have found useful for anticipating events.

Another way of stating the above is that an individual can be viewed as continually attempting to impose order and coherence, to extract meaning from, to understand, to anticipate, and, thus, to exercise control over the onrushing events in which he or she is forever immersed. This is done by making choices—choices about how to interpret events, choices among alternative courses of action, choices among evaluations of their courses of action. What we want to document in this chapter is that the outcome that follows a particular choice is, at least in part, a function of the expectation or perceived probability that the outcome in question will result from the choice. There is a prior question, however. What determines the perceived probabilities? What are some of the variables that influence our perception that one outcome is more or less likely than another? This is the question we take up first. It is important to keep in mind that we will be discussing only situations in which the individual believes he or she may be able to exert control over the outcome.

DETERMINANTS OF SUBJECTIVE PROBABILITIES

As used here, the term *subjective probability* is very similar in meaning to what Stotland (1969) refers to as hope: an expectation greater than zero of achieving some goal. There are degrees of hopefulness, of course, and these can be viewed as differing levels of subjective probability. The importance of hope, of some reasonable subjective probability of success at one's endeavors, has been widely accepted, as Stotland correctly points out. As we shall see in Chapter 7, lack of hope is implicated in what have been termed *apathy deaths* (Nardini, 1952) and, at the other extreme, some have seen in hopefulness the very key to human existence. Cohen (1964), for example, argues that "... when the chance of success is relatively small, ... most people look at the bright side of things, seeing it as brighter than it is. ... This phenomenon makes sense biologically, for had our ancestors faced danger and difficulty too realistically they might have shrunk from it or lost courage. Survival might have required some excess of boldness" (pp. 32–33).

If one's subjective probability of goal attainment is of such importance, we need to explore some of its determinants. A good place to begin is indicated by that psychometric maxim that has been the bane of many a rejected applicant: "Past performance is the best predictor of future performance."

Experience

For tasks that are familiar and with which a person has experience, it seems reasonable to suppose that one's subjective probability of success on future attempts at the task is, to a large extent, determined by one's history of successes and failures on the task itself, that is, the objective probability of success. If, at the beginning of the 1962, 1963, 1964, or 1965 baseball seasons, Hank Aaron had predicted that his batting average would be exactly the same as the preceding year, he would never have erred by more than 1 percent. His averages were .327 (1961), .323 (1962), .319 (1963), .328 (1964), and .318 (1965).

Even in the absence of such consistency, there is evidence that one's subjective probability of success on familiar tasks is responsive to one's experience. Feather (1968), for example, asked subjects to complete a series of 15 anagrams. For half the subjects, the first five anagrams were very easy, whereas for the remaining subjects, the first five were insoluble. For all subjects, the last ten anagrams had been pretested to be at about the 50 percent difficulty level, that is, the chance of any one of the last ten anagrams being solved by a member of the particular population from which the subjects had been drawn was approximately 50 percent. Prior to seeing each anagram, subjects were asked to estimate their chances of solving it. Subjects who were initially confronted with insoluble anagrams tended first to decrease their rated chances of solving the next anagram and then increase their rated chances as they got into the last ten (50 percent difficulty). For subjects initially confronted with very easy anagrams, the opposite effect occurs: their rated chances of solving the next anagram increased over the first five trials and then began to decrease as they start experiencing the more difficult (for them) final ten anagrams. Similar effects of experience on subjective probabilities have been reported in a number of studies (cf. Feather, 1966; Feather and Saville, 1967).

Further, it does not appear to be necessary that the person have a precise standard against which to compare his or her performance in order for future subjective probabilities on the task to be influenced. The global feedback that one has succeeded or failed in the past appears to be sufficient. Jessor and Readio (1957), for example, asked fourth graders to throw darts over a screen at a target lying on the floor, a target which could not be seen by the subjects. For either 10 of 20 throws or 3 of 20 throws subjects were told that they had hit the target. Before the 21st trial, subjects were asked whether or not they expected to hit the target on the next trial and how many times out of the next five trials they expected to hit the target. On both of these measures, subjects who believed they had previously hit the target 50 percent of the time indicated significantly higher expectations than subjects who believed they had previously hit the target only 15 percent of the time (3 out of 20).

Thus, on a task with which one has experience, the subjective probability of success on future attempts at the task is determined in part by the objective probability of past successes and/or the feedback—independent of actual performance—that one has succeeded or failed in the past. It is possible to distinguish, however, between simply being able to predict one's performance and being aware that one's performance—even though it may be improving—is going to fall short of the level required to attain the goal. It seems plausible that the awareness of the discrepancy between performance level and required performance may be crucial to one's expectation that success will follow renewed efforts at the task.

To illustrate the above distinction, Diggory and Morlock (1964) asked subjects to sort a pack of 70 cards, each with one of several complex designs printed on it. Subjects were given 10 25-second trials at sorting the deck, and the goal was to sort 40 cards correctly on at least one of the trials. The experimenter supposedly timed the subject on each trial, but, in actuality, the experimenter kept track of how many cards were correctly sorted and stopped the subject after he had sorted a predetermined number correctly on each trial. Thus, the experimenter was able to control the subject's level of performance on a given trial and all subjects improved, that is, sorted more cards correctly on each succeeding trial. Before each trial, subjects were asked what they thought the chances were of reaching the goal on at least one of the remaining trials and how many cards they thought they would sort correctly on the next trial. Responses to the latter measure, which is an index of one's level of aspiration, showed a steady increase over trials as subjects realized they were indeed improving. However, the subjective probability of reaching the goal declined over trials as it became apparent that, at the rate at which their performance was improving, they would probably not attain the goal.

Diggory and Morlock (1964) argue that in situations analogous to the one in their experiment, in which the ultimate goal is a fixed level of performance or competence and not simply improvement or being able to accurately predict one's performance, that the estimated subjective probability of success is a better index of the degree of encouragement of discouragement than is the level of aspiration. Let us use this as a working hypothesis for the moment, since later we are going to try to determine the effects, if any, of the degree of encouragement or discouragement. The argument we will develop is that the subjective probability of reaching a goal is an important determinant of the quality and persistence of the performance in attempts to attain that goal. Given that purpose, it would have been nice if Diggory and Morlock had actually timed their subjects or had reported the number of incorrectly sorted cards on each trial so that we could determine if performance began to deteriorate as the subjective probabilities declined.

For now, let us summarize by saying that the evidence appears to indicate that subjective probabilities are responsive to objective probabilities when the latter are available or can be inferred from the discrepancy between the performance level and the goal. It appears to be the case, however, that for many—if not most—of the goals we pursue there are no objective probabilities available. Life would be worse than dull if all the tasks we performed were tasks on which we had sufficient past experience to determine our objective probability of success.

How do people arrive at an estimate of their subjective probability of success on novel tasks or for obtaining new goals?

Social Comparison

Before attending to the how in the above question, it might be well to say a word about the why—why would anyone even bother to attempt to estimate his or her subjective probability of success on novel tasks or in uncertain situations? Why not just plunge in and try?

Evidence abounds that people abhor uncertainty. Janis (1951), for example, notes that during World War II residents of London actually seemed relieved when bombs began falling. The waiting each night for the bombing to begin was the most difficult period. Uncertainty appears to arouse anxiety, and anxiety—as most of us know—is not very pleasant. Thus, simple uncertainty reduction and the consequent reduction in anxiety is a partial answer to the why. Further, Festinger (1954) and others have pointed out that ". . . a person's cognition (his opinions and beliefs) about the situation in which he exists and his appraisals of what he is capable of doing (his evaluation of his abilities) will together have bearing on his behavior. The holding of incorrect opinions and/or inaccurate appraisals of one's abilities can be punishing or even fatal in many situations" (p. 117). It is not difficult to imagine examples in which an inaccurate assessment of one's abilities and subjective probability of success could, indeed, be fatal.

As for the how part of the question, since many of our opinions, beliefs, and abilities cannot be validated by physical reality or by past experience with specific tasks, we must have something on which to base our self-assessments so that the anxiety produced by uncertainty will not drive us up the wall. Festinger (1950, 1954) has hypothesized that people solve these self-assessment problems by substituting social reality for physical reality when the latter cannot be used to assess an opinion or an ability. That is, we compare ourselves with others whom we have reason to believe will be similar to ourselves with respect to the ability in question. An amateur photographer would compare the quality of his products with other amateurs, not with a professional. Only when we can compare our abilities with others who are similar in other relevant characteristics can we establish stable evaluations of those abilities. The evidence for this statement seems clear-cut (cf., Radloff, 1966).

There is a complication, however. As Festinger (1954, p. 124–125) points out, in our society, there is a value placed on doing better and better. The consequence is a unidirectional drive upward with respect to abilities. That is, we are not satisfied to know that we are about as good as Sam or Sue or Judy at tennis or woodcarving or whatever; we want to be slightly better than the people we compare ourselves with. Thus, given a range of people with whom we could compare ourselves, we will be inclined to choose as a comparison those whom we anticipate may be slightly better with respect to the ability in question. As

Wheeler (1966) puts it, "The comparer is attempting to confirm the similarity he has assumed. The comparer is attempting to prove to himself that he is almost as good as the very good ones; he would experience subjective feelings of failure only if he found a greater ability difference than expected" (p. 30).

There is, in fact, some evidence for such upward comparison. Wheeler (1966), for example, administered a fake test to groups of seven subjects with the ostensible purpose of detecting those who qualified for a particular course. Following the test, each subject was led to believe that he had scored 310 on the test and that his was the middle score in the group, that is, the fourth from the top. Subjects were also given information about the approximate position of the top (550–600) and bottom (25–75) scores and were asked to indicate the person in the group whose score they would most like to know. As can be seen in Table 5.1, most subjects chose to see scores ranked slightly above their own. Further, Wheeler presents questionnaire response evidence that most subjects did, indeed, assume their own score was closer to the score immediately above them than it was to the score immediately below. The latter, of course, is merely suggestive since it may represent only a post hoc justification of their previous upward choices. In any event, there does appear to be some evidence that people tend to choose for comparison those who may be slightly better at the particular ability than they are and, it is at least plausible, that they do this to confirm an assumed similarity upward.

If this assumed similarity upward is a general phenomenon, it would have important implications for an individual's assessment of his or her subjective probability of success at unfamiliar and novel tasks. The increase in confidence of success might help insure success, particularly in that region of maximum uncertainty in which the chances of success and failure are about equal. More-

TABLE 5.1*
Percentage of Subjects Choosing to See the Scores
Associated With Various Ranks of the Personality
Test[a]

Rank	% Choosing
1	5.0
2	33.1
3	48.8
4 = Subject's Own Score	—
5	7.4
6	5.8
7	0.0

*(Copyright 1966 by Academic Press, New York. Reprinted by Permission.)
[a](From Wheeler, 1966, p. 29.)

over, such a bias upward may not be peculiar to novel tasks. Howell (1972) notes that in laboratory studies people are consistently overconfident in evaluating their own skill, that is, they do not benefit as much from past experience in evaluating their own skill as they do in making judgments of events which are controlled by external factors. People seem quite adept at attributing their failures to temporary lapses of motivation or attention or effort (Heider, 1958), but seldom do they perceive themselves as failing because of lack of ability. People, of course, do differ in these tendencies as Weiner and Kukla (1970) have documented. However, if we assume that our society does value achievement, generally, such face-saving attributions for failure are likely to be widespread and result in the sort of persistent overevaluation of one's own skill as indicated by Howell. Somewhat paradoxically, it appears that the proverbial average person assumes he or she is slightly better than average.

There appear to have been few, if any, studies directly addressed to the question of how observation of others performing a task on which people themselves have no experience affects assessments of their own subjective probability of success at the task. There have been several studies, however, which have included reporting performance norms of fictitious groups to subjects. The subjects were then asked to estimate their own chances of success at the task. Groups, such as these, used to reduce uncertainty about the appropriateness of values, beliefs, and attitudes or to assess relative abilities are termed *reference groups*.

Assuming that the appropriate reference group for college students interested in assessing their intellectual abilities is one of other college students, Festinger (1942) presented individual college student subjects with two tasks: (1) a series of synonym tests on which they were to provide synonyms beginning with *a, b,* or *c* for lists of words; and (2) a series of information tests requiring specific answers to questions. In response to the question, "What score do you expect to get on the next trial?," subjects raised their expectations when told they had been performing below the average performance of high school students and lowered their expectations when told they had been performing above the average performance of graduate students. There is also evidence that on tasks for which the individual has a clear assessment of his abilities, for instance, familiar tasks, information about the performance of some reference group has little effect (cf., Chapman and Volkmann, 1939).

The level of aspiration studies done by Festinger and Chapman and Volkmann are consistent with the position being developed here in at least two important respects: (1) people do use information about the performance of various reference groups to roughly estimate their own subjective probability of success at the task; and (2) a person's own past experience at a task, when such exists, is a more important determinant of his subjective probability estimates than is information about the performance of reference groups. However, the level of aspiration studies say nothing about the third component of this argument, namely, that people generally assume they are slightly better than average within their own reference groups. In addition to the studies by Wheeler (1966) and Howell (1972) mentioned earlier, there are incidental findings from various studies that offer tentative evidence for this third factor.

Several studies have attempted to manipulate subjects' expectations for performance on a task by informing them prior to the task that subjects similar to themselves either did very well or very poorly on the tasks. When the probability of success—as determined by the performance of similar subjects—is reported as being very low (20 percent or 30 percent), subjects consistently estimate that their own probability of success is significantly higher, that is, close to 50 percent (cf., Feather and Saville, 1967). Feather (1966), for example, told one group of college student subjects that anagrams they were about to attempt were more difficult than most and that only about 30 percent of college students are able to solve them. Prior to attempting the first anagram, the mean probability of success estimated by this group was .54. A similar upward distortion of one's own chances is also reported by Feather (1963).

It is true that in these same studies there is generally a downward distortion among subjects who are told that others like themselves have generally succeeded, for instance, that they have an 80 percent or a 70 percent chance of success as determined by the previous performances of others. However, these downward distortions in the objective probabilities are always considerably less than the upward distortions among subjects who are told that others like themselves have generally failed. For example, in the study by Feather (1966), subjects told that only about 30 percent of their peers were able to solve the anagrams estimated their own initial probability of success as .54, an upward distortion of +.24. On the other hand, in the same experiment, subjects told that about 70 percent of their peers were able to solve the anagrams estimated their own initial probability of success as .63, a downward distortion of only −.07.[1] A similar effect was found by Feather and Saville (1967). In the latter study, subjects were either told, "You should find these anagrams easier than most. About 70 percent of previous Psychology I students were able to solve them correctly in the time allowed . . ." or, "You should find these anagrams more difficult than most. About 30 percent of previous Psychology I students were able to solve them correctly in the time allowed" (Feather and Saville, 1967, p. 227). Subjects given the former (70 percent) instructions estimated their own initial probability of success as .61, a downward distortion of −.09. Subjects given the 30 percent instructions estimated their initial probability of success as .56, an upward distortion of +.26.

Lest someone think that such asymmetrical distortions of one's own chances vis-á-vis those of his or her peers occur only in anticipation of solving anagrams

[1] Feather did not test for the significance of this difference in magnitude of distortion, but it appears to be a reliable effect.

or only among male subjects or only in research by Feather or only in Australia, let me hasten to add that none of these things is true. Feather and Saville used both male and female subjects and report no differences in initial probability estimates as a function of sex—Feather (1966), in fact, used only female subjects, so it is clearly not a phenomenon peculiar to males in a male-achievement dominated culture. Further, other researchers using very different tasks have reported analogous distortion effects.

There are no doubt several factors involved in the sort of subjective probability estimates we are discussing. Regression effects (Campbell and Stanley, 1966) or a tendency to avoid extreme responses may both be involved, but there is no reason why either of these would produce the asymmetry of distortions which is generally found. The social comparison hypothesis of a tendency to assume similarity upwards, to believe that one is a little above average, to think that one is a little more capable than most of one's peers taken in conjunction with regression and/or the tendency to avoid extreme responses may partially explain the asymmetry. When the reported performance norms of one's peers are very low (20 percent or 30 percent), all of these forces push one's own subjective estimates upwards (toward 50 percent). When the reported performance norms of one's peers are very high (70 percent or 80 percent) these forces are not all pushing in the same direction. The disposition to assume similarity upwards would tend to push one's own subjective estimates even higher (toward 90 percent), but regression and the tendency to avoid extreme responses would oppose. The result could be the sort of asymmetrical distortions generally found.

Whatever accounts for the asymmetry, it is worth noting that the result is a general elevation of the subjective probability of success when the objective probability of success is less than .5, that is, when the objective probability of success indicates that the rational decision is to not even try. By elevating the subjective probability of success upwards when it is below .5, one can justify trying and one can rationalize continuing to pursue the goal—whatever that may be. It is conceivable, then, that at least part of the asymmetry is accounted for by the desire to pursue valued goals and at the same time appear rational to one's self. As we mentioned in Chapter 2, there is a fair amount of evidence that motivation influences cognition (McClelland and Atkinson, 1948). Perhaps one's desire for a goal influences one's subjective probability that the goal can be attained.

Goal Value

The hypothesis that the value of the goal one is pursuing may influence one's subjective probability of attaining that goal has been around a long time. Several people have commented on the conditions under which such an influence may be particularly salient. McGregor (1938), for example, has argued that ambiguity and importance are essential features of situations in which one might reasonably expect subjective factors to play a role in one's predictions. If ambiguity and importance are both zero, then, according to McGregor, we can anticipate that subjective factors will not influence the prediction. The subjective factor McGregor was particularly concerned with was wishful thinking, which Webster defines as the interpretation of facts as one would like them to be, rather than as they really are. If one is pursuing a desired goal, presumably one would like for the probability of success to be high. In McGregor's terms, our question here is whether variations in the importance (value, desirability, valence) of the goal one is pursuing do, indeed, make a difference in one's subjective evaluations of the probability of attaining that goal.

There have been a number of questionnaire studies of wishful thinking (for example, McGregor, 1938; Cronbach and Davis, 1944; Cantril, 1938; Lefford, 1946). The general procedure in such studies has been to ask subjects to rate both the likelihood that a number of social or political events are going to occur and the desirability of the occurrence of each of those same events. The general finding in these studies has been that the more likely the perceptible occurrence of an event, the more desirable that event is rated. Perhaps this might be stated in reverse: the more desirable an event is rated, the more likely its occurrence is perceived to be. Or could it be stated both ways? The ambiguity, of course, stems from the correlational nature of the studies. Although either direction of causality may be of interest, we are concerned here only with the desirability—likelihood direction. For our purposes, then, these studies are ambiguous. Upon close examination, there are also methodological flaws. As Carlsmith (1962) has pointed out, the events judged were usually remote from and unimportant to the subjects. In addition, response biases may have contributed significantly to the correlation obtained since the scales were similarly worded for both desirability and likelihood ratings, and both desirability and likelihood ratings were usually obtained at the same time.

A further difficulty with questionnaire studies of the influence of the desirability of an event or goal on the perceived likelihood of the goal is that they have usually been based on correlations between the mean belief (likelihood) ratings of all subjects with the mean value (desirability) ratings of all subjects. As Miller (1973) points out, it would be more appropriate to correlate the two sets of ratings for each subject and then find the mean of these correlations. To demonstrate his point that the previous studies (for example, McGuire, 1960) had exaggerated the magnitude of wishful thinking by correlating mean ratings, Miller asked 60 subjects to rate both the truth probabilities and how desirable they felt each of 18 propositions to be. He then correlated the mean truth and desirability ratings of the 18 propositions and obtained an $r = .68$. However, when he correlated the belief and desirability ratings of each subject, transformed these into z scores, obtained the mean z score, and transformed this back into a correlation, the r was only .43. Miller's conclusion is that the questionnaire studies of wishful thinking have generally overestimated its magnitude.

If we couple this sort of computational inflation with the possibility of response biases and ambiguity of causality inherent in correlational studies, it may very well be that wishful thinking does not exist, that all along it has been a figment of imaginative minds and poor research. There appear to be both theoretical approaches and empirical research which would be congenial with such an interpretation. Rotter's (1954) social learning or expectancy-reinforcement theory postulates that reinforcement or goal value and the expectation for goal achievement are, in general, independent. As for research, there are several studies which, taken at face value, indicate that Rotter may be correct.

In the Jessor and Readio (1957) study mentioned earlier, in addition to giving false feedback to the fourth graders who were trying to hit a target they could not see, an attempt was made to examine the influence of different values of hitting the target. That is, some subjects received one small piece of candy (M & M's) for each hit, a second group received two for each hit, and a third group received three for each hit. Before the 21st trial, subjects were asked their expectations of hitting the target on subsequent trials. The amount of reward received for previous hits (one, two, or three M & M's) had no effect on the estimates of future success. It is not clear, however, that this can really be taken as negative evidence for the proposition that goal value influences the perceived likelihood of attaining the goal. For one thing, Jessor and Readio (1957) apparently made no attempt to establish that the three levels of goal value in their study were perceived by subjects as intended. Are three M & M's significantly more valuable to subjects than two M & M's? I doubt it.

A later study by Hess and Jessor (1960) suffers from a similar ambiguity of interpretation. In this study, college-student subjects were asked to participate in two successive card games. In the first, they learned expectancies for the occurrence of a valued event; they won either 5¢ or 25¢ if a marked card was turned up and lost either 5¢ or 25¢ if a blank card was turned up after a deck of ten cards had been cut. The sequence of reinforcement was controlled by the experimenter[2] such that a marked card appeared on .3, .5, .7 of a series of 40 trials. In the second game, the subject's winning depended not upon the appearance of a marked card on the top of the deck, but on the accuracy of the subject's predictions that a marked or a blank card would appear. Consistent with the previous study, the value of the event had no effect, either on the rate of learning the probability of its occurrence or on the final level of perceived probability of the event. As in the previous study, no attempt was made to establish that subjects perceived 25¢ for being correct as a significantly more valuable goal than 5¢. While one might more plausibly defend this manipulation of value than the difference in M & M's used in the previous study, unfortunately subjects were playing with provided money. It is also true that the procedure was complex, and subjects may not have accurately perceived or fully understood their task.

---

[2] The experimenter apparently needed some experience at Las Vegas since the marked cards had been "shaved" so that the experimenter could tell where to cut the deck in order to control the sequence of reinforcements.

Beyond specific criticisms of studies that have found no effect of goal value on expectations for goal occurrence, there is the classic difficulty of concluding anything from null hypothesis outcomes. Fortunately, there have been several studies which indicate that goal value does affect one's subjective probability of goal attainment.

Marks (1951) hypothesized that childrens' stated expectations would vary with the desirability or undesirability of a goal such that, given the same objective probability of the goal's occurrence, for a desirable goal the subjective probability would be higher, whereas for an undesirable goal the subjective probability would be lower. To test this hypothesis, fifth and sixth graders were told that for each of a series of 10 decks of 10 cards they would either win a point (5 decks) or lose a point (5 decks) if a picture card was drawn.[3] The objective probability for drawing a picture card was either .1, .3, .5, .7 or .9. Before each trial, the probability and desirability of the appearance of a picture card was made clear by the experimenter announcing, for example, "This time we have *7 pictures* and *3 blank* cards. If you pick a picture, you'll get a point" (or "I'll take a point away") (p. 339). Before each selection, the subject was asked if he or she expected to pick a picture. The stated expectations were greatly influenced by the desirability of the outcomes. At each probability level (.1, .3, .5, .7, .9), the number of yes responses was significantly greater when picking a picture was desirable than when it was undesirable. A similar result is reported by Irwin (1953) using college students as subjects. Unfortunately, with both of these studies, the results may simply reflect what subjects desired and not what they actually expected.

By way of comment, it should be pointed out that all of the above studies have employed relatively trivial goals—getting a point; 5¢, 25¢; and M & M's. Hence, one might seriously question the generalizability of any of this research regardless of the outcome, that is, regardless of whether or not the conclusion of a specific study indicates that goal values do influence the perceived likelihood of attaining the goal. Another general problem with most of the research, for our purposes, is that the tasks confronting subjects were frequently simply guessing tasks. Consider the Marks study as an example. With prior knowledge that a deck of 10 cards placed face-down on a table contained, say, five picture cards, the subject was to point to a card that he believed was a picture card. Pure guessing. There is no way that subjects could rationally believe that they might become more skillful at such a task. There is no way that subjects could convince themselves that with a little more effort they might do better on subsequent trials. This is an important point because our own goal here is to see if one's subjective probability of reaching a goal influences the quality and persistence of one's performance in attempts to attain that goal.

Fortunately, several studies have utilized both more meaningful goals and goals

---

[3] Actually the subject simply pointed to 1 of the 10 cards in each deck, all 10 cards having been placed face down on a table.

which were contingent upon performance, and not simply upon correct guesses. Worell (1956), for example, selected[4] three tasks which differed in intrinsic value or interest for his subjects: a level-of-aspiration board, a rotary pursuit task, and a tapping task. The subjects were fifth and sixth grade boys and, assuming that they valued athletic ability in themselves, Worell further differentiated the three tasks by informing subjects that the three differed in terms of their ". . . relative merit in providing information about a person's athletic abilities . . . for example, coordination, timing, and balance" (p. 49). The level-of-aspiration board was described as the most important and the tapping task as the least important. Subjects' expectations for their performance were significantly greater on the low- and medium-value tasks than on the high-value tasks. Thus, we have the suggestion that with nontrivial tasks requiring skilled performance, goal-value does influence expectations. Worell even comes up with an old saying to underscore the plausibility of the pattern of results, that is, that subjects believed their probability of a good performance was less on the most valued task—"The good things are always hard to get."

A problem with old sayings is that they often come in contradictory pairs. What about, "The best things in life are free?" Before we become enamored of Worell's finding, let us note an even more plausible alternative explanation for it. The effect of goal value may simply be a function of the use of three different tasks. As Carlsmith (1962) points out, ". . . the effect of 'reinforcement value' is completely confounded with the effect of a particular task. Persons familiar with the level-of-aspiration board describe it as a task in which success is likely to be perceived as a matter of pure chance. If this is true, and if success at rotary pursuit is not perceived as due to chance, then it is reasonable that a subject would expect to improve more with practice on the task involving skill" (p. 25).

Whether Carlsmith's interpretation is correct or not, subsequent research has not supported Worell's conclusion. If anything, it appears that when nontrivial goals are involved and subjects believe that goal attainment is at least in part a function of their skill and/or effort expended, then increasing the value or importance of the goal increases their subjective probability of achieving the goal. A study by Diggory, Riley, and Blumenfeld (1960) illustrates this effect nicely. The procedure employed was essentially the same task mentioned earlier in our discussion of the distinction between one's level of aspiration for a given performance and one's overall subjective probability of goal attainment. It will be recalled that subjects were asked to sort a pack of 70 cards, each with one of a number of different designs printed on it. They were given ten 25-second trials at sorting the deck and the goal was to sort 40 cards correctly on at least one trial. The experimenter supposedly timed the subject on each trial, but in actuality he kept track of how many cards were correctly sorted and stopped the

---

[4] Selection was based on a pretest in which the tasks were ranked.

subject after he had sorted a predetermined number correctly on each trial.[5] This allowed the experimenter to control each subject's performance. Prior to each trial, subjects were asked to estimate their subjective probability of sorting 40 cards correctly on at least one of the remaining trials. It is clear, of course, that these estimates would be a function of the controlled performances across trials.

Of concern here, however, is the fact that Diggory et al. were also interested in whether or not goal value would affect the estimates, and they manipulated subjects' motivation to perform the task. They use *motivation* to refer to subjects' ". . . supposed intensity of desire to achieve the required standard of performance . . . not because the performance is especially important in itself but because it is instrumental to some reward or benefit which is contingent on the performance" (Diggory, 1966, p. 131). Low motivation subjects were simply asked to sort the cards and given some mumbo-jumbo about the experimenter being interested in the acquisition of skill in complex performances. For high motivation subjects, on the other hand, the task was built up as a preliminary test and selection device designed to find college students who might profit from government-financed training in the physical sciences with vague allusions to NASA, Sputnik, and all that. Note, however, that both high and low motivation subjects perform the same task, at the same level (due to the method of timing trials) and get the same feedback. The effect of motivational level (goal value) is depicted in Figure 5.1. As can be seen in the figure, subjects with high motivation have consistently higher estimates of their probability of success than subjects with low motivation.

Diggory (1966) also presents some evidence that when subjects are not asked to estimate their probability of success on each trial—where sequence effects might be maximal—but, say, only on before the first, sixth, and ninth trials, similar effects occur on probability estimates as a function of motivation. Further, some research by Sylvia Farnham-Diggory (also reported in Diggory, 1966) indicates that the probability of success estimates of children working for a valued prize are also elevated in comparison to those of children working for no prize or one low in value. Thus, it begins to appear as if the old studies of wishful thinking were onto something after all—in spite of their flaws. It appears, at least, that when one perceives the outcome to be to some extent dependent on one's own effort or skill, increasing the value of the goal then increases one's subjective probability of attaining that goal.

McGregor (1938) suggested that two variables influence the extent to which subjective factors play a role in predictions, particularly in wishful thinking: importance and ambiguity. We have seen that importance or goal value does make a difference. There is the suggestion in Figure 5.1 of the operation of

---

[5] Diggory (1966) reports that of 2,232 subjects recruited for a number of experiments employing this procedure, fewer than 31 indicated any suspicion of this deception.

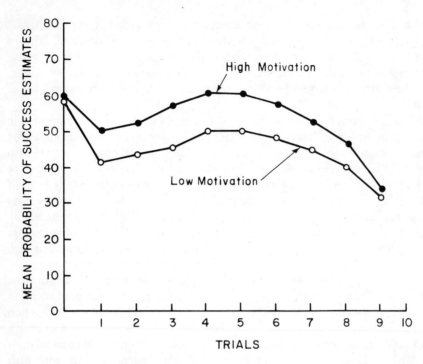

FIG. 5.1 Estimated probability of success by trials as a function of motivation. (Data from Diggory, et al., 1960. Graph from Diggory, 1966, p. 148. Copyright 1966 by John Wiley and Sons. Reprinted by Permission.)

McGregor's second factor, ambiguity. As can be seen in the figure, the two curves representing probability estimates appear to get closer together on trials 7, 8, and 9 as the deadline (trial 10) approaches. It appears that when, after repeated attempts at the task, the goal has not been reached, a reality constraint begins to dampen the effect of goal value on probability estimates. The situation becomes less and less ambiguous as the deadline approaches and one can see that he or she is still some distance from the goal. Hence, subjective estimates become more realistic. There is, in fact, some evidence that this occurs.

Time Perspective

With tasks that are partially skill- and effort-dependent, it could be the case that the individual perceives that more time—a deadline further in the future—will allow better preparation or more practice and, hence, that his or her probability of success at the task is greater. It is a frequently recurring theme of utopian novels (cf., Hilton, 1933) that longevity is the key to serenity—not because of the absence of a fear of death—but because with an infinite life span, one could master all tasks, learn all languages, and do anything one wished.[6] There is a widespread belief that if one had eternity at one's disposal, all things would be possible.

Nisan (1972) conducted one of several studies which appear to document this idea. He hypothesized that temporal distance from the goal one is to pursue brings about an increase in the expectancy for success on skill-dependent tasks; to check on this, he asked 100 male college students to read descriptions of a test they were to take now or after four weeks. The test had 12 items at each of two levels of difficulty. For one group of items, it was reported that only 25 percent of those who attempt them are able to answer correctly (high difficulty) and, for the second group of items, it was reported that 50 percent get them correct (medium difficulty). The test was described as one requiring "quick orientation and inference" (p. 176), a description which subjects could plausibly construe as indicating that both skill and effort would make a difference. When asked to rate their chances of answering the items correctly, there were reliable trends for both levels of difficulty to indicate higher expectancies for the test to be taken in four weeks.

One thing that might modify such an effect, of course, is the extent and nature of one's previous experience with the task. If a person has already put forth what he or she knows is his or her best effort on a given task and has failed, then it is unlikely that putting the task off for a few days or weeks is going to make much difference in subjective estimates of the probability of success on the task. Evidence on this point comes from a study by House (1973), in which male and female college students were asked to attempt one of two series of 20 anagrams. The anagram lists were so constructed that in comparison with norms reported by the experimenter, subjects were induced to believe that they had either passed or failed. Following their performance, subjects were asked to rate their expectations for performance on a second, similar anagrams task, which they would take either immediately, in 3 weeks, or after 21 weeks. Subjects who had just succeeded on the first anagrams test rated their performance expectancies significantly higher for the task 21 weeks in the future, than for a retake either immediately or after three weeks. For subjects who had failed, there were no differences as a function of when the task would be attempted again.

There are a couple of ambiguities in the above results, however. It appears (House, 1973) that when subjects were indicating their expectations about performance either immediately or after 3 weeks, they actually anticipated taking another anagrams task at one of these two times. On the other hand, when indicating their performance expectancies for 21 weeks later ". . . subjects were aware that they would not actually be taking a test at this distant time" (p. 281). This confounding could easily account for the results. Another difficulty,

---

[6] It is interesting in this connection that *serenity* means both tranquility or repose and clearness or brightness. Peace may very well come with understanding.

for present purposes, is that the anagrams task was described as being very intelligence-dependent, with practice having little effect. It is doubtful if subjects fully believed this, but it may have attenuated any tendency for subjects to convince themselves that they could do better in the future. Some research which overcomes both of these problems is reported by Diggory (1966).

Using the same card-sorting task described earlier, in which subjects are given a pack of 70 cards with different designs on them, Diggory and his associates attempted to manipulate the nearness of the deadline against which subjects were working. To do this, some subjects were scheduled for one hour appointments, but were told at the outset that the experimenter was not quite sure how many trials at the card-sorting task they would have time for. Again, however, all subjects believed that the goal was to sort 40 cards correctly on at least one of the trials. The experimenter did promise all subjects that there would be time for at least ten trials, and that after the tenth trial he would check the time and tell them precisely how many more trials they would have. Thus, for trials zero to nine, the deadline was at some vague point in the future for all subjects. At trial ten, one-fourth of the subjects were told they had one more trial, one-fourth were told they had two more trials, one-fourth were told they had four more, and the remaining subjects were told they had eight more trials. The mean changes in the probability of success estimates between trials nine and ten are indicated below (from Diggory, 1966, p. 144).

Number of Remaining Trials	1	2	4	8
Mean Change Between Trials 9–10	−5.25	−3.00	0.00	+1.13

It appears that the estimated probability of success remains higher when the deadline against which one is working is at some vague point in the future (as it was for trials zero to nine) and when the deadline is clarified, the further it is in the future, the higher the subjective probability of reaching the goal.

With respect to this question of deadlines, Diggory (1966) underscores our earlier distinction between the old level of aspiration (LA) research, in which subjects estimate their performance on the next task and the research we have been discussing which addresses subjects' overall estimates of their probability of reaching a specific goal; He points out that:

> ... [no] student of LA thought to consider how important, in determining our estimate of the likelihood that we will achieve an ultimate goal, is the amount of time or number of opportunities we have to reach it, but time, or more precisely limitation of time, puts the term to all our strivings. None of us has infinite time to accomplish anything, and it is a rare society indeed that can afford all of its constituent individuals very large amounts of time to accomplish even the most mundane tasks. We all face deadlines, whether they are long or short or whether they are imposed by other people, natural circumstances, or by ourselves is no matter; they are there (Diggory, 1966, p. 126).

We have been emphasizing skill-dependent tasks and tasks on which subjects believe their effort will make a difference. There is some evidence that the sorts of effects we have been discussing may generalize to tasks on which skill and effort are both irrelevant. Strickland, Lewicki, and Katz (1966), for example, asked subjects to place bets either before or after[7] throwing dice in a game. With dice, of course, the outcome is purely chance. Apparently subjects convinced themselves that they could influence the outcome of dice throwing, however, because they bet more and took lower probability bets when betting before the dice had been thrown. Whether or not this is really a function of subjects' convincing themselves that they will be able to influence the outcome needs to be clarified.

In any event, it does appear to be the case that for tasks which are dependent on one's level of skill and/or the amount of effort one expends, the greater the temporal distance to the goal or the greater the number of attempts to attain the goal which remain, the higher one's subjective probability of attaining the goal. But there may be a complication. The fewer the remaining trials to attain a goal, the more effort one is likely to have already expended. That is, with each succeeding trial, one exerts more effort and, at the same time, reduces the number of trials remaining. As we have just seen, the latter (reduction in remaining trials) would tend to lower the subjective probability of success. What effect does the cumulative increase in effort expended have on the subjective probability of goal attainment?

Effort Expended

There are reasons to believe that the more effort one has expended in pursuit of a goal, the more likely that person is to believe that he or she will, in fact, attain the goal. Both dissonance theory (Brehm and Cohen, 1962; Festinger, 1957) and attribution theory (Kelley, 1967; Jones and Davis, 1965) lead to the prediction that subjective probabilities of success will increase with increases in the amount of effort expended. According to dissonance theory, the cognition that one has expended a large amount of effort in pursuit of a goal would be dissonant with the cognition that the subjective probability of goal attainment is low. One way in which this dissonance could be reduced, of course, is to convince oneself that the subjective probability of success is not so low after all. According to attribution theory, the perception that one has expended a large amount of effort can be explained by adopting the belief that the subjective probability of success is relatively high. The hidden assumption is that people view themselves as rational, and rational people do not waste effort on unattainable goals. Yaryan and Festinger (1961) offer evidence pertinent to the effort—subjective probability question. They asked 60 female high school students to participate in an experiment about studying for exams. All 60 subjects were led to believe that half of the subjects in the experiment would be required to stay for two

---

[7] In the after condition, subjects did not know what number had been thrown when placing their bets. They simply knew the dice had already been thrown.

hours, while the other half of the subjects would be done after one hour. They were further informed that they would not find out which group they would be in until after a preliminary task had been completed. Half of the subjects were assigned to a high-preparatory-effort condition, in which they were required to memorize a set of definitions so that they would be ready in case they were one of the ones selected to take the IQ test which would be given in the second hour of the experiment. The remaining subjects were assigned to a low-preparatory-effort condition, in which they only had to take a minute or two to look over the definitions, that is, these subjects did not have to memorize them. On a subsequent questionnaire, subjects who had just been through the more effortful preparation indicated that they believe they were significantly more likely to be selected to take the IQ test.

Unfortunately for us, there are a number of ambiguities in the Yaryan and Festinger study. First, there is an important time differential between the high- and low-preparatory-effort conditions. Subjects in the former spent 25 to 30 minutes memorizing definitions before indicating their expectancy about being selected for the IQ test. Subjects in the latter (low-effort) condition only spent a couple of minutes looking over the definitions before indicating their expectancies. Thus, subjects in the high-effort condition might have been more likely to believe they had been selected simply because they had been in the experimental setting a much longer time. Along this line, Johnson and Steiner (1965) point out that the experimenter spent more time with subjects in the high-effort condition and, since all subjects had been told that the experimenter knew who would take the IQ test, it seems possible that subjects in the high-effort condition interpreted the amount of time the experimenter devoted to them as indicating that she knew they would be taking the test. A further difficulty with the Yaryan and Festinger result is that we do not really know whether or not subjects wanted to take the IQ test. It could be plausibly argued that the subjects did, in fact, perceive taking the test as a valuable and interesting experience—one they could tell their friends about and, perhaps, one which would give them some information about their abilities. On the other hand, one could just as plausibly argue that the subjects did not want to take the test and that the real goal was to be in the group which could leave after only an hour instead of the group staying two hours and taking the test.

Thus, taken at face value, the Yaryan and Festinger study appears to support the idea that the more effort one has expended in connection with the occurrence of an event, the greater one's subjective probability of the event occurring. If such an effect were real, it would oppose the tendency for subjective probabilities to decline with repeated goal attempts as the deadline approaches within which the goal must be reached. As we have seen, however, the Yaryan and Festinger result cannot be taken at face value, and, hence, the question arises as to whether or not there is other research bearing on the issue.

Another way of looking at the question of effort expenditure and subjective probability of success is to ask whether or not effort expenditure has any effect on the perceived value of the goal. We have already seen that increasing the value or importance of the goal increases the subjective probability of goal attainment. If increases in effort expended to attain a goal increase the value of the goal, then we would have another reason for expecting that increases in effort will result in increased subjective probability of success. There is, in fact, a fair amount of evidence that the more stressful the initiation which one must undergo to become a member of a group, the greater the attractiveness of the group (see Hendrick and Jones, 1972, pages 152–195, for a review). Other research which bears on the effort expenditure, goal value issue comes from the decision-making literature. It is a common finding that when given a choice between two alternatives, the relative attractiveness of the chosen alternative increases after the decision. Further, the closer the two alternatives are in attractiveness prior to the decision, the greater the relative increase in attractiveness of the chosen alternative after the decision (cf., Brehm, 1956). If we assume that a decision between two alternatives which were initially closer together in attractiveness is more difficult than a decision between two alternatives which were initially farther apart in attractiveness, then the latter finding is further evidence that expending effort does increase the perceived value of the goal.

Taken together, the congruence of the dissonance and attribution predictions along with the above research do provide tentative support for the hypothesis that the more effort one has expended in pursuit of a goal, the higher one's subjective probability of success, other things equal, of course. It is regrettable that most of the research which was directly stimulated by the Yaryan and Festinger result was focussed on establishing alternative explanations for the finding rather than on the conditions under which the result might indeed be true. In any event, it is still an important question of whether effort expenditure per se increases one's subjective probability of success. For now, the answer appears to be a tentative "yes" and we shall proceed, but the evidence is not overwhelming. Before proceeding, however, let us briefly summarize the material we have covered in this chapter.

Summary

We began with a brief discussion of the importance of one's perception that there is freedom of choice among life's events, that is, among the alternatives faced in succeeding moments. It was pointed out that one of the purposes of this chapter is to document the idea that the outcome which follows a particular choice is in part a function of the expectation or perceived probability that the outcome in question will result from the choice. Thus, the first order of business was to examine the determinants of one's subjective probability of attaining a particular outcome or reaching a particular goal.

As one might expect, the most important determinant of the subjective probability of success on familiar tasks is one's own past experience on the task. Further, on such tasks, the simple knowledge that one has succeeded or failed—

even if one cannot accurately evaluate and adjust one's performance—is sufficient to determine one's subjective probability of success. In connection with this point, we were led to make a distinction between one's level of aspiration and one's overall subjective probability of goal attainment: the latter appears to be a better index of one's degree of encouragement or discouragement. We then turned to an examination of the processes by which people evaluate their probability of success on unfamiliar tasks and it appears that people do this by comparing themselves with others. Further, we found an interesting asymmetry in the form of an assumed similarity upwards, that is, the average person apparently believes he or she is a little better than average. The general result of this asymmetry is an elevation of the subjective probability of success when the objective probability is below .5. It was pointed out that at least part of the asymmetry may be accounted for by the desire to pursue valued goals and at the same time appear rational—presumably rational people would not pursue goals where the chance of failure is predominant. This led us to a discussion of the effect of goal value and the evidence appears to indicate that increasing goal value increases one's subjective probability of attaining the goal. Similarly, the greater the time remaining for goal attainment, the higher the subjective probability of attaining the goal. Finally, we examined some tentative evidence which appears to indicate that the more effort one has already expended in pursuit of a goal, the higher one's subjective probability of success. This may be an important factor in sustaining performance for goals which are difficult to achieve or goals which require extended periods of effort and persistence.

We have explored these determinants of one's subjective probability of goal attainment in some detail because it is a basic hypothesis of the position being developed here that one's subjective probability of success is the key to intrapersonal self-fulfilling prophecies. Thus, we need to construct a general framework for looking at the interrelationships among objective probabilities, subjective probabilities, and effort.

A THEORETICAL ANALYSIS

As will become apparent, many of the ideas to be discussed in this section are not new. Specific similarities to existing theoretical positions will be indicated at several points. As will also become apparent, however, the particulars of the model developed below differ from existing formulations in a number of ways.

Dichotomous Processes

In the last section we examined some of the determinants of the perceived probability of success. It appears that when one has little experience on a task or, as McGregor (1938) would put it, in ambiguous situations, subjective factors come into play to distort the objective probability of success. When the objective probability of success is low, there appears to be a general tendency to convince oneself that it is somewhat higher, a tendency which we referred to as wishful thinking. There was also some evidence that, when the objective probability of success is very high, there is a general tendency to distort downward, that is, to convince oneself that the probability is actually somewhat lower. The latter tendency, which we have not previously given a name, might be called anticipatory face-saving and is similar to what Archibald (1974) refers to as "defensive effort." That is, if the objective probability of success is high, it would be most embarrassing to fail. Hence one can mitigate or forestall any potential embarrassment by convincing oneself that the probability of success is actually somewhat lower.

Thus we have two antagonistic cognitive processes, one operating to distort the perceived probability of success upward when the objective probability is low (wishful thinking) and one operating to distort the perceived probability of success downward when the objective probability is high (anticipatory face-saving). The notion of opposing processes which underlie behavior is an old one which can be traced through an almost endless series of transformations and variations. For example, Murphy and Murphy (1968) point out that the ancient Chinese concepts of yin and yang ". . . of contrasts of opposites, and the changes resulting from the interplay of them foreshadow such concepts as multiple determinism, dualism, and conflict is psychoanalytic thought" (p. 133). Freud, of course, transformed these ideas into the interplay of Eros (yang) and Thanatos (yin) without doing great violence to the basic notions. It may be a mistake to speak of transforming the ideas. Rather, it appears that many people have independently felt a need to introduce explanatory concepts which are predicated on a duality of underlying processes. The similarity of the various guises in which the idea has appeared may simply attest to the pervasiveness of the evidence for such conceptions.

In any event, Tolman, Miller, Lewin, Bruner, Rotter, and Atkinson—to take only those theorists whose works are most pertinent to the present argument— have all postulated the existence of opposing psychological processes underlying behavior. This is not to say that the ideas contained in any of these earlier formulations bear a one-to-one relation with the development here. There is, however, a remarkable similarity of the basic assumptions and premises common to all of these formulations as Feather (1959), Deutsch (1968), and others have pointed out. All are concerned with some form of expectancies or anticipations and all postulate a duality of dynamic processes underlying perception and behavior. Whether the discussion is cast in terms of positive and negative goal gradients, approach and avoidance tendencies, perceptual sensitization and perceptual defense, positive and negative valence, or motive to succeed and motive to avoid failure, the common thread of meaning is clear.

The theoretical position most directly relevant to our purposes is Atkinson's (1957) theory of achievement motivation. Atkinson defines an expectancy as the anticipation that performance of a behavior will be followed by a particular outcome. Further, he defines motives as dispositions to strive for particular kinds of satisfactions. He hypothesizes that in situations in which one perceives that performing an act or sequence of acts will be instrumental in achieving a goal, two motives are likely to be aroused: (1) the disposition to approach success (motive to succeed); and (2) the disposition to avoid failure (motive to avoid failure). The cognitive consequences of these two motives, when aroused, are very similar to what we have referred to as wishful thinking and anticipatory face-saving, respectively. As we shall see, however, the position developed below differs from Atkinson's in several fundamental respects. With this brief historical digression to place our ideas in context, let us return to wishful thinking and anticipatory face-saving and see where they lead.

In addition to evidence for the existence of these two processes, we saw earlier that the two processes are apparently not equal. That is, wishful thinking appears to be somehow more potent and leads to a greater absolute magnitude of distortions in perceived probability than anticipatory face-saving. A plausible way in which one might account for this asymmetry can be found in the nature of the populations from which subjects were drawn to participate in the various studies. All of the studies we have cited which bear on the existence of such an asymmetry were carried out either in the United States or Australia. It seems to be a safe assumption that in both of these countries success and achievement are highly valued. Further, most of the studies cited utilized college students as subjects, subpopulations in both countries that are even more achievement- and success-oriented than the parent populations from which they were drawn (cf., Atkinson, 1958). Consequently, it is eminently plausible that, in such groups, wishful thinking would be predominant.

Granting, then, for the sake of argument, the existence and simultaneous operation of the two processes we have described, we are left with the questions of: (1) the shape of the functions which relate wishful thinking and anticipatory face-saving to the objective probability of success; and (2) the interaction or combination of the two processes. The very simplest possibilities which appear to be consistent with the data are the following. Since wishful thinking appears to be operative mainly when the objective probability of success is low, we conjecture that wishful thinking is a decreasing function of the objective probability of success. As the objective probability of success increases, wishful thinking decreases. On the other hand, since anticipatory face-saving is useful or needed only when the objective probability of success is high—when it is low, one already has a face-saving excuse for failure—we conjecture that anticipatory face-saving is an increasing function of the objective probability of success, that is, they increase together. As for how wishful thinking and anticipatory face-saving combine, the simplest possibility is that they summate algebraically.

One other question remains about the relationship of these two processes to the objective probability of success. Earlier we mentioned ambiguity as a sine qua non of the operation of wishful thinking and anticipatory face-saving. One implication of this is that there will be little, if any, distortion when the objective probability of success is extreme, that is, very close to one or very close to zero. At the extremes of one and zero, there is little ambiguity—success is either a sure thing or failure cannot be avoided. Given this lack of ambiguity at the extremes, we would expect wishful thinking and anticipatory face-saving to operate only above some minimal objective probability of success and below some maximum objective probability. When there is absolutely no chance of failure, for example, there is little need to leave oneself an out or an excuse for failure by distorting the probability of success downward.

By way of summary, we can formulate the above argument into a set of three postulates:

Postulate I: As the ambiguity of task requirements increase, there is an increase in the extent to which wishful thinking and anticipatory face-saving determine the perceived probability of success.

Postulate II: Above some minimal and below some maximum objective probability of success, the magnitude of wishful thinking declines and the magnitude of anticipatory face-saving increases as the objective probability of success increases.

Postulate III: Wishful thinking and anticipatory face-saving summate algebraically to distort one's perception of the probability of success.

The value of these postulates is dependent, of course, on where they lead, on what can be shown to follow from them.

If we depict in graphic form the relationships mentioned in the second postulate and assume that we are discussing some mythical average person in a culture such as our own, we would have a graph similar to that in Figure 5.2. Note that in the figure we have incorporated the asymmetry discussed in the preceding section. In other words, we are assuming that we are depicting the processes of an individual from a culture such as our own in which achievement and success are highly valued and, consequently, an individual for whom wishful thinking predominates. We have also incorporated into Figure 5.2 the reality constraints imposed by extreme probabilities. It can be seen that neither process operates when the objective probability of success is very close to zero or one.

One other point about Figure 5.2 that is important to note is that it depicts the relative magnitudes of processes for one hypothetical person. It should be the case that people will differ in the relative predominance of these two processes and we shall explore the consequences of this in the following section. For now, it is only necessary to point out that people should also differ in the minimum and maximum objective probabilities of success where these two processes come into play. That is, some people may begin thinking wishfully whenever there is even the slightest chance of success whereas others may not allow themselves to dream until the objective probability is considerably higher. Thus, in Figure 5.2 the points C_1 and C_2 may vary for different people. The

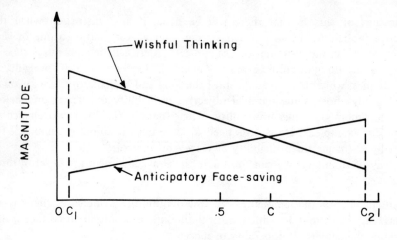

OBJECTIVE PROBABILITY OF SUCCESS

FIG. 5.2 Relative magnitudes and relations to the objective probability of success of wishful thinking and anticipatory face-saving. Wishful thinking dominant.

consequence of this, of course, is that for group data—assuming we could obtain independent measures of the two processes—we would expect wishful thinking to be represented by an inverted U-curve skewed to the high objective probabilities and anticipatory face-saving to be represented by an inverted U-curve skewed to the low objective probabilities.

Now, to determine the total magnitude and direction of distortion produced by the two processes whose individual magnitudes are depicted in Figure 5.2, we simply subtract the magnitude of anticipatory face-saving from the corresponding magnitude of wishful thinking for every possible value of objective probability. If we do this and plot the results against the objective probability of success, we obtain a diagram such as that depicted in Figure 5.3. In Figure 5.3, the points C_1, C, and C_2 correspond to the same points along the abscissa in Figure 5.2. It should again be pointed out that the solid line in Figure 5.3 depicts the distortion for one person for whom wishful thinking is the predominant process. Following the reasoning in the preceding paragraph, the curve for a group of people for each of whom wishful thinking predominates, but for whom the points C_1 and C_2 vary would be represented by a line similar to the dotted line in Figure 5.3.

One point to note about Figure 5.3 is that, for an individual for whom wishful thinking predominates, the point at which the distortion shifts from positive to negative is actually somewhat higher than .5. That is, for the entire range between points C_1 and C, such an individual actually distorts the objective probability of success upwards—he or she believes that it is somewhat greater than it really is. Between the points C and C_2, on the other hand, such an

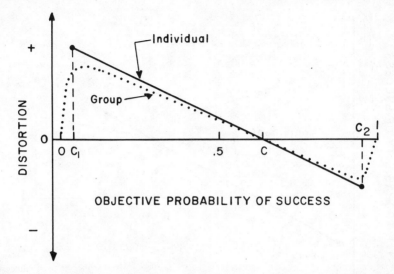

FIG. 5.3 Total magnitude and direction of distortion of the objective probability of success produced by wishful thinking and anticipatory face-saving for an individual and a group with wishful thinking predominant.

individual distorts the objective probability of success downward, that is, they convince themselves that it is somewhat lower than it really is.

Another way of looking at the relationships in Figure 5.3 is to plot the subjective probability of success versus the objective. This is done in Figure 5.4. The dashed line at a 45-degree angle in Figure 5.4 represents the relation between objective and subjective probabilities when there is no distortion. If this were the case, then for every value of the objective probability, the subjective probability would be precisely the same. The solid line in Figure 5.4 corresponds to the solid line in Figure 5.3 and represents the distortion for an individual for whom wishful thinking predominates. As can be seen, in the region between C_1 and C, the objective probability of success is overestimated and in the region between C and C_2, it is underestimated. The dotted line in Figure 5.4 corresponds to the dotted line in Figure 5.3 and represents the mean distortion for a group of people for each of whom wishful thinking is predominant.

We have been discussing the distortions of objective probability using the example of a person for whom wishful thinking is predominant. The only reason for selecting this particular example is because most of the research discussed in the preceeding section was conducted in a culture for which it seemed plausible to assume and, in fact, has been documented (cf., McClelland, 1961), that success and achievement are highly valued. Thus, the asymmetry of distortion which is depicted in Figure 5.4 is, for the most part, congruent with the empirical research described earlier. However, it should be clear that in other cultures or in some sub-populations within our culture in which achievement and

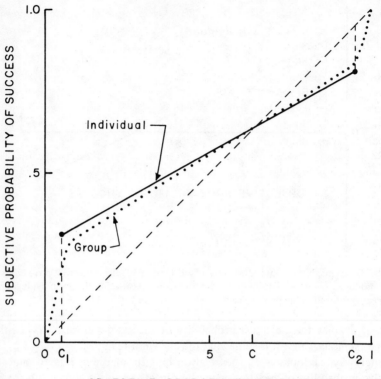

FIG. 5.4 Objective versus subjective probability of success for an individual and a group with wishful thinking predominant.

success are not dominant values, the likelihood that wishful thinking will predominate in any randomly selected group or individual might be very small. More generally the question is, what happens to the relationship in Figure 5.4 when wishful thinking is not dominant? How do individual differences in the relative dominance of wishful thinking and anticipatory face-saving influence the resulting distortion of the objective probability of success?

Individual Differences

The individual difference of interest is the relative predominance of the two processes discussed above. As with most individual differences, it should be obvious that there is an infinite number of possible gradations—from total dominance of wishful thinking coupled with complete absence of anticipatory face-saving to the reverse. With the help of a few additional assumptions, it would be possible to depict each of these gradations by a line similar to the solid line in Figure 5.4. This infinite set of lines, each representing an individual's distortion of the objective probability of success, would differ in slope, in vertical displacement, in the points at which they crossed the dashed line in Figure 5.4, and in the points at which the realities imposed by very high or very low objective probabilities eliminated distortion (C_1 and C_2 in the figure). However, we shall not do violence to any aspects of the model and it will be considerably more convenient to cast our discussion in terms of two types—one for whom wishful thinking predominates (as in Figure 5.4) and one for whom anticipatory face-saving is the stronger tendency.

We shall assume that the slopes of the functions relating anticipatory face-saving and wishful thinking to the objective probability of success are the same regardless of which function has the greater mean magnitude. Also, we shall continue to assume that there will be little distortion when the objective probability of success is very near zero or very near one. The only difference, then, from the development in the section on dichotomous processes is that we shall depict the distortions for an individual for whom anticipatory face-saving is of relatively greater magnitude than wishful thinking. Thus, corresponding to Figure 5.2 for someone for whom wishful thinking is stronger, we have Figure 5.5 for someone for whom anticipatory face-saving is dominant.

There are several points of comparison between Figures 5.2 (wishful thinking predominant) and 5.5 (anticipatory face-saving predominant). First, note that in both figures, points C_1 and C_2 correspond. It is true, of course, that the precise points on the objective probability continuum where C_1 and C_2 are located, that is, where the reality constraints imposed by very high and very low probabilities

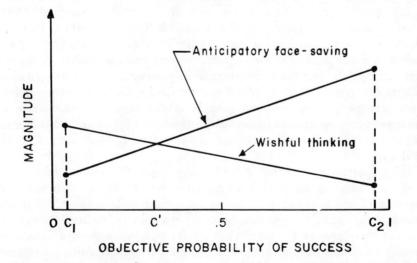

FIG. 5.5 Relative magnitudes and relations to the objective probability of success of wishful thinking and anticipatory face-saving. Anticipatory face-saving dominant.

would eliminate distortion, are expected to differ from person to person. However, there is no reason to expect such variation to affect the development here. Secondly, note that in Figure 5.2, the point C is somewhat higher than an objective probability of .5 while in Figure 5.5, the corresponding point C', is somewhat lower than an objective probability of .5.

Let us now follow precisely the same line of argument outlined in the dichotomous processes section. First, we subtract the magnitude of anticipatory face-saving from the corresponding magnitude of wishful thinking at every level of objective probability to obtain the magnitudes and directions of distortion produced by these two processes. Then, if we plot the (distorted) subjective probability of success versus the objective probability of success it can be shown that we obtain a relation such as that depicted by the solid line in Figure 5.6. As can be seen, in the region between C_1 and C', the objective probability of success is overestimated and, in the region between C' and C_2, the objective probability of success is underestimated. The dotted line in Figure 5.6 represents the relationship between objective and subjective probability of success for a group of people for whom anticipatory face-saving is predominant. Again, the only assumption necessary to obtain the group line from the individual is that points C_1 and C_2 would differ from person to person.

Of major interest here is the contrast between Figures 5.4 and 5.6. These two figures depict the hypothesized relationships between objective and subjective probabilities when either wishful thinking or anticipatory face-saving is dominant. In order to facilitate the comparison, Figure 5.7 was constructed, representing a composite of the essential features of both Figures 5.4 and 5.6. Note that the higher line in Figure 5.7 indicates both a greater overall subjective probability of success and a greater subjective probability of success at every level of objective probability for the individual for whom wishful thinking is more pronounced. Further, for such an individual there is a considerably greater region in which he or she overestimates the objective probability of success as compared to the individual for whom anticipatory face-saving is predominant (C_1 to C versus C_1 to C', respectively). Conversely, for one in whom anticipatory face-saving is pronounced, there is a large region in which he or she underestimates the objective probability of success (C' to C_2). The corresponding region of underestimation is much smaller for one in whom wishful thinking is stronger (C to C_2).

It is important to note that in the region between C' and C in the figure the difference between the two types represented is clearest. That is, in the region between C' and C, the person who is most concerned about saving face or being prepared for failure or protecting his or her ego is underestimating the objective probability of success. On the other hand, in the region between C' and C, the person for whom wishful thinking is dominant is overestimating the objective probability of success. In the regions from C_1 to C' and C to C_2 both types are overestimating and underestimating, respectively, and the differences in these regions are of some magnitude, but they do not differ in direction of distortion.

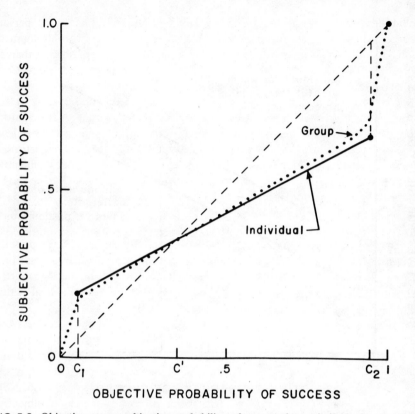

FIG. 5.6 Objective versus subjective probability of success for an individual and a group with anticipatory face-saving dominant.

In the next section, we shall argue that the subjective probability of success is a crucial determinant of the decision of how much effort one should expend on a task and, via this cognitive decision route, is the key to intra-personal self-fulfilling prophecies. At that point, we shall return to the differences in subjective probabilities between our two types. Before turning to the question of the relation between the perceived probability of success and action or of effort expenditure, it might be well to say a little more about related ideas. Specifically, it might help to focus the perspective here a little more sharply to contrast it with some notions developed by Atkinson (1957) and Feather (cf., Atkinson and Feather, 1966) within the framework of research on achievement motivation.

There are several similarities between the present model and Atkinson's (1957). For example, Atkinson (1958) assumes that ". . . the relative strength of a motive influences the subjective probability of the consequence consistent with that motive—biases it upwards. In other words, the stronger the achievement motive relative to the motive to avoid failure, the higher the subjective

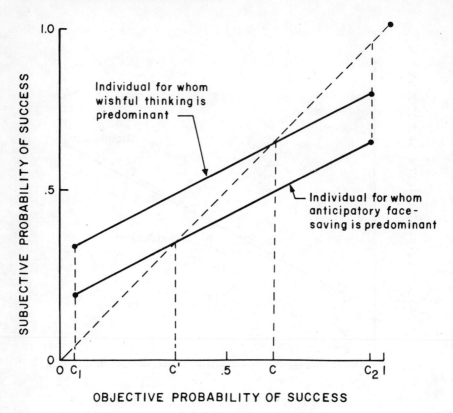

FIG. 5.7   Relationships between objective and subjective probabilities for two individuals.

probability of success given stated odds" (p. 333). Atkinson's focus, however, is on the motive to achieve and the motive to avoid failure. Whatever influence these motives have on the subjective probability of success is incidental and, in fact, appears to have been mentioned as an afterthought in his 1957 *Psychological Review* article in conjunction with the interpretation of some experimental results. It should be clear by now that the focus of the present model is somewhat different. We have explicitly addressed the determinants of the subjective probability of success, a problem largely ignored by Atkinson, McClelland, Feather, and other achievement—motivation theorists.

There is, of course, a similarity between the two cognitive processes at the core of the present model and the two antagonistic motives, to achieve success and to avoid failure, which have been the focus of most research on achievement—motivation. Yet, as a result of the differential focus on cognition versus motivation, the two models lead to quite different predictions. It follows from Atkinson's model that a person for whom the motive to avoid failure is predominant will avoid all tasks unless forced or constrained to perform. As we shall see, this is not the case for a person for whom anticipatory face-saving is relatively stronger than wishful thinking. Such a person may perceive his or her chances of success to be somewhat lower than a person for whom wishful thinking predominates, but for neither person does it follow that they will avoid all tasks.

Another important way in which Atkinson's formulation differs from that being developed here is a consequence of his assumption that the probability of success and the incentive value of success are negatively related, that is, as the probability of success increases, the incentive value of success decreases. He also assumes that the (anti-) incentive value of failure is a negative linear function of the probability of success. As Diggory (1966) points out, Atkinson ". . . quite consciously leaves no room for questions of fact on this issue. His theory asserts that if, for example, the incentive value (I) . . . of a goal has the hypothetical maximum value of 1.00, then the probability of success $P(s)$ for that goal is zero, and if $I = .90$, $P(s) = .10$; $I = .10$, $P(s) = .90$. Thus a perfect negative correlation between goal attractiveness and $P(s)$ is *built into* the theory" (p. 123). We, of course, have not assumed such a relationship between goal value and the probability of success. In fact, we have already attempted to document the idea that increasing the incentive value of a goal may increase rather than decrease the subjective probability of success.

An additional way in which Atkinson's model differs from the present one is, in part, a consequence of his assumptions about the relationship between incentive value and probability of success. For Atkinson (1958), the resultant tendency to approach success (T_a) is determined by the algebraic summation of approach and avoidance tendencies, thus:

$$T_a = (Ms \times Ps \times Is) + (Maf \times P_f \times -I_f).$$

In this equation Ms = Motive to Succeed, Ps = Probability of Success, Is = Incentive Value of Success or $(I - Ps)$, Maf = Motive to Avoid Failure, P_f = Probability of Failure, and I_f = Incentive Value of Failure of $(-Ps)$. It can be shown, using the formula and employing the assumptions made by Atkinson (that $Is = I - Ps$ and $I_f = -P_s$) that when constrained to perform, a person for whom the motive to avoid failure is stronger than the motive to succeed will be least inclined to approach tasks of intermediate difficulty because it is here that the value of $(Maf \times P_f \times -I_f)$ is most negative. That is, if given a choice between two tasks, one of which has to be performed, and the perceived probability of success on one task is .25 while on the second it is .50, the person in whom the motive to avoid failure is dominant will choose the former (.25). As we shall see in the next section, the current model makes the opposite prediction for everyone, even those for whom anticipatory face-saving is dominant. The word opposite may not be quite right, however, because the model being developed here applies to situations of free choice in which the individual believes he or she is free to select or reject any or all tasks. As we have already seen, in discussing people for whom the motive to avoid failure is dominant, Atkinson's model predicts they will reject all tasks unless forced to perform.

It also follows from the Atkinson formulation that a person in whom the motive to succeed is dominant will be most inclined to approach tasks of intermediate difficulty because it is here that $(Ms \times Ps \times Is)$ is a maximum. That is, if given a choice between two tasks one of which has a probability of success of .75 and one of which has a probability of success of .50, the person in whom the Motive to Succeed is dominant will choose the latter. As we shall see, given the same choice, the present model leads to the prediction that all people, including those in whom wishful thinking is dominant, will choose the former.

Thus, in spite of the not-so-accidental analogy between the dual cognitive processes postulated in the dichotomous processes section and the dual motives at the core of Atkinson's formulation, there are fundamental differences between the two models. It is true that over the last two decades there has been a series of attempted revisions of the basic Atkinson equation (cf., Weiner, 1965; Atkinson and Cartwright, 1964) and some clarifications of points not clear originally (cf., Feather, 1966). As a result, some new predictions have been generated, but none of these reformulations has questioned the key assumptions. Rather, they have simply attempted to add new components to the basic equation in an effort to make it fit the facts better.

For now, let us go back to the current model and pick up where we left off—we need to get from thought to action. We have seen that wishful thinking and anticipatory face-saving operate to distort the objective probability of success. Further, it was demonstrated that, regardless of which of these two processes is dominant, the distortion produced may be determined in essentially the same way—by subtracting the magnitude of anticipatory face-saving from the magnitude of wishful thinking for every value of objective probability—and we have seen that the relationship between objective and subjective probability retains essentially the same shape for both types. The result is an overestimate of low probabilities and an underestimate of high probabilities. The types differ primarily in the height of the curve relating objective to subjective probability as can be seen in Figure 5.7. As a result of this, however, the two differ in terms of where the crossover from over- to under-estimation occurs and in terms of the relative portion of the objective probability continuum which is over- or under-estimated.

Earlier it was pointed out that a basic idea to be developed here is that one's subjective probability of success is the key to intra-personal self-fulfilling prophecies. Thus, we need to see how the subjective probability of success might plausibly be related to goal-directed behavior and effort. Further, we need to see whether the sorts of individual differences we have been discussing might be expected to make a difference in behavior.

Effort and Goal-Seeking Behavior

In concluding their comprehensive review of the literature on human and animal motivation, Cofer and Appley (1964) argue for the rejection of the concept of drive. They point out that since the term was introduced by Woodworth in 1918, it has dominated thinking about human motivation even though the classical operational definition of drive, that is, deprivation, does not apply to most human motives and, in fact, is even of questionable relevance to hunger and thirst (cf., Cofer and Appley, 1964, pp. 818–821). In place of drive, Cofer and Appley argue for the incorporation of some form of learned anticipations into all thinking about motivation. Specifically, they propose for consideration what they refer to as the operation of an *anticipation–invigoration mechanism*, in which stimuli which have been associated with some consummatory behavior produce an anticipation which ". . . arouses or excites the organism, alerts it, enhances its responsiveness to the available stimuli. . . . Such stimuli, of course, may also play a role in guiding or directing the *behavior which ensues and which anticipation has aroused*, to one degree or another" (pp. 821–822, emphasis added). Thus, it follows that people will seek out good or valued outcomes and will similarly exert effort to avoid bad outcomes. What any given individual will consider good and what bad is unimportant as is the fact that what one considers good, another may consider bad and vice versa. Whether or not one believes that there is no accounting for taste, taste is unimportant here.

Implicit in the above discussion of Cofer's and Appley's anticipation–invigoration mechanism is an assumption which has been made explicit by Heider (1958) in his naive analysis of action. Heider calls attention to the fact that the perceived cause of a task outcome is an important determinant of one's performance on the task. If, for example, attaining a valued outcome is perceived to be a function of one's own effort and little else, then something like an anticipation–invigoration mechanism comes into play and effort is likely to be expended in pursuit of the goal. On the other hand, if the outcome is perceived to be largely a function of luck or chance, it is unlikely that effort will be expended in pursuit of the goal. Thus, a component of anticipation is the perception that one's own actions and effort will be efficacious. When this component is missing, there will be no invigoration.

As Heider puts it, the perception that one can (or cannot) influence the course of events is a function of the person's perception of his or her own power and/or ability to bring about the event in question. A part of this perception is what Heider refers to as the *environmental forces*. The environmental forces are a mixture of the difficulty of the task and the extent to which opportunity and luck play a part in the outcome. Heider defines the concept of can as a relationship between the person and the environment in which there is an ". . . absence of imposed restraining environmental forces" (p. 85) and cannot is the situation in which the imposed environmental restraining forces are perceived to be more important determinants of task outcome than one's own effort. In the latter situation, we assume that the person will not try as hard or will not try at all.

There is a very commonsense ring to the above. When one perceives that the task outcome will be due mainly to factors beyond one's control and irrelevant to one's effort or skill, there is little point in bringing a great deal of effort and/or expertise to bear on the task. It probably would not make much difference, at least as far as can be determined. On the other hand, things are seldom so clear-cut, at least, with important real-life tasks. The aspiring job applicant can never be quite sure whether her self-presentation, composure, and articulateness in the interview will make a difference. Perhaps they have already decided to whom to give the job and are just going through the motions of interviewing some female candidates to avoid charges of sex discrimination. Thus, even in tasks where one is sure that skill and effort do make a difference, there often remain elements of chance or of unpredictability. Usually these elements are not chance—in the sense of randomness—but are, nevertheless, unpredictable. We generally operate with rather imperfect knowledge. We simply cannot know everything we need to know to make absolutely certain predictions about succeeding at a task, even a task as simple as driving to the store.

It is interesting in this connection that Kukla's (1972) recent analysis of perceived task difficulty and its relationship to intended effort defines "Difficulty . . . only for skill situations in which probabilistic concepts are not applicable" (p. 458). The point here, of course, is that this is an artificial and unrealistic distinction. Probabilistic concepts are applicable to skill situations and most people appear to be aware of it. There are numerous aphorisms and bits of folk wisdom which express an understanding of this inseparability. Statements of intentions are often accompanied with disclaimers to the effect that one cannot foresee all contingencies: "The Lord willing" and "If the creek don't rise." Kukla does acknowledge that ". . . a more general concept, specifying the relationship between difficulty and effort when chance also influences outcome, is surely to be desired" (p. 458).

It should come as no surprise that our candidate for this more general concept is the subjective probability of success. Kukla, in fact, considers this as a possibility, but rejects it in the belief that the probability of success is a result of the decision about how much effort one is going to expend in pursuit of the goal. Formally, Kukla states that:

> For each action X, the subject constructs a function F_x which associates to each possible level of *effort* (E) a unique probability function P_{xe}; that is, $F_x(E) = P_{xe}(xi)$. $P_{xe}(x^i)$ is then the subjective probability of obtaining the outcome x^i to actions, X, given an effort of magnitude E (Kukla, 1972, p. 457).

In other words, the subjective probability of success is known only after one has decided how much effort he or she will expend on the task.

There is, no doubt, a certain amount of circularity between the assessment of subjective probability and the decision about how much effort to expend. However, it seems to fit better with everyday experience to think of the subjective probability of success as determining effort expenditure. It does not ring true to think of a person as saying, "I am going to expend E amount of effort. If I do, my subjective probability of success is . . ." Rather, it seems more plausible that people assess (roughly) their subjective probability of success and then decide whether or not the situation warrants doing whatever they can to help insure the desired outcome. Although Heider's (1958) comments on this question are open to various interpretations, it can be argued that implicit in his discussion and examples of the concepts of can and trying is the assumption that the assessment of can is primary (cf., pp. 82–89). Throughout his discussion are examples in which the assessment of can has apparently already been made and the question is simply whether or not one will put forth the effort necessary. As he says, ". . . the experience of 'I can' is a knowledge that one is able to reach a goal or to produce an effect if one only wills it" (p. 86). In the section on determinants of subjective probabilities, we reviewed a number of ways in which one might arrive at a rough estimate of his or her subjective probability of success on a task without explicitly considering the amount of effort that one intends to expend: by taking a quick check of one's past history of successes and failures on similar tasks, by comparing one's general ability level with those of others who have succeeded or failed on the task, and by seeking justification for effort already expended on the task.

Let us suppose, then, that the assessment of one's subjective probability of success is primary, that—contrary to Kukla's argument—it does precede and determine decision-making about task performance. Stotland (1969) sees this supposition as simply a restatement of the ancient truism that ". . . hopefulness is a necessary condition for action" (p. 7) and as not really being controversial at all. The important question, of course, is what follows from the perception that one has a certain probability of success. If differences in the perceived probability of success result in no behavioral differences of note, the subjective probability of success would be of little interest. How, then, does the subjective probability of success relate to performance?

Before proposing an answer to this question, it might be well to recall that we have set a couple of boundary conditions to our discussion. We are focussing only on valued (desired) goals and we are assuming a free-choice situation in which the person is not forced to perform but can freely choose to do so or not. Under these circumstances we hypothesize that there is a direct relationship between the subjective probability of success through effort and the probability that one will exert at least the minimum effort required for success. When the perceived probability of success is high, one is more likely to do whatever is required, even though the effort needed may be very great. On the other hand, when the perceived probability of success is very low, one is less likely to do enough, even though the effort required for success may be very small. We shall review evidence for this in Chapter 6.

The above hypothesis is very similar to Stotland's (1969) basic proposition that one's ". . . motivation to achieve a goal is, in part, a positive function of its perceived probability of attaining the goal" (p. 7) and follows rather directly from our earlier discussion of Cofer's and Appley's anticipation–invigoration mechanism. We have added something, however, in an attempt to side-step the issue focussed on by Kukla (1972), that is, the question of the intensity with which one pursues a chosen task. Specifically, by phrasing the hypothesis in terms of the probability that one will exert at least the minimum effort required for success, we avoid the complication of task difficulty. That is, two tasks for which one assesses his or her subjective probability of success to be approximately the same may differ in terms of the amounts of effort required. One may require several weeks of concentrated effort whereas the other may require nothing more than a few minutes of attentive concern or thought. As the hypothesis is phrased, however, we would predict that in both cases the likelihood of exerting whatever effort is required would be the same.

To go back for a moment to the two personality types depicted in Figure 5.7—one for whom wishful thinking predominates and one for whom anticipatory face-saving predominates—it can be seen that at any point on the objective probability continuum, the subjective probability is greater for the person with wishful thinking dominant. It follows from the above hypothesis that for every level of objective probability, the person for whom anticipatory face-saving is dominant will be less likely to exert the effort required for success. It is also important to note that the difference between the two personality types is most pronounced when the objective probability of success is around .5. In Figure 5.7 it can be seen that in the region around .5, the two types differ in the direction of distortion. That is, between C' and C in the figure, the person with wishful thinking dominant is overestimating the objective probability of success while the person for whom anticipatory face-saving is dominant is underestimating the objective probability of success. Yet it is this region around .5 which is the region of greatest uncertainty about task outcome—the region where we would expect effort to make the greatest difference in insuring success or lack of effort to be a major factor in failure. This is precisely the region in which a little effort would be likely to tip the balance toward success.

The general hypothesis, then, is that the subjective probability of success is the key to intra-personal self-fulfilling prophecies. As the subjective probability of success increases, the likelihood that one will exert whatever effort is required for success also increases. Our task in Chapter 6 will be to explore evidence which bears on this hypothesis. Unfortunately, in studies which have examined the determinants of performance, relatively few investigators have treated the subjective probability of success per se as an independent variable, and even fewer have actually measured subjective probabilities. Thus, in order to look at what effect the subjective probability of success has on performance, we shall have to make use of some indirect evidence, evidence from studies which have manipulated and/or measured other variables. Consequently, a word is in order about how some of these other variables relate to subjective probability.

A Rose by Any Other Name . . .

One of the variables that has frequently been utilized in studies of human performance is anxiety. In fact, anxiety has been utilized as a variable or explanatory construct in studies of almost everything. Lazarus and Averill (1972), in commenting on this state of affairs, point out that ". . . one is struck by the tendency to make anxiety the central mediating construct in virtually every form of behavior, pathological or normal, human or animal" (p. 245). There are at least two consequences of this: (1) the literature on anxiety is huge; and (2) several authors have recommended abandoning the concept because it has been used in so many different ways (cf., Rotter, 1954; Sarbin, 1968). Fortunately for us, there is no need to review the anxiety literature. It will suffice for our purposes to point out the similarity between two components of anxiety as a concept and one's subjective probability of success. In spite of the diverse usage of the concept which has led some to recommend its abandonment, there appears to be a core of meaning which we can extract. There appears to be widespread agreement that there are both anticipatory and uncertainty components to anxiety. Regardless of the theoretical orientations of those who have used the concept, anxiety is usually seen as centering around the belief that something is or is not going to happen—something about which the person does not know quite what to do or even what it is.

Given these two aspects of anxiety, it seems reasonable to suppose that, in situations requiring effort expenditure and/or skilled performance for goal attainment, anxiety and one's subjective probability of success will be related, but not linearly. When anxiety is high, it may be possible to use this information to infer that the subjective probability of success is intermediate, that is, there is maximum uncertainty. On the other hand, when anxiety is low, this may mean that the subjective probability of success is either very high or very low. In either case, uncertainty is relatively low. With this relationship in mind, we may be able to extract, from studies of the relationship of anxiety to performance, evidence pertinent to our hypothesis that the subjective probability of success is the key to performance.

Another potential source of data bearing on the hypothesis is the growing body of literature on helplessness. Mandler (1972) refers to helplessness as a state of arousal which results when one perceives there are no task- or situation-relevant behaviors available. Further, he points out that "Helplessness is . . . an immediate reaction to the situation and is somewhat stimulus-bound. The person does not know what to do in this particular situation. However, one can assume that if this builds up over a variety of situations one might get to a generalized feeling of not knowing what to do in any situation, which, of course, is parallel to the notion of hopelessness" (p. 371). Although Mandler never discusses his ideas specifically in terms of the subjective probability of success, it seems clear that his arguments could be rephrased in terms of perceived probabilities. He is, of course, focussing on only that end of the continuum where the subjective probability of success is very low and where we would expect the person to be least likely to attempt whatever was required.

Thus, in addition to studies directly addressing the question of the influence of subjective probabilities of success on performance there are at least two other areas of research which may offer some pertinent data-research on anxiety and on helplessness. In the preceding section, we mentioned a third additional area. It was pointed out that some evidence exists that people who differ in the relative strength of the need for achievement and the motive to avoid failure also differ in their perceived probability of success, given stated objective probabilities. That is, people who have a strong motive to succeed tend to see their subjective probability of success as somewhat higher, given the same circumstances, than do people who are less oriented toward achievement. Thus, strength of the motive to achieve may serve as an indirect index of the perceived probability of success.

Another individual difference variable which may be related to differences in the subjective probability of success is Rotter's (1966) distinction between the belief in external versus internal locus of control. Rotter's position is that in the course of events people develop different generalized and generalizable expectancies about the extent to which they will be able to control the reinforcements they receive. Due to their particular reinforcement history, some people develop a belief in internal control, that is, they perceive that events affecting them are generally contingent upon their own behavior. Others develop a belief in external control, that is, they perceive that events affecting them are generally a result of luck, chance, fate, the behavior of others, and are not usually a result of their own behavior. As Rotter (1966) points out, "These generalized expectancies will result in characteristic differences in behavior in a situation culturally categorized as chance determined versus skill determined, and they may act to produce individual differences within a specific condition" (p. 2). In a situation in which one's effort and/or ability can be seen as at least a partial determinant of success, it seems reasonable to assume that people who have a strong generalized belief in internal control will have a higher subjective probability of success and, by our hypothesis, will be more likely to succeed.

There are several other variables which could plausibly be assumed to relate systematically to differences in subjective probability of success—things such as self-esteem (Rosenberg, 1965), ego-strength (Barron, 1953), and, possibly, even field dependence versus field independence (Witkin, Dyk, Faterson, Goodenough, and Karp, 1962). Since there have been only a handful of studies which have examined the relationships of these and other such variables to performance, we shall not take the time to define them all here. The only reason for mentioning them is to indicate some other areas of research that might conceivably bear on our hypotheses about subjective probabilities and effort to achieve a goal.

With this brief digression to call attention to some of the aliases under which the subjective probability of success has appeared, let us see what evidence there is that the subjective probability of success makes a difference in performance. This is what we take up in Chapter 6.

Summary

In this section, an attempt was made to develop several hypotheses about the relationships between objective probabilities of success, subjective probabilities, and the likelihood that one will expend whatever effort or exercise whatever skill necessary to insure success. Beginning with two antagonistic cognitive processes which vary in relative dominance from person to person, it was postulated that these two processes combine to distort the objective probability of success. The general result is an overestimation of low objective probabilities and an underestimation of high objective probabilities. Individual differences in the relative dominance of these two processes were shown to affect the proportion of the objective probability continuum which is over- or underestimated. The greater the relative dominance of wishful thinking, the greater the proportion of the objective probability continuum which is overestimated. The greater the relative dominance of anticipatory face-saving, the greater the proportion of the objective probability continuum which is underestimated.

Although an attempt was made to point out the similarities between the present model and earlier theoretical statements, it was also pointed out that the model differs in several fundamental respects from the most closely related theory, Atkinson's (1957) model of risk-taking behavior. This led to a discussion of how the subjective probability of success might plausibly be related to effort, and it was hypothesized that as the subjective probability of success increases, the likelihood that one will do whatever is necessary to insure success also increases. Now we shall see how this hypothesis fares.

6
Performance

It appears to be widely believed that most people never realize their full potential. There are many reasons for the persistence and pervasiveness of such a belief. It is, for example, a comfort to think that one could have been a concert pianist or a Nobel Laureate or whatever, if one had simply practiced more or studied harder. It is also possible that the dominance of behaviorism in American Psychology during the early part of this century has had an influence on the acceptance of the belief. Generations of college students were, and still are, exposed to the writings of Watson, Skinner, and their latter-day disciples. The behaviorist position is clear and appealingly simple. With the proper scheduling of rewards one can even be (or create) a concert pianist who is also a Nobel Laureate.

On a more mundane level, it does seem to be the case that goals which people both desire and have the ability to achieve often go aglimmering. On the other hand, people who appear to have no more or even less ability, often achieve those very goals. How can such an irrational state of affairs be accounted for? Surely—hopefully—it's not all a matter of chance. The implications of that possibility are too terrifying to consider and, besides, we all know that it's not just luck. What, then, are some of the variables which affect the pursuit of goals, which influence the quality and persistence of performance?

KEY VARIABLES DETERMINING PERFORMANCE

It will be recalled that, in Chapter 1, a self-fulfilling prophecy was defined as an expectation that leads to its own fulfillment. There appears to be no reason to apply this definition only to expectations of negative events or to events with punitive consequences. However, a recent review by Archibald (1974) considers a number of existing explanations for intrapersonal self-fulfilling prophecies and focuses exclusively on the anticipation of negative events. In the sections that follow, we shall have occasion to examine some of the same evidence that Archibald reviews, but we shall not be limited to research on anticipation of negative events. Utilizing the ideas developed in the preceding chapter, we shall see how one's subjective probability of success relates to performance. Whether the goal of performance is avoiding negative events or embracing positive ones is immaterial. Let us begin by looking at how one's history of success and failure at a task influences performance.

Prior Success and Failure

In Chapter 5, it was hypothesized that the subjective probability of success is the key to performance. Specifically, the hypothesis is that the greater one's subjective probability of success, the greater the likelihood that one will do whatever is required to achieve success. As we also saw in the last chapter, prior successes at the same or similar tasks do, indeed, increase one's subjective probability of success and, conversely, prior failures lower one's subjective probability of success. The question now is whether or not these variations in the subjective probability of success actually affect subsequent performance.

Feather (1966) obtained some evidence pertinent to this question in a study mentioned briefly in the section on the determinants of subjective probability. Female undergraduates were asked to attempt a series of 15 anagrams and, prior to performing each, they were asked to estimate their chances of solving that anagram correctly. For half of the subjects, the first 5 anagrams were very easy, while for the remaining subjects, the first 5 were insoluble. For all subjects, the last 10 anagrams were the same and had been selected so that the subjects had approximately a 50 percent chance of solving each. As anticipated, subjects who were initially confronted with 5 easy anagrams increased their estimates of the probability of success for each succeeding anagram, while subjects initially confronted with 5 insoluble anagrams decreased their estimates. The former subjects increased their estimates from .57 (prior to the first anagram) to .76 (prior to the sixth), while the latter subjects decreased their estimates from .61 (prior to the first) to .19 (prior to the sixth). On trials 6 through 15, which involved the same ten anagrams for all subjects, the group that began the 6th trial with a higher mean subjective probability of success (.76) performed significantly better than the group that began with a lower mean subjective probability of success. These data, then, appear to support the hypothesis relating subjective probability to performance.

Given that the last 10 anagrams in the above study were the same for all subjects and that these anagrams had been selected to be at about the 50 percent difficulty level, we would expect that the estimates of success of subjects who had initially encountered 5 very easy anagrams would decline after trial 6 as they began to encounter an occasional anagram they could not solve. On the other hand, the estimates of subjects who had initially encountered 5 insoluble anagrams should rise after trial 6 as they began to encounter some anagrams that they could solve. This is precisely what occurred. Further, some evidence from a study by Feather and Saville (1967) indicates that such fluctuations in one's subjective probability of success are followed by fluctuations in performance.

In the Feather and Saville study, male and female college students were each asked to attempt a series of 13 anagrams. As in the previous experiment by Feather, the last 10 anagrams were the same for all subjects and were of approximately 50 percent difficulty. The first 3 anagrams seen by a given subject were some combination of very easy and impossible. Eight combinations are possible, and all 8 were employed with different subjects: Easy, Easy, Easy—Easy, Easy, Impossible—____—____—Impossible, Impossible, Impossible. Again, initial experience on the first 3 anagrams had a significant effect on probability of success estimates. Subjects who had experienced uniform success on the first 3 estimated their probability of success on the fourth as significantly higher than did subjects who had experienced uniform failure on the first 3. Again we would expect probability estimates to decrease for the initial uniform success group as they began the 50 percent difficulty items (trials 4–13) and to increase for the initial uniform failure group as they began these same items. Of interest here is the finding that subjects who had experienced uniform success initially obtained higher scores on trials 4–8 than on 9–13, whereas subjects who had experienced uniform failure initially obtained lower scores on trials 4–8 than on 9–13. Thus, increases in subjective probability of success are followed by better performance and decreases in the subjective probability of success are followed by poorer performance.

The studies by Feather and Feather and Saville do not, of course, establish or document the mechanism by which a higher subjective probability of success leads to improved performance. It would, in fact, be rather surprising if there were only one mechanism or process involved. It is possible that a number of different things are responsible for the improvement in performance that follows an increase in subjective probability of success. For example, subjects who experienced predominant success on the first few anagrams may have become more interested in the task, paid closer attention, worked faster, developed work methods or habits which helped insure subsequent success, or any combination of these. On the other hand, subjects who had experienced predominant failure on the first few anagrams may have lost interest, become anxious and distractible, or convinced themselves that the task was a silly one on which it was not worth trying. We shall return to some of these possibilities in the following sections. For now, let us take a closer look at this notion of prior success and failure.

It may be useful, for analytic purposes, to think of one's subjective probability of success as comprised of two components. That is, one's subjective probability of success can be conceived of as a sum of a general subjective probability which has been arrived at from experience with related tasks and as a specific subjective probability having to do with the task at hand. There is nothing particularly new about this idea. It has been stated explicitly by Rotter (1954) in terms of general and specific expectancies and is central to much of the work on achievement motivation. The achievement motive and the motive to avoid failure are considered to be relatively stable dispositions to approach success and avoid failure, respectively, which interact with experience in particular situations to determine performance. As we saw in Chapter 5, a person with a strong motive to achieve is likely to have a higher subjective probability of success, given stated odds, than a person for whom the motive to avoid failure is dominant.

Taking this point of view, then, that one's subjective probability of success has a general and a specific component, leads immediately to the implication that in sequential performances or attempts at a task, the two components should be most influential at different stages of performance. That is, initially, one's generalized subjective probability of success should be most influential in determining the level of performance but, as one gains experience on the task at hand, the subjective probability specific to the task becomes increasingly influential. Feather (1965) presents some tentative evidence for this line of reasoning. Subjects' initial estimates of their probability of success on an anagrams task were found to be correlated with the strength of their motive to achieve success. The stronger the motive to succeed, the higher the initial probability estimates when the task was perceived to be of moderate difficulty. When the task was described as easy, there was no relationship between need for achievement and initial probability estimates. Feather also found a significant positive correlation between need for achievement and performance scores in the moderate difficulty condition, but not in the easy condition. Both of these findings are consistent with the argument above, if we assume that need for achievement is an indirect index of one's general subjective probability of success. Also, in the same study, Feather obtained estimates of what each subject's subjective probability of success had been at the midpoint and just prior to the end of the work period. Neither of these probability estimates were related to the strength of the subject's need for achievement (or to their scores on a measure of anxiety). However, both the middle and terminal probability estimates were significantly related to performance. The higher the probability estimates, the higher the level of performance.

Unfortunately for us, the latter finding is ambiguous. Feather obtained the middle and terminal probability estimates in a post-performance questionnaire. The estimates were—or very likely could have been—influenced by each subject's knowledge of how he or she had actually performed. Thus, there is some evidence for the notion that people approach skill and effort dependent tasks with an internalized notion of their ability and of their probable chances of success on such tasks. Further, these dispositional estimates do relate to performance—the higher the initial estimates, the better the initial performance. With increasing experience on the specific task, it should be the case that the influence of these generalized expectancies for success fade and performance should be more closely related to subjective probabilities established through past experience on the task at hand. It is the evidence for the latter that seems weakest at this point.

There is further pertinent evidence in a couple of studies which were addressed to the effects of belief in internal versus external control of reinforcement on performance. To examine the latter studies, we need to make use of a point made in the last chapter. There it was mentioned that in a situation in which one's effort and/or ability can be seen as at least a partial determinant of success, it seems reasonable to assume that people who have a strong generalized belief in internal control (Rotter, 1966) will have a higher initial subjective probability of success.

The two pertinent studies are by Feather (1968) and Ryckman, Gold, and Rodda (1971). In both studies, subjects who had been selected on the basis of responses to the I–E scale as either internals or externals were asked to attempt 15 anagrams and were given 30 seconds per anagram. In both studies, the first 5 anagrams were either very easy or impossible and the last 10 were at the 50 percent difficulty level. Further, in both studies, subjects were asked to estimate their probability of success on each anagram immediately prior to attempting that anagram. Results from both experiments indicate that subjects who have a strong belief in internal control of reinforcement estimate their chances of success initially, that is, on the first trial, to be somewhat higher than subjects who have a stronger belief in external control of reinforcement.[1] Further, subjects for whom the first 5 anagrams were easy increase their estimated probabilities of success on subsequent trials and perform significantly better on subsequent trials than subjects for whom the first 5 anagrams were impossible. However, analyses of variance in both studies reveal that belief in internal versus external control of reinforcement was not significantly related to performance on the last 10 anagrams. Thus, there is some additional evidence that the general component of one's subjective probability of success is directly related to initial performance on an unfamiliar task, but not to later performance on the same task. Later performance on the task appears to be determined, at least in part, by the specific subjective probabilities developed by one's experiences of success and failure on the task itself.

We have seen that there appear to be both dispositional and situational components to one's subjective probability of success and that these two

---

[1] Unfortunately, Feather's male external subjects were not really believers in external control of reinforcement. They scored very close to the midpoint of the I–E scale (see Feather, 1968, p. 39). Hence the statement here applies only to his female subjects.

components appear to be differentially influential on performance at different stages of a task. The specific determinant of the situational component that we have been discussing is one's history of success and failure on the task. It should be clear that there are other aspects of situations, and we need to see whether these other aspects also influence performance and if such influences might plausibly be mediated by changes in the situational component of one's subjective probability of success.

Feedback

Conceptually, feedback is very similar to prior success and failure, and on tasks for which there are clear performance criteria which one can see for oneself, it is impossible to separate the two. Yet there are many tasks on which such clear standards of success and failure are not immediately obvious and on which it is possible to examine the effects of feedback independently of actual performance.

To take an extreme example, Kobler and Stotland (1964) have argued that suicide can sometimes be viewed as the result of implicit and explicit communications from others that one's situation is hopeless, that there is nothing that can be done. They point out that studies of suicide "... suggest that when the response to attempted suicide was positive and active, only a small percentage (2 or 3 percent) subsequently committed suicide. Conversely, there are strong indications that actual suicide follows upon a helpless, fearful response to communication of suicide intent" (p. 10). They buttress their argument with an in-depth study of a small, private psychiatric hospital in which there had been an epidemic of suicides in a period of six months, although suicide had been very rare among patients in this hospital in previous years. The interview and case history data indicate that each of the patients who did commit suicide had made prior suicidal gestures and that the prior gestures had been met with indications from the hospital staff that they did not know what to do to prevent suicides. For a number of reasons, the hospital staff's self-confidence in their ability to help patients establish new goals and purposes in life had so deteriorated that suicide attempts were met with despair and the expectation that actual suicides would follow, which they did.

There are many ambiguities of interpretation in a study such as that by Kobler and Stotland. We have no way of knowing, to take just one example, whether or not the patients resident in the hospital when the epidemic of suicide occurred generally had valid reasons for believing that their situations were, indeed, more hopeless than the patients of previous years. In spite of this and other ambiguities, the Kobler and Stotland argument has a certain plausibility to it. In Chapter 4, we reviewed a number of studies which indicated myriad ways in which the hospital staff might have communicated their expectations and fears even while trying not to. Further, if the patients perceived these inadvertent communications to mean that they were suicide types, whatever that may be, then it is not surprising that suicide was the eventual outcome.

A recent attributional analysis of achievement behavior by Weiner, Heckhausen, Meyer, and Cook (1972) is relevant here. Following Heider, Weiner et al. point out that one may distribute the causes of success and failure on a task to four elements: ability, effort, task difficulty, and luck. Further, they argue that these four elements may be conceptualized as varying along two attributional dimensions which they term *stability* and *locus of control* in the manner depicted in Table 6.1. Thus, one is assumed to attribute the causes of success and/or failure on a task to either fixed or variable factors which may be internal or external to oneself. How one distributes or allocates responsibility for success or failure among these four factors is further hypothesized to be an important determinant of subsequent performance. Thus, if one is led to believe that one has failed and that the failure was primarily due to a lack of ability, one's expectation of future success on the same task is likely to be lower than if one is led to believe that the failure was due to lack of effort. Or to go back to our example of someone who has made a suicide attempt, if those around them could convince them that their despair and self-perceived failure at life are not the result of an inability to cope or of the difficulty of living a useful and interesting life, then the prognosis would appear much brighter. On the other hand, if someone who has made a suicide attempt perceives that others believe he or she is indeed unable to cope or that living a useful and interesting life may be beyond their grasp, the prognosis would appear very poor.

Weiner et al. argue that, when making attributions for the causes of one's success or failure, internal attributions (to ability or effort) serve to magnify emotional or affective responses to the outcome in comparison to external attributions (task difficulty or luck). Thus, success is particularly pleasant and failure particularly unpleasant if they are believed to be due to one's level of ability or to the amount of effort one expended. Successes and failures that are believed to be due to the difficulty of the task or to luck have less emotional

TABLE 6.1
Attributions of Stability and Locus of Control[a]

		Attributions of locus of control	
		Internal	External
Attributions of stability	Fixed	Ability	Task difficulty
	Variable	Effort	Luck

[a]From Weiner et al., 1972. (Copyright 1972 by the American Psychological Association. Reprinted by permission.)

impact. Again, the example of one who has attempted suicide is pertinent. If they perceive their situation to be dismal primarily because of their own lack of ability or effort, their despair may be particularly bleak. More directly relevant to our purposes here, however, is the argument by Weiner et al. that changes in one's expectations of future success and failure are primarily influenced by allocations of the causes for past success and failure along the stability dimension. As they put it:

> ... failure ascribed to low ability or a hard task (stable factors) should produce greater decrements in the subsequent expectancy of success than attributions of failure to a lack of effort or bad luck (variable factors). This is intelligible because effort subsequently can be increased, just as luck may improve. ... On the other hand, attributions of failure to low ability or a hard task ... are likely to produce similar decrements in the expectancy of goal attainment, for both ability and task difficulty are perceived as remaining relatively constant over time (p. 240).

Thus, we need to be more precise in our discussion of the effects of feedback on performance. One cannot naively assume that success will always lead to an increase in the probability of future success and failure will always lead to a decrease. Unfortunately, there has been a fair amount of research that was predicated on just this assumption (cf., Moulton, 1965). Success that one attributes to luck may actually lead to a decrease in the subjective probability of future success or, conversely, failure that one attributes to luck may actually lead to an increase. The hypotheses developed in Chapter 5 are, then, consistent with the position taken by Weiner et al. (1972). Specifically, success-failure feedback influences performance via changes in the subjective probability of success. Success or failure feedback which leads to an increase in the probability of future success will lead to an improvement in performance.

Some evidence on the above comes from the second experiment reported in Weiner et al. (1972) in which 39 German male high school students were given 5 trials of a digit—symbol substitution task. On each trial, subjects were interrupted after they had completed various portions of the task, but before they were able to finish. Hence, failure was induced on each trial, and, following each trial, subjects were asked to what extent their failure was due to lack of effort, lack of ability, luck, or the difficulty of the task. They were also asked to indicate their perceived probability of success on the next trial. As anticipated, the more the subjects attribute their failure to lack of ability and task difficulty (stable factors), the greater the decrease in the probability of success for the next trial. Further, the more they attribute failure to lack of ability and task difficulty, the more slowly they actually perform[2] on subsequent trials. On the other hand, subjects who attribute their failure predominantly to luck or lack of effort subsequently indicate higher subjective probabilities of success and perform more quickly on later trials. Weiner et al. (1972) conclude that "... per-

---

[2] This relationship was significant only for task difficulty and performance.

haps any causal ascription for failure which maintains 'hope' will have a facilitating effect, or at least not result in performance decrements" (p. 246). This, of course, is precisely what we would predict. As long as one's subjective probability of success is maintained, performance will be maintained.

Most studies have not looked at the attributions subjects make about the causes of success and failure in as much detail as Weiner et al., but there have been several additional studies which have examined the relationship between expectancy changes following success-failure feedback and subsequent performance. Steiner (1957), for example, found that subjects with positive self appraisals tended to avoid internal attributions to explain their poor performance on a word-formation task. In a better controlled study, Zajonc and Brickman (1969) employed a reaction time task, in which subjects were to throw a switch as quickly as possible following the onset of a stimulus light. After several blocks of trials on this task, feedback was introduced independently of performance. One-third of the subjects were each led to believe they were achieving the reaction time required for success on only 20 percent of the trials; one-third were each told they were achieving 80 percent successes; and one-third continued with no feedback. In general, subjects tended to raise their expectations for subsequent performance after success and to lower them after failure. However, those subjects who received failure feedback and who ". . . resisted lowering their expectancies, or lowered them relatively less, subsequently improved, while those who lowered them more did not improve" (p. 153). This, of course, is consistent with the position being developed here. It should also follow that subjects receiving success feedback, who raised their expectations the most, improved the most in later performance, but under success feedback there was essentially no relation between expectancy change and later performance. Zajonc and Brickman speculate that the latter finding may be due to a ceiling effect on performance among subjects who had high expectations initially.

Thus, it again appears that, relatively speaking, increases in one's subjective probability of success lead to increments in performance, while decreases lead to decrements in performance. One of the genuine difficulties in this line of research is indicated by the qualification in the foregoing sentence. Specifically, how do we know what feedback really means to a given subject. As Zajonc and Brickman point out, ". . . many of the low expectancy subjects expected to win 4 times out of 10. It is possible that 4 successes out of 10 was perceived by such subjects as equally challenging and equally rewarding to achieve as the 8 wins out of 10 expected by other subjects" (p. 154). Another way of saying this is that in order to know what feedback on a given task means to a subject, we have to know what that subject's goal is, what he or she is trying to achieve. Along this line, Locke (1967) points out that feedback or knowledge of results is generally believed to have two functions, informational (how one has done) and motivational (goal setting), and that previous research has generally confounded the two. That is, often no attempt is made to determine if different goals are set by groups given knowledge of results and groups not given such information.

In an attempt to test the hypothesis that the setting of different performance goals was actually responsible for increments in performance previously attributed to the informational component of knowledge of results, Locke (1967) designed a simple experiment in which male and female subjects were asked to work a number of math problems. Each problem consisted of three two-digit numbers to be added and was presented on a separate three- by five-inch card. Subjects worked for an hour during which there were five trial blocks. Half of the subjects received feedback (knowledge of results) at the end of each block of trials, and half did not. In addition, half of each of these two groups were instructed to, "Do your best", and half were given a specific number of problems[3] to try to work on each trial (hard goal). Subjects assigned to the four groups had been matched in arithmetic ability on the basis of a pretest. The results indicate that both the knowledge of results–hard goal and no knowledge of results–hard-goal groups do progressively better over trials than the two do-your-best groups. Further, within the do-your-best and hard-goal groups, feedback makes no difference. Locke (1967) concludes that the results ". . . support the hypothesis that motivational effects previously attributed to differential [knowledge of results] were actually a function of differential performance goals associated with the [knowledge of results] conditions" (p. 327).

Before we take a closer look at how performance goals influence performance, it might be well to briefly summarize the material covered so far. We began this chapter by examining some research on the effects of prior success and failure on subsequent performance. We found that prior success tends to increase one's subjective probability of success and that such increases are followed by improved performance. On the other hand, prior failure appears to lower one's subjective probability of success and such decreases are followed by poorer performance. Further, fluctuations in one's probability of success are followed by fluctuations in performance. We then made the point that one's subjective probability of success on a given task appears to have two components: (1) a general or dispositional component; and (2) a situational component. The general component appears to be most influential in determining initial performance on a task and, as one gains experience on the task, this influence fades and the situational component as determined by one's experience on the task at hand becomes a better predictor of performance. In an attempt to become more precise about the determinants of the situational component of one's subjective probability of success, we then turned to an attributional analysis of feedback.

---

[3] On Trial Block 1, a given subject in this condition was assigned a goal about 10 percent higher than that achieved by a matched subject in the do-best condition. On succeeding trials, goals for hard-goal subjects averaged 11 percent higher than the matched do-best subjects.

We have seen that one cannot assume that success feedback will necessarily lead to an increase in one's subjective probability of success on a task and, conversely, failure feedback will not necessarily lead to a decrease. The important variable is the perceived reason for one's past success or failure. Somewhat paradoxically, failure may lead to an increase in one's subjective probability of success and improved performance, if the failure is attributed to luck or lack of effort. Turning to a closely related issue, we saw that feedback may not always mean what it is intended to mean, that is, it is necessary to know what particular goal, subgoal, or level of performance a person is striving to attain in order to know how a given instance of feedback will be interpreted. Thus, we need to look at how goals and incentives influence performance.

Incentives and Goals

It follows from the hypotheses in Chapter 5 that as the probability of attaining a valued goal increases, the probability that one will do whatever is called for to reach that goal also increases. It is a truism, of course, that different people value different things and even in relatively well-controlled laboratory experiments, different subjects may be pursuing different goals. Some may do what the experimenter requests because they are intellectually curious about research; some may only want the money; some may want approval from the (usually) higher-status experimenter; and some may simply want to master whatever task is set for them. By our hypotheses, then, in order for feedback to enhance performance, it must increase the subjective probability that whichever of these goals the subject is really pursuing is likely to be achieved.

In line with this reasoning, French (1958) hypothesized that people who are achievement-oriented will improve in performance of a group task when given positive feedback about their apparent efficiency and mastery of the task. Conversely, she hypothesized that people who are less achievement-oriented, but more concerned with affiliation and social relations, would improve more in performance of the same task when given positive feedback about their apparent ability to work well together. To test these hypotheses 256 Air Force trainees were selected from a larger group of potential subjects who had been tested for the strength of their achievement and affiliation motivations. Half of the subjects were high in achievement motivation and low in affiliation motivation, and half were high in affiliation motivation and low in achievement motivation. Subjects were assigned to motivationally homogeneous 4-person groups and were assigned a story construction problem. That is, for 3 10-minute work periods they were to attempt to construct a story out of 20 phrases or short sentences which had been written on cards and distributed among the group members, 5 to each member. Group members were not allowed to show their cards to others, and the entire task had to be done by conversation.

The variable of interest here was termed *task* versus *feeling feedback* and was manipulated during a break between work periods. For half of the groups the experimenter said, "This group is working very efficiently," and mentioned five specific task-related behaviors that had been observed (task feedback). For the remaining groups the experimenter said, "This group works very well together," and mentioned five specific behaviors of a social nature (feeling feedback). The argument here, of course, is that for achievement-oriented groups the task feedback is more likely to increase the subjective probability of attaining the goal of interest to them and, thus, facilitate performance, whereas for the affiliation-oriented groups the feeling feedback is more likely to have this effect. The results indicate that this is precisely what occurred. In terms of the number of points obtained on the problem solution, task feedback was more effective with the achievement-oriented groups and feeling feedback resulted in better performances by the affiliation-oriented groups.

There is an interesting methodological sidelight to the above experiment. Initially, the experimenter was unaware of the motivational composition of any given group. This was done, of course, in an attempt to forestall any possible experimenter bias. However, French reports that it "soon became apparent" (p. 407) that there were systematic differences among the groups. The affiliation groups were much quieter whereas violent arguments—and one actual fight— erupted in the achievement-oriented groups. Although initially unaware of the composition of a group at the beginning of each experimental session, French correctly guessed the motivational orientation of 78 percent of the groups. Hence, it is quite possible that some bias did creep into the manner in which the feedback was given.

Konstadt and Forman (1965) report an experiment that was conceptually very similar to French's. Focusing on the distinction of Witkin et al. (1962) between field dependence and field independence, Konstadt and Forman point out that a salient characteristic of field-dependent individuals is their relatively non-analytic, global approach to problems. That is, in comparison to field-independent individuals, the field-dependent appears to be unable to separate a problem from its context. It follows that, when attempting to perform in the presence of others, particularly in the presence of authority figures, a field-dependent person should be overly attuned to signs of approval and disapproval from those others. Another way of saying this is that the field-dependent individual is more likely to view approval or disapproval from others as pertinent positive or negative feedback about their performance, since for such people the performance problem is less likely to be separated from the human environment. Hence, for the field-dependent person, approval or disapproval is more likely to increase or decrease the subjective probability of goal attainment and result in improved or diminished performance than for the field-independent individual. The more analytical field independent is more likely to separate the performance problem from the irrelevant human context, and his or her performance is correspondingly less likely to be affected by signs of approval and disapproval.

Based on responses to an Embedded Figures Test, Konstadt and Forman (1965) identified 19 fourth graders as field independent and 19 as field dependent and asked these 38 subjects to perform a letter cancellation task. For the letter cancellation task, subjects were tested in small groups containing both field-dependent and field-independent subjects, and each group was tested twice—once with an approving examiner and once with a disapproving examiner. Approval and disapproval conditions of testing were defined by comments made by the examiner at frequent, specified intervals during the test sessions. As anticipated, the performance of field-dependent subjects deteriorated significantly more than that of field-independent subjects when the examiner expressed disapproval.

There are, of course, numerous circumstances where it is fairly safe to assume that everyone involved will have the same goal. In such situations, anything that can be reasonably assumed to increase the perceived probability of goal attainment should facilitate performance. As an example, in a study by Johnson and Foley (1969), male and female undergraduates were all assigned the same task. They were divided up into same-sex pairs, and all pairs were to discuss a set of 10 questions concerning a chapter in their textbook. Following the discussions, knowledge of the material in the chapter was assessed with a 30-item, multiple-choice questionnaire. The only difference among the various pairs of subjects was the reason they had been given for performing this exercise. Some pairs were told it was simply a time-filler; others were told it was a new approach to learning, which was of undetermined value; and others were told it was a new approach to learning which had been demonstrated to be highly successful. Thus, the latter subjects should have had a higher subjective probability that this approach would help them learn the material. Results indicate that the latter group did, indeed, do best on the subsequent multiple-choice test. Further, they reported covering significantly more questions than the other groups, had higher self-ratings of satisfaction, and still did better when the amount of material covered was statistically equated across groups. Thus, they not only covered more material but learned better the material that was covered. Johnson and Foley (1969) conclude that ". . . the belief that participation in a new teaching method will be a personally valuable experience apparently facilitates effort which, in turn, facilitates performance" (p. 10).

The fact that there are some situational incentives or goals that can safely be assumed to be valued by all in those situations has implications for a point discussed in the preceding section. There the point was made that one's subjective probability of success on any given task has both situational and dispositional components. If it is true that increasing the value of a goal increases one's subjective probability of success, as the evidence cited in the section on goal values appears to suggest, then it should follow that, as we increase the incentive to perform in a given situation, the dispositional component of one's subjective probability of success will become relatively less influential as a determinant of performance.

Some evidence pertaining to the above reasoning comes from a study by Atkinson and Reitman (1956), in which male subjects who were either high or low in need for achievement were asked to perform a series of arithmetic problems[4] under one of two conditions. It should be recalled that earlier the point was made that subjects high in need for achievement have a higher subjective probability of success (dispositionally) than subjects low in need for achievement, given the same objective odds. For approximately half the subjects, in the Atkinson—Reitman study, the experimenter simply emphasized the importance of doing well on the task (achievement condition), whereas for the remaining subjects the importance of doing well was emphasized and a five-dollar prize was offered for the person having the highest score (multi-incentive). The results indicate that in the former condition, but not in the multi-incentive condition, subjects high in need for achievement both attempted significantly more problems than did subjects low in need for achievement and solved significantly more problems correctly. Further, an analysis of math aptitude scores available on approximately two-thirds of the subjects indicated that there was no relationship between need for achievement and quantitative ability. Similar results on the relationship between need for achievement and performance as a .function of incentives are reported by Atkinson (1958). Thus it appears that, as the situational incentive to perform is increased, the dispositional component of one's subjective probability of success becomes less influential in affecting the level of performance.

We have been focusing primarily on variables that lead to an increase in one's subjective probability of success and to subsequent increments in performance. We have not paid too much attention to the negative side, to decreases in subjective probabilities and to decrements in performance. In the following three sections, we shall focus on several factors that appear to deleteriously influence performance. We shall begin with a situational factor, proceed next to one that is a mixture of situational and dispositional components, and then to one that is primarily dispositional in nature. The situational factor with which we begin is a facet of feedback that we did not discuss earlier—the discrepancy between how one expects to perform on a given task and one's actual performance on that task.

Expectancy—Performance Discrepancies

There are several theoretical reasons for anticipating that a discrepancy between how one expects to perform in a particular situation and how one actually performs may be detrimental to subsequent performance. Consider a person who performs more poorly than he or she expected. Many skilled tasks require close and constant attention, and, when an element of doubt about one's ability intrudes into consciousness as a result of a poor performance, part of one's

---

[4] There was another task also, but the results on that task appear to have been confounded by the introduction of an extraneous variable in *one* of the conditions immediately prior to the performance of the task.

attention in subsequent attempts at the task may not be focused on the task itself. If such attention-destroying doubts are allowed to build and become the center of consciousness, they could seriously interfere with performance. There is an element of folk wisdom that appears to have as its goal the prevention of such a chain of events, that is, the idea that failure should be quickly followed by another attempt at the task. One should get right back in the saddle immediately after being thrown. That way, self-doubts about one's ability to control the horse don't have time to build to the point that one is really unable to exercise control.

Similarly, there are reasons for believing that, when one has exceeded one's expectations, performance may also deteriorate. When one has done better at a task than one expected, one may fall into the trap of thinking that one has mastered the task, may relax too soon, and may be a little less careful on subsequent attempts. Consequently, subsequent attempts may not go quite so smoothly. Pride may not only precede, it may actually cause a fall—and in things other than horsemanship.

In an article that aroused a great deal of interest and controversy, Aronson and Carlsmith (1962) proposed another hypothesis to account for the performance decrements that follow both positive and negative deviations from expectations. According to dissonance theory (Brehm and Cohen, 1962; Festinger, 1957), when a person is aware simultaneously of two items of information or cognitions that are psychologically inconsistent, that person experiences a motivational state termed cognitive dissonance. The motivational state is directed toward the reduction of dissonance, and this can usually be done by changing one of the cognitions or by adding additional items of information to resolve the apparent inconsistency. For example, the two cognitions that "I was extremely rude to X" and "I am a courteous person" are psychologically inconsistent. Courteous people are not rude. However, the dissonance aroused by the pairing of these two could be reduced by adopting another cognition such as "X deserved it" or by reinterpreting one of the original two—"I was not really rude, I simply said what needed to be said." Aronson and Carlsmith (1962) point out that, in most dissonance-arousing situations, a cognition about the self is involved. As they put it, "... instead of stating that dissonance exists between two inconsistent cognitions, it may be more useful to state that dissonance exists between a cognition about the self (i.e., a self-relevant performance expectancy) and a cognition about behavior which is inconsistent with this expectancy" (p. 178). Thus, a person who has a clear conception of his or her ability on a particular task should experience dissonance if they do better or worse than expected. The interesting aspect, of course, is that even a performance which is better than anticipated will produce dissonance and psychological discomfort.

To test their hypothesis, Aronson and Carlsmith paid 40 female undergraduates to take a bogus social sensitivity test, described as being a valid, reliable, and accurate measure of how sensitive an individual is to others. The test materials consisted of 100 cards, on each of which were three photographs of young men. The subjects' task was to identify which of the three men pictured on each card was schizophrenic. Unknown to the subjects was the fact that all of the pictures were of apparently normal men and had been taken from a college yearbook. The test was administered in five parts of 20 trials or cards each, with a three-minute rest period between trials. At the end of each of the first four blocks of 20 trials, the experimenter appeared to score the subjects' responses and then reported a false score to the subjects. Half of the subjects were told that they had gotten either 16 or 17 correct on each of the first four blocks, and half were told they had gotten either 4 or 5 correct on each block. Thus, at the beginning of the fifth block, the former subjects had a high expectancy and the latter had a low expectancy. On the fifth block of trials, again by false feedback, 10 subjects in each of the expectancy conditions were led to believe they had scored 17 correct (high performance) and the remaining 10 subjects in each expectancy condition were led to believe they had scored 5 correct (low performance). The experimenter then informed all subjects that he had forgotten to time their speed on the fifth block of 20 trials and asked them to repeat the fifth block.

The dependent measure was simply the number of choices that were changed on the repeat performance; the means for each condition on this measure are indicated in Table 6.2. As would be expected and as can be seen in the table, those who expected to do well and actually did well on the fifth test changed the fewest responses on the retake. Further, as anticipated, those who expected to do well and who actually did poorly changed the most responses. Of particular interest, however, is the finding that those who expected to do poorly and who actually did well also changed a large number of responses. Aronson and Carlsmith conclude that the interaction depicted in Table 6.2 ". . . reflects the drive to confirm a self-relevant performance expectancy regardless of whether the expectancy concerns a positive or negative event" (p. 181).

TABLE 6.2
Mean Number of Responses Changed on the Retake of
Trial Block Number 5[a,b]

		Score obtained on fifth test	
		High	Low
Score expected on fifth test	High	3.9	11.1
	Low	10.2	6.7

[a]From Aronson and Carlsmith, 1962. Copyright 1962 by the American Psychological Association, Washington, D.C. Reprinted by Permission.
[b]Interaction $F = 69.8$, $df = 1/39$, $p < .001$

As was mentioned earlier, the Aronson and Carlsmith study aroused a great deal of commentary and stimulated a host of subsequent studies. Before looking at some of the criticisms, it might be well to point out the similarity between Aronson's and Carlsmith's hypothesis and interpretation of results—". . . drive to confirm a self-relevant performance expectancy . . ."—and the hypotheses developed in Chapter 5. When one has a low subjective probability of success on a task, the expectation is that one will fail and one is less likely, according to our hypotheses, to do things that might lead to success. In the Aronson and Carlsmith study, subjects who expected to do poorly and who did well could have insured success on the retest by sticking with their responses, but they did not. In other words, they were unlikely to do the very thing that would have led to success. On the other hand, subjects who expected to do well (a high subjective probability of success) could insure success either by sticking with their responses when they had done well on the fifth trial (which they did) or by changing their responses when they had done poorly (which they did). Thus, subjects with a high subjective probability of success were more likely to do those things required to insure success.

Along this line, one of the more interesting criticisms of the Aronson—Carlsmith study has been made by Waterman and Ford (1965). They hypothesize that the differences between the high and low expectancy groups in the original study may not have been due to dissonance produced by performance inconsistent with expectations, but to differential recall of performance. That is, by giving subjects in the high expectancy groups consistent feedback on the first 80 trials that they were doing well, the experimenter may have induced them to acquire a consistent method for making choices. Thus, it would be easier for them to reapply the rule on the repeat of the fifth block and to recall what their initial responses to that block had been. Then they could stick with those responses if they had done well on the fifth set of pictures or they could change them if they had done poorly. On the other hand, the consistently poor scores given the low expectancy subjects over the first four trial blocks may have decreased their interest in the whole experiment. Thus, they may have paid less attention to their choices and would consequently be less able to recall them. It is also unlikely that they developed a consistent strategy for making choices since, up until the fifth block, whatever they did was incorrect. Note that this interpretation of the Aronson—Carlsmith results is consistent with the position being developed here, but is not, of course, congruent with the dissonance interpretation of those data.

To check on their idea, Waterman and Ford (1965) carried out an experiment which was a slight modification of the original Aronson—Carlsmith study. Male undergraduates were asked to inspect 100 triads of faces, and, from each set of three, they were to identify the schizophrenic. Again, by false feedback on the first four blocks of trials, subjects were led to believe that they were either doing very well (high expectancy) or very poorly (low expectancy). As in the Aronson–Carlsmith study, half of the subjects in each expectancy condition were led to believe they did very well on the fifth block (high performance), half thought they did very poorly on the fifth block (low performance), and all subjects were requested to retake the fifth block of the test. However, on the retake subjects were asked to try to remember as accurately as possible which of the faces in each set they had initially selected in addition to indicating which of the faces they now believed to be schizophrenic. In support of their hypothesis, Waterman and Ford found that high-expectancy subjects were significantly better able to recall their original choices to the fifth trial than were low-expectancy subjects. Further, there was no interaction between expectancy and performance on the recall scores. It appears that differential recall may, at least partially, explain the results in the original study. If it is true that subjects who have a low subjective probability of success on a task lose interest and fail to attend to details of performance, then it should come as no surprise that when they accidentally turn in a good performance, they are unlikely to be able to reconstruct or duplicate that performance if the occasion arises.

There have been several successful replications of the Aronson and Carlsmith (1962) study (e.g., Brock, Edelman, Edwards, and Schuck, 1965). However, additional data in these same supportive studies as well as other studies support a number of criticisms of the original results. For example, Ward and Sandvold (1963) pointed out that the emphasis on the reliability and validity of the test in the initial instructions to subjects coupled with the fact that the original subjects were paid for participation may have been sufficient to motivate consistency seeking on the part of subjects whose performance on the fifth block was inconsistent with their expectations. That is, the instructions and the pay may have made subjects feel they ought to be consistent because the experimenter expected it. Further, Hendrick and Jones (1972) point out that the experimenter in the Aronson–Carlsmith study was presumably aware of the hypothesis being tested and of the condition to which any given subject had been assigned. Thus, the experimenter may have inadvertently behaved differently toward subjects in the different conditions, perhaps signaling his own expectancies of hypothesis confirmation in various ways. To make an increasingly long story short, it is clear that the precise conditions under which the hypothesis proposed by Aronson and Carlsmith holds true are not yet known. It may turn out that the hypothesis is false or that the empirical result may be genuine, but have nothing to do with dissonance.

In any event, there is another critique of the Aronson–Carlsmith procedure, which is of particular interest here. Zajonc and Brickman (1969) and Cottrell (1967) point out that one of the ambiguities in the original study is that there was no objective criterion against which performance could be compared—none of the photos depicted a true schizophrenic. As Zajonc and Brickman (1969) put it, "While the subject changes his responses as a function of feedback, the completely arbitrary criteria of correctness makes it impossible to determine whether the subject's performance *actually* improves or deteriorates in a given condition" (p. 150). This does not mean that the line of research begun by Aronson and Carlsmith is useless for our purposes. It does mean that perhaps we have been discussing that research in the wrong terms.

Instead of the effects of disconfirmed expectancies on performance, the research may need to be rephrased in terms of uncertainty about one's ability on variation in responding. Clearly, those subjects whose expectancies were disconfirmed on the fifth block should have become less certain of their ability in the situation than subjects whose expectancies were confirmed. Given that the high-expectancy group had been getting feedback that they were 80 to 85 percent successful and the low-expectancy group's feedback indicated they were 20 to 25 percent successful, the disconfirmations should have had the effect of moving the subjective probability of success closer to .5 for both groups, that is, down for the high-expectancy group and up for the low-expectancy group. It is also clear that the subjects whose expectancies were disconfirmed varied their responses significantly more on the retake of the fifth block and that they varied their responses more than either the low-expectancy subjects whose expectancies were confirmed, or the high-expectancy subjects whose expectancies were confirmed, that is, subjects who had a lower and higher subjective probability of success, respectively.

While the responses of the latter two groups are similar, it seems reasonable to suppose that the motivations underlying those responses are not similar. The high-expectancy-confirmed group has presumably found an appropriate pattern of responding, and they stick with it. The low-expectancy-confirmed group has apparently become convinced that nothing they do will lead to success, and they continue to plod along in their rut. It is only those whose expectancies have been disconfirmed and who are, thus, uncertain about what to do whose responses begin to fluctuate. This pattern of results is very similar to that suggested in our brief discussion of anxiety earlier.

There it was conjectured that in situations requiring effort expenditure and/or skilled performance for goal attainment, anxiety and one's subjective probability of success will be related, but not linearly. When anxiety is high, it should be the case that the subjective probability of success is intermediate or vice versa— either way, there is maximum uncertainty. On the other hand, when anxiety is low, this may mean that the subjective probability of success is either very high or very low. In either case, uncertainty is relatively low. This line of reasoning and the results discussed above suggest that one effect of high anxiety or an intermediate probability of success may be variability in responding. Further, if it is correct that a high probability of success leads to little variability because one thinks they have found the best set of responses, and a low probability of success leads to little variability because one thinks nothing will work, then it follows that the variability that accompanies an intermediate probability of success (high anxiety) should decrease one's chances of success in relation to another with a high probability of success, and increase one's chances of success in relation to another with a low probability of success. While this certainly seems plausible, let us back up a little and look at some of the research on the relationship between anxiety and performance before we get too far out on a limb.

Anxiety

There has been a great deal of comment and speculation about the detrimental effects of anxiety on learning and performance. For example, drawing on his own observations of the classroom behavior of school children, Holt (1964) argues that anxiety leads to behaviors that make genuine learning all but impossible. The pressure to produce and to get the right answer, which he believes is pervasive in the classroom, is seen as instilling such a deep and all-consuming fear of displeasing adults (teachers) that children resort to various strategies, which can result in correct answers without their even having to understand the problem that was posed or the question that was asked. One such strategy is the guess-and-look, in which the student begins an answer while scrutinizing the teacher's face for any sign that he or she is on the right track. Another is the mumble strategy, which often appears effective because the teacher who asks a question may be so eager to hear the right answer—since it will indicate that he or she is an effective teacher—that anything even remotely resembling the right answer will be accepted, so the class can forge ahead to the next topic. Holt believes that the real villain in these tragic daily scenarios, the thing that drives children into these narrow and defensive strategies, is an anxiety about pleasing adults (teachers) at all costs. As he puts it (1964), "Perhaps they are thrown too early, and too much, into a crowded society of other children, where they have to think, not about the world, but about their position in it" (p. 43).

The thrust of Holt's argument is that the sorts of self-defeating strategies to produce, which result from the anxiety-arousing classroom atmosphere in which one has to shine brighter than one's classmates, usually lead to an impulsiveness that destroys genuine performance and problem solving.

> . . . When a child gets right answers by illegitimate means, and gets credit for knowing what he doesn't know, and knows he doesn't know, it does double harm. First, he doesn't learn, his confusions are not cleared up; secondly, he comes to believe that a combination of bluffing, guessing, mind reading, snatching at clues, and getting answers from other people is what he is supposed to do at school; that this is what school is all about; that nothing else is possible (p. 146).

Holt's thesis is certainly a provocative one and, to anyone who has spent much time in a classroom, it has a great deal of face validity. The potential biases that may have entered into Holt's choice of anecdotes to support his argument are, however, rather obvious. Hence we need to examine the relationship between anxiety and performance a little more closely.

If anxiety is really related to one's subjective probability of success in the manner we have hypothesized, then it should be the case that by changing his or her perceived probability of success, a highly anxious person could be induced to behave as one who was less anxious. Conversely, it should be the case that by changing the perceived probability of success, a person who was without anxiety initially could be induced to behave as if he or she were indeed highly anxious. We have assumed that high anxiety is associated with an intermediate probability of success and low anxiety with either a high or a low probability of success. Thus, if the performance of a person who is initially rather anxious is met with repeated failure, his or her probability of success should fall to a very low level and he or she would consequently behave as one low in anxiety. On the other hand, consider the performance of a person who is initially low in anxiety because of a high perceived probability of success. If the latter's performance is met with repeated failure, his or her probability of success should decrease toward .5, and he or she should consequently show behavior increasingly like that of one who is high in anxiety.

If we assume that their low-anxiety subjects had an initial high probability of success, then a study by Marlett and Watson (1968) appears to support the above reasoning. We are also still entertaining Holt's hypothesis that impulsiveness is a characteristic of the highly anxious. Based on their responses to the Alpert–Haber (1960) Test Anxiety Scale, Marlett and Watson selected 28 high-anxiety ninth-grade boys and 28 low-anxiety boys. Each subject was seated before a panel with four switches and was assigned the task of learning the correct sequence of two button presses, which would prevent a loud buzzer from sounding (failure). Over a series of 12 trials, each subject repeatedly failed to find the correct sequence, that is, the buzzer always sounded following his two button presses. Contrary to what we would expect, on the first trial, highly anxious subjects showed a significantly greater initial hesitation: on trial one, they responded more slowly than low-anxious subjects. However, beginning with trial two, the results appear to be consistent with our expectations. With repeated failure, the initially high-anxiety subjects responded increasingly more slowly and the initially low-anxiety subjects responded increasingly more quickly. There was also greater redundancy of responding among the initial high-anxiety subjects. They were significantly more likely to repeat sequences of button presses that had already been tried. Further, some questionnaire data indicate that the highly anxious subjects spent significantly more time worrying about their performance. As Marlett and Watson (1968) note, "The high-test anxious person spends a part of his task time doing things which are not task oriented. He worries about his performance, worries about how well others might do, ruminates over choices open to him, and is often repetitive in his attempts to solve the task" (p. 203). All of these things, of course, increase the probability of failure.

Some results very similar to the above are reported in an earlier study by Feather (1963). The task in Feather's study was a word-association game, in which subjects were to draw a card and to then think of a word that might correctly be associated with the word printed on the card according to some unspecified rules. After each of 120 such trials the experimenter simply replied, "That's correct," or, "That's incorrect," to a subject's answer, and the subject's goal was to try to discover the (nonexistent) rules. Some subjects were told they were correct 80 percent of the time; some were told they were correct 50 percent of the time; and some were correct only 20 percent of the time (high failure). The latter group took significantly longer to complete the task. On the other hand, subjects who believed they were succeeding 80 percent of the time were least variable in their responses. That is, these subjects were behaving as if they had discovered a rule by which to respond, even though there were no rules. This corresponds with the point made earlier about the low response variability among high expectancy–high performance subjects in the Aronson–Carlsmith study, that is, those subjects with a high probability of success.

In both the Marlett and Watson (1968) and Feather (1963) studies, there is evidence that high anxiety or an intermediate probability of success is associated with heightened response variability or uncertainty. It is as if the attention of such subjects wanders. They take longer to respond. They report thinking about irrelevant things. If there were some way to focus the attention of such subjects on the task at hand, presumably their performance could be improved. At least, the variability in their responding might be decreased.

Some data pertinent to this point are reported in a study by Brody (1964). Male high school students who had scored either high or low on an anxiety test were told that either a circle or a square would be tachistoscopically presented on a screen before them at subliminal levels and they were simply asked to write down what they thought they saw. There were 200 such trials and on all trials a blank slide was actually projected on the screen. Each subject went through the experiment twice: once as just described, and once under what Brody refers to as *induced muscular tension*. That is, at the ready signal prior to each trial the subject was to squeeze a dynamometer and keep it squeezed until the slide was presented on that trial. Thus, in the latter condition, it is likely that subjects attended more closely to the slide presentation. The results indicate that highly anxious subjects vary their responses significantly less in the induced tension condition than in the nontension condition. Thus, it may be that wandering attention and irrelevant ruminations account for some of the response variability among highly anxious subjects. It is somewhat paradoxical that this same variability in response may both decrease their chance of success, in comparison to someone with a high subjective probability of success, and increase their chance of success, in comparison to someone with a low subjective probability of success. As we have pointed out, both of the latter two may be low in anxiety and low in response variability, but for different reasons.

There are, of course, problems with all three of the preceding studies (Marlett–Watson, Feather, Brody). We have made some assumptions in interpretation that may not be appropriate: in none of the studies are the results really clear cut, and in none of the studies have all of the variables of interest here been measured. Further, there is one problem that is common to all three studies. Neither Marlett and Watson nor Feather nor Brody used a task on which performance could really be measured, that is, there were no objective criteria of improvement on the tasks. There have been a number of studies, however, relating anxiety to actual performance. Russell and Sarason (1965), for example, found that highly anxious subjects took significantly longer to solve a set of anagrams than did subjects who were less anxious. There are, unfortunately, many possible explanations for such a result. While it may seem plausible that high-anxiety subjects, having a lower perceived probability of success, were more distractible and tended to let their attention wander, we have no evidence from this particular study that this occurred. It may simply be that the low-anxiety subjects in the Russell and Sarason study were more intelligent and, hence, could solve anagrams faster.

A study by Harleston, Smith, and Arey (1965), which also used anagram solution as the performance criterion, offers a little better evidence on some possible mediating mechanisms. Harleston et al. were interested in physiological arousal relationships, as indicated by change in heart rate, test-anxiety scores, and problem-solving. They point out that there have been several successful attempts to relate physiological indices to performance, but that studies relating anxiety-scale scores to physiological changes are scattered and inconsistent. Subjects for this particular study were 42 female undergraduates, who had been selected on the basis of their responses to a test-anxiety questionnaire as either low, medium, or high anxious. Subjects were given 20 minutes to solve as many of 60 anagrams as possible. During this 20-minute period and for 5 minutes before and 5 minutes after, each subject's heart rate was recorded from her right thumb by a photocell amplifier unit. In the 5 minute pretest or base line recording period, the mean heart rate did not differ among the three groups.

For purposes of analysis, two percentage-change scores were calculated for each subject, taking the ratios of her mean heart rate during the first 5 minutes of testing and during the entire 20 minutes of testing to her mean heart rate during the 5-minute pretest or baseline period. Both of these percentage-change scores were significantly correlated to the subject's test-anxiety scores. The higher a subject's test-anxiety score, the greater her increase in heart rate during the first 5 minutes of testing and during the entire 20 minutes of testing. Further, there were tendencies for the highly anxious subjects to solve fewest anagrams and to have longer solution times than low-anxious subjects on the ones they did solve. Unfortunately, these tendencies were not significant.

However, when the three groups of subjects were condensed into two—those with the largest percentage-change scores on heart rate and those with the smallest, subjects with the smaller percentage-change scores performed significantly better both in terms of number of anagrams solved and quickness of solution.

There are several important points that need to be noted in connection with the above results. First, there is the theoretically important suggestion that high anxiety may result in significantly greater arousal in a performance situation and that this excessive arousal may interfere with performance. Hull (1943), Zajonc (1965), and many others have presented evidence and theoretical rationales for the often-noted finding that, on complex tasks or even when learning simple tasks, an increase in arousal increases task-irrelevant responses at the expense of task-relevant responses. This coincides nicely with our earlier discussion that high anxiety or an intermediate probability of success increases response variability. It should be pointed out that in Archibald's (1974) discussion of mechanisms underlying intrapersonal self-fulfilling prophecies of negative events, he distinguishes between *anxiety distraction* and *energizing arousal* and treats them separately. From the point of view taken here, this is an artificial and inappropriate distinction since arousal is presumed to produce the irrelevant responses or distraction. Further, in contrast to Archibald's discussion, the reasoning here is presumed to apply to anticipation of both positive and negative events.

A second point that stems from the Harleston et al. study concerns the anxiety scale employed. The classification of subjects into low-, medium-, and high-anxious groups was done on the basis of their responses to an anxiety scale developed by Harleston (1962). None of the other studies we have discussed in this chapter employed Harleston's scale to assess the anxiety level of the participants. One of the real difficulties in making sense out of research in this area is indicated by this. There is, in fact, a profusion of different anxiety scales. Everyone seems to have created his or her own anxiety scale to suit his or her particular research needs or theoretical conceptions, and there have been relatively few systematic attempts to relate the various scales. Thus, it may be untenable to assume that a subject assigned to the high-anxiety group in Study A on the basis of responses to Scale X is psychologically isomorphic with a subject assigned to the high-anxiety group in Study B on the basis of responses to Scale Y.

Fortunately, the attempts that have been made to interrelate various anxiety scales appear to have yielded rather consistent results, results which happen to coincide with the distinction, discussed in the section on prior success and failure, between dispositional and situational components of one's subjective probability of success. Alpert and Haber (1960), for example, make the point that two divergent positions appear to have developed among those involved in the construction of anxiety scales. The first position is characterized by the assumption that each individual has a relatively stable or constant level of internal anxiety. Taylor's (1953) general anxiety scale which was constructed from MMPI items appears to be the archtype here. The second position is characterized by the assumption that anxiety is situationally aroused and situationally specific. The Test Anxiety Scale developed by Mandler and Sarason (1952) is an example of a scale designed to measure anxiety aroused specifically in testing and performance situations. Other types of situations would presumably require other scales to measure whatever anxiety they aroused.

The two positions discussed above have evolved into a distinction between trait and state anxiety (Spielberger, 1972), which is, conceptually, very similar to our distinction between the dispositional and situational components of one's subjective probability of success. Further, if we assume that college undergraduates have a good deal of personal experience in academic testing situations, Alpert and Haber (1960) present some evidence that appears to reinforce the position developed earlier that, as one gains experience in a situation, the situationally specific component of one's subjective probability of success becomes increasingly important in determining performance. Alpert and Haber administered a variety of trait and state anxiety scales to male Stanford undergraduates and correlated the responses on the scales to verbal-aptitude scores, grade-point averages, and grades. The results indicate that "... the variable which the specific scales measure, and which the general scales do not, is involved in academic performance to such an extent that the specific scales are better predictors of academic performance than are the general anxiety scales" (p. 209).

Since the subjects in the study by Alpert and Haber were Stanford undergraduates, who are generally considered to be among the most capable and academically competent undergraduates, it seems safe to assume that those scoring low in test anxiety had a high subjective probability of success in such academic performance settings. Further, if we assume high test anxiety corresponds to an intermediate probability of success, then the results indicate that the higher the perceived probability of success, the better the performance. It is important to note that the criteria of performance in this study were not artificial laboratory tasks, but real-life indices—college grades and grade-point averages.

It appears that the literature on the relationship between anxiety and performance is generally consistent with and supportive of the position developed earlier on the relationship between one's subjective probability of success and one's performance. Further, the anxiety literature suggests several possible processes that might mediate the relationship between subjective probability and performance: response variability at the intermediate levels of perceived probability coupled with increased arousal, production of irrelevant responses, and distraction. Unfortunately, studies of anxiety and performance have rarely directly measured the variables that are of most importance to our argument, such as the subjective probability of success. Hence, we shall not pursue that literature further because of the necessity to continue to make translating assumptions which, while plausible, may or may not be valid. Let us get back on firmer terrain.

Most of the anxiety literature we have discussed appears to relate primarily to the situational component of one's subjective probability of success. Recently another body of literature has emerged that is *clearly* related to the dispositional component of one's subjective probability of success—and without any translation of variables. That is the literature we take up next.

Learned Helplessness

The perception that one is helpless in a particular situation clearly corresponds to a very low subjective probability of success. It follows, according to the hypothesis in Chapter 5, that the perception of helplessness decreases the likelihood of initiating and sustaining task-relevant behaviors and thereby decreases the likelihood of success. As we shall see, it almost always insures failure. Although many people have been interested in the diverse behavioral phenomena associated with helplessness, the most comprehensive treatment of the subject is found in the work of Seligman (cf., 1975, for a review). It is worth noting, particularly since we have paid no attention to comparative research in the preceding chapters, that Seligman's work on human helplessness stems from his own earlier research on the relationship of fear conditioning to instrumental learning in animals.

The initial finding that appears to have stimulated this line of research is reported by Overmier and Seligman (1967). Using a two-compartment shuttle-box with a barrier between the two compartments, Overmier and Seligman found that dogs placed in the shuttlebox behaved very differently if they had previously been subjected to certain classical conditioning procedures than if they had not. If the floor on either side of the barrier was electrified, naive dogs quickly learned to jump the barrier into the other side and, thus, escape the shock. On the other hand, if the dogs had previously learned to associate a tone with an inescapable electric shock while restrained in a harness, they failed to escape shock when later placed in the shuttlebox. The key words here are *inescapable* and *while restrained*. That is, it seemed as if the latter dogs had learned during the prior experience with inescapable shock that their responses were to no avail, hence their motivation to initiate responses which might lead to escape in the shuttlebox was absent.

Before it could be concluded that there was an intervening expectation that responding would be useless, there was another possible explanation of the results that had to be ruled out. That is, it might have been the case that the prior electric shock itself produced some physiological damage or change or deficit that led to reduced responding. To check on this possibility, Seligman and Maier (1967) assigned naive, mongrel dogs to one of three groups. Dogs assigned to an escape group were secured into a rubberized cloth hammock and received 64 unsignaled electric shocks presented at varying intervals. These dogs could (and did) learn to escape or turn off the shock by simply pressing their heads against one of two panels on either side of their head. Dogs assigned to a yoked-control group were put in the same hammock and each was also shocked 64 times. However, these dogs could not terminate the shock by pressing their heads against a panel. Rather, the duration of the shock on each trial for this group was set equal to the mean duration of the corresponding trial in the escape group. Thus, the responses of dogs in the yoked-control group were irrelevant to termination of the shock, whereas the responses of dogs in the escape group controlled the shock. Both groups, however, experienced the same amounts of shock. A second or normal-control group of dogs were not placed in the hammocks and received no shocks.

Subsequently, dogs in all three groups were placed in a shuttlebox and given 10 trials of escape avoidance training. The major results are indicated in Table 6.3. As can be seen in the table, the responses of naive dogs who have received no pretreatment are very similar to dogs in the escape group, both in terms of the latency of responding in the shuttlebox and in terms of the number of successful escapes. On the other hand, dogs previously exposed to electrical shocks which they could not control (the yoked group) are much slower to respond and generally fail to escape the escapable shock in the shuttlebox. Thus, it is not the prior shock itself or any physiological changes resulting from it that produces the previously noted failure to escape in the shuttlebox. Rather, it appears to be the prior learning that responding is pointless that destroys the motivation to try, to initiate responses that might be instrumental to goal attainment.

With this very brief look at the sort of research from which Seligman's notions about learned helplessness have emerged, let us turn to the theory he has constructed, and then we shall look at some evidence for the existence and effects of learned helplessness in humans.

TABLE 6.3
Indices of Shuttlebox Escape–Avoidance[a]

Group	Mean latency (in seconds)	Percent of dogs failing to escape on at least 9 of 10 trials	Mean number of failures to escape
Escape	27.00	0	2.63
Normal	25.93	12.5	2.25
Yoked	48.22	75	7.25

[a]From Seligman & Maier, 1967. (Copyright 1967 by the American Psychological Association, Washington, D.C. Reprinted by Permission.)

Seligman's (1975) theoretical statement is very compatible with the position developed in Chapter 5, although his terminology and emphases are somewhat different. Drawing on a massive literature on operant conditioning, Seligman notes that it has been repeatedly demonstrated that humans and animals can and do learn about the contingencies between their responses and the outcomes they receive. Specifically, he points out that organisms learn not only when their responses produce outcomes but they also learn in those situations ". . . in which the probability of the outcome is the same whether or not the response of interest occurs" (p. 46). They learn, in other words, that in some situations their responses have nothing to do with the outcome. Three things are involved (Seligman, 1975, p. 47):

| Information about the contingency [between responses and outcome] | → | Cognitive representation of the contingency (learning, expectation, perception, belief) | → | Behavior |

The important part of this diagram is the cognitive representation of the contingency, the expectation that responses and outcomes either are or are not related. Learned helplessness is said to occur when one has formed the expectation with respect to some outcome that the outcome occurs independently of all his or her voluntary responses.

In Seligman's view, the consequences of learned helplessness should be apparent in three realms: motivation, cognition, and emotion. Motivationally, one's perception that outcomes are independent of one's responses destroys the impetus to initiate responses. Seligman (1975) argues that, "For voluntary responding to occur, an incentive must be present in the form of an expectation that responding may succeed. In the absence of such an expectation, that is, when an organism believes responding is futile, voluntary responding will not occur" (p. 50). Cognitively one's perception that outcomes are independent of one's responses interferes with subsequent learning in situations in which outcomes are not independent of responses. Emotionally, if the outcome that is perceived to be independent of one's responses is a traumatic one, such as shock, learned helplessness results in an increase in emotional responses. It follows from Seligman's statement of the theory that learned helplessness and its motivational, cognitive, and emotional effects can be wiped out by changing the expectation that one's outcomes and responses are independent, that is, by inducing the expectation that one's responses will make a difference in the outcome one receives.

Seligman (1975) marshalls an impressive array of experimental and anecdotal evidence in support of the above. Further, there is a rapidly growing body of experimental studies that were specifically designed to test various aspects of the learned helplessness model with human subjects. Hiroto (1974), for example, hypothesized that subjects pretreated for a number of trials with an inescapable aversive stimulus (a 110-db tone presented through earphones) would be slower to learn to escape (turn off the tone) in a subsequent task than subjects who had not experienced the aversive pretreatment. Further, he noted the conceptual similarity between learned helplessness and a belief in external control of reinforcement, which we mentioned earlier. Externals tend to perceive reinforcements to be independent of their responses—a function of chance, luck, fate— and, hence, should be particularly susceptible to learned helplessness effects. Internals, on the other hand, tend to believe more strongly that they control the reinforcements they receive, generally, and should be more resistant to adopting the perception that outcomes are independent of their responses. In addition, Hiroto included a difference in instructional set, that is, some subjects were told explicitly that there was something they could do to escape the tone (skill conditions), whereas other subjects were told that the way to stop the tone was up to the experimenter, but that they could try to guess (chance conditions).

After having experienced inescapable tones, escapable tones, or no pretreatment, all subjects were tested with 18 signaled 10-second trials. A 5-second red light preceded the onset of the 5-second 110 db tone. The appropriate response, by which subjects could either avoid the tone—during the first 5 seconds of a trial—or escape the tone—during the last 5 seconds—was moving a knob to one side of a manipulandum on one trial and to the opposite side on the next trial. The results indicate that subjects pretreated with inescapable tone failed to escape the aversive tone on over 50 percent of the 18 trials, while subjects pretreated with escapable tone failed to escape on only 13 percent of the trials and subjects in the no pretreatment condition failed to escape on only 11 percent. Further, Hiroto points out that "Both locus of control and skill—chance instructional set factors produced an effect similar to inescapability. In view of the parallel effects between the 3 factors, I suggest that a single process may underlie learned helplessness, externality, and the perceptual set of chance—the expectancy that responding and reinforcement are independent" (p. 192).

From the point of view of the position taken in Chapter 5, that is a most felicitous conclusion, but, unfortunately, it does not appear warranted. One serious confounding in Hiroto's study is that subjects assigned to the inescapable and escapable pretreatment conditions were not yoked in terms of exposure to the aversive stimulus. That is, subjects in the inescapable condition received 5 seconds of the aversive noise on each trial during pretreatment, whereas subjects in the escape condition escaped during the pretreatment trials after an average of only 1.4 seconds of exposure to the tone. Thus, as Hiroto himself and others (cf., Wortman and Brehm, 1975) have pointed out, it is possible that the greater stress experienced by subjects in the inescapable condition may account for the results.

A second issue raised by the similarity between Hiroto's pretreatment to his testing situation is the extent to which learned helplessness is specific to the situation in which one's responses have proved to be ineffective. Earlier we distinguished between situational and dispositional components of one's objective probability of success and reviewed some evidence that indicated these two components are most influential at different stages of performance. It is relatively clear (Seligman, 1975) that people and animals can learn that in a specific situation their responses and their outcomes are independent. In such situations, the perception of helplessness ensues and responding ceases—*in those situations*. If this were all there was to the phenomena of learned helplessness, most would be willing to acknowledge that it occurs, that it has been well documented in the learning literature, and we could go on to the next topic. However, the really interesting and important question about the perception of helplessness is the extent to which it generalizes. In the language used earlier, the question is the extent to which low situationally specific subjective probabilities of success contribute to or become transformed into a low dispositional subjective probability of success.

Surprisingly, there is not much research on the circumstances under which helpless does and does not generalize. Seligman (1975) argues very persuasively that generalization of helplessness is at the core of those diverse psychological states that are loosely referred to as depression. The evidence for such an inference is rather tenuous, however. There is some evidence that helplessness effects do generalize to different types of tasks.

Noting the conceptual similarity between the instrumental behaviors called forth by escapable versus inescapable aversive stimulation and the cognitive behaviors brought into play by soluble versus insoluble problems, Hiroto and Seligman (1975) designed a 12-condition experiment that was essentially four replications of the sort of escape, yoked-inescape, and control conditions used in the studies mentioned above. In the first set of those conditions, escape and yoked-inescape subjects were pretreated with 45 exposures of an aversive 90 db tone, which the former could escape by learning a sequence of button presses (instrumental responses), while the latter could not. These two groups, together with a no-pretreatment control group were then tested for helplessness, using an escapable aversive tone and the sort of human shuttlebox manipulandum described in the study by Hiroto (1974). In the second replication, the pretreatment was the same (tone and button pressing), but subjects were tested for helplessness on an anagram solution (cognitive) task. In the third and fourth sets of three conditions, series of soluble or insoluble discrimination tasks were used during pretreatment, and either the tone-shuttlebox or anagram tasks were used in testing for helplessness. The design is summarized in Figure 6.1.

The results for one set of conditions, the instrumental pretreatment—cognitive test are illustrative. In this set, the subjects pretreated with inescapable aversive tones do much more poorly on an anagram-solution task than subjects pretreated with a series of aversive tones from which they could learn to escape by pressing a button or control subjects who were not exposed to the pretreatment tones. The results for the other three sets of conditions were essentially the same. Subjects pretreated with either inescapable aversive tones or insoluble

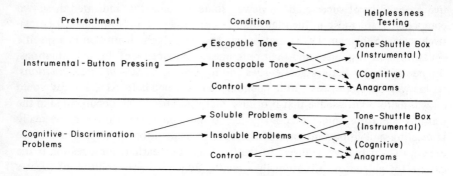

FIG. 6.1   Schematic of the design utilized by Hiroto and Seligman (1975).

discrimination problems did more poorly on a subsequent anagram or human shuttlebox task than did non-pretreated controls or subjects pretreated with escapable aversive tones or soluble discrimination problems, respectively. Hiroto and Seligman (1975) point out that this cross modal (instrumental–cognitive and cognitive–instrumental) generality of learned helplessness is important, in that it suggests the development of a dispositional (traitlike) expectation that attempts at task solution are futile.

There is, unfortunately, a problem with the Hiroto and Seligman (1975) design. As Wortman and Brehm (1975) point out:

> A trivial reason why subjects without perceived control may show helplessness effects on the test task is that, if they are unable to exert control on the training task after many trials, they simply may not believe the experimenter when he tells them that the test task is solvable. For example, consider the subjects . . . who were exposed to an instrumental pretreatment and an instrumental test task. Subjects in the No Escape condition were shown a manipulandum and were specifically told that there was something they could do to end the noise bursts. Even though there was a large number of trials (45), the subjects found themselves unable to make any progress toward eliminating the bursts. Subjects were then shown a second manipulandum, and again told that there was something they could do to eliminate the noise bursts. After trying every conceivable type of response and not being able to eliminate noise bursts earlier, it is certainly possible that subjects would conclude that there was, in fact, no solution to the problem, and that the experimenter had not been truthful with them. . . . in that light it is not surprising that they were not quick to find a solution on the second task (p. 304).

The question of the extent to which perceived helplessness in one situation generalizes to other situations has still not received a clear answer. The evidence is still fragmentary and a number of the learned helplessness experiments with humans are ambiguous because of serious methodological flaws.

In line with our earlier discussion, it seems reasonable to suppose that one of the key factors influencing generalizability of learned helplessness is one's attribution of the cause of his or her failure in a given situation. If the repeated failures that result in the perception of learned helplessness are attributed to lack of ability, we would expect the effects of helplessness to generalize only to those situations perceived to call for the same ability. If the failures are attributed to task difficulty, the generalization of helplessness should be limited to similar tasks. If the failures are attributed to luck or to lack of effort, the perception of helplessness would not even develop in the first place. In any event, it is apparent that ". . . considerably more effort must be spent both in demonstrating that helplessness does generalize to new and different situations, and in delineating the factors that affect generalization" (Wortman and Brehm, 1975, p. 326).

It is true that much remains to be done. The potential importance of a clear understanding of the phenomena associated with helplessness and its obverse is great, however, and bodes well for future research on the topic. As Seligman (1975) points out, the concept of learned helplessness may cast new light on the perennial nature–nurture controversy:

> . . . I believe that motivation and emotion are more plastic than cognition, more shaped by the environment. I am no longer convinced that special, intensive training will raise a child's IQ by twenty points, or allow him to talk three months early, or induce him to write piano sonatas at age five, as Mozart did. On the other hand, I *am* convinced that certain arrangements of environmental contingencies will produce a child who believes he is helpless—that he cannot succeed—and that other contingencies will produce a child who believes that his responses matter—that he can control his little world. If a child believes he is helpless he will perform stupidly, regardless of his IQ. If a child believes he is helpless he will not write piano sonatas, regardless of his inherent musical genius. On the other hand, if a child believes that he has control and mastery, he may outperform more talented peers who lack such a belief (pp. 136–137).

That, of course, is precisely the point we have been trying to make.

We have discussed a number of variables that effect performance and we have assumed throughout that performance is goal directed. People work in order to achieve goals and it is not too important whether the goal is subsistence or perfection of a particular skill or to salt away a certain amount of money. Their subjective probability of attaining the goal appears to be the crucial determinant of performance. Further, the research on learned helplessness indicates some of the psychological consequences that ensue when one's goal is relinguished, when one's subjective probability of success approaches zero. But what about the other end of the scale? What happens when one's goal is achieved?

SOME COMMENTS ABOUT GOAL ATTAINMENT

It is apparently an index of the times we live in, with the emphasis on becoming as opposed to being, that there has been relatively little research on the consequences of goal attainment. One often hears that, as we free more and more people from menial and semimechanical work and assure more and more people of a reasonable standard of living, leisure behavior is going to become a problem. The nature of the problem that would be posed by an increase in the amount of leisure time available to the average person is unclear, however. If *leisure behavior* simply means engaging in activities with different goals from those pursued in one's workaday world, then it is difficult to see what the problem will be.

On the other hand, if leisure behavior is a euphemism for pointless activity or purposelessness, then there is indeed going to be a problem of monstrous proportions. One of the strongest messages that comes across when people are questioned about their lives and their work is that a steady diet of pointless activity deadens the spirit. Life becomes tasteless, odorless, and flat. Consider the comments of a washroom attendant at the Palmer House in Chicago:

> Most of the time I'm sitting down here reading, a paper or a book. . . . The day goes. . . . I'm not particularly proud of what I'm doing. . . . Outside of my immediate family, very few people know what I do. . . . I've become inured to it now. It doesn't affect me one way or the other. The years piled up and now it doesn't even occur to me, doesn't cross my mind. . . . The whole thing is obsolete. It's on its way out. This work isn't necessary in the first place. It's so superfluous. It was *never* necessary. It's just a hustle (Terkel, 1975, p. 155–157).

The problem, of course, is that a total absence of purpose can be devastating to one's self-esteem or sense of worth even, or perhaps particularly, if one is well paid, well fed, and has a nice home in the suburbs.

It does seem rather strange, then, that for decades most psychological theories pertinent to performance clearly implied that purposelessness is, in fact, everyone's ultimate goal. Lewin (1940), for example, explicitly assumes that the intention to achieve a particular goal corresponds to the induction of a tension state within the person, which persists until the goal is achieved. When the goal is achieved the tension is released. "Conceptually, tension refers to the state of one system relative to the state of surrounding systems. The essence and the purpose of this construct is to include a tendency for change in the direction of equalization of the state of neighboring systems" (Lewin, 1951, p. 11). The final goal, then, is the absence of tension, total quiescence of the organism. Similarly, drive theorists such as Hull (1943) have long argued that people are spurred to activity only as a result of some external or internal stimulation, which persists until a response is made that terminates the stimulation. Once the stimulation ends, the organism supposedly lapses into a temporary nirvana, that reputedly blissful state of being in which there are no desires and no passions (it always sounds suspiciously like death).

It is true, of course, that more recently the thrust of theoretical explanation for performance and goal-seeking behavior has changed. There is increasingly widespread recognition that some conceptualization is called for which can account for the fact that humans and animals do not lapse into a stuporous nirvana when strong drives and stimuli are absent. All of the preceding chapters are, in fact, predicated on the view that people can be viewed as continuously attempting to impose some sort of order on, to extract some meaning from, to understand, to anticipate, and, thus, to control the onrushing events in which they find themselves immersed. White's (1959) notion of effectance motivation is very similar to this position:

> Putting it picturesquely, we might say that the effectance urge represents what the neuromuscular system wants to do when it is otherwise unoccupied or is gently stimulated by the environment. Obviously there are no consummatory acts; satisfaction would appear to lie in the arousal and maintaining of activity rather than in its slow decline toward bored passivity. . . . Strongly aroused drives, pain, and anxiety, however, can be conceived as overriding the effectance urge and capturing the energies of the neuromuscular system. But effectance motivation is persistent in the sense that it regularly occupies the spare waking time between episodes of homeostatic crisis (p. 321).

This notion that people will engage in activity for its own sake or in order to avoid periods of inactivity has been humorously incorporated into folk wisdom in the form of Parkinson's Law: "Work expands so as to fill the time available for its completion" (Parkinson, 1957, p. 33). There have, in fact, been several experimental verifications of Parkinson's law with human subjects.

Aronson and Landy (1967), for example, asked two groups of male and female subjects to rank three sets of photographs of people in terms of various psychological traits. The first set was to be ranked in terms of apparent intelligence, the second in terms of perceived warmth, and the third in terms of perceived honesty. The experimenter was then "unexpectedly" called out of the room, and it was made clear that he would be gone for either 5 minutes or 15 minutes. During the absence the subjects were to do the rankings, and when he returned the rankings would be recorded. While the experimenter was out of the room, the subject's behavior was observed via a peephole in the wall and the actual amount of time spent handling the photographs was recorded. As anticipated, subjects who thought the experimenter would be back in 15 minutes spent significantly longer (mean = 640 seconds) doing the rankings than did subjects who thought they only had five minutes (mean = 288 seconds). "Thus, while work does not necessarily expand to fill *all* of the time available, it does tend to expand and fill more time when more time *is* available" (Aronson and Landy, 1967, p. 280).

The answer to our question about the consequences of goal attainment appears to be more complex, then, than that assumed by drive and drive-stimulus reduction theorists. People do not simply become quiescent when a goal is attained and await the next internal or external impetus to action. Further, if they perceive that goal completion would be followed by periods of inactivity, they tend to prolong their approach to the goal, to stretch it out to fill at least part of the time, which would otherwise be empty. There are obvious limits to this imposed by the existence of other goals and fatigue, so perhaps we should rephrase the question and inquire about the consequences of goal attainment for the pursuit of other goals and for the experience of fatigue.

Concerning the former, Child and Whiting (1950) present some questionnaire data obtained from 151 male undergraduates who were asked to write out descriptions of two goal-attainment incidents they had experienced—one that had been preceded by a period of frustrated attempts and one of simple goal attainment without any appreciable frustration. The subjects then responded to a number of questions about each incident. The most frequently reported response to goal attainment was relaxation and enjoyment of the goal. However, one of the most apparent results of goal attainment was an increase in the person's confidence that other, similar goals must also be attainable. As Child and Whiting (1950) put it, ". . . there is strong evidence that renewed striving as a response to goal attainment is positively associated with an increase in confidence as a result of the attainment of the goal in the particular incident" (p. 675). Further, in line with the attributional analysis discussed earlier, the questionnaire responses also revealed an association, albeit a weak one, between renewed striving following goal attainment and self-blame for the frustration that preceded attainment. In other words, the more subjects saw the previous failures as their fault, the more likely they were to renew striving following success. Apparently, they perceived their own efforts to make a difference.

There are, of course, ambiguities of interpretation with the sort of retrospective data reported by Child and Whiting. Further, as we saw in the section on learned helplessness, the extent to which success or failure on one task or in one situation leads to shifts in the subjective probability of success on other tasks and in other situations is still an open question. The theoretical position developed earlier, that is, that one's subjective probability of success has both dispositional and situational components, assumes that generalization does occur. Similarly, the works of Rotter (1966), Seligman (1975), and numerous others are predicated on the assumption of generalization, but that, of course, does not make it so. The assumption does lead to a perspective which, for the moment at least, appears to facilitate the attempt to understand the available evidence.

As for the consequences of goal attainment on fatigue, it seems obvious that fatigue is produced by effort expended in pursuit of the goal. It is generally assumed that the only relationship between goal attainment and fatigue is that with goal attainment, effort ceases, and the effects of fatigue stop accumulating and begin to dissipate. Somewhat paradoxically, however, it appears that part of the enjoyment associated with goal attainment may stem from allowing oneself to experience fatigue. It seems plausible that a process that might contribute to one's ability to sustain performance for long periods of time is the underestimation of the amount of fatigue that one is experiencing. The veridical perception of the amount of fatigue one is experiencing would be very unpleasant and could interfere with continued performance. To illustrate this point, Walster and Aronson (1967) use the following example:

> Suppose a person embarked on a 10-mile hike. Near the end of the hike we would expect him to be perfectly aware that he was extremely fatigued. The very thought of hiking for an additional 10 miles might appear noxious or even impossible. If, however, the same person had embarked on a 20-mile hike, walking at the same pace, and in the same manner as the 10-mile hiker, at the end of 10 miles he might feel less fatigued; the experience of great fatigue would be incompatible with his knowledge that he must hike an additional 10 miles. Thus, we would expect him to suppress such a feeling or underestimate its intensity . . . (p. 42).

In other words, if two people who have each performed at the same level on the same task for the same amount of time have different perceptions of how far off the goal is, the one who perceives the goal to be closer should be the more fatigued.

To test this idea, Walster and Aronson (1967) designed a very simple two-condition experiment in which, for repeated trials, subjects in both conditions were asked to perform highly fatiguing tasks. One task was marking Xs in squares of graph paper at the rate of one X per second, the pace being set by a metronome, for 10 minutes. The second fatiguing task involved measurement of the subject's visual threshold. In addition, prior to beginning either of these tasks, subjects had been required to dark-adapt for 45 minutes and to answer a lengthy questionnaire. After dark-adaptation, subjects in the long-expectancy condition were told there would be five trials at the X-marking and visual-threshold task, whereas subjects assigned to the short-expectancy condition were told there would only be three trials. On each trial, subjects were asked to indicate how fatigued they were on a scale ranging from zero ("as fresh as I have ever been") to 13.5 ("as tired as I have ever been"). The results on this measure show essentially no differences between the long- and short-expectancy groups on Trials 1 and 2. However, on Trial 3, the short-expectancy group indicated a sizeable increase in experienced fatigue, whereas the long expectancy group did not. It appears that, "The expectancy of continued performance mitigates the veridical perception of one's own fatigue. Individuals tend to underestimate the extent of their fatigue until they feel that they have virtually completed their task" (Walster and Aronson, 1967, p. 45).

Such misattribution, in conjunction with the effort justification hypothesis discussed earlier, may indeed play a part in sustaining performance over long periods of time. Unfortunately, there has not yet been much research on long term, real-life goals. Hence, it is impossible to know at this point if the sorts of variables we have been discussing play a role in the pursuit of such goals. Needless to say, I am convinced they do, and there are a handful of studies that support the extension to real-life situations. We have already examined some on the relationship of anxiety to college grades. McClelland (1965), to take only one further example, reports that among Wesleyan University students, need for achievement, as measured in 1947, was predictive of the occupations of those same students 14 years later, in 1961. Thus, there have been a few beginnings, but much remains to be done.

SUMMARY

We began this chapter with an examination of the effects of prior success and failure on subsequent performance of the same task. It appears that prior success tends to raise one's subjective probability of success for future performance and that such increases in the subjective probability of success are followed by improved performance. On the other hand, prior failure appears to lower one's subjective probability of success and such decreases are followed by poorer performance. Further, the evidence appears to indicate that one's subjective probability of success has two components: a dispositional and a situational component. The former appears to be most influential in determining initial performance on an unfamiliar task. As one gains experience on a task, the influence of the dispositional component fades and the situational component, as determined by one's experience in the task at hand, becomes a better predictor of performance.

We then turned to an attributional analysis of feedback. It appears that the perceived reasons for one's success or failure are more important in determining future performance than success or failure per se. Failure may, in fact, lead to an increase in one's subjective probability of success and in one's improved performance if the failure is attributed to luck or lack of effort. Further, feedback of success or failure may not always mean what it is intended to mean. It is necessary to know the particular goal or level of performance a person is striving to attain in order to understand how feedback will be interpreted and what effect it will have on performance. It also appears that increasing the incentive to perform in a particular situation decreases the influence of the dispositional component of one's subjective probability of success.

Next, we examined some research on the discrepancy between expectancy and performance and reinterpreted these data in terms of the effects of uncertainty on variability in responding. This led to a discussion of several studies, which have related anxiety to performance. The literature on anxiety and performance appears quite consistent with several of the hypotheses developed earlier. Again the data suggest the operation of both situational and dispositional determinants of one's subjective probability of success and point to maximum distraction, arousal, and response variability when the perceived probability of success is at an intermediate level. It was argued that such behaviors should decrease the likelihood of a successful performance if compared with the behaviors of someone with a high subjective probability of success and, simultaneously, increase the likelihood of a successful performance if compared with the behaviors of someone with a low subjective probability of success.

While the research on anxiety seemed to focus on the intermediate levels of probability, the next topic discussed was primarily concerned with the effects of very low levels of the subjective probability of success. The work on learned helplessness indicates that the perception of independence between one's outcomes and responses is a motivational disaster. The important, and still open, question about the helplessness research is the extent to which such effects generalize and become dispositional characteristics. Finally, we made a few comments about the consequences of goal attainment. In contrast to earlier conceptualizations, it appears that the most important things about goal attainment are what it means for the pursuit of other goals and for the experience of fatigue.

7
Expectations, Health, and Disease

... medicine will eventually flounder in a sea of irrelevancy unless it learns more of the relations of the body ... to the total environment, ... the past, and the aspirations of human beings.

Dubos, 1965

Only in the past three decades has modern medicine begun to take seriously the view that environmental, social, and psychological factors play important roles in both health and disease. Not too many years ago the suggestion that such abstract phenomena as aspirations or expectations could actually influence susceptibility to illness or the course of a disease once it has been contracted would have been met with derision in scientific medical circles. As the evidence has mounted, however, the view that "... all illness is to some extent affected by the way that men perceive their life situations and react to them" (Hinkle and Wolff, 1958, p. 1385) has won increasing acceptance. In the present chapter we shall explore some of the evidence that aspirations and expectations do play a role in health and disease. We begin with one of the oldest known influences of expectations in medicine, placebo effects, then turn to the topic of general susceptibility to illness, and end up with a brief examination of voodoo and apathy deaths.

PLACEBO EFFECTS

The term *placebo* had been around for a long time. The generally agreed upon translation of this Latin verb form is "I shall please," and many consider placebos as substances given or procedures employed purely to pacify patients.

Of course, it is less than clear why pacification is not considered beneficial in and of itself. As we shall see, however, placebos have beneficial effects above and beyond that of "mere" pacification.

Interest in placebos and placebo effects appears to have increased rather dramatically in the past few years. Shapiro (1960), for example, reports that more articles on placebos appeared in the medical literature in the period from 1954 to 1957 than in the entire first half of the twentieth century. There are a number of possible reasons for this rather belated surge of interest. One of the more interesting alternatives has to do with the nature of medicine itself down through the ages. That is, as a number of medical historians have pointed out, up until about a hundred years ago nearly all medications and therapeutic procedures were, in effect, placebos. Only with the development of specifically effective medications, vaccines, and procedures could interest in placebo effects per se emerge without posing too much of a threat to medical practitioners. As long as the only effects produced were placebo effects, medicine would have been totally destroyed by having that point publicized.

There are, of course, other factors involved in the recent surge of interest in placebos. Increased public exposure to advertising and other information about drugs has made more people aware of the curious fact that many medicines which, when they are initially introduced, appear to work wonders, later turn out to be completely ineffective. It seems rather natural that people would begin to wonder about the initial cures produced.

Whatever combination of reasons really accounts for the relatively recent focusing of explicit attention on placebos, it seems clear that people have long been aware of the existence of placebo-like effects. Unfortunately, awareness that such effects occurred was not sufficient to prevent practitioners from continuing to make the mistake of placing their own faith in untested and unevaluated medications and procedures. Shapiro (1960) gives the following example:

> Trousseau, who was able to say, "you should treat as many patients as possible with the new drugs while they have the power to heal" was [also] able to claim diseases (such as neuralgia, nervous dyspnoea, anginia pectoris and rheumatism) to be cured, modified and rapidly checked by the use of magnets, "which it is impossible to refer to the patient's imagination!" (p. 116).

We all have our little blind spots. As Rosenthal and Frank (1956) point out, ".... the relief of any particular complaint by a given medication is not sufficient evidence for the specific effect of the medicine on this complaint unless it can be shown that the relief is not obtained as a placebo effect" (p. 296).

Let us see, then, what effects placebos do have. Can the belief or expectation that a particular substance will produce psychological and physiological change actually produce those changes? Even if the substance is pharmacologically inert? Is there any good evidence, in short, that placebos can relieve complaints and produce cures? Probably the most common symptom and the most frequently mentioned presenting complaint in all of medicine is pain. Hence, pain relief seems a reasonable area in which to begin an examination of placebo effects.

Pain Relief

Early attempts to study pain in the laboratory by experimentally producing pain in humans resulted in several red herrings being introduced into the literature. For example, consider the procedure employed by Hardy, Wolff, and Goodell (1940) of focusing heat on the skin and having subjects report just noticeable increases in intensity as well as the time when the heat became painful. The fact that the skin temperature at which the pain threshold occurred was relatively constant and close to the temperature at which tissue destruction began led to the mistaken belief that tissue destruction was the necessary and sufficient condition for pain. Yet anecdotal evidence appears to indicate that, given tissue damage of approximately the same magnitude, reports of pain vary with the significance or meaning attached to the damage (Beecher, 1959; Melzack, 1961). Further, given the same physiological disorders, members of some cultures are much more likely to report associated pain than are members of other cultures (Zola, 1966). There are also numerous reports of people being injured during some highly-charged emotional event and not even being aware of their injury until later.

While these examples hint at the role of expectations in pain perception, there are problems of interpretation in each. Zola's (1966) finding, for example, may be due to cultural differences in stoicism or the inclination to adopt the sick role (Mechanic, 1966) and not to actual differences in pain perception. The experience of pain seems so attention-compelling and primitive when it occurs that it is difficult for most people to believe the extent to which the perception of pain is dependent on nonphysiological factors. Hence, we need some clear experimental evidence that avoids the interpretive ambiguities of anecdotes.

As we have already noted, however, experimentation with pain perception is itself a tricky business and there is another precaution suggested by past research on pain. Beecher (1962) points out that "... some 15 groups of investigators have ... utterly failed to demonstrate any dependable effect of even large doses of powerful narcotics on the experimental pain threshold in man. Yet ... small doses of these same narcotics are universally effective in lessening or relieving completely the pain of great wounds" (p. 439). There are, as Beecher (1966) and others have demonstrated, qualitative differences between experimentally produced threshold pain and the pain associated with various injuries and somatic disorders. *In vitro is not in vivo*. To look at the effect of placebos on pain relief, then, we shall confine ourselves to some exemplary experimental studies—to avoid ambiguities of interpretation—carried out in connection with pathological pain—to avoid having to make any assumptions about whether the results will generalize to real life.

Beecher, Keats, Mosteller, and Lasagna (1953) compared the effectiveness of placebos as pain relievers with the effectiveness of morphine, codeine, and acetylsalicylic acid. Subjects in the study were hospital patients who were experiencing postoperative[1] pain. The patients were given alternately a placebo capsule or one of the analgesic drug capsules every two hours—usually beginning this alternation thirty hours after surgery. The capsules were given only as necessary for pain and evaluations of pain relief were made by persons unaware of the nature of the agents employed. The evaluations of pain relief consisted of the patients' statements as to whether or not the pain had subsided and were made at one hour and two hour intervals after each administration. Data on the first two pairs of doses are presented in Table 7.1. As can be seen in the table, in each group of patients the analgesic drug was somewhat more effective. However, in three of the four groups this difference in pain relief effectiveness was very small. Further, in all groups placebos brought relief 25 to 40 percent of the time.

A number of studies have found similar results. Beecher (1955), for example, cites 15 reports involving a total of 1,082 patients in which placebos were found to have an average significant effectiveness of 35.2 ± 2.2 percent. One possibility suggested by such repeated findings, a possibility that apparently occurred to many people, is that there are stable individual differences among patients in the tendency to show a positive reaction to placebos. The attempts to identify such patients with tests of suggestibility or intelligence or other personality variables or by demographic factors have generally been unsuccessful and/or inconsistent (Shapiro, 1971). There seem to be two reasons for this general failure. First, if placebo effects are really a function of the patients' expectations or faith or hope or anticipation of improvement or relief, then those expectations and anticipations are likely to be specific to certain situations. What inspires faith in one situation for one patient and leads to improvement may be missing in a second situation or perceived differently by a second patient in the same situation. Secondly, it seems that those seeking to identify personality variables that will differentiate placebo reactors from nonreactors have been looking at the wrong variables. There is some evidence in the literature that, if one were to develop a test of the extent to which people were in touch with their internal states and aware of bodily reactions, then placebo reactors might well be identifiable psychometrically.

For example, consider the following study by Jellinek (1946). Starting with a headache remedy, Drug A, composed of three ingredients (a, b, and c), Jellinek

---

[1] Patients who had had surgery of the central nervous system or the gastrointestinal tract, and those with prolonged nausea were not included.

TABLE 7.1
Analgesic Potency of Agents Administered Orally Compared With a Placebo[a]

Number of patients	Agent	% Relief	Agent	% Relief	Difference in % relief
52	Placebo	40.0	Acetylsal. acid (300 mgm.)	50.0	+10.0
36	Placebo	25.5	Acetylsal. acid (600 mgm.)	54.9	+29.4
44	Placebo	33.9	Codeine (60 mgm.)	38.7	+ 4.8
40	Placebo	31.5	Morphine (10 mgm.)	40.7	+ 9.2

[a]From Beecher, *et al.* 1953, p. 394. Copyright 1953 by the Williams and Wilkins Co., Baltimore, Maryland. Reprinted by Permission.

compared the effectiveness of Drug A, Drug B (composed of *a* and *c*), Drug C (composed of *a* and *b*), and Drug D (a placebo) in relieving headaches. All drugs were made to appear identical in size, shape, and taste. For four periods of two weeks, four groups of subjects were asked to take tablets whenever a headache occurred and to return at the end of each two-week period. Each group of subjects took a different drug (A, B, C, or D) during each two-week period. Thus, each group served as its own control and the order of using different drugs could be counterbalanced. At the end of each two-week period, subjects reported the number of headaches for which they had taken a drug and the number of headaches relieved. From these data, a success rate was calculated by dividing the number relieved by the number treated.

At the end of eight weeks, the overall mean success rates for the four kinds of tablets were: A = .84, B = .80, C = .80, and D = .52. A hasty conclusion here might be that there was essentially no difference in the effectiveness of A, B, and C and that all three were about 30 percent more effective than the placebo, D. However, Jellinek points out that such a conclusion would be both meaningless and misleading. To illustrate his point, he separated the data for those subjects for whom the placebo had some effect from the data for those subjects for whom the placebo had no effect and presented the following table (see Table 7.2). As can be seen in the table, among those subjects not showing a reaction to the placebo, there are consistent (and significant) differences among the three drugs in terms of their effectiveness. Drug A is consistently the most and Drug B the least effective. On the other hand, among subjects reacting to the placebo, the differences in effectiveness of Drugs A, B, and C are neither significant nor consistent.

Similar results are reported in the study by Beecher et al. (1953), which was discussed above. When subjects showing a positive reaction (pain relief) from

TABLE 7.2
Clinical Tests on Comparative Effectiveness of
Analgesic Drugs

Gp.	Subjects Not Reacting to Placebo				Subjects Reacting to Placebo			
	Drugs				Drugs			
	n	A	B	C	n	A	B	C
1	14	.90	.65	.86	36	.76	.87	.83
2	26	.88	.66	.70	23	.76	.84	.87
3	20	.85	.60	.71	30	.89	.85	.76
4	19	.91	.82	.86	31	.86	.90	.83
All	79	.88	.67	.77	120	.82	.87	.82

[a]From Jellinck, 1946. (*Biometrics*, 1946, *2*, 87–91. With permission from the Biometric Society.)

placebos were separated from those not showing such a reaction, it was found that in the former group there were no differences in relief obtained from aspirin or morphine and codeine. Among placebo nonreactors, however, aspirin was significantly more effective than morphine or codeine.

Thus, there appears to be some evidence that placebo reactors are somewhat less able to discriminate their internal reactions. This makes more plausible the possibility that they may be responding predominantly to expectations developed in the situation at hand, expectations that are presumably the same regardless of which particular tablet is ingested. Unfortunately, however, the above studies made no attempt to assess patient expectations and to relate expectations to the likelihood of showing a placebo reaction. A study which made an attempt to overcome these shortcomings is reported by Lasagna, Mosteller, von Felsinger, and Beecher (1954).

In this study, postoperative patients on general surgical, urologic, orthopedic, and gynecologic wards were selected for study if morphine or a similar narcotic had been prescribed by the hospital staff for pain relief. From a group of 93 patients who had been administered alternate doses of placebo and morphine, 27 were selected who had responded in a fairly consistent fashion to the injections: 11 were always relieved of pain by placebo injections; 13 were never relieved; and 3 were usually not relieved. These 27 patients were then studied intensively via interviews, projective tests, intelligence tests, and the collection of various demographic data. The types of surgery and anesthetic were similar for the reactors and nonreactors. Further, the two groups could not be differentiated on the basis of their intelligence test results or observations by ward personnel. However, all of the reactors were very positive and enthusiastic about their hospital care—in fact, all of the placebo reactors found the hospital care to be wonderful, while only 4 of the 16 nonreactors felt this way. This could reasonably be assumed to be an indirect assessment of positive expectations, were it not for the unfortunate fact that the interviews were conducted after patients had or had not obtained relief from the placebo injections. Thus, the placebo reactors had, in fact, experienced less pain than the nonreactors, and the interview data may simply reflect that fact.

Most discussions of placebo effects clearly implicate the patients' expectations as being important in the production of such effects (cf., Goldstein, 1962). It is somewhat surprising, then, that there appear to have been no studies which have directly assessed expectations about the likelihood of pain relief prior to administration of a placebo. It follows from our previous discussion (Chapter 5) that, the greater the perceived probability of pain relief, the greater the actual relief experienced. As for the physiological mechanism by which expectations might have such an influence, Melzack and Wall (1965) point out that pain is generally considered to be the sensory component of an imperative protective reflex and that, "It is now firmly established . . . that stimulation of the brain activates descending efferent fibers . . . which can influence afferent conduction at the earliest synaptic levels of the somesthetic system. Thus it is possible for central nervous system activities subserving attention, emotion, and memories of prior experience to exert control over the sensory input" (pp. 975–976).

Rather than pursue the literature on pain relief, suppose we grant that placebos can indeed reduce pain—this, in fact, seems clear—and that the expectation of pain relief is a key mediating variable. Someone might still point out that pain is a very subjective experience and, in the final analysis, its magnitude is not verifiable by an outside observer. Our purpose might better be served, then, by asking if there are any documented instances of concrete, verifiable physiological changes being produced by placebos and if there is any evidence that such changes are related to expectations that they will occur.

Physiological Changes

Although not generally recognized, evidence that placebos can produce objective physiological changes has been around for some time. A number of relatively sophisticated double-blind experiments that included placebo control conditions were carried out in the late 1940s and early 1950s to evaluate the effects of specific drugs. We, of course, are not interested in the various drugs themselves, but only in the placebo conditions.

An example is a study by Wolf (1954), which reports an evaluation of mephenesin (Tolserol) requested by E.R. Squibb and Sons. The subjects were 31 patients in a New York hospital who were suffering from a variety of disorders, but for all of whom anxiety and tension were prominent among their complaints. The purpose of the study was to see if Tolserol exerted a specific effect on subjective anxiety and tension. Squibb furnished the investigator with six batches of pills, all of which were identical in taste, shape, and smell, but some of which were placebos. The period of observation was broken down into two-week intervals, and each patient was given medication from a new batch of pills every two weeks (two pills, four times a day). Thus, each patient served as his or her own control, and neither the person administering the pills, nor the patient, nor the persons recording symptoms and signs (for evidence of anxiety relief) knew whether a patient was taking a placebo or Tolserol at any given time.

The results comparing placebos and Tolserol are of little interest here. However, three patients had major toxic reactions while taking placebos. One developed a severe rash that went away as soon as she stopped taking the pills. A second developed nausea, overwhelming weakness, and palpitations about 15 minutes after every dosage. The third patient developed epigastric pain, watery diarrhea, urticaria, and edema of the lips within 10 minutes of taking her pills. After 48 and again after 96 hours, a second and third trial of pills produced the same reactions. Further, "This patient was [then] shifted to another batch. When the same reaction followed again, she was given no further pills. When the batches were finally identified, it was found that she had had her severe reactions with both mephenesin and placebos" (Wolf, 1954, p. 340).

A number of other experiments have also documented physiological reactions and changes to placebos and, conversely, the absence of physiological reactions and changes to pharmacologically active substances. Wolf (1950) points out that the effects of a drug are not necessarily the same each time it is administered because the pharmacologic action may either enhance or oppose other forces acting on the particular organ or system at the same time. Among the other forces that may interact with the pharmacologic action are those due to: the state of the organ or system at the time of administration; the setting in which administration takes place; and previously established habits and conditioning associated with various aspects of administration.

In support of the above points, Wolf (1950) and Abbott, Mack, and Wolf (1952) report a number of experiments and observations on a human subject with a large gastric fistula in whom it was possible to observe and measure directly several aspects of the gastric mucous membrane and its activity. For example, administration of an antihistamine had a depressing effect upon both gastric blood flow and acidity when the stomach was in an average state and the patient was relatively relaxed and contented. On the other hand, administration of the same drug had no effect on either blood flow or acidity when the patient was tense and angry. Further, a series of eight experiments on the same patient involving the oral administration of urogastrone revealed that, ". . . when the stomach was not hyperaemic and hypersecretive, the agent induced an evident inhibition of secretion associated with pallor and diminution of turgidity. When, on the other hand, the agent was administered in the presence of gastric hyperfunction, little or no effect was noted" (Wolf, 1950, p. 101).

There is much additional evidence that placebos can and do produce physiological changes and that the effects of pharmacologically active drugs are modified by a number of extraneous situational, cognitive, and physiological factors. However, we need to go back to the second part of the question that began this section and see if there is any evidence that expectancies mediate such effects (or noneffects).

Toward the end of a lengthy review of data on the benefits of and adverse reactions to oral contraceptives, Pincus (1966) reports the following experiment. Two groups of Puerto Rican women were given an effective oral contraceptive (Enovid)—one group with no mention of possible side effects and the second group with an admonition that certain effects might occur, such as nausea, dizziness, and headaches. A third group of women was given a placebo[2] instead of birth-control pills along with the same admonition that side effects might occur. Reports of physical ill-being such as nausea, vomiting, and headache were approximately the same in the two groups expecting such effects to occur—regardless of whether they were taking Enovid or a placebo. Further, the frequency of such problems was much higher in both of these groups than among the women taking Enovid but not expecting side effects to occur.

Although this result is certainly compatible with the view taken here, there are several difficulties with Pincus's study. First, they may simply reflect a difference in recall. Women admonished to expect certain effects may attend to those effects more closely when they do occur and hence recall them more easily when later questioned about their occurrence. Secondly, the two groups who were led to believe that side effects would occur lived in a different city from the women given Enovid with no admonition about side effects. The latter group lived in a different city from the former two groups. Thus, there may have been systematic differences among the groups, but even if there were not regional or cultural differences in the tendency to report illness, the experimenters obviously were not blind as to the condition to which the subjects had been assigned and may have biased the results obtained.

Fortunately, there are additional data which bear on the expectation—placebo—physiological change sequence. Wolf (1950), for example, reports several studies in which it was suggested to patients that a substance they were about to receive would abolish their nausea and vomiting. The patients were then given doses of Ipecac, a substance which normally induces nausea by relaxing the stomach and interrupting its contractile activity. Within 20 minutes of administration, nausea and vomiting stopped and did not return until the following day.

---

[2] The women in this group were asked not to abandon their use of vaginal (diaphragm and jelly) contraceptives for several months.

In a somewhat better controlled study: Strupp, Levenson, Manuck, Snell, Hinrichsen, and Boyd (1974) employed a double-blind procedure to investigate the effects of expectations on bronchodilation in asthmatics. The subjects were 13 asthmatic college students, each of whom participated individually in 3 experimental sessions. During each session a nurse, who was blind as to the substance she was administering, had subjects inhale either a placebo or a bronchodilator (Isuprel). After each inhalation the subjects breathed for 60 breaths into a respiratory resistance unit, which recorded both the pressure and flow of their breath from which the total respiratory resistance was calculated by dividing the former by the latter. Prior to each of the two inhalations at a given experimental session, the nurse described the placebo or dilator she was about to administer as either being neutral ("this is a test substance which has no effect and is used only to calibrate our equipment" p. 339), a bronchodilator ("this is a substance frequently used to help people open up their airways and breathe more easily" p. 339), or a bronchoconstrictor ("the substance is known to produce marked airway constriction in individuals with your predisposition" p. 339).

Since the interpretation of the changes in total respiratory resistance is ambiguous when an actual bronchodilator was administered following a suggestion, we shall attend only to the data from administration of the placebo inhalant. As expected, when described as a neutral substance, the placebo produced no changes in respiratory resistance. However, when described as a bronchoconstrictor[3], the placebo produced a marginally significant ($p < .10$) increase in respiratory resistance for the group as a whole. Further, as in our earlier discussion of pain relief, the data indicate a striking ". . . tendency for some subjects to consistently react to the *pharmacological* effect of the inhalant and for others to react more prominently to the *suggested* effect" (p. 341). It would have been nice for our purpose if the design had included some way of checking on the extent to which the suggestions influenced expectancies, but it did not. We would anticipate, of course, that the suggestions were most effective in influencing the expectancies of people who were subsequent reactors.

It appears that we can tentatively answer the two questions with which we began this section in the affirmative. Placebos can produce objective, physiological changes and it seems to be the case that the expectations that such changes will occur are at least partial determiners of their occurrence. There are other lines of research that strengthen these conclusions. For example, there is evidence that enthusiastic physicians who communicate their optimism for a particular procedure or course of treatment to their patients have higher success rates than skeptical physicians, in both surgery (Beecher, 1961) and other types

---

[3] Strupp, *et al.* did not administer the placebo following the suggestion that it was a bronchodilator.

of treatment (Fisher, Cole, Rickels, and Uhlenhuth, 1964). Rather than pursue this topic of the extent to which expectations can influence physiology solely in the context of placebo effects, let us take it to a somewhat more general level and inquire if there is any evidence or reason to believe that expectations influence our states of health and disease.

HEALTH AND DISEASE

It seems to be the case that most people blame illness or disease on external factors, which somehow invade the body and make a mess of things—the disease is seen as being due to something they ate, or they caught, or which happened to them. Implicit in such reasoning is an idea that can be traced throughout medical history, but appears to have become most firmly established, in the minds of laymen and health workers alike, only in the last 100 years. This idea is the doctrine of specific etiology (Dubos, 1965) and, simply put, implies that for each disease there is *a* cause—usually a microbe or germ or a deficiency of some sort that produces the disease.

After having been around for centuries, this doctrine became entrenched as scientific medicine's party line only in the late nineteenth and early twentieth centuries. According to Dubos (1965), the reasons for the overestablishment of the doctrine at this particular point in history were the repeated successes of the followers of Louis Pasteur and Robert Koch in demonstrating the applicability of Pasteur's germ theory of disease to the identification of specific microbes responsible for many of the acute infectious diseases that were ravaging the world's populations. As Dodge and Martin (1970) point out:

> For one disease after another, specific causative pathogens were isolated and specific curative agents were developed. The traditional multicausal perspective, stressing the loss of a maintenance equilibrium involving man as a whole and varying factors in his total environment, was slowly being relinquished in the face of the overwhelming evidence in favor of the germ theory. Indeed, during this period Pasteur attested before the Paris Academy of Medicine that the discovery of specific causes heralded the end of the "old medicine" (p. 13).

The "old medicine" has been gradually reasserting itself, however. The doctrine of specific etiology simply leaves too many questions unanswered. How, for example, can it account for the fact (Engel, 1975) that many people who are exposed to the tubercle bacillus never develop tuberculosis? Or, more generally, how could it account for the finding that the features "... of a disease are determined more by the response of the organism as a whole than by the characteristics of the causative agent" (Dubos, 1965, p. 327). There is obviously more involved than the mechanistic unfolding of a disease process initiated by the invasion of a microbe.

It is an added testimony to Pasteur's greatness, if any were needed, that in later life he recognized the limitations of the doctrine of specific etiology. As Selye (1956) relates, Pasteur had been

... sharply criticized by many of his enemies for failing to recognize the importance of the *terrain* (the soil in which disease develops). They said he was too one-sidedly preoccupied with the apparent cause of disease: the microbe itself. There were, in fact, many debates about this between Pasteur and his great contemporary, Claude Bernard; the former insisted on the importance of the disease-producer, the latter on that of the body's own equilibrium. Yet Pasteur's work on immunity induced with serums and vaccines shows that he recognized the importance of the soil. In any event, it is rather significant that Pasteur attached so much importance to this point that on his deathbed he said to Professor A. Rénon who looked after him: "Bernard was right. The microbe is nothing, the soil is everything"[4] (p. 205).

My own interest in the possibility that expectations may influence health and disease was initially triggered by some data bearing on *le terrain*, that is, on the susceptibility of the host. We shall take a brief look at those data and then turn to a possible mediating mechanism between social–psychological factors and susceptibility. We shall then examine some evidence on life changes, social stress, and illness which appears to support the hypothesized relationships.

General Susceptibility to Illness

It is well known that the probability of illness increases greatly as one descends the socioeconomic scale. From a psychological point of view, this is an interesting, but ambiguous, fact. Expectancies might conceivably be involved, but there are too many nonpsychological explanations that could more plausibly account for it. Low socioeconomic status is, for example, related to: (1) more congested living conditions; (2) poorer sanitation facilities; (3) poorer general levels of nutrition; and (4) more stressful working conditions. The first two of these factors would increase the probability of exposure to infectious agents and the last two would lay the groundwork for the onset of the chronic diseases which have become the bane of life in the twentieth century.

Suppose it were true, however, that, within homogeneous social groups, there were sizeable differences in the frequencies with which members experienced illness and contracted diseases. Then the usual processes invoked to explain social class differences in the incidence and prevalence of illness would not be applicable. Consider the following study by Hinkle, Pinsky, Bross, and Plummer (1956). It involved 226 men who had been continuously employed for at least 20 years in the installation and repair division of a telephone company in the center of a large city. Most of the men had been between 16 and 24 years of age

---

[4] *Bernard avait raison. Le germe n'est rien, c'est le terrain qui est tout.* (Copyright 1956 by McGraw-Hill Co., New York, Reprinted by Permission.)

when first employed and were, thus, steadily employed at the same company for the first two decades of adult life. Nearly all of them had completed high school and had had some additional technical training beyond that; nearly all were married and had children; and most of them owned or rented individual houses. As Hinkle et al. (1956) point out, "Insofar as it can ever be said that a large group of men share an equal opportunity to encounter the external causative agents of disease, the statement can probably be made of this group" (p. 223). In short, these men worked for the same company, at the same jobs, over the same period of time; shared the same climate, environment, working conditions, level of income, and sanitation facilities; and were exposed to the same metropolitan community influences. Further, a required medical examination and history taken prior to employment insured that all men had been in good health at the time of initial employment. Men having other than minor physical defects were rejected, as were those for whom there was any evidence of peculiar behavior.

The data available on each man consisted of his complete medical history over a 20-year period. Specifically, the company had a record of the initial-employment physical examination and medical history; records of physical examinations and medical histories, performed at intervals of several years over the 20-year period; a complete work attendance record for each man, listing each absence and the reason for it; and a record of every visit to the company's medical department, including descriptions of the reason for each visit. Further, when any of the men were hospitalized, copies of their hospital records were obtained and included in their medical folder. From these records, a tabulation was made for each man of all illness episodes he had experienced over the 20-year period. Before commenting on the results, it is worth pointing out a number of similar studies that have been conducted.

During the early and middle 1950s, Hinkle and his colleagues investigated the frequency and distribution of illness episodes in a number of different populations: Hungarian refugees, Chinese graduate students and professionals, female telephone operators, recent college graduates, and the skilled workmen we have been discussing above. In each of these and other populations, data relating to health, life experiences, and background over a 20-year period were derived from a number of sources, including extensive interviews, physical examinations, medical records, and reports of relatives and friends. In some of the studies, for example in the investigation of health and illness among Chinese graduate students and professionals, the data were obtained almost entirely from verbal reports of the subjects themselves. In other studies, such as that of the 226 telephone installers and repairmen, the health history data were obtained from objective medical records, which had been continuously maintained for 20 years.

The major results in each of these studies, regardless of the method of data collection and regardless of the particular population examined, were essentially the same, and we shall discuss them together. One of the most striking findings to emerge is that, within each group, during the two decades of young adult life, 25 percent of the individuals experienced approximately 50 percent of all illness episodes while another 25 percent experienced less than 10 percent of all illness episodes. Further, those experiencing the greater number of illness episodes were not simply having recurring bouts with some chronic malady. They were found to have more different major and minor syndromes involving more different organ systems and falling into more different etiological categories. The fact that the effect occurs for major as well as minor illnesses casts some doubt on the possibility that it could be accounted for by differences in the tendency to report sickness or by differential inclinations to take the sick role. Some people apparently have a greater general susceptibility to illness of all kinds—regardless of type or the causal agents apparently involved.

In addition, Hinkle and Wolff (1958) point out that the examination of illness patterns over extended periods of time reveals that each person has a rather constant mean rate of illness episodes. However, from time to time, there occur clusters of illness episodes, usually of several years duration, within which the individual's episode rate is significantly elevated. They point out that, "It was . . . common to observe that peak periods of illness occurred in the absence of any significant change in activity, diet, or exposure to infection, trauma, toxic materials or other physical aspects of the environment" (pp. 1381–1382). The occurrence of these clusters of diseases seems to argue against genetic influences being a major factor. Why should a cluster occur at a particular point in a person's life if only inherited dispositions were responsible? Such dispositions might be necessary, but hardly sufficient.

Thus, within homogeneous social groups, illness is not randomly distributed. It appears that some people have a greater general susceptibility than others. Also, for any given individual, illness is not randomly distributed over the course of his or her life. There is a tendency for illness episodes to occur in clusters. It also appears that physical aspects of the environment and genetic influences do not offer fully adequate explanations for either of these findings.[5]

When I first came across Hinkle's research, I was genuinely awed by the implications. I am not quite sure what I had been assuming, but it was probably something to the effect that, even if illness was not randomly distributed across populations, it was randomly distributed within populations. If you were lucky, you stayed healthy. If not, well, that's the way it goes. Others have, apparently, shared my initial reaction to Hinkle's findings. In commenting on a paper by Hinkle (1961), in which much of the earlier research is summarized, Lemkau

---

[5] It is important to note that illness episodes are *not* independent events. Having one disease generally increases the probability of subsequent diseases, and this increase comes about via purely physiological mechanisms. Hence, the phenomena we are discussing may not have anything to do with expectations. Our purpose, however, is hypothesis generation, not proof.

(1961) says that, as far as etiological research is concerned, "A host factor so tremendous and so undiscriminating as seems to me to be theoretically implied by Dr. Hinkle's present data . . . leaves me, at least, most uncomfortable in relation to the value of research regarding definable specific diseases" (p. 297).

The intriguing question, to me, was what lay behind an increase in the general susceptibility to illness. There were numerous speculations, suggestions, and anecdotes in the literature that seemed to implicate expectations as contributing factors in general susceptibility. Engel (1968), for example, had suggested that a psychological giving-up of attempts to cope with one's problems and life situation often preceded the onset of illness. Hinkle, Christenson, Kane, Ostfield, Thetford, and Wolff (1958), in a detailed comparison of the characteristics of a sample of subjects who had experienced a large number of illness episodes over a 20-year period with those of a similar sample who had experienced relatively few episodes, found that the former were more likely to view their lives ". . . as difficult, demanding, and unsatisfactory" (p. 293). Such retrospective perceptions may, unfortunately, be the results of rather than the precursors of the greater frequency of illness experienced. In any event, this implication, that the perceived inability to obtain valued goals in life could—somehow—result in physiological changes that increased one's susceptibility to illness, seemed to run through much of the psychosomatic literature. Before looking at some of the pertinent evidence, however, it might be well to say a little about the somehow.

Stress and Psychosomatics

Although both terms in the above heading have been around for a long time, only in the last half century have they come into prominent and frequent use in medicine. The term psychosomatic highlights the inappropriateness of discussing mind and body as if they were separate. Although the term itself is yet to be indexed in some of the more mechanistically oriented physiology textbooks (cf., Vander, Sherman, and Luciano, 1970), the idea that the mind and body are mutually interdependent seems to have passed beyond the realm of serious debate. Many questions remain, of course, about the nature of this interdependence.

As for the term stress, it was introduced by Selye to designate a stereotyped, nonspecific response of the body to any demand made upon it. As is now well known, the internal changes Selye discovered were the indices that begin to develop in stage two of what he later named the *general adaptation syndrome*. It appears to be the case that, in response to diverse stressors, the body goes through three stages: an initial alarm reaction in which resistance to the stressor falls below normal; a stage of resistance in which all of the body's resources are mobilized to resist the effects of the stressor; and, if the stressor is not removed or successfully neutralized, an eventual stage of exhaustion in which resistance again drops below normal. It was, of course, true that each different type of stressor produced some specific effects that were peculiar to itself. Extreme cold produced some effects that an injection of Formalin did not and vice versa. However, both extreme cold and an injection of Formalin produced evidence of the operation of the general adaptation syndrome.

For our purposes, there are two questions of interest here. First, is it possible that the body's own response to diverse assaults on its integrity, the general adaptation syndrome, could alter the organism's general susceptibility to illness? Secondly, if the answer to the first question is yes, then it would become important for us to know if social–psychological, as well as physical, stressors can produce the general adaptation syndrome?

Without going into the details of the neural and endocrine processes involved, the answer to the first question does, indeed, appear to be yes. Chronic overproduction of pro- and antiinflammatory adrenocorticoids, which occurs during the alarm reaction and resistance stages, has been implicated as a causative factor in a series of diseases of adaptation (Appley and Trumbull, 1967; Selye, 1956). Among these are diseases of the heart, blood vessels, and kidney; high blood pressure; eclampsia; rheumatic and rheumatoid arthritis; inflammatory diseases of the skin and eyes; infections; allergic and hypersensitivity diseases; cancer; and metabolic diseases. The story of how Selye and other workers related these various diseases of resistance to the nonspecific effects of stress makes interesting reading but would, unfortunately, take volumes to relate. It is important to add a note of caution before we proceed, however. Selye (1956) points out that "*no disease is exclusively caused by maladaptation*, but derangements of our adaptive mechanisms do play a decisive role in the development of many diseases" (pp. 203–204).

Let us go back to the second question above. Granting that the sort of systemic stress that Selye has elucidated can set the stage for diseases of various kinds, is there any evidence that social and psychological variables can lead to or invoke the general adaptation syndrome with both its beneficial and potentially harmful effects? If such evidence existed, it would be easy to see how psychosocial stimuli might be related to disease.

Levi (1974) presents a conceptual model, depicted in Figure 7.1, in which stress is, in fact, the main mediating mechanism between psychological and social variables and disease. As can be seen in the figure, the relationships among the various components form a cybernetic system with continuous feedback. Thus, the hypothesis underlying the model is that psychosocial changes can act as stressors which, in predisposed individuals, may lead to disease of one type or another. In the model the box entitled Precursors of Disease refers to malfunctions in various organ systems produced by stress which have not resulted in disease, but which—if continued—will. In proposing the model, Levi is careful to point out that the evidence that extrinsic psychosocial stimuli can cause disease is not at all clear.

It is easy to understand why the evidence is not clear. The problem is not lack of expertise or the equipment and methodology needed to test the model. These

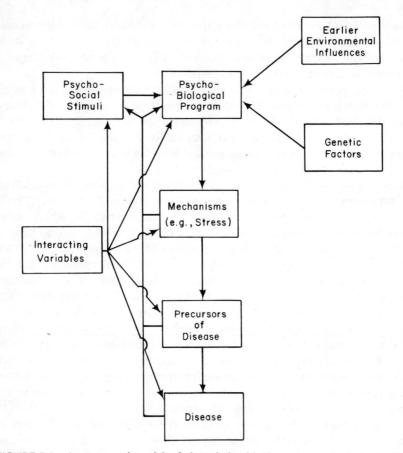

FIGURE 7.1. A conceptual model of the relationship between psychosical stimuli and disease. (From Levi, 1974, p. 10. Copyright 1974 by Charles C Thomas, Publisher. Reprinted by Permission.)

have been available for many years. The reason the entire model cannot be subjected to a series of straightforward experimental tests is that most investigators believe such tests could not be morally justified. One simply cannot subject humans to severe, prolonged psychosocial stressors and see if disease develops.

Hence, investigators who were interested in the sorts of relationships depicted in the model appear to have resorted to one or the other of two general approaches to obtaining evidence on the existence and nature of those relationships. The first approach has been to either expose subjects to mild social and psychological stressors and measure physiological response variables known to be associated with the General Adaptation Syndrome or to measure the same variables among participants in naturally occurring social–psychological stressor situations. The second approach, which we shall consider in the next section, consists of attempts to quantify the amount of social–psychological change individuals have experienced and to relate this directly to the number and severity of illness episodes they have experienced.

Let us consider a couple of examples of the first approach, one in which subjects are experimentally exposed to relatively mild social psychological stressors and one which measured the effects of "naturally occurring" stressors.

The former is illustrated in some of the work by Bogdonoff and his associates (Back and Bogdonoff, 1964; Bogdonoff, Klein, Back, Nichols, Troyer, and Hood, 1964), in which the amount of free fatty acids released into the blood were measured in response to several different situations. The presence of free fatty acids in the blood is a fairly sensitive indicator of epinephrine and nonepinephrine release and, hence, of the activation of the parasympathetic and sympathetic branches of the autonomic nervous system. Chronic overactivation of the parasympathetic system has been implicated as a contributing factor in maladies as diverse as asthma and ulcers, while chronic overactivation of the sympathetic system may result in hypertension (cf., Moss, 1973). Further, Back and Bogdonoff (1967) report some well-founded suspicion that it is free fatty acids, rather than cholesterol, that are deposited on the walls of arteries and may, thus, eventually increase the probability of coronary artery occlusion.

Back and Bogdonoff (1967) did not, of course, gather any evidence on the correlates of long term excesses of free fatty acid in the blood, and therein lies the limitation of such research. They did find, however, that free fatty acid levels were higher among subjects participating in an experiment with a group of strangers than among subjects participating in the same experiment with a group of acquaintances. Back and Bogdonoff discuss this and similar findings in terms of the buffering effect of being surrounded by a group of friends and acquaintances, that is, it appears that the subject ". . . who comes into the experiment in a group feels shielded from the experimental situation and reacts as if protected against the laboratory and its influences" (p. 387). One might be tempted to extrapolate from such findings to those epidemiological studies that have found that people living in large family units or near supportive and trusting friends are less prone to have a myocardial infarction (cf., Stout, Morrow, Brandt, and Wolf, 1964)—but we shall resist that temptation.

The second example of a study that has focused on the Psychosocial Stimuli → Stress indicators part of the model in Figure 7.1 used the naturally occurring situation of men undergoing the Navy's underwater demolition team training course (Rubin and Rahe, 1974). For two months, detailed daily serum uric-acid, cholesterol, and corticoid variations were recorded for a group of 32 trainees, 12 of whom dropped out without completing this "extremely stressful" training course. A number of findings emerged from the study that are pertinent here. For example, elevations in mean serum cholesterol levels occurred repeatedly in situations evocative of anxiety and fear of failure, and the 12 men who eventually dropped out had had higher initial cholesterol levels than the 20 men who completed the course. All of the results may be concisely summarized by noting that variations in each biochemical indicator could be logically related to the day-to-day demands made upon the men.

We could continue with examples of such research, but the literature on the psychophysiology and psychoendocrinology of stress in humans is so enormous that it would be impossible to review it comprehensively here. However, several recent selective reviews of that literature (Levi, 1974; Oken, 1967) conclude that it is now well established that psychological and social stimuli can trigger in humans the types of physiological–endocrine responses known to occur in the general adaptation syndrome in rats and other subhuman animals. This is necessary information, of course, and helps bolster one's faith in the first half of the sort of hypothetical sequential chain depicted in Figure 7.1. But as Levi (1974), Singleton (1974), and others have pointed out, such studies tell us only that psychosocial stimuli could lead to precursors and disease by explicating a plausible mediating link. They leave open the question of whether or not psychosocial stimuli are really related to disease. Fortunately, there is a growing body of literature that addresses precisely this question.

Life Change and Illness

Basic to the notion of stress is the idea that the adaptive capabilities of the body are finite, only so much can be endured before its ability to adjust is temporarily exhausted. This idea can be traced through the works of many physicians, psychologists, and physiologists, has recently been popularized in Toffler's (1971) *Future Shock*, and seems well supported by experimental research with rats and other subhuman animals (cf., Selye, 1956). The body's adaptive capabilities are called into play, of course, whenever one experiences change of any sort—whether it be the invasion of a microbe, walking up a flight of stairs, or divorcing one's husband. If we consider one's general susceptibility to illness to be inversely related to the state of one's adaptive capabilities at any given point in time, it follows, then, that the more changes one has recently experienced, the greater one's susceptibility to illness.

Employing a self-administered questionnaire that elicited information about major social readjustments and status changes the respondent had experienced over the preceding ten-year period, Rahe, Meyer, Smith, Kjaer and Holmes (1964) report a series of studies bearing on the above reasoning. In one study, two samples of employees at a tuberculosis sanitorium responded to the questionnaire. One group of employees had actually contracted tuberculosis, and the time of onset was known to within three months because of periodic checkups which all employees had to take. The second group consisted of nontuberculous employees who were matched, person-by-person, to those who had contracted the disease in terms of age, sex, race, education, social class, and marital status. The questionnaire data revealed that for the nontuberculous group major social readjustments were generally dispersed over the preceding ten years. However, in the tuberculous group there was a tendency for many more such readjustments to have occurred in the two years immediately preceding the onset of illness.

In another study reported in the same paper, 40 tuberculous outpatients, 40 patients with newly diagnosed cardiac disease, and 40 matched (but healthy) control subjects responded to the same questionnaire. The major results of this study are depicted in Figure 7.2 where it can be seen that in both the cardiac and tuberculous patients, but not the controls, there was a mounting frequency of reported readjustments in the years immediately preceding illness onset.

There are a number of ambiguities apparent in the above two studies. First, there is the fact that the results are based on retrospective reports, that is, subjects were asked to recall major social stresses and readjustments over the past ten years. It is true that control subjects had the same task and that they did not show the mounting frequency of stresses characteristic of the groups who succumbed to illness, but it may be that there is something about having a

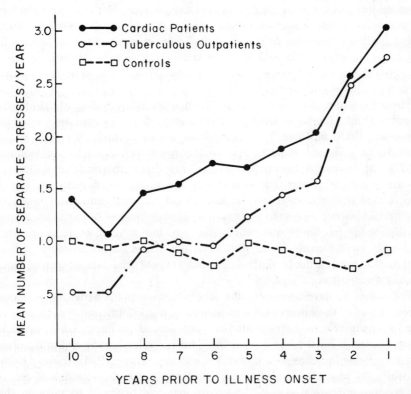

FIGURE 7.2. Relationships of recalled major stresses to years preceding illness onset. (From Rahe et al., 1964, p. 39. Copyright 1964 by Pergamon Press, Reprinted by Permission.)

major illness that makes people more introspective. They begin mulling over the past more than healthy people. Then, the apparent mounting frequency of illness in the recent past for such people may simply reflect the fact that recent events are more easily recalled than events of eight, nine, or ten years ago. We shall look at a couple of prospective studies which overcome this ambiguity below, but first there is another difficulty to be mentioned.

In studies such as those by Rahe et al. (1964), the results are cast entirely in terms of the number of stresses experienced and in broad categories such as personal or economic readjustments. It is clear, of course, that some personal and economic readjustments are more difficult than others, hence it would be valuable to have some estimates of the magnitude of adjustment necessitated by various events. To accomplish this, Holmes and Rahe (1967) requested a large heterogeneous sample of subjects to rate a number of life change events in terms of the amount of readjustment that would be necessitated if they were involved in the event or if the event should happen to them. The ratings were made by assigning marriage an arbitrary value, such as 50 on a scale from 1 to 100, and each subject was asked to assign a number to each event on the basis of whether it took more or less readjustment than marriage. The rank order of the 43 events rated and the mean value of perceived readjustment necessitated—in relation to marriage—are given in Table 7.3. In the table it can be seen, for example, that being fired from one's job is perceived to necessitate much less readjustment than the death of one's spouse.

There have now been a series of studies demonstrating widespread consensus about the rank ordering of the amount of adaptive or coping behavior evoked by the events listed in Table 7.3. There are occasional cultural differences in the perceived adjustment required for specific events (cf., Masuda and Holmes, 1967), but, in general, the relative rank orderings have proven to be significantly similar in various groups. The rated values of readjustment necessitated by the events thus allows a more precise estimate of the total amount of stress an individual has been subjected to at various periods in his or her life. One simply multiplies the frequency with which any event has occurred by its rated value and adds up the result for all the events the person has experienced in that period. The result is the total life-change units experienced in some span of time, usually six months or a year.

Following the development of the schedule of recent experience—the name given to one of the questionnaire formats soliciting information about which of the life-change events respondents have experienced—Holmes, Rahe, and their colleagues have carried out a series of additional retrospective and prospective studies relating life change to illness. For example, Rahe (1974) reports a study in which 84 physician–subjects were asked to fill out the schedule of recent experience, indicating any of the events that had occurred to them in the immediately preceding 12-month period. Of the 84 subjects: 41 had life-change unit totals of at least 250 for the preceding year; 32 had totals between 150 and

TABLE 7.3
Rank Order and Ratings of Readjustment Necessitated
by 43 Events[a]

Rank	Life event	Mean value
1	Death of spouse	100
2	Divorce	73
3	Marital separation	65
4	Jail term	63
5	Death of close family member	63
6	Personal injury or illness	53
7	Marriage	50
8	Fired at work	47
9	Marital reconciliation	45
10	Retirement	45
11	Change in health of family member	44
12	Pregnancy	40
13	Sex difficulties	39
14	Gain of new family member	39
15	Business readjustment	39
16	Change in financial state	38
17	Death of close friend	37
18	Change to different line of work	36
19	Change in number of arguments with spouse	35
20	Mortgage over $10,000	31
21	Foreclosure of mortgage or loan	30
22	Change in responsibilities at work	29
23	Son or daughter leaving home	29
24	Trouble with in-laws	29
25	Outstanding personal achievement	28
26	Wife begin or stop work	26
27	Begin or end school	26
28	Change in living conditions	25
29	Revision of personal habits	24
30	Trouble with boss	23
31	Change in work hours or conditions	20
32	Change in residence	20
33	Change in schools	20
34	Change in recreation	19
35	Change in church activities	19
36	Change in social activities	18
37	Mortgage or loan less than $10,000	17
38	Change in sleeping habits	16
39	Change in number of family get-togethers	15
40	Change in eating habits	15
41	Vacation	13
42	Christmas	12
43	Minor violations of the law	11

[a]From Holmes and Rahe, 1967, p. 216. Copyright 1967 by
Pergamon Press, Elmsford, N.Y., Reprinted by Permission.

250; and 11 had totals of less than 150. Nine months later, these same 84 subjects were contacted and interviewed about illness episodes that had occurred in the intervening nine months. Of those subjects who had initially had life change totals greater than 250, 59 percent reported a significant health change during the nine months. Of those with initial totals between 150 and 250, only 25 percent reported such change, and, of those with initial totals less than 150, only one reported a change in health status. Thus, it appears that the more life change one has experienced in the recent past, the greater one's likelihood of becoming ill.

Unfortunately, this conclusion is tempered somewhat by the fact that both the life-change information and illness data were obtained via self-report. Hence, it may be that the relation between the two is spuriously inflated by a tendency for some people to talk about their troubles, while others are generally more reserved and/or tend not to pay much attention to such problems. A study that partially overcomes this interpretive ambiguity is reported by Rubin, Gunderson and Arthur (1971).

The latter study is one of a series of prospective studies in which the schedule of recent experience was administered to Navy enlisted men prior to their embarking on an extended cruise. Upon their ships' return to base some months later, the health records were obtained from the ships' infirmaries, and illness episodes experienced during the cruise—which presumably were verified by infirmary personnel—were related to total life-change events experienced in the 18 months prior to the beginning of the cruise. Although the correlations are not particularly large, those subjects with higher total life-change units at the start of the cruise tended to have more illnesses during the cruise. It should be noted, however, that the subjects in these studies were, for the most part, young, single males in excellent physical condition. Hence, the studies provide rather stringent tests of the hypothesis that increased life changes increase susceptibility to illness.

Even so, there is still the nagging suspicion that we may be seeing a tendency to report illness rather than illness per se. Perhaps those sailors who show up at the infirmary least often have the same problems—headaches, colds, fever—but they are more stoical and keep their problems to themselves, assuming they will feel better tomorrow. Partially in response to this criticism, Wyler, Masuda, and Holmes (1971) investigated the relationship between life change and seriousness of illness. For this study, data were obtained from a total of 232 patients on the inpatient medical, surgical, psychiatric, and gynecological services of several different hospitals. Each patient completed the schedule of recent experience for the six-month, one-year, and two-year periods immediately preceding, that is, they indicated each event that had occurred to them and whether it had occurred in the preceding six months, year, or two years. In addition, each patient's admitting diagnosis was coded into one of 126 categories on a seriousness of illness scale developed by Wyler. The magnitudes of life-change events in each of the three time periods preceding hospital admission (6 months, 1 year, 2 years) were significantly correlated with the seriousness of the patients' illnesses. The greater the magnitude of life-change experienced, the more serious the illness. Further, Wyler et al. (1971) present evidence that this relationship holds for illnesses with chronic, ill-defined onset—such as hypertension or diabetes—but not for those with acute, well-defined onset.

It is, indeed, beginning to appear that "Subjects' recent life changes, perceptions of symptoms, and selected demographic, psychosocial and occupational characteristics appear to act in combination to precipitate illness episodes" (Rahe, 1974, p. 76). We could continue to cite research that supports this general conclusion. Before proceeding, however, let us take a moment and summarize the material covered so that we can pick up the line of argument upon which we intended this research to bear.

We began this chapter by looking at placebo effects, and it appears that placebos can relieve subjective symptoms such as pain and produce objective physiological changes. Also, it appears that the belief or expectation that such effects will be produced is an important factor in their occurrence. We then turned to the more general question of whether expectations might influence health and disease. As background for this question it was first necessary to establish that there are reliable differences among people in their general susceptibility to illness—differences that apparently cannot be fully accounted for by genetic predisposing factors or by aspects of the physical environment. Further, social and psychological factors, such as expectations, had been repeatedly implicated as being of etiological significance in the literature on general susceptibility to illness. If such factors are indeed to be considered of etiological significance in disease, the process or mechanism by which they might be mediated needed to be explored. Thus we turned to a brief examination of some of the work on stress, the general adaptation syndrome, and diseases of adaptation and suggested a model linking psychosocial stimuli and disease via stress. Since most of the work on stress and disease had been done with animals, it seemed appropriate to next establish the point that psychosocial stimuli do produce in humans physiological and endocrine responses, which could lead to the sorts of diseases of adaptation known to be produced by stress in animals. Having thus obtained a plausible mediating link between psychosocial stimuli and disease in humans, we examined some data on life change and illness, which indicates that the occurrence of such stimuli are indeed related to disease.

Given, then, that social and psychological variables are of etiological significance in illness—but, neither necessary or sufficient, of course—we can go back to the question with which we began and ask about a specific type of social–psychological variable. That is, are expectations about one's ability to obtain valued goals in life related to one's general susceptibility to illness?

Expectations and Illness

The common psychological core of the many definitions of stress in the literature is the perception of threat. Interference or anticipated interference with goal-directed behaviors is generally believed to result in renewed attempts to both cope with the interference and obtain the goal, and a beginning of psychological and physiological defense processes. If the demands for such adaptive responding are too great or continue for too long, then, as we have seen, one's general susceptibility to illness is increased. It is crucial not to lose sight of the fact, however, that it is the perception of threat that initiates this chain. The question of interest here is whether threat perception is followed by an increase in susceptibility to illness only among those who, following the perceived threat, develop an expectation of being unable to cope. The evidence for the influence of such intervening expectations is far from conclusive, but it comes from a variety of sources.

There are, for example, repeated hints and pertinent bits of data in the life change–illness literature discussed in the preceding section that it is the expectation that one is not going to be able to handle some demanded change or readjustment that is important. Hinkle and Wolff (1958) report an exploratory study in which descriptions of the life situations of 68 subjects were rated by independent observers who were unaware of the medical histories of the subjects. These ratings were then plotted against frequency of illness episodes. The illness episode rates were significantly higher during those years for which the observers had estimated that subjects would perceive their situations as unsatisfactory and themselves as unable to make adequate adaptations. There is a similar suggestion in the study mentioned earlier (Hinkle, et al., 1958) in which detailed life history data were collected from 10 frequently-ill and 10 seldom-ill Chinese professionals. Observers unaware of the medical histories of the 20 subjects could not discriminate the two groups with respect to the extent to which they had achieved socially valued goals in life, realized their potential, or fulfilled the responsibilities of their positions in life. However, members of the two groups were notably different in terms of the way they themselves perceived their lives. Members of the frequently-ill group were much more likely to have definite praiseworthy and socially desirable goals, even when those goals were unrealistic. As Hinkle et al. (1958) point out, actual life situations appear less important than the way those situations are perceived. Similarly, it will be recalled that in Chapter 6 the point was made that it is impossible to know if another has succeeded or failed solely on the basis of objective performance— one must know the goal that the other is attempting to achieve.

There is another way of looking at the extent to which the expectation of being unable to cope is a factor in increasing one's general susceptibility to illness. Consider the life events listed in Table 7.3. These 43 events differ in a number of ways in addition to the magnitude of readjustment necessitated by their occurrence. One way in which they differ is the extent to which the events are under the control of the person involved. For example, one usually has no control over such events as the death of a close friend or the change in health of a family member, whereas one is usually able to, at least partially, exert some influence over such events as marital reconciliation or a change to a different line of work. These two pairs of events were specifically chosen as illustrations, because the sum of the life-change units for each pair is 81. Hence, in terms of the amount of readjustment necessitated should either of these pairs occur, there would be no difference according to the mean values listed in the table. However, Paykel (1974), in summarizing a series of studies that employed variations on the schedule of recent experience, reports that he distinguished ". . . those events which were at least partly under the respondent's control and could be initiated by him from those outside his control and found that the uncontrolled events were perceived as more stressful" (p. 152).

There are, of course, a number of explanations for the findings we have just mentioned that do not implicate expectations as a contributing factor. The finding by Hinkle et al. (1958), for example, that the more frequently ill Chinese were more likely to view their life situations as demanding and unamenable to successful adaptation may have been due to the fact that they were more often in poor health. However, there is a growing experimental literature that corroborates the notion that the expectation of control over noxious stimuli does reduce the stress produced by such stimuli. Of particular interest here are those studies that have demonstrated that the perception of control over aversive stimuli—as opposed to real control—decreases the intensity of those physiological responses usually taken as indicators of stress.

An example is a study by Geer, Davison, and Gatchel (1970), in which 40 male college students were instructed to press a reaction time key with their finger as soon as they felt an electric shock through an electrode attached to their ankle. During the first set of trials the shock lasted for six seconds on each trial, regardless of how fast the subject responded. During the second set of trials, the shock lasted for three seconds, again this was true regardless of how fast the subject responded. However, half of the subjects were told at the beginning of the second set of trials, ". . . if your speed of reaction time is as fast or faster than the average of your reaction times in Part I, shock duration will be decreased in length from six seconds to three seconds. Thus, if you can react quickly enough, you can significantly cut down the duration of shock you receive on each trial" (Geer, et al., 1970, p. 733). These subjects, then, were led to expect that their responses would make a difference in the outcomes they received. The remaining subjects were simply told that, in the second set of trials, the ". . . shock duration will be decreased in length from six seconds to three seconds" (p. 733).

As a measure of autonomic activity and arousal during the experimental session, each subject's skin conductance was continuously recorded via electrodes attached to the palm and wrist of the subject's nonpreferred hand. Two results with this measure are of interest here. First, during the second set of trials, the skin conductance responses of subjects who (incorrectly) perceived that they could control the amount of shock received diminished significantly more rapidly than the skin conductance responses of subjects who believed (correctly) that they could not control the amount of shock received. Secondly, using spontaneous fluctuations in skin conductance as an index of general autonomic arousal, subjects who perceived they could control the amount of shock received had significantly fewer such fluctuations. Geer et al. (1970) explain their results along relatively simple and familiar (cf., Chapter 6) learning lines:

> ... that is, human beings tend to find less stressful those aversive situations over which they at least believe they have some degree of control. Indeed, such situations in real life are probably, as a rule, less stressful. The instructions to our perceived control subjects then enable these individuals to label the situation as one in which they are not helpless. Their subsequent behavior is then affected in the same way as it has been in the past, when control was available (p. 737).

As we saw in the last chapter, the self-label that one is not helpless has significant motivational effects. It apparently can also diminish the magnitude of physiological indices of stress.

Two related studies that employed a different physiological index of stress are reported by Hokanson, DeGood, Forrest, and Brittain (1971). In both studies subjects' systolic blood pressures were recorded while they worked on a complex matching task. Aversive stimulation in the form of electric shock occurred whenever the subject failed to complete a matching response sequence within a certain time interval. The timing mechanism was set for each subject's work rate, so that each received a shock about once every 45 seconds. In the first study, subjects in one group were told that they could signal for a one-minute rest period whenever they felt the need by simply saying, "Stop" or "Time." Subjects in a second group were told that rest periods of one minute would occur from time to time and that they would know when they could rest by the appearance of a red light on the panel in front of them. Thus, the former group believed they could control their time-outs, and the latter group did not. Subjects in the two groups were yoked. For every time-out taken by a subject in the perceived control group, the yoked subject received a corresponding rest period at the same point in time relative to the beginning of the task. The main result of interest here is that over the entire course of the experimental session the yoked subjects exhibited significantly higher systolic blood pressure levels than the subjects who perceived they could control their time-outs from the aversive task.

There is a problem of interpretation here, however. Is the perception of control the important variable or is it possible that the subjects who could choose when to take their time-outs did so at the most "... psychologically propitious moments, that is, when they were especially fatigued, tense, etc." (Averill, 1973, p. 291). Taking their rest periods at such moments would increase the effectiveness of rest. Subjects in the other condition, of course, may have had rest periods imposed at less propitious moments. Hence, their rest periods would be less restful and less effective in reducing blood pressure. On the other hand, perhaps this is not really an alternative explanation, but simply another way of making the same point. Hokanson et al. (1971) point out that the yoked-subjects

> ... were in an aversive situation over which they had relatively little control (time-outs are imposed), and as such were undergoing conditions which presumably develop the learned-helplessness syndrome. From this viewpoint, the differential systolic responses obtained ... may reflect enhanced stress responding among the yoked controls, rather than attenuated systolic levels in the experimental group (p. 68).

There is another result of interest in the second study reported by Hokanson et al. In the latter experiment, essentially the same task was used as in the first, but all subjects were allowed to take rest periods whenever they chose. However, in order to take a rest, subjects had to indicate that they wanted to do so 30 seconds in advance, by depressing a switch with their free hand and they had to continue to work for the 30 seconds. Thus, a brief anticipatory period occurred prior to each rest period. The results indicate that a discernible reduction in systolic blood pressure occurs during these periods when the subjects were anticipating a rest. Further, this reduction in systolic pressure occurs even though there was no detectable relaxation in their work rate on the matching task.

These results are consistent with Lazarus' (1966) theoretical notion that the perceived availability of coping responses—a rest period in this case—over which one has control or believes one has control should diminish stress reactions. Further, Hokanson et al. point out that the higher systolic pressures of subjects who lacked control over their rest periods is "at least reminiscent [of the] ... feelings of time urgency, a sense of unrelenting external demands, and behavioral patterns of compulsive activity to ward off impending harm" (p. 68), which have been identified as characteristic of those most likely to develop coronary problems (Friedman and Rosenman, 1974).

There have been a number of other studies investigating the effects of the expectation that one will be able to cope with aversive stimuli. As Averill (1973) points out, although a number of those studies are open to alternative explanations, it has generally been found that in comparison to conditions in which subjects expect to have no control over aversive stimuli, conditions which instill the expectation of control reduce physiological and endocrine stress responses. There are a number of possible processes that might account for this. For example, the expectation of control over aversive stimuli may, in effect, modify the perceived nature of those stimuli—they become less of a threat even though their physical characteristics remain the same. Or, as Averill points out, the expectation of control may imply that one can regulate the administration of those stimuli to oneself and, hence, one can insure that one will be in the appropriate receptive state when they occur.

Thus, while it does seem to be the case that the expectation of control over aversive stimuli reduces stress in humans, we have yet to see any clear experimental evidence that the absence of this expectation increases the probability of stress-induced disease. As in our earlier discussion of the stress—disease link, this is a problem that cannot be experimentally investigated in humans. However, there is a good deal of pertinent animal research. Weiss (1971), for example, reports an experiment in which some rats could avoid or escape an electric shock by performing a wheel-turning response. The shocks were either preceded by a signal (a beeping tone) or, in a second set of conditions, no signal preceded the shock. For each animal that could avoid or escape the shock—whether or not it was preceded by a signal—there were two matched animals: one was yoked and received exactly the same shocks but had no control over the shock; a second one received no shock. Thus, there were six conditions of interest here, composed by the combination of signal—no signal and avoidance—yoked—no shock. The stress-session part of the experiment lasted for 48 hours with the shock level initially set at 1.6 ma and increased by .6 ma every 12 hours.

The main dependent measure in Weiss' experiment was the length of gastric ulcer lesions that were produced by these conditions in the lower, glandular area of the rats' stomachs. The data, presented graphically in Figure 7.3, show two things of particular interest. First, it is clear that the animals that could avoid or escape the shock ulcerated significantly less than the yoked animals, which experienced exactly the same shocks in the same sequence but could not avoid or escape the shock[6]—and this occurred regardless of whether or not the shock was preceded by a signal. Secondly, comparing the signal—no signal conditions, it is also clear that the predictability of the shock in the signal conditions reduces its stressfulness for both the avoidance—escape and yoked rats. Thus, both controllability and predictability of aversive stimulation ameliorate its ulcerogenerative effects.

There are a number of other experiments in the literature that have produced similar results. None that I know of has clearly separated out the effects of perceived control from actual control and predictability. However, it is clear that the expectation of control is an element of actual control and may be involved in predictability, even though it would, of course, be nonveridical in the latter

---

[6] This, of course, is the opposite result to Brady's (1958) famous "executive monkey" study. Weiss points out that Brady's non-random assignment of the more reactive monkeys to "executive" positions may account for his result.

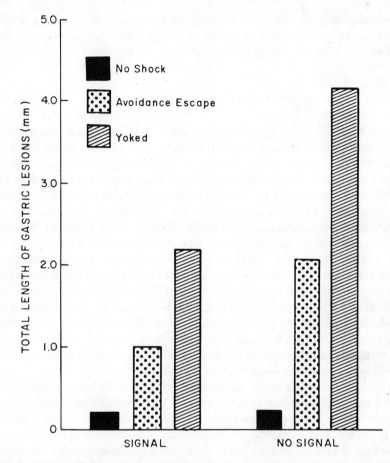

FIGURE 7.3.   Median length of gastric lesions for the no shock, avoidance-escape, and yoked groups in the signal and no signal conditions. (From Weiss, 1971, p. 6. Copyright 1971 by the American Psychological Association. Reprinted by Permission.)

case. In any event, results such as those by Weiss taken in conjunction with the research by Hokanson et al. and Geer et al. discussed earlier, in which perceived control did decrease the magnitude of nonpathological stress indicators, at least makes plausible the hypothesis that the expectation of control over aversive stimulation will reduce the magnitude or delay the onset of stress-induced pathology.

It is clear that we are beginning to get on shaky ground again. The experimental underpinnings are fewer and further apart. Rather than retreat now, however, let us push on one final step further. We have seen that expectations may be influential in almost every facet of one's life—from thought processes to interpersonal relations to striving for goals to the occurrence of disease. In the spirit of tentative reconnaissance, then, let us ask if there is any evidence that expectations may be implicated in the termination of life.

EXPECTATIONS AND DEATH

The study that alerted me to the possibility that expectations may, indeed, play a role in death was an investigation of the mortality rate among people admitted to the Orthodox Jewish Home for the Aged in Chicago (Lieberman, 1961). During the period between 1947 and 1959, 860 applicants were placed on the home's waiting list after an initial physical and mental screening. Of these 860, 700 actually were admitted to the Home and 78 withdrew their applications. The waiting period prior to admission for the 700 averaged 6.4 months following the completion of the screening tests and interviews, and the remaining 82 people (860 − 700 − 78 = 82) died while on the waiting list. Lieberman computed the mortality rate for those admitted to the home for the first year following admission and found a 24.7 percent first-year mortality for the 700 admissions. The comparable rate among those who died while on the waiting list was only 10.4 percent, ". . . less than half the rate for the first year of institutionalization" (p. 517). Some additional data indicate that this differential result was not due to any detectable differences in age or physical status of those admitted versus those on the waiting list.

There are, no doubt, many possible explanations for the above result. There may, for example, have been some implicit criterion for early admission, such as those most in need being given preference. Lieberman does not present sufficient medical history data to evaluate such a possibility. However, the explanation that seemed most cogent to me had to do with the perceptions that most people have of homes for the aged. It is unfortunate, but it appears to be true that most people view entrance into such homes as the end of the line. These are places where one goes to die, where hope ends and one—quite literally—has nothing to look forward to. It seemed possible that such perceptions, when translated into an expectation for oneself upon entrance to such an institution, might actually have been partly responsible for the increased mortality rate among those admitted to the home.

Thus alerted to the possibility that expectations may play a role in the occurrence and/or timing of death, I began to find other bits and pieces of pertinent evidence ranging from second- and third-hand anecdotes to quasi-experimental results. Also, I found that the idea itself was not at all new, but had been around for a long time.

Cannon (1942), for example, not only suggested that expectations might be a factor in voodoo death, but even outlined the physiological processes that might mediate such a result. Cannon focused on the physiological effects of extreme fear or terror resulting from the anticipation that one is doomed to die because someone has "pointed a bone" or tabooed food has been ingested or one has somehow been hexed by a sorcerer or medicineman. Among a number of examples Cannon cites is the following one taken from a letter written to him by a Dr. S. M. Lambert of the Western Pacific Health Service. A physician, Dr. P. S. Clarke, was working with Kanakas on the sugar plantations of North Queensland.

> One day a Kanaka came to his hospital and told him he would die in a few days because a spell had been put upon him and nothing could be done to counteract it. The man had been known by Dr. Clarke for some time. He was given a very thorough examination, including an examination of the stool and the urine. All was found normal, but as he lay in bed he gradually grew weaker. Dr. Clarke called upon the foreman of the Kanakas to come to the hospital to give the man assurance, but on reaching the foot of the bed, the foreman leaned over, looked at the patient, and then turned to Dr. Clarke saying, "Yes, doctor, close up him he die" (i.e., he is nearly dead). The next day, at 11 o'clock in the morning, he ceased to live. A postmortem examination revealed nothing that could in any way account for the fatal outcome (p. 171). (Reproduced by permission of the American Anthropological Association from the *American Anthropologist, 44*(2), 1942.)

It is, of course, quite possible that in the late 1930s, when this incident apparently occurred, many things that could have caused death would not have been detected by postmortem examination—some subtle or esoteric poison, perhaps, about which Dr. Clarke had no knowledge.

It is also possible that the physiological effects of prolonged and intense fear, Cannon's preferred interpretation, produced the result. The intense emotional arousal brought about by such fear would result in a tremendously increased production of epinephrine, a rapid pulse, a loss of fluids from the blood to the tissues and, as the heart continued to beat more and more rapidly—partly to compensate for the falling blood pressure due to loss of fluids from the blood, a state of shock would ensue. The ultimate result of such a sequence of events might well be, according to Cannon, a state of constant contraction of the heart or death in systole.

As an illustration that such phenomena are not entirely curiosities of the distant past or peculiarities of uncivilized savages, consider this more recent example from *Newsweek* (Alpern and Cumming, 1976). In March 1976 in a small North Carolina town, several people attending a seance heard the prediction that a local woman, Mrs. Dorothy Ramsey, would die on April 10, "probably in an auto accident." The woman about whom the prediction was made had a history of emotional problems and, when informed of the forecast, became increasingly distraught and nervous. On April 10, she locked herself in her house and refused to go out. The next morning she was found, dead. An autopsy revealed traces of alcohol and drugs in the blood, a combination which could have produced the fatal result, depending on the concentration of each. However, there is another possibility. The fatal combination may have been the belief of impending disaster—Mrs. Ramsey apparently took the prediction of death seriously—and detectable physiological effects produced by the alcohol and drugs. This is not to say that the pharmacological effects of the latter produced death. Richter (1957) quotes a former coroner of the city of Baltimore, Dr. R. S. Fisher, as saying ". . . a number of individuals die each year after taking small, definitely sublethal doses of poison, or after inflicting small, nonlethal wounds on themselves; apparently they die as a result of the belief in their doom" (p. 197).

As a result of some of his own work with rats, Richter (1957) himself has proposed a physiological mechanism that might mediate between hopelessness and death, a mechanism which differs from the chain of events suggested by Cannon. While Cannon's hypothesis deals with the results of intense arousal and overactivation of the sympathicoadrenal system, Richter's hypothesis deals, instead, with what have been termed *apathy deaths* (cf., Garrity, 1974).

Richter found that rats firmly held in his hand prior to being put in a water-filled jar, from which there was no escape, would swim around for a few minutes and then sink to the bottom and die. Further, electrocardiogram, body temperature, and respiratory-rate recordings indicated that, contrary to Cannon's hypothesis, these rats died with a slowing down of the heart, a drop in body temperature, and a decrease in respiration rate. Following death, autopsies revealed that the rats' hearts were grossly enlarged and filled with blood, i.e., the rats died in diastole—the ventricular muscles had become increasingly relaxed. Richter interprets these results as evidence for the importance of hopefulness in sustaining life and supports his interpretation by demonstrating two things:

1. Rats put into water-filled jars without having been previously held until they ceased struggling would swim for two and one half days (approximately 60 hours) before dying.
2. Rats held in the hand and released and then held and released again for a few times prior to being put in the jar—rats taught, in other words, that the situation was not hopeless—would also swim for extended periods of time before dying.

There are numerous reports of apparently similar apathy deaths in situations such as concentration camps and prisoner of war camps where escape seems impossible and the detention period is indefinite (cf., Bettelheim, 1943; Seligman, 1975; Strassman, Thaler, and Schein, 1956). For example, Nardini (1952), a medical officer among American prisoners of war of the Japanese in the Philippine Islands for three and one-half years, reports a number of instances of fatal withdrawal, in which prisoners simply lay down and awaited death.

The situation does not have to be as extreme as that of a concentration camp for such phenomena to occur, however. Engel (1968) believes that the important variable is not the external situation, but a sense of psychological impotence which he refers to as the *giving up–given up complex*—". . . a feeling that for briefer or longer periods of time one is unable to cope with the changes in the environment" (pp. 359–360). Similarly, Seligman (1975), argues that "The psychosomatic effects of exertion of will—active control over outcomes—and the will to live cannot be overestimated. Of all psychosomatic variables, this one may be the most powerful" (p. 184).

There are a number of additional lines of research that might be mentioned in connection with the possibility that expectations contribute to the occurrence and timing of death. For example, the life change–illness research discussed earlier has recently been extended to investigate the life situations of victims of myocardial infarctions prior to death (cf., Rahe and Romo, 1974). Reports of spouses and other close relatives indicate that these sudden death victims had significantly elevated life-change scores on the schedule of recent experience in the six months immediately preceding death. It could plausibly be argued that the expectation of being unable to cope with these rising demands for adjustment were a factor in the precipitation of the infarctions. However, the multiple ambiguities in such data are obvious: lack of matched controls; memory for recent events is better than for distant events; spouses do not necessarily know how the deceased perceived particular events. Hence, such data do not help to establish our hypothesis any more rigorously. Similarly, Engel's (1971) analysis of newspaper accounts of sudden death in unusual circumstances are intriguing and he repeatedly implicates expectations as contributing factors—both the expectation of being unable to cope with some life situation and the belief that one has nothing to live for. But again, such data are ambiguous.

This is an area in which it will, of course, be impossible to do the sort of experimental research which would erase the ambiguities once and for all. The evidence that is available, however, seems to strongly suggest that expectations do play a role in the occurrence and timing of death.

SUMMARY

Beginning with some data on placebos and ending with some observations on death and dying, we have seen that expectancies produce effects ranging from pain relief to an increase in one's general susceptibility to illness and may even influence death itself. We briefly explored some physiological and endocrine responses that could link various psychosocial stimuli, such as expectations to disease, and selectively reviewed a number of studies that indicate expectancies do produce in humans the sorts of physiological responses that if prolonged could lead to malfunctions and disease. We have switched back and forth several times from research with humans to research with animals because experimental research on several aspects of the model linking expectancies to illness and death (Figure 7.1) cannot be morally justified with humans and, hence, no human data were available.

In spite of the obvious need for more research and in spite of the equally obvious tenuousness of several links in the chain of reasoning presented, it seems to me that the evidence we have discussed in this chapter cannot be dismissed. It is true that much more needs to be known and known more precisely. But it is also true that "... the states of health or disease are the expressions of the success or failure experienced by the organism in its efforts to respond adaptively to environmental challenges" (Dubos, 1965, p. xvii), and environmental challenges are not limited to invading microbes.

8
Perspective

In the preceding chapters, we have seen that there is abundant evidence for the existence and influence of both interpersonal and intrapersonal expectancies. However, the diversity of the issues we have confronted and the variety of sources from which we have drawn might raise a question about the most appropriate metaphor to describe what we have been exploring. Is it a forest with a few bare spots here and there or a desert with a few isolated stands of trees? We have been discussing two broad categories of expectations: (1) those having to do with the characteristics and behaviors of others; and (2) those having to do with one's own subjective probabilities of success at various endeavors. The intimate relation between these two and the phenomena that seem to make the forest metaphor more appropriate are seen most clearly in interpersonal interaction.

If we define norms as relatively stable rules about behavior that are based on agreement or consensus and that are enforced by appeals to values or other suprapersonal agents, then it can be easily observed that there are certain categories of people to whom various groups of norms are applied by those around them. People similarly categorized have the same subset of norms applied to them and are said to occupy the same role. Once a person has been categorized as occupying a given role, certain definite behaviors are expected of them. This aspect of roles is similar to the type of expectations discussed in Chapters 2 and 3. Once we categorize another as having a particular characteristic, we assume or anticipate that they will have certain additional characteristics.

The concept of role, however, shifts the focus to the interaction with the categorized other and also calls our attention to the normative nature of our expectations. As Secord and Backman (1964) point out, in an interaction

> ... the other person is not only *expected* to behave in a certain way; he *should* behave
> in that way. Failure on his part to meet expectations is likely to be met with surprise,

disgust, anger, or indignation. This normative quality of expectations stems from the fact that only when one is able to anticipate consistently the behaviors of others can one maximize one's reward–cost outcomes. The extent to which expectations are normative varies in proportion to the importance of the rewards and costs involved (p. 455).

We must be able to anticipate the behaviors of others with some consistency, so that we can evaluate our own chances of success and, hence, choose among alternative courses of action.

When people behave inappropriately—as defined by the expectations of those with whom they are interacting, the result depends on a number of factors, not the least of which is the relative power or status of the interactants. When the inappropriate one is low in status, the reward and punishment options available to others are fairly obvious and may range from the strategic use of rewards in an attempt to shape the other's behavior to more drastic measures involving assorted punishments, including incarceration. The sort of residual rule-breaking discussed in Chapter 4 is, of course, a violation of the normative expectations to which most people subscribe about what it takes to be "sane," and, as we saw, the sanctions applied to the rule-breakers or norm-violators were often severe. On the other hand, when the inappropriate one is relatively high in status or power, the options available to those with whom they are interacting are more constrained. Here the alternatives may be reduced to such tactics as breaking off the interaction and seeking other interaction partners whose behaviors are more predictable and who thus allow us to anticipate the course of interaction more reliably.

Our expectations about what characteristics and behaviors of others go together serve us in another way when we attempt to evaluate our own chances of success at various tasks—tasks not necessarily related to interaction. As we saw in Chapter 5, it appears that, on tasks with which we have no experience, we evaluate our chances of success by comparing ourselves with others. We base such judgments in part on how others with characteristics similar to our own have done on the tasks—on our expectations about the relationships between those characteristics and successful behavior on the tasks. We use these expectations directly to establish our subjective probability of success.

As we saw in Chapters 6 and 7, our perception of the probability of success or, more generally, of our ability to cope with demands made upon us often seems to have the quality of a self-fulfilling prophecy. The perception of a high probability of success seems to enhance performance on a variety of tasks. At the other extreme, the perception of helplessness or of a very low probability of success seems to be a motivational disaster—the perception itself insuring failure by destroying the will to respond, to make an effort toward goal attainment. Further, the stress induced by the perception of being unable to cope may even increase our susceptibility to illness; conversely, the perception of being in control, of being master of one's fate, may reduce the likelihood of experiencing the detrimental effects of prolonged stress in response to various environmental and psychosocial stimuli.

To summarize, that expectations are of crucial importance in a variety of interpersonal and intrapersonal processes is well supported by the research we have examined. That this variety of processes may profitably be considered within the framework developed in Chapter 5 is, at this point, less clear. Nevertheless, the line of argument we have pursued suggests a number of directions for future research, research that can directly assess the viability of the argument itself.

DIRECTIONS FOR RESEARCH

In the preceding chapters, a number of studies have been cited in support of particular points. Often the results of these studies were ambiguous because of some methodological flaw or artifact or because the authors did not ask quite the right—for our purpose—questions. It would, of course, bear on the line of argument in the previous chapters if each such ambiguity were clarified, and it was for this reason that an attempt was made to be explicit about the imperfections of each bit of evidence used in constructing the argument. Clarification of these numerous ambiguities is, then, one direction of research suggested by the model. However, in addition to these isolated weak links that are in need of rewelding, there are several general areas of research suggested by the model, areas in which there has been relatively little work. Let us briefly examine four of these.

Goals and Interaction Strategies

Frequently in interpersonal interaction there occur ambiguous situations in which we are not quite sure how to relate to a particular other or what we can anticipate or expect from them. As we discussed in Chapter 4, a number of authors have pointed out that in such undefined situations, individuals can be seen to engage in a series of maneuvers designed to locate the position of the other in some known social system or cast the other in an appropriate role vis-à-vis themselves, by eliciting certain types of information and relying on what cues the other presents, even if they are minimal.

Weinstein (1966), for example, argues that one of the primary tasks facing an individual who wishes to achieve his or her goals in the interaction is to make certain that inappropriate evaluative judgments of his or her assumed identity are not made. This is done by a series of metacommunicational tactics, such as

... the icon (short for identity confirmation). Here we are concerned with the actor's droppings—name dropping, place dropping, experience dropping, and the like. "After 25 years of experience in this business . . ." or, "Back at Harvard. . . ." One function of such acts is to legitimize information given . . . the question of credibility shifts to the preface with the actor in essence saying believe what I say because of what I am. . . . (p. 397).

Weinstein identifies a number of other such tactics but, although they are eminently plausible and fit well with the day-to-day experience of most people, there are few hard data on the conditions under which such interpersonal ploys are employed or on the functions they serve. Specifically, there is very little research relating intrapersonal goals that may be achieved through interaction to the sorts of interpersonal ploys and strategies employed. The needed fine-grained analysis of ongoing interaction that would help establish some of the parameters and functions of the sort of interpersonal maneuvers involved has simply not been done.

The Development of Implicit Theories

In their review of research on structural representations of implicit personality theories, Rosenberg and Sedlak (1972) cite only five studies of personality perception in children. The state of the field is really not quite that bad, although it is surprising how few pertinent empirical data there are. It appears that there have been almost as many articles reviewing (and bemoaning) the paucity of literature in this area as there have been articles reporting research.

Of particular importance is the possibility that patterns of expectations among characteristics of others change, that is, are organized differently, at different stages of development and that these changes are interpretable in psychologically meaningful ways in terms of the stage of life of the subjects. This developmental approach to implicit theories would, of course, be most valuable if it were done on an individual level and if the evolving patterns of expectations could be shown to make a difference in the perceivers' behaviors toward others.

Subjective Probability of Success

There are a number of possible lines of research suggested by the model developed in Chapter 5. One could, for example, treat anticipatory face-saving and wishful thinking as independent, but enduring, dispositions and construct personality scales to measure the two—checking on the assumption of independence by determining the discriminant validity of the constructed scales. Another possibility is to ignore the question of whether the two processes are independent and deal only with their sum, treating the sum as equivalent to the dispositional component of one's subjective probability of success.

The latter approach is very close to that advocated in Chapter 6 in connection with the issue of the generality of learned helplessness. However, the issue is not just with learned helplessness, but with its obverse, which we might call *learned competence*. With both learned helplessness and learned competence, in a specific situation the questions are to what extent and under what conditions does this specific learning generalize and decrease or increase the dispositional component of one's subjective probability of success. It seems reasonable to suppose that one of the key factors influencing generalizability of learned helplessness or learned competence is one's attribution of the cause of success or failure in a given situation, but there has been relatively little research on this and there are, no doubt, other factors affecting generalization.

Expectations and Physiology

The evidence on the relationships between expectations and physiological changes seems to be one of the more intriguing, but less solid, bodies of evidence we have considered. As we saw in Chapter 7, there are numerous reasons for this lack of conclusiveness. However, the issues involved are too important to allow one to be satisfied with the present state of knowledge in this area.

There are some signs that research on these issues is gaining momentum and becoming more sophisticated in the process. The research on the physiological effects of perceived control over aversive stimuli is, for example, a promising beginning, but it is just a beginning. Much remains to be learned. There is also an exciting new area of research, biofeedback, that is directly relevant to the issues raised in Chapter 7, and biofeedback research is also in its infancy. Can we learn to monitor and control our own internal reactions to stressful stimuli? If so, and there is mounting evidence that at least some of our internal responses to such stimuli can be dampened, if not completely eliminated, then we may be able to make some headway against those chronic diseases such as hypertension that have become the bane of life in modern, urban, pressure-filled societies.

A FINAL WORD

We have inquired into the nature and consequences of expectations in a wide variety of settings and have examined both interpersonal and intrapersonal expectancies. It appears that this apparent variety of *inter-* and *intra*personal processes are in fact closely related. There are, of course, many unanswered questions pertinent to the line of argument developed in the preceding chapters and the attempt was made to be as explicit as possible about these weak links. Even so, it appears that, for both interpersonal and intrapersonal prophecies, ". . . the ultimate function of prophecy is not to tell the future, but to make it" (Wagar, 1963, p. 66).

Aronson, E., & Carlsmith, J. M. Performance expectancy as a determinant of actual performance. *Journal of Abnormal and Social Psycholoogy*, 1962, *65*, 178–182.

Aronson, E., & Landy, D. Further steps beyond Parkinson's law: A replication and extension of the excess time effect. *Journal of Experimental Social Psychology*, 1967, *3*, 274–285.

Asch, S. E. Forming impressions of personality. *Journal of Abnormal and Social Psychology*, 1946, *41*, 258–290.

Ashmore, R. D. Prejudice: Causes and cures. In B. Collins, (Ed.), *Social psychology*. Reading, Mass.: Addison-Wesley, 1970.

Atkinson, J. W. Motivational determinants of risk-taking behavior. *Psychological Review*, 1957, *64*, 359–372.

Atkinson, J. W. Towards experimental analysis of human motivation in terms of motives, expectancies, and incentives. In J. W. Atkinson, (Ed.), *Motives in fantasy, action, and society*. Princeton: Van Nostrand, 1958.

Atkinson, J. W., & Cartwright, D. Some neglected variables in contemporary conceptions of decision and performance. *Psychological Reports*, 1964, *14*, 575–590.

Atkinson, J. W., & Feather, N. T., (Eds.). *A theory of achievement motivation*. New York: Wiley, 1966.

Atkinson, J. W., & Reitman, W. R. Performance as a function of motive strength and expectancy of goal attainment. *Journal of Abnormal and Social Psychology*, 1956, *53*, 361–366.

Averill, J. R. Personal control over aversive stimuli and its relationship to stress. *Psychological Bulletin*, 1973, *80*, 286–303.

Back, K. W., & Bogdonoff, M. D. Plasma lipid response to leadership, conformity, and deviation. In P. H. Leiderman & D. Shapiro, (Eds.), *Psychobiological approaches to social behavior*. Stanford, California: Stanford, 1964.

Back, K. W., & Bogdonoff, M. D. Buffer conditions in experimental stress. *Behavioral Science*, 1967, *12*, 384–390.

Baker, J. P., & Crist, J. L. Teacher expectancies: A review of the literature. In J. D. Elashoff & R. E. Snow (Eds.), *Pygmalion reconsidered*. Worthington, Ohio: Charles A. Jones, 1971.

Baldwin, A. L. Personal structure analysis: A statistical method for investigating the single personality. *Journal of Abnormal and Social Psychology*, 1942, *37*, 163–183.

Bannister, D., & Mair, J. M. *The evaluation of personal constructs*. London: Academic Press, 1968.

Barron, F. An ego-strength scale which predicts response to psychotherapy. *Journal of Consulting Psychology*, 1953, *17*, 327–333.

Baughman, E. Rorschach scores as a function of examiner difference, *Journal of Projective Techniques*, 1951, *15*, 243–249.

Bayton, J. A., McAlister, L., & Hamer, J. Race–class stereotypes. In C. W. Backman & P. F. Secord, (Eds.), *Problems in social psychology*. New York: McGraw-Hill, 1966.

Beach, L., & Wertheimer, M. A free response approach to the study of person cognition. *Journal of Abnormal and Social Psychology*, 1961, *62*, 367–374.

Becker, H. S. *Outsiders: Studies in the sociology of deviance*. New York: The Free Press of Glencoe, 1963.

Becker, H. S. Labeling theory reconsidered. In H. S. Becker, *Outsiders* (2nd ed.). New York: The Free Press, 1973.

Beecher, H. K. The powerful placebo. *Journal of the American Medical Association*, 1955, *159*, 1602–1606.

Beecher, H. K. *Measurement of subjective responses*. New York: Oxford University Press, 1959.

Beecher, H. K. Surgery as placebo: A quantitative study of bias. *Journal of the American Medical Association,* 1961, *176,* 1102–1107.

Beecher, H. K. Nonspecific forces surrounding disease and the treatment of disease. *Journal of the American Medical Association*, 1962, *179*, 437–440.

Beecher, H. K. Pain: One mystery solved. *Science*, 1966, *151*, 840–841.

Beecher, H. K., Keats, A. S., Mosteller, F., & Lasagna, L. The effectiveness of oral analgesics (morphine, codeine, acetylsalicylic acid) and the problem of placebo "reactors" and "nonreactors." *Journal of Pharmacology and Experimental Therapeutics*, 1953, *109*, 393–400.

Beez, W. V. Influence of biased psychological reports on teacher behavior and pupil performance. *Proceedings of the 76th Annual Convention of the American Psychological Association*, 1968, *3*, 605–606.

Benedetti, D. T., & Hill, J. G. A determiner of the centrality of a trait in impression formation. *Journal of Abnormal and Social Psychology*, 1960, *60*, 278–280.

Berne, E. *Transactional analysis in psychotherapy*. New York: Grove Press, 1961.

Bettelheim, B. Individual and mass behavior in extreme situations. *Journal of Abnormal and Social Psychology*, 1943, *38*, 417–452.

Blanchard, W. A. Relevance of information and accuracy of interpersonal prediction: A methodological note. *Psychological Reports*, 1966, *18*, 379–382.

Bogdonoff, M. D., Klein, R. F., Back, K. W., Nichols, C. R., Troyer, W. G., & Hood, C. Effect of group relationship and of the role of leadership upon lipid mobilization. *Psychosomatic Medicine*, 1964, *26*, 710–719.

Boring, E. G. *A history of experimental psychology* (2nd ed.). New York: Appleton-Century-Crofts, 1950.

Bossom, J., & Maslow, A. H. Security of judges as a factor in impressions of warmth in others. *Journal of Abnormal and Social Psychology*, 1957, *55*, 147–148.

Brady, J. V. Ulcers in "executive" monkeys. *Scientific American*, 1958, *199* (October), 95–100.

Brehm, J. W. *A theory of psychological reactance*. New York: Academic Press, 1966.

Brehm, J. W. Postdecision changes in the desirability of alternatives. *Journal of Abnormal and Social Psychology*, 1956, *52*, 384–389.

Brehm, J. W., & Cohen, A. R. *Explorations in cognitive dissonance*. New York: Wiley, 1962.

Brigham, J. C. Ethnic stereotypes. *Psychological Bulletin,* 1971, *76*, 15–38.

Brock, T. C., Edelman, S. K., Edwards, D. C., & Schuck, J. R. Seven studies of performance expectancy as a determinant of actual performance, *Journal of Experimental Social Psychology*, 1965, *1*, 295–310.

Brody, N. Anxiety, induced muscular tension, and the statistical structure of binary response sequences. *Journal of Abnormal and Social Psychology*, 1964, *68*, 540–543.

Bruner, J. S., Perceptual theory and the Rorschach test, *Journal of Personality*, 1948, *17*, 157–168.

Bruner, J. S. Personality dynamics and the process of perceiving. In R. R. Blake & G. V. Ramsey, (Eds.), *Perception: An approach to personality*. New York: Ronald Press, 1951.

Bruner, J. S. Primary group experience and the process of acculturation. *American Anthropologist*, 1956, *58*, 605–623.

Bruner, J. S., Shapiro, D., & Tagiuri, R. The meaning of traits in isolation and in combination. In R. Tagiuri & L. Petrullo (Eds.), *Person perception and interpersonal behavior*. Stanford, Calif.: Stanford, 1958.

Bruner, J. S., & Tagiuri, R. The perception of people. In G. Lindzey, (Ed.), *Handbook of social psychology*. Reading, Mass.: Addison-Wesley, 1954.

Brunswik, E. *Systematic and representative design of psychological experiments*. Berkeley: University of California Press, 1949.

Bugental, D. E., Love, L. R., & Gianetto, R. M. Perfidious feminine faces. *Journal of Personality and Social Psychology*, 1971, *17*, 314–318.

Burgers, J. M. Causality and anticipation. *Science*, 1975, *189*, 194–198.

Burke, W. W. Social perception as a function of dogmatism. *Perceptual and Motor Skills*, 1966, *23*, 863–868.

Campbell, D. T. Stereotypes and the perception of group differences. *American Psychologist*, 1967, *22*, 817–829.

Campbell, D. T., & Stanley, J. C. *Experimental and quasi-experimental designs for research*. Chicago: Rand-McNally, 1966.

Cannon, W. B. "Voodoo" death. *American Anthropologist*, 1942, *44*, 169–181.

Cantril, H. The prediction of social events. *Journal of Abnormal and Social Psychology*, 1938, *33*, 364–389.

Carlsmith, J. M. *Strength of expectancy: Its determinants and effects*. Unpublished Doctoral Dissertation, Harvard University, 1962.

Carson, R. C. *Interaction concepts of personality*. Chicago: Aldine, 1969.

Cauthen, N. R., Robinson, I. E., & Krauss, H. H. Stereotypes as contexts of meaning. *Proceedings of the 79th Annual Convention of the American Psychological Association*, 1971, *6*, 353–354. (a)

Cauthen, N. R., Robinson, I. E., & Krauss, H. H. Stereotypes: A review of the literature 1926–1968 *Journal of Social Psychology*, 1971, *84*, 103–125. (b)

Chaikin, A. L., Sigler, E., & Derlega, V. J. Nonverbal mediators of teacher expectancy effects. *Journal of Personality and Social Psychology*, 1974, *30*, 144–149.

Chapman, D. W., & Volkmann, J. A social determinant of the level of aspiration. *Journal of Abnormal and Social Psychology*, 1939, *34*, 225–238.

Chapman, L. Illusory correlation in observational report. *Journal of Verbal Learning and Verbal Behavior*, 1967, *6*, 151–155.

Chapman, L., & Chapman, J. Genesis of popular but erroneous psycho-diagnostic observations. *Journal of Abnormal Psychology*, 1967, *72*, 193–204.

Chapman, L., & Chapman, J. Illusory correlation as an obstacle to the use of valid psycho-diagnostic signs. *Journal of Abnormal Psychology*, 1969, *74*, 271–280.

Child, I. L., & Whiting, J. W. Effects of goal attainment: Relaxation versus renewed striving. *Journal of Abnormal and Social Psychology*, 1950, *45*, 667–681.

Chu, F. D., & Trotter, S. *The madness establishment*. New York: Grossman, 1974.

Cofer, C. N., & Appley, M. H. *Motivation: Theory and research*. New York: Wiley, 1964.

Cohen, A. R. Cognitive tuning as a factor affecting impression formation. *Journal of Personality*, 1961, *29*, 235–245.

Cohen, J. *Behaviour in uncertainty: And its social implications*. New York: Basic Books, 1964.

Cottrell, N. B. The effect of dissonance between expected and obtained performance upon task proficiency and self-estimates of task proficiency. *Journal of Social Psychology*, 1967, *72*, 275–284.

Cronbach, L. J. Processes affecting scores on "understanding of others" and "assumed similarity." *Psychological Bulletin*, 1955, *52*, 177–193.

Cronbach, L. J., & Davis, B. Belief and desire in wartime. *Journal of Abnormal and Social Psychology*, 1944, *39*, 446–458.

Dailey, C. A. The effects of premature conclusions upon the acquisition of understanding of a person. *Journal of Psychology*, 1952, *33*, 133–152.

D'Andrade, R. G. Trait psychology and componential analysis. *American Anthropologist*, 1965, *67*, 215–228.

D'Andrade, R. G. Memory and the assessment of behavior. In H. M. Blalock, (Ed.), *Measurement in the social sciences: Theories and strategies*. Chicago: Aldine, 1974.

Denzin, N. K. The self-fulfilling prophecy and patient–therapist interaction. In S. P. Spitzer & N. K. Denzin, (Eds.), *The mental patient: Studies in the sociology of deviance*. New York: McGraw-Hill, 1968.

Denzin, N. K., & Spitzer, S. P. Paths to the mental hospital and staff predictions of patient role behavior. *Journal of Health and Human Behavior*, 1966, 7, 265–271.

Deutsch, M. Field theory in social psychology. In G. Lindzey & E. Aronson, (Eds.), *Handbook of social psychology* (2nd ed.). Reading, Mass.: Addison-Wesley, 1968.

Diggory, J. C. *Self-evaluation: Concepts and studies*. New York: Wiley, 1966.

Diggory, J. C., & Morlock, H. C., Jr. Level of aspiration, or probability of success? *Journal of Abnormal and Social Psychology*, 1964, 69, 282–289.

Diggory, J. C., Riley, E. J., & Blumenfeld, R. Estimated probability of success for a fixed goal. *American Journal of Psychology*, 1960, 73, 41–55.

Dion, K., Berscheid, E., & Walster, E. What is beautiful is good. *Journal of Personality and Social Psychology*, 1972, 24, 285–290.

Dodge, D. L., & Martin, W. T. *Social stress and chronic illness*. Notre Dame, Indiana: University of Notre Dame Press, 1970.

Dornbusch, S. M., Hastorf, A. H., Richardson, S. A., Muzzy, R. E., & Vreeland, R. S. The perceiver and the perceived: Their relative influence on the categories of interpersonal perception. *Journal of Personality and Social Psychology*, 1965, 1, 434–440.

Dubos, R. *Man adapting*. New Haven: Yale University Press, 1965.

Duncan, S., & Rosenthal, R. Vocal emphasis in experimenters' instruction reading as unintended determinant of subjects' responses. *Language and Speech*, 1968, 11, 20–26.

Ehrlich, H. J., & Rinehart, J. W. A brief report on the methodology of stereotype research. *Social Forces*, 1965, 43, 564–575.

Eisenberg, L. The human nature of human nature. *Science*, 1972, 176, 123–128.

Ellsworth, P. C., & Carlsmith, J. M. Effects of eye contact and verbal content on affective response to a dyadic interaction. *Journal of Personality and Social Psychology*, 1968, 10, 15–20.

Engel, G. L. A life setting conducive to illness: The giving up–given up complex. *Bulletin of the Menninger Clinic*, 1968, 32, 355–365.

Engel, G. Sudden and rapid death during psychological stress. *Annals of Internal Medicine*, 1971, 74, 771–782.

Engel, G. L. A unified concept of health and disease. In T. Millon, (Ed.), *Medical behavioral science*. Philadelphia: W. B. Saunders, 1975.

Erikson, K. T. *Wayward puritans*. New York: Wiley, 1966.

Ervin-Tripp, S. M. Sociolinquistics. In L. Berkowitz, (Ed.), *Advances in experimental social psychology* (Vol. 4). New York: Academic Press, 1969.

Exline, R. V., & Winters, L. C. Affective relations and mutual glances in dyads. In S. S. Tomkins & C. E. Izard, (Eds.), *Affect, cognition, and personality*. New York: Springer, 1965.

Eysenck, H. J., & Crown, S. National stereotypes: An experimental and methodological study. *International Journal of Opinion and Attitude Research*, 1948, 2, 26–39.

Farina, A., Allen, J. G., & Saul, B. B. The role of the stigmatized person in affecting social relationships. *Journal of Personality*, 1968, 36, 169–182.

Farina, A., Chapnick, B., Chapnick, J., & Misiti, R. Political views and interpersonal behavior. *Journal of Personality and Social Psychology*, 1972, 22, 273–278.

Farina, A., Holland, C. H., & Ring, K. Role of stigma and set in interpersonal interaction. *Journal of Abnormal Psychology*, 1966, 71, 421–428.

Farina, A., & Ring, K. The influence of perceived mental illness on interpersonal relations. *Journal of Abnormal Psychology*, 1965, 70, 47–51.

Feather, N. T. Subjective probability and decision under uncertainty. *Psychological Review*, 1959, *66*, 150–164.

Feather, N. T. The effect of differential failure on expectation of success, reported anxiety, and response uncertainty. *Journal of Personality*, 1963, *31*, 289–312.

Feather, N. T. The relationship of expectation of success to need achievement and test anxiety. *Journal of Personality and Social Psychology*, 1965, *1*, 118–126.

Feather, N. T. Effects of prior success and failure on expectations of success and subsequent performance. *Journal of Personality and Social Psychology*, 1966, *3*, 287–298.

Feather, N. T. Change in confidence following success or failure as a predictor of subsequent performance. *Journal of Personality and Social Psychology*, 1968, *9*, 38–46.

Feather, N. T., & Saville, M. R. Effects of amount of prior success and failure on expectations of success and subsequent task performance. *Journal of Personality and Social Psychology*, 1967, *5*, 226–232.

Felipe, A. Evaluative versus descriptive consistency in trait inferences. *Journal of Personality and Social Psychology*, 1970, *16*, 627–638.

Festinger, L. Wish, expectation, and group standards as factors influencing level of aspiration. *Journal of Abnormal and Social Psychology*, 1942, *37*, 184–200.

Festinger, L. Informal social communication. *Psychological Review*, 1950, *57*, 271–282.

Festinger, L. A theory of social comparison processes. *Human Relations*, 1954, *7*, 117–140.

Festinger, L. *A theory of cognitive dissonance.* Evanston, Ill.: Row, Peterson, 1957.

Filer, R. N. The clinician's personality and his case reports. *American Psychologist*, 1952, *7*, 336. (Abstract)

Fisher, S., Cole, J., Rickels, K., & Uhlenhuth, E. H. Drug-set interaction: the effect of expectations on drug response in outpatients. *Neuropsychopharmacology*, 1964, *3*, 149–156.

French, E. G. Effects of the interaction of motivation and feedback on task performance. In J. W. Atkinson, (Ed.), *Motives in fantasy, action, and society.* Princeton, N.J.: Van Nostrand, 1958.

Friedman, M., & Rosenman, R. H. *Type A behavior and your heart.* New York: Knopf, 1974.

Friedman, N. *The social nature of psychological research: The psychological experiment as a social interaction.* New York: Basic Books, 1967.

Friendly, M. L., & Glucksberg, S. On the description of subcultural lexicons: A multidimensional approach. *Journal of Personality and Social Psychology*, 1970, *14*, 55–65.

Gardner, T. D., & Barnard, J. W. Intelligence and the factorial structure of person perception. *American Journal of Mental Deficiency*, 1969, *74*, 212–217.

Garrity, T. F. Psychic death: Behavioral types and physiological parallels. *Omega*, 1974, *5*, 207–215.

Gauron, E. F., & Dickinson, J. K. Diagnostic decision-making in psychiatry: 1. Information usage. *Archives of General Psychiatry*, 1966, *14*, 225–232.

Geer, J. H., Davison, G. C., & Gatchel, R. I. Reduction of stress in humans through nonveridical perceived control of aversive stimulation. *Journal of Personality and Social Psychology*, 1970, *16*, 731–738.

Gergen, K. J. Social psychology as history. *Journal of Personality and Social Psychology*, 1973, *26*, 309–320.

Gibbins, K. Communication aspects of women's clothes and their relation to fashionability. *British Journal of Social and Clinical Psychology*, 1969, *8*, 301–312.

Gibby, R. G. Examiner influence on the Rorschach inquiry. *Journal of Consulting Psychology*, 1952, *16*, 449–455.

Gilbert, G. M. Stereotype persistence and change among college students. *Journal of Abnormal and Social Psychology*, 1951, *46*, 245–254.

Goffman, E. *The presentation of self in everyday life*. Garden City, N.Y.: Doubleday-Anchor, 1959.

Goffman, E. *Asylums*. Garden City, N.Y.: Doubleday-Anchor, 1961.

Goffman, E. *Stigma: Notes on the management of spoiled identity*. Englewood Cliffs, N.J.: Prentice-Hall, 1963.

Goffman, E. *Frame analysis: an essay on the organization of experience*. Cambridge, Mass.: Harvard University Press, 1974.

Goldfarb, A. Reliability of diagnostic judgments made by psychologists. *Journal of Clinical Psychology*, 1959, *15*, 392–396.

Golding, S. L., & Rorer, L. G. Illusory correlation and subjective judgment, *Journal of Abnormal Psychology*, 1972, *80*, 249–260.

Goldstein, A. P. *Therapist–patient expectancies in psychotherapy*. New York: Pergamon Press, 1962.

Gove, W. Who is hospitalized: A critical review of some sociological studies on mental illness. *Journal of Health and Social Behavior*, 1970, *11*, 294–303.

Grosz, H. J., & Grossman, K. G. Clinician's response style: A source of variation and bias in clinical judgment. *Journal of Abnormal Psychology*, 1968, *73*, 207–214.

Guilford, J. P. *Psychometric methods* (2nd ed.). New York: McGraw-Hill, 1954. (Originally published 1936.)

Hakel, M. Significance of implicit personality theories for personality research and theory. *Proceedings of the 77th Annual Convention of the American Psychological Association*, 1969, *4*, 403–404.

Hamilton, D. L. The structure of personality judgments: Comments on Kuusinen's paper and further evidence. *Scandanavian Journal of Psychology*, 1970, *11*, 261–265.

Hamilton, D. L., & Gifford, R. K. Influence of implicit personality theories on cue utilization in interpersonal judgment. *Proceedings of the 78th Annual Convention of the American Psychological Association*, 1970, *5*, 415–416.

Hammond, K. R., (Ed.). *The psychology of Egon Brunswik*. New York: Holt, Rinehart, and Winston, 1966.

Hammond, K. R., Hursch, C. J., & Todd, F. J. Analyzing the components of clinical inference. *Psychological Review*, 1964, *71*, 438–456.

Hammond, K. R., Wilkins, M. M., & Todd, F. J. A research paradigm for the study of interpersonal learning. *Psychological Bulletin*, 1966, *65*, 221–232.

Haney, C. A., & Michielutte, R. Selective factors operating in the adjudication of incompetency. *Journal of Health and Social Behavior*, 1968, *9*, 233–242.

Harding, J., Proshansky, H., Kutner, B., & Chein, I. Prejudice and ethnic relations. In G. Lindzey & E. Aronson, (Eds.), *Handbook of social psychology* (2nd ed.). Reading, Mass.: Addison-Wesley, 1969.

Hardy, J. D., Wolff, H. G., & Goodell, H. Studies on pain: A new method for measuring pain threshold: Observations on spatial summation of pain. *Journal of Clinical Investigation*, 1940, *19*, 649–657.

Harleston, B. W. Test anxiety and performance in problem-solving situations. *Journal of Personality*, 1962, *30*, 557–573.

Harleston, B. W., Smith, M. G., & Arey, D. Test-anxiety level, heart rate, and anagram problem solving. *Journal of Personality and Social Psychology*, 1965, *1*, 551–557.

Hastorf, A. H., Richardson, S. A., & Dornbusch, S. M. The problem of relevance in the study of person perception. In R. Tagiuri & L. Petrullo, (Eds.), *Person perception and interpersonal behavior*. Stanford, Calif.: Stanford University Press, 1958.

Hastorf, A. H., Schneider, D. J., & Polefka, J. *Person perception*. Reading, Mass.: Addison-Wesley, 1970.

Heider, F. *The psychology of interpersonal relations*. New York: Wiley, 1958.

Helson, H. *Adaptation-level theory*. New York: Harper & Row, 1964.

Hendrick, C., & Jones, R. A. *The nature of theory and research in social psychology*. New York: Academic Press, 1972.

Hersh, J. B. Effects of referral information on testers. *Journal of Consulting and Clinical Psychology*, 1971, *37*, 116–122.

Hess, H. F., & Jessor, R. The influence of reinforcement value on rate of learning and asymptotic level of expectancies. *Journal of General Psychology*, 1960, *63*, 89–102.

Higgins, E. T., & Rholes, W. S. Impression formation and role fulfillment: A "holistic reference" approach. *Journal of Experimental Social Psychology*, 1976, *12*, 422–435.

Hilgard, E. R. *Theories of learning* (2nd ed.). New York: Appleton-Century-Crofts, 1956.

Hilton, J. *Lost horizon*. New York: Simon & Schuster, Pocket Books, 1939. (Originally published by William Morrow, 1933.)

Hinkle, L. E. Ecological observations of the relation of physical illness, mental illness, and the social environment. *Psychosomatic Medicine*, 1961, *23*, 289–296.

Hinkle, L. E., Christenson, W. N., Kane, F. D., Ostfeld, A., Thetford, W. N., & Wolff, H. G. An investigation of the relation between life experience, personality characteristics, and general susceptibility to illness. *Psychosomatic Medicine*, 1958, *20*, 278–295.

Hinkle, L. E., Pinsky, R. H., Bross, I. D., & Plummer, N. The distribution of sickness disability in a homogeneous group of "healthy adult men." *American Journal of Hygiene*, 1956, *64*, 220–242.

Hinkle, L. E., & Wolff, H. G. Ecologic investigations of the relationship between illness, life experiences, and the social environment. *Annals of Internal Medicine*, 1958, *49*, 1373–1388.

Hiroto, D. S. Locus of control and learned helplessness. *Journal of Experimental Psychology*, 1974, *102*, 187–193.

Hiroto, D. S., & Seligman, M. E. P. Generality of learned helplessness in man. *Journal of Personality and Social Psychology*, 1975, *31*, 311–327.

Hokanson, J. E., DeGood, D. E., Forrest, M. S., & Brittain, T. M. Availability of avoidance behaviors in modulating vascular-stress responses. *Journal of Personality and Social Psychology*, 1971, *19*, 60–68.

Hollander, E. P. Conformity, status, and idiosyncrasy credit. *Psychological Review*, 1958, *65*, 117–127.

Holmes, D. S. Dimensions of projection. *Psychological Bulletin*, 1968, *69*, 248–268.

Holmes, T. H., & Rahe, R. H. The social readjustment rating scale. *Journal of Psychosomatic Research*, 1967, *11*, 213–218.

Holt, J. *How children fail*. New York: Pitman, 1964.

Holt, R. R. Clinical judgment as a disciplined inquiry. *Journal of Nervous and Mental Disease*, 1961, *133*, 369–382.

Horowitz, M. J. A study of clinicians' judgments from projective test protocols. *Journal of Consulting Psychology*, 1962, *26*, 251–256.

House, W. C. Performance expectancies and affect associated with outcomes as a function of time perspective. *Journal of Research in Personality*, 1973, *7*, 277–288.

Howell, W. C. Uncertainty and confidence in human decision-making. Paper read at American Psychological Association Convention, 1972.

Hull, C. L. *Principles of behavior: An introduction to behavior theory*. New York: Appleton-Century-Crofts, 1943.

Inkeles, A., & Levinson, D. J. National character: The study of modal personality and sociocultural systems. In G. Lindzey & E. Aronson, (Eds.), *Handbook of social psychology* (2nd ed.). Reading, Mass.: Addison-Wesley, 1969.

Irwin, F. W. Stated expectations as functions of probability and desirability of outcome. *Journal of Personality*, 1953, *21*, 329–335.

Jackson, D. N. The measurement of perceived personality trait relationships. In N. F. Washburne, (Ed.), *Decisions, values, and groups* (Vol. 2). New York: Pergamon, 1962.

Jackson, D. N., & Messick, S. J. Individual differences in social perception. *British Journal of Social and Clinical Psychology*, 1963, *2*, 1–10.

Janis, I. L. *Air war and emotional stress*. New York: McGraw-Hill, 1951.

Jellinek, E. M. Clinical tests on comparative effectiveness of analgesic drugs. *Biometrics Bulletin*, 1946, *2*, 87–91.

Jessor, R., & Readio, J. The influence of the value of an event upon the expectancy of its occurrence. *Journal of General Psychology*, 1957, *56*, 219–228.

Johnson, H. H., & Foley, J. M. Some effects of placebo and experiment conditions in research on methods of teaching. *Journal of Educational Psychology*, 1969, *60*, 6–10.

Johnson, H. H., & Steiner, I. D. Effort and subjective probability. *Journal of Personality and Social Psychology*, 1965, *1*, 365–368.

Jones, E. E. Authoritarianism as a determinant of first-impression formation. *Journal of Personality*, 1954, *23*, 107–127.

Jones, E. E., & Davis, K. E. From acts to dispositions: The attribution process in person perception. In L. Berkowitz, (Ed.), *Advances in experimental social psychology* (Vol. 2). New York: Academic Press, 1965.

Jones, E. E., & Gerard, H. B. *Foundations of social psychology*. New York: Wiley, 1967.

Jones, R. A., & Cooper, J. Mediation of experimenter effects. *Journal of Personality and Social Psychology*, 1971, *20*, 70–74.

Jones, R. A., & Rosenberg, S. Structural representations of naturalistic descriptions of personality. *Multivariate Behavioral Research*, 1974, *9*, 217–230.

Jones, S. C., & Panitch, D. The self-fulfilling prophecy and interpersonal attraction. *Journal of Experimental Social Psychology*, 1971, *7*, 356–366.

Karlins, M., Coffman, T. L., & Walters, G. On the fading of social stereotypes: Studies in three generations of college students. *Journal of Personality and Social Psychology*, 1969, *13*, 1–16.

Katz, D., & Braly, K. Racial stereotypes of one hundred college students. *Journal of Abnormal and Social Psychology*, 1933, *28*, 280–290.

Katz, M. M., Cole, J. O., & Lowery, H. A. Studies of the diagnostic process: The influence of symptom perception, past experience, and ethnic background on diagnostic decisions. *American Journal of Psychiatry*, 1969, *125*, 937–947.

Kelley, H. H. The warm–cold variable in first impressions of persons. *Journal of Personality*, 1950, *18*, 431–439.

Kelley, H. H. Attribution theory in social psychology. *Nebraska symposium on motivation* (Vol. 15). Lincoln, Neb.: University of Nebraska Press, 1967.

Kelley, H. H., & Stahelski, A. J. Social interaction basis of cooperators' and competitors' beliefs about others. *Journal of Personality and Social Psychology*, 1970, *16*, 66–91.

Kelly, G. A. *The psychology of personal constructs*. New York: Norton, 1955.

Kirscht, J. P., & Dillehay, R. C. *Dimensions of authoritarianism: A review of research and theory*. Lexington, Ky.: University of Kentucky Press, 1967.

Kleck, R. Physical stigma and task oriented interactions. *Human Relations*, 1969, *22*, 53–60.

Kleck, R., Ono, H., & Hastorf, A. The effects of physical deviance upon face-to-face interaction. *Human Relations*, 1966, *19*, 425–436.

Kobler, A. L., & Stotland, E. *The end of hope: A social–clinical study of suicide*. New York: The Free Press, 1964.

Koltuv, B. B. Some characteristics of intrajudge trait intercorrelations. *Psychological Monographs*, 1962, *76*(33, Whole No. 552).

Konstadt, N., & Forman, E. Field dependence and external directedness. *Journal of Personality and Social Psychology*, 1965, *1*, 490–493.

Kostlan, A. A method for the empirical study of psychodiagnosis. *Journal of Consulting Psychology*, 1954, *18*, 83–88.

Kostlan, A. A reply to Patterson. *Journal of Consulting Psychology*, 1955, *19*, 486.

Krauss, H. H. Schizophrenia: A self-fulfilling, labeling process. *Psychotherapy: Theory, research, and practice*, 1968, *5*, 240–245.

Krishna, D. "The self-fulfilling prophecy" and the nature of society. *American Sociological Review*, 1971, *36*, 1104–1107.

Kruskal, J. B. Multidimensional scaling by optimizing goodness of fit to a nonmetric hypothesis. *Psychometrika*, 1964, *29*, 1–27. (a)

Kruskal, J. B. Nonmetric multidimensional scaling: A numerical method. *Psychometrika*, 1964, *29*, 115–129. (b)

Kukla, A. Foundations of an attributional theory of performance. *Psychological Review*, 1972, *79*, 454–470.

Kuusinen, J. Affective and denotative structures of personality ratings. *Journal of Personality and Social Psychology*, 1969, *12*, 181–188.

Laing, R. D., & Esterson, A. *Sanity, madness, and the family*. Baltimore: Penguin, 1970. (Originally published by Tavistock, 1964.)

Lambert, W. E., Hodgson, R. C., Gardner, R. C., & Fillenbaum, S. Evaluational reactions to spoken languages. *Journal of Abnormal and Social Psychology*, 1960, *60*, 44–51.

Lanzetta, J. T., & Hannah, T. E. Reinforcing behavior of "naive" trainers. *Journal of Personality and Social Psychology*, 1969, *11*, 245–252.

Lasagna, L., Mosteller, F., von Felsinger, J. M., & Beecher, H. K. A study of the placebo response. *American Journal of Medicine*, 1954, *16*, 770–779.

Lazarus, R. S. *Psychological stress and the coping process*. New York: McGraw-Hill, 1966.

Lazarus, R. S., & Averill, J. R. Emotion and cognition: With special reference to anxiety. In C. D. Spielberger, (Ed.), *Anxiety: Current trends in theory and research*. New York: Academic Press, 1972.

Leary, T. *Interpersonal diagnosis of personality*. New York: Ronald Press, 1957.

Lefford, A. The influence of emotional subject matter on logical reasoning. *Journal of General Psychology*, 1946, *34*, 127–151.

Lemert, E. M. *Social pathology*. New York: McGraw-Hill, 1951.

Lemert, E. M. Paranoia and the dynamics of exclusion. *Sociometry*, 1962, *25*, 2–20.

Lemkau, P. V. Discussion. *Psychomatic Medicine*, 1961, *23*, 296–297.

Lester, D. Attempts to predict suicidal risk using psychological tests. *Psychological Bulletin*, 1970, *74*, 1–17.

Levi, L. Psychological stress and disease: A conceptual model. In K. E. Gunderson & R. H. Rahe, (Eds.), *Life stress and illness*. Springfield, Ill.: Thomas, 1974.

Levy, L. H. A note on research methodology used in testing for examiner influence in clinical test performance. *Journal of Consulting Psychology*, 1956, *20*, 286.

Lewin, K. Formalization and progress in psychology. *University of Iowa Studies in Child Welfare*, 1940, *16*, 9–42.

Lewin, K. *Field theory in social science* (D. Cartwright, Ed.). New York: Harper, 1951.

Lieberman, M. A. Relationship of mortality rates to entrance to a home for the aged. *Geriatrics*, 1961, *16*, 515–519.

Liebow, E. *Tally's corner: A study of Negro streetcorner men*. Boston: Little, Brown & Company, 1967.

Linsky, A. S. Community homogeneity and exclusion of the mentally ill: Rejection versus consensus about deviance. *Journal of Health and Social Behavior*, 1970, *11*, 304–311.

Lippmann, W. *Public opinion*. New York: Harcourt, Brace, 1922.

Locke, E. A. Motivational effects of knowledge of results: Knowledge or goal setting? *Journal of Applied Psychology*, 1967, *51*, 324–329.

Lott, A. J., Lott, B. E., Reed, T., & Crow, T. Personality-trait descriptions of differentially liked persons. *Journal of Personality and Social Psychology*, 1970, *16*, 284–290.

Luft, J. Implicit hypotheses and clinical predictions. *Journal of Abnormal and Social Psychology*, 1950, *45*, 756–759.

Luft, J. Monetary value and the perception of persons. *Journal of Social Psychology*, 1957, *46*, 245–251.

Mackie, M. Arriving at "truth" by definition: The case of stereotype inaccuracy. *Social Problems*, 1973, *20*, 431–447.

MacLeod, R. B. The phenomenological approach to social psychology. *Psychological Review*, 1947, *54*, 193–210.

Mandler, G. Helplessness: Theory and research in anxiety. In C. D. Spielberger, (Ed.), *Anxiety: Current trends in theory and research*. New York: Academic Press, 1972.

Mandler, G., & Sarason, S. B. A study of anxiety and learning. *Journal of Abnormal and Social Psychology*, 1952, *47*, 166–173.

Marks, R. W. The effect of probability, desirability, and "privilege" on the stated expectations of children. *Journal of Personality*, 1951, *19*, 332–351.

Marlett, N. J., & Watson, D. Test anxiety and immediate or delayed feedback in a test-like avoidance task. *Journal of Personality and Social Psychology*, 1968, *8*, 200–203.

Masling, J. The effects of warm and cold interaction on the interpretation of a projective protocol. *Journal of Projective Techniques*, 1957, *21*, 377–383.

Masling, J. The effects of warm and cold interaction on the administration and scoring of an intelligence test. *Journal of Consulting Psychology*, 1959, *23*, 336–341.

Masuda, M., & Holmes, T. H. The social readjustment rating scale: A cross-cultural study of Japanese and Americans. *Journal of Psychosomatic Research*, 1967, *11*, 227–237.

McClelland, D. C. *The achieving society*. Princeton, N.J.: Van Nostrand, 1961.

McClelland, D. C. N achievement and entrepreneurship: A longitudinal study. *Journal of Personality and Social Psychology*, 1965, *1*, 389–392.

McClelland, D. C., & Atkinson, J. W. The projective expression of needs: I. The effect of different intensities of the hunger drive on perception. *Journal of Psychology*, 1948, *25*, 205–222.

McDermott, J. F., Harrison, S. I., Schrager, P. W., Killins, E., Lindy, J., & Waggoner, R. W. Social class and mental illness in children: The diagnosis of organicity and mental retardation. *Journal of the American Academy of Child Psychiatry* 1967, *6*, 309–320.

McDermott, J. F., Harrison, S. I., Schrager, J., & Wilson, P. T. Social class and mental illness in children: Observations of blue-collar families. *American Journal of Orthopsychiatry*, 1965, *35*, 500–508.

McGregor, D. The major determinants of the prediction of social events. *Journal of Abnormal and Social Psychology*, 1938, *33*, 179–204.

McGuire, W. J. A syllogistic analysis of cognitive relationships. In M. J. Rosenberg, C. I. Hovland, W. J. McGuire, R. P. Abelson, & J. W. Brehm, *Attitude organization and change*. New Haven, Conn.: Yale University Press, 1960.

McGuire, W. J. Suspiciousness of experimenter's intent. In R. Rosenthal & R. L. Rosnow, (Eds.), *Artifact in behavioral research*. New York: Academic Press, 1969.

Mechanic, D. Response factors in illness: The study of illness behavior. *Social Psychiatry*, 1966, *1*, 11–20.

Meehl, P. E. Some ruminations on the validation of clinical procedures. *Canadian Journal of Psychology*, 1959, *13*, 102–128.

Meichenbaum, D. H., Bowers, K. S., & Ross, R. R. A behavioral analysis of teacher expectancy effect. *Journal of Personality and Social Psychology*, 1969, *13*, 306–316.

Melzack, R. The perception of pain. *Scientific American,* 1961, *204,* 41–49.

Melzack, R., & Wall, P. D. Pain mechanisms: A new theory. *Science,* 1965, *150,* 971–979.

Mensh, I. N., & Wishner, J. Asch on "forming impressions of personality": Further evidence. *Journal of Personality,* 1947, *16,* 188–191.

Merton, R. K. *Social theory and social structure* (Rev. ed.). New York: The Free Press, 1957.

Miller, C. E. On the assessment and existence of "wishful thinking." Paper presented at the 45th Annual Meeting of the Midwestern Psychological Association, Chicago, Ill., May 10–12, 1973.

Miller, D., Sanders, R., & Cleveland, S. E. The relationship between examiner personality and obtained Rorschach protocols: An application of interpersonal relations theory. *American Psychologist,* 1950, *5,* 322–323. (Abstract)

Minor, M. W. Experimenter-expectancy effect as a function of evaluation apprehension. *Journal of Personality and Social Psychology,* 1970, *15,* 326–332.

Moss, G. E. *Illness, immunity, and social interaction: The dynamics of biosocial resonation.* New York: Wiley, 1973.

Moulton, R. W. Effects of success and failure on level of aspiration as related to achievement motives. *Journal of Personality and Social Psychology,* 1965, *1,* 399–406.

Murphy, G., & Murphy, L. B., (Eds.), *Asian psychology.* New York: Basic Books, 1968.

Nardini, J. E. Survival factors in American prisoners of war of the Japanese. *American Journal of Psychiatry,* 1952, *109,* 241–247.

Newcomb, T. An experiment designed to test the validity of a rating technique. *Journal of Educational Psychology,* 1931, *22,* 279–289.

Newcomb, T. Autistic hostility and social reality. *Human Relations,* 1947, *1,* 69–86.

Newton, R. L. The clinician as judge: Total Rorschachs and clinical case material. *Journal of Consulting Psychology,* 1954, *18,* 248–250.

Nisan, M. Dimension of time in relation to choice behavior and achievement orientation. *Journal of Personality and Social Psychology,* 1972, *21,* 175–182.

Norman, W. T. Toward an adequate taxonomy of personality attributes: Replicated factor structure in peer nomination personality ratings. *Journal of Abnormal and Social Psychology,* 1963, *66,* 574–583.

Nunnally, J. C. *Popular conceptions of mental health: Their development and change.* New York: Holt, Rinehart, and Winston, 1961.

Oken, D. The psychophysiology and psychoendocrinology of stress and emotion. In M. H. Appley & R. Trumbull, (Eds.), *Psychological stress: Issues in research.* New York: Appleton-Century-Crofts, 1967.

Osgood, C. E. Studies on the generality of affective meaning systems. *American Psychologist,* 1962, *17,* 10–28.

Osgood, C. E., Suci, G. J., & Tannenbaum, P. H. *The measúrement of meaning.* Urbana, Ill.: University of Illinois Press, 1957.

Overmier, J. B., & Seligman, M. E. P. Effects of inescapable shock upon subsequent escape and avoidance responding. *Journal of Comparative and Physiological Psychology,* 1967, *63,* 28–33.

Parkinson, C. N. *Parkinson's law, and other studies in administration.* Boston: Hougton-Mifflin, 1957.

Passini, F. T., & Norman, W. T. A universal conception of personality structure? *Journal of Personality and Social Psychology,* 1966, *4,* 44–49.

Pastore, N. Attributed characteristics of liked and disliked persons. *Journal of Social Psychology,* 1960, *52,* 157–163.

Patterson, C. H. Diagnostic accuracy or diagnostic stereotypy, *Journal of Consulting Psychology,* 1955, *19,* 483–485.

Paykel, E. S. Recent life events and clinical depression. In K. E. Gunderson & R. H. Rahe, (Eds.), *Life stress and illness*. Springfield, Ill.: Thomas, 1974.

Peabody, D. Trait inferences: Evaluative and descriptive aspects. *Journal of Personality and Social Psychology Monograph*, 1967, *7*(Whole No. 644).

Pheterson, G. I., Kiesler, S. B., & Goldberg, P. A. Evaluation of the performance of women as a function of their sex, achievement, and personal history. *Journal of Personality and Social Psychology*, 1971, *19*, 114–118.

Phillips, L., & Draguns, J. G. Classification of the behavior disorders, *Annual Review of Psychology*, 1971, *22*, 447–482.

Pincus, G. Control of conception by hormonal steroids. *Science*, 1966, *153*, 493–500.

Plath, S. *The bell jar*. New York: Harper and Row, 1971.

Radloff, R. Social comparison and ability evaluation. *Journal of Experimental Social Psychology Supplement 1*, 1966, 6–26.

Rahe, R. H. Life change and subsequent illness reports. In K. E. Gunderson & R. H. Rahe, (Eds.), *Life stress and illness*. Springfield, Ill.: Thomas, 1974.

Rahe, R. H., Meyer, M., Smith, M., Kjaer, G., & Holmes, T. H. Social stress and illness onset. *Journal of Psychosomatic Research*, 1964, *8*, 35–44.

Rahe, R. H., & Romo, M. Recent life changes and the onset of myocardial infarction and coronary death in Helsinki. In E. K. Gunderson & R. H. Rahe, (Eds.), *Life stress and illness*. Springfield, Ill.: Thomas, 1974.

Regan, D. T., Straus, E., & Fazio, R. Liking and the attribution process. *Journal of Experimental Social Psychology*, 1974, *10*, 385–397.

Richter, C. P. On the phenomenon of sudden death in animals and man. *Psychosomatic Medicine*, 1957, *19*, 191–198.

Rosenberg, M. *Society and the adolescent self-image*. Princeton, N.J.: Princeton University Press, 1965.

Rosenberg, M. J. When dissonance fails: On eliminating evaluation apprehension from attitude measurement. *Journal of Personality and Social Psychology*, 1965, *1*, 28–42.

Rosenberg, S., & Jones, R. A. A method for investigating and representing a person's implicit theory of personality: Theodore Dreiser's view of people. *Journal of Personality and Social Psychology*, 1972, *22*, 372–386.

Rosenberg, S., Nelson, C., & Vivekananthan, P. S. A multidimensional approach to the structure of personality impressions. *Journal of Personality and Social Psychology*, 1968, *9*, 283–294.

Rosenberg, S., & Olshan, K. Evaluative and descriptive aspects in personality perception. *Journal of Personality and Social Psychology*, 1970, *16*, 619–620.

Rosenberg, S., & Sedlak, A. Structural representations of implicit personality theory. In L. Berkowitz, (Ed.), *Advances in experimental social psychology*. New York: Academic Press, 1972.

Rosenhan, D. L. On being sane in insane places. *Science*, 1973, *179*, 250–258.

Rosenthal, D., & Frank, J. D. Psychotherapy and the placebo effect. *Psychological Bulletin*, 1956, *53*, 294–302.

Rosenthal, R. *Experimenter effects in behavioral research*. New York: Appleton-Century-Crofts, 1966.

Rosenthal, R. On the social psychology of the self-fulfilling prophecy: Further evidence for Pygmalion effects and their mediating mechanisms. New York: MSS Modular Publications, 1973, Module 53, 1–28.

Rosenthal, R., & Jacobson, L. *Pygmalion in the classroom*. New York: Holt, Rinehart, and Winston, 1968.

Rotter, J. B. *Social learning and clinical psychology*. New York: Prentice-Hall, 1954.

Rotter, J. B. Generalized expectancies for internal versus external control of reinforcement. *Psychological Monographs*, 1966, *80* (Whole No. 609).

Rubin, R. T., Gunderson, E. K., & Arthur, R. J. Life stress and illness patterns in the U.S. Navy–v. prior life change and illness onset in a battleship's crew. *Journal of Psychosomatic Research,* 1971, *15,* 89–94.

Rubin, R. T., & Rahe, R. H. U.S. Navy underwater demolition team training: Biochemical studies. In K. E. Gunderson & R. H. Rahe, (Eds.), *Life stress and illness.* Springfield, Ill.: Thomas, 1974.

Rubovits, P. C., & Maehr, M. L. Pygmalion analyzed: Toward an explanation of the Rosenthal–Jacobson findings. *Journal of Personality and Social Psychology*, 1971, *19,* 197–203.

Rubovits, P. C., & Maehr, M. L. Pygmalion black and white. *Journal of Personality and Social Psychology*, 1973, *25,* 210–218.

Rushing, W. A. Individual resources, societal reaction, and hospital commitment. *American Journal of Sociology*, 1971, *77,* 511–526.

Russell, D. G., & Sarason, I. G. Test anxiety, sex, and experimental conditions in relation to anagram solution. *Journal of Personality and Social Psychology*, 1965, *1,* 493–496.

Ryckman, R. M., Gold, J. A., & Rodda, W. C. Confidence rating shifts and performance as a function of locus of control, self-esteem, and initial task experience. *Journal of Personality and Social Psychology*, 1971, *18,* 305–310.

Saenger, G., & Flowerman, S. Stereotypes and prejudicial attitudes, *Human Relations*, 1954, *7,* 217–238.

Sanders, R., & Cleveland, S. E. The relationship between certain examiner personality variables and subjects' Rorschach scores. *Journal of Projective Techniques*, 1953, *17,* 34–50.

Sarbin, T. R. Role theory. In G. Lindzey, (Ed.), *Handbook of social psychology.* Reading, Mass.: Addison-Wesley, 1954.

Sarbin, T. R. On the futility of the proposition that some people be labeled "mentally ill." *Journal of Consulting Psychology*, 1967, *31,* 447–453.

Sarbin, T. R. Ontology recapitulates philology: The mythic nature of anxiety. *American Psychologist*, 1968, *23,* 411–418.

Sarbin, T. R., & Kamiya, J. Contributions to role-taking theory: The experimental separation of qualities of self and of role. Unpublished manuscript, 1952, cited in T. R. Sarbin, Role theory. In G. Lindzey, (Ed.), *Handbook of social psychology.* Reading, Mass.: Addison-Wesley, 1954.

Sarbin, T. R., Taft, R., & Bailey, D. *Clinical inference and cognitive theory.* New York: Holt, Rinehart, and Winston, 1960.

Schachter, S. *Emotion, obesity, and crime.* New York: Academic Press, 1971.

Scheff, T. J. *Being mentally ill: A sociological theory.* Chicago: Aldine, 1966.

Scheff, T. J. The labeling theory of mental illness. *American Sociological Review*, 1974, *39,* 444–452.

Schur, E. M. *Labeling deviant behavior.* New York: Harper & Row, 1971.

Scodel, A., & Mussen, P. Social perception of authoritarian and nonauthoritarians. *Journal of Abnormal and Social Psychology*, 1953, *48,* 181–184.

Secord, P. F. Stereotyping and favorableness in the perception of Negro faces. *Journal of Abnormal and Social Psychology*, 1959, *59,* 309–314.

Secord, P. F., & Backman, C. *Social psychology.* New York: McGraw-Hill, 1964.

Secord, P. F., & Berscheid, E. Stereotyping and the generality of implicit personality theory. *Journal of Personality*, 1963, *31,* 65–78.

Secord, P. F., Bevan, W., & Katz, B. The Negro stereotype and perceptual accentuation. *Journal of Abnormal and Social Psychology,* 1956, *53,* 78–83.

Seligman, M. E. P. *Helplessness: On depression, development, and death.* San Francisco: Freeman, 1975.

Seligman, M. E. P., & Maier, S. F. Failure to escape traumative shock, *Journal of Experimental Psychology*, 1967, *74*, 1–9.

Selye, H. *The stress of life.* New York: McGraw-Hill, 1956.

Shapiro, A. K. A contribution to a history of the placebo effect. *Behavioral Science*, 1960, *5*, 109–135.

Shapiro, A. K. Placebo effects in medicine, psychotherapy, and psychoanalysis. In A. E. Bergin & S. L. Garfield, (Eds.), *Handbook of psychotherapy and behavior change.* New York: Wiley, 1971.

Shapiro, D., & Tagiuri, R. Sex differences in inferring personality traits. *Journal of Psychology*, 1959, *47*, 127–136.

Shepard, R. N. The analysis of proximities: Multidimensional scaling with an unknown distance function. I. *Psychometrika,* 1962, *27,* 125–140.   (a)

Shepard, R. N. The analysis of proximities: Multidimensional scaling with an unknown distance function, II. *Psychometrika*, 1962, *27*, 219–246.   (b)

Sherif, M., & Hovland, C. I. *Social judgment.* New Haven, Conn.: Yale University Press, 1961.

Sherman, R. C., & Ross, L. B. Liberal-conservatism and dimensional salience in the perception of political figures. *Journal of Personality and Social Psychology*, 1972, *23*, 120–127.

Shrauger, S., & Altrocchi, J. The personality of the perceiver as a factor in person perception. *Psychological Bulletin*, 1964, *62*, 289–308.

Sines, L. K. The relative contribution of four kinds of data to accuracy in personality assessment. *Journal of Consulting Psychology*, 1959, *23*, 483–492.

Singleton, W. T. Comment. In K. E. Gunderson & R. H. Rahe, (Eds.), *Life stress and illness.* Springfield, Ill.: Thomas, 1974.

Skinner, B. F. *The behavior of organisms: An experimental analysis.* New York: Appleton-Century-Crofts, 1938.

Smedslund, J. The concept of correlation in adults. *Scandinavian Journal of Psychology*, 1963, *4*, 165–173.

Smedslund, J. Note on learning, contingency, and clinical experience. *Scandinavian Journal of Psychology,* 1966, *7,* 265–266.

Snow, R. E. Unfinished pygmalion. *Contemporary Psychology*, 1969, *14*, 197–199.

Spielberger, C. D., (Ed.). *Anxiety: Current trends in theory and research.* New York: Academic Press, 1972.

Starr, B. J., & Katkin, E. S. The clinician as an aberrant actuary: Illusory correlations and the incomplete sentences blank. *Journal of Abnormal Psychology*, 1969, *74*, 670–675.

Steiner, I. D. Self-perception and goal-setting behavior. *Journal of Personality*, 1957, *25*, 344–355.

Stotland, E. *The psychology of hope.* San Francisco: Jossey-Bass, 1969.

Stout, C., Morrow, J., Brandt, E. N., & Wolf, S. Unusually low incidence of death from myocardial infarction. *Journal of the American Medical Association,* 1964, *188,* 845–849.

Strassman, H. D., Thaler, M. B., & Schein, E. H. A prisoner of war syndrome: Apathy as a reaction to severe stress. *American Journal of Psychiatry*, 1956, *112*, 998–1003.

Stricker, L. J., Jacobs, P. I., & Kogan, N. Veridicality of implicit personality theories. *Proceedings of the 78th Annual Convention of the American Psychological Association*, 1970, *5*, 157–158.

Strickland, L. H., Lewicki, R. J., & Katz, A. M. Temporal orientation and perceived control as determinants of risk-taking. *Journal of Experimental Social Psychology*, 1966, *2*, 143–151.

Stritch, T. M., & Secord, P. F. Interaction effects in the perception of faces. *Journal of Personality*, 1956, *24*, 270–284.

Strupp, H. H., Levenson, R. W., Manuck, S. B., Snell, J. D., Hinrichsen, J. J., & Boyd, S. Effects of suggestion on total respiratory resistance in mild asthmatics. *Journal of Psychosomatic Research*, 1974, *18*, 337–346.

Sullivan, H. S. *The interpersonal theory of psychiatry*. New York: Norton, 1953.

Szasz, T. *The myth of mental illness*. New York: Dell, 1961.

Szasz, T. *Ideology and insanity*. Garden City, New York: Doubleday-Anchor, 1970.

Tagiuri, R. Introduction. In R. Tagiuri & L. Petrullo, (Eds.), *Person perception and interpersonal behavior*. Stanford, Calif.: Stanford University Press, 1958.

Taylor, J. A. A personality scale of manifest anxiety. *Journal of Abnormal and Social Psychology*, 1953, *48*, 285–290.

Temerlin, M. Suggestion effects in psychiatric diagnosis. *Journal of Nervous and Mental Disease*, 1968, *147*, 349–353.

Temerlin, M. K., & Trousdale, W. W. The social psychology of clinical diagnosis. *Psychotherapy: Theory, Research and Practice*, 1969, *6*, 24–29.

Terkel, S. *Working*. New York: Avon Books, 1975. (Originally published by Pantheon Books, A Division of Random House, Inc., 1972.)

Thomas, W. I., & Thomas, D. S. *The child in America*. New York: Knopf, 1928.

Thorndike, E. L. A constant error in psychological ratings. *Journal of Applied Psychology*, 1920, *4*, 25–29.

Thorndike, R. L. Review of Pygmalion in the classroom. *American Educational Research Journal*, 1968, *5*, 708–711.

Toffler, A. *Future shock*. New York: Bantam, 1971.

Tolman, E. C. *Purposive behavior in animals and men*. New York: Appleton-Century-Crofts, 1932.

Tolman, E. C. Egon Brunswick 1903–1955. *American Journal of Psychology*, 1956, *69*, 315–324.

Towbin, A. When are cookbooks useful? *American Psychologist*, 1960, *15*, 119–123.

Tversky, A., & Kahneman, D. Availability: A heuristic for judging frequency and probability. *Cognitive Psychology*, 1973, *5*, 207–232.

Vander, A. J., Sherman, J. H., & Luciano, D. S. *Human physiology: The mechanisms of body function*. New York: McGraw-Hill, 1970.

Wagar, W. W. *The city of man*. Boston: Houghton-Mifflin, 1963.

Walster, B., & Aronson, E. Effect of expectancy of task duration on the experience of fatigue. *Journal of Experimental Social Psychology*, 1967, *3*, 41–46.

Ward, W. C., & Jenkins, H. M. The display of information and the judgment of contingency. *Canadian Journal of Psychology*, 1965, *19*, 231–241.

Ward, W. D., & Sandvold, K. D. Performance expectancy as a determinant of actual performance: A partial replication. *Journal of Abnormal and Social Psychology*, 1963, *67*, 293–295.

Warr, P. B., & Knapper, C. *The perception of people and events*. New York: Wiley, 1968.

Wason, P. C. On the failure to eliminate hypotheses in a conceptual task. *Quarterly Journal of Experimental Psychology*, 1960, *12*, 129–140.

Waterman, A. S., & Ford, L. H. Performance expectancy as a determinant of actual performance: Dissonance reduction or differential recall? *Journal of Personality and Social Psychology*, 1965, *2*, 464–467.

Watzlawick, P., Beavin, J. H., & Jackson, D. D. *Pragmatics of human communication*. New York: Norton, 1967.

Weiner, B. The effects of unsatisfied achievement motivation on persistence and subsequent performance. *Journal of Personality*, 1965, *33*, 428–442.

Weiner, B., Heckhausen, H., Meyer, W. U., & Cook, R. E. Causal ascriptions and achievement behavior: A conceptual, analysis of effort and reanalysis of locus of control. *Journal of Personality and Social Psychology*, 1972, *21*, 239–248.

Weiner, B., & Kukla, A. An attributional analysis of achievement motivation. *Journal of Personality and Social Psychology*, 1970, *15*, 1–20.

Weinstein, E. A. Toward a theory of interpersonal tactics. In C. W. Backman & P. F. Secord, (Eds.), *Problems in social psychology*. New York: McGraw-Hill, 1966.

Weiss, J. M. Effects of coping behavior in different warning signal conditions on stress pathology in rats. *Journal of Comparative and Physiological Psychology*, 1971, *77*, 1–13.

Wenger, D. L., & Fletcher, C. R. The effect of legal counsel on admissions to a state mental hospital: A confrontation of professions. *Journal of Health and Social Behavior*, 1969, *10*, 66–72.

Wheeler, L. Motivation as a determinant of upward comparison. *Journal of Experimental Social Psychology Supplement 1*, 1966, 27–31.

White, R. W. Motivation reconsidered: The concept of competence. *Psychological Review*, 1959, *66*, 297–333.

Wiener, M., & Mehrabian, A. *Language within language: Immediacy, a channel in verbal communication*. New York: Appleton-Century-Crofts, 1968.

Wiggins, N., Hoffman, P. J., & Taber, T. Types of judges and cue utilization in judgments of intelligence. *Journal of Personality and Social Psychology*, 1969, *12*, 52–59.

Wilde, W. A. Decision-making in a psychiatric screening agency. *Journal of Health and Social Behavior*, 1968, *9*, 215–221.

Wishner, J. Reanalysis of "Impressions of personality." *Psychological Review*, 1960, *67*, 96–112.

Witkin, H. A., Dyk, R. B., Faterson, H. F., Goodenough, D. R., & Karp, S. A. *Psychological differentiation*, New York: Wiley, 1962.

Wolf, S. Effects of suggestion and conditioning on the action of chemical agents in human subjects—the pharmacology of placebos. *Journal of Clinical Investigation*, 1950, *29*, 100–109.

Wolf, S. Effects of placebo administration and occurrence of toxic reactions. *Journal of the American Medical Association*, 1954, *155*, 339–341.

Worell, L. The effect of goal value upon expectancy. *Journal of Abnormal and Social Psychology*, 1956, *53*, 48–53.

Wortman, C. B., & Brehm, J. W. Responses to uncontrollable outcomes: An integration of reactance theory and the learned helplessness model. In L. Berkowitz, (Ed.), *Advances in experimental social psychology*, New York: Academic Press, 1975.

Wyler, A. R., Masuda, M., & Holmes, T. H. Magnitude of life events and seriousness of illness. *Psychosomatic Medicine*, 1971, *33*, 115–122.

Yaryan, R. B., & Festinger, L. Preparatory action and belief in the probable occurrence of future events. *Journal of Abnormal and Social Psychology*, 1961, *63*, 603–606.

Zajonc, R. B. The process of cognitive tuning in communication. *Journal of Abnormal and Social Psychology*, 1960, *61*, 159–167.

Zajonc, R. B. Social facilitation. *Science*, 1965, *149*, 269–274.

Zajonc, R. B., & Brickman, P. Expectancy and feedback as independent factors in task performance. *Journal of Personality and Social Psychology*, 1969, *11*, 148–156.

Zanna, M. P., & Hamilton, D. L. Attribute dimensions and patterns of trait inferences. *Psychonomic Science*, 1972, *27*, 353–354.

Zola, I. K. Culture and symptoms—an analysis of patients' presenting complaints. *American Sociological Review*, 1966, *31*, 615–630.

Author Index

263

Subject Index

A

Achievement motivation, 147–148
Anticipatory face-saving, *see* Subjective probability of success
Anticipation-invigoration mechanism, 158–162
Anxiety, *see also* Performance
Anxiety, 163, 185–190, 188–191
  attention decrements, 187–190
  critiques of research, 188–191
  distraction, 189
  effects, 185–191
  relation to subjective probability of success, 186–191
Attribution theory, 16–25, 143–145, 172–174

B

Behaviorism, 24, 166
  purposive, 24

C

Choice, 126–127
Communication of expectations, 5, 104–125, 241
  behavioral assimilation, 121–122
  defining the situation, 116–117
  immediacy, 120–121

Communication of expectations (*contd.*)
  information management, 117–118
  interaction with the stigmatized, 112–116
    difficulty of monitoring reactions, 114
    elicitation by the stigmatized, 115
    phantom acceptance, 113
    stigma theories, 112
    uneasiness of normals, 113
  liking and cooperation, 119–120
  projected self-definitions, 116–124
  punctuation of interaction, 122-123
  role-taking, 116–124
  studies of experimenter bias, 104–106
    eye contact, 106
    projection as possible mediator, 105–106
    voice inflection, 106
  teacher-pupil interaction, 106–112
    evaluation apprehension, 109–110
    generalizability of data, 111–112
    naturally occurring expectancies, 111–112
    possible mediators, 107–110
    Pygmalion effect, 106–108
  working consensus, 125

D

Death, 234–238
  apathy deaths, 236–237
  mechanisms, 236

271